Enlightenment's Frontier

The Lewis Walpole Series in Eighteenth-Century Culture and History

The Lewis Walpole Series, published by Yale University Press with the aid of the Annie Burr Lewis Fund, is dedicated to the culture and history of the long eighteenth century (from the Glorious Revolution to the accession of Queen Victoria). It welcomes work in a variety of fields, including literature and history, the visual arts, political philosophy, music, legal history, and the history of science. In addition to original scholarly work, the series publishes new editions and translations of writing from the period, as well as reprints of major books that are currently unavailable. Though the majority of books in the series will probably concentrate on Great Britain and the Continent, the range of our geographical interests is as wide as Horace Walpole's.

ENLIGHTENMENT'S FRONTIER

The Scottish Highlands and the Origins of Environmentalism

Fredrik Albritton Jonsson

Yale
UNIVERSITY
PRESS
New Haven & London

Published with assistance from the Annie Burr Lewis Fund.

Copyright © 2013 by Yale University.
All rights reserved.
This book may not be reproduced, in whole or in part, including illustrations, in any form (beyond that copying permitted by Sections 107 and 108 of the US Copyright Law and except by reviewers for the public press), without written permission from the publishers.

Yale University Press books may be purchased in quantity for educational, business, or promotional use. For information, please e-mail sales.press@yale.edu (US office) or sales@yaleup.co.uk (UK office).

Set in Electra type by IDS Infotech Ltd., Chandigarh, India.
Printed in the United States of America.

Library of Congress Cataloging-in-Publication Data

Jonsson, Fredrik Albritton, 1972–
Enlightenment's frontier : the Scottish Highlands and the origins of environmentalism / Fredrik Albritton Jonsson.
pages cm. — (The Lewis Walpole series in eighteenth-century culture and history)
Includes bibliographical references and index.
ISBN 978-0-300-16254-7 (clothbound : alk. paper)
1. Environmentalism—Scotland—History—18th century. 2. Enlightenment—Scotland. 3. Scotland—Intellectual life—18th century. 4. Highlands (Scotland)—Environmental conditions—History—18th century. I. Title.
GE199.G7J66 2013
304.209411'509033—dc23
201204030

A catalogue record for this book is available from the British Library.

This paper meets the requirements of ANSI/NISO Z39.48–1992 (Permanence of Paper).

10 9 8 7 6 5 4 3 2 1

Contents

Acknowledgments   vii

Introduction: The Enlightenment in the Peat Moss   1

PART ONE A NEW WORLD IN THE NORTH

1 The Moral Geography of Scotland   11

2 Natural History and Civil Cameralism   43

3 Improving the Scottish Climate   69

PART TWO RIVAL ECOLOGIES

4 Alternate Highlands   93

5 Rival Ecologies of Global Commerce   121

6 Larch Autarky   147

PART THREE STATIONARY HIGHLANDS

7 Coal Exhaustion in 1789   167

Contents

8 Overpopulation and Extirpation   188

9 Wasteland Island   213

10 "A Stationary Condition for Ever"   232

Conclusion: The Ghosts of the Enlightenment   262

Maps   265

List of Abbreviations   267

Notes   269

Index   331

Illustrations follow page 164

Acknowledgments

This book has been much longer in the making than I might have hoped. On the way, I have incurred a great many intellectual and institutional debts. Long ago, Simon Schaffer prodded me into giving the eighteenth century a chance. A circle of friends in Cambridge, including James Delbourgo, Jamie Elwick, Bryan Garsten, Ryan Hanley, and the late Emile Perreau-Saussine, provided a brilliant, broad model of the life of the mind, at a time when I had little idea of what I should be doing. Later, at the University of Chicago, my dissertation adviser, John Brewer, encouraged my first serious forays into the Scottish Enlightenment with his characteristic combination of learning, wit, and wisdom. Jan Goldstein, Steve Pincus, and Alison Winter also offered exacting criticism as well as warm support. At Colorado State University, my former colleagues Mark Fiege, Jared Orsi, and Thaddeus Sunseri bear considerable responsibility for my fall from the heights of intellectual history into the sublunar realms of environmental history. I am very grateful to all of them for this turn of events. I am also indebted to several other friends and colleagues at Colorado State, including Ruth Alexander, Elizabeth Jones, Prakash Kumar, Ann Little, Diane Margolf, Alison Smith (now at the University of Toronto), and Doug Yarrington for their encouragement. Overseas, a number of scholars in the fields of Scottish history, Enlightenment thought, environmental history, political economy, and the history of science have responded with kind interest and patience to my questions over the years, including Thomas Ahnert, Linda Andersson-Burnett, David Arnold, Brett Bennett, Maxine Berg, Brian Bonnyman, Richard Drayton, Jim Endersby, Nigel Leask, Jim Livesey, Fabien Locher, Andrew Mackillop, Allan Macinnes, Nicholas Phillipson, John Robertson, John Scanlan, Chris Smout, Sverker Sörlin, Emma Spary, Frank

Trentmann, Paul Warde, and Charles Withers. In North America, I owe a similar debt to John Broich, Bob Bucholz, Jim Caudle, Will Cavert, Deborah Cohen, Chris Dudley, Fonna Forman-Barzilai, Jo Guldi, Ted McCormick, Minakshi Menon, Chris Otter, Mark Philips, Richard Sher, Brent Sirota, Phil Stern, Paul Sutter, Abby Swingen, James Vaughn, Carl Wennerlind, Paul Wood, and Anya Zilberstein. At the University of Chicago, I have had the great fortune of joining a stellar group of colleagues, including Ralph Austen, Dipesh Chakrabarty, Jim Chandler, Constantin Fasolt, Cornell Fleischer, Cam Hawkins, Adrian Johns, Jonathan Lyon, Kathy Morrison, Liz Moyer, Emily Osborn, and Tara Zahra. I am particularly grateful to Paul Cheney, who has been a comrade in arms in eighteenth-century history for several happy years. Many thanks also to past and present students at Chicago, including Venus Bivar, Maura Capps, Arnab Dey, Kyle Gardner, Josh Large, David Lyons, Kirsty Montgomery, Peter Simon, Heather Welland, and Sheila Wille. Finally, let me express my very great appreciation for the thoughtful and thorough appraisal of my manuscript afforded by the two anonymous reviewers for Yale University Press and the exceptional assistance provided by the editors at the press, Chris Rogers, Christina Tucker, and Laura Jones Dooley.

Thanks to the editor at the American Historical Review and the University of Chicago Press for allowing me to include a revised version of my article "Rival Ecologies of Global Commerce: Adam Smith and the Natural Historians."

In the process of writing this book, I have presented drafts of the argument at the American Society for Environmental History conference, the California Institute of Technology, Colorado State University, Columbia University, the Huntington Library, the Institute of Historical Research in London, the Newberry Library, the North American Conference of British Studies, Queens University Belfast, the Social Science History conference, the University of Cambridge, the University of Edinburgh, the University of Glasgow, the University of Saint Andrews, and Yale University. I am deeply obliged to these many audiences for the challenging questions and encouraging comments I have received over the years. None of these conversations would have been possible without research funding and access to the archives. I gratefully acknowledge the generous support of the Mellon Foundation, the Institute of Historical Research in London, the College of Liberal Arts at Colorado State University, and the Social Science Division and the Franke Center for the Humanities at the University of Chicago. I also wish to express my gratitude to the staff at the following libraries and archives: the University of Chicago Special Collections, the National Library of Scotland, the National Archives of Scotland, the British Library, the National Archives at Kew, the Huntington

Library, the Bodleian Library, the University of Edinburgh Special Collections, the University of Glasgow Special Collections, the Library of the Royal Botanic Gardens in Edinburgh, the Center for History of Science at the Royal Swedish Academy of the Sciences, Stockholm, the University of Aberdeen Special Collections, the Royal Highland and Agricultural Society and its librarian, Willie Johnston, as well as the Blair Castle muniments and their archivist, Jane Anderson. Thanks also to my research assistant, Colin Rydell, for laboring heroically with last-minute revisions and to University of Chicago GIS specialist Chieko Maene for the quick work in making the maps.

Let me tip my hat as well to five old friends who have never failed to remind me that there is more to life than eighteenth-century peat bogs: Anders Brunstedt, Tom Bullock, Robert Chiappetta, Torbjörn Persson, and Jens Spinger. *Stort tack!*

The greatest debts are the most difficult to express properly. Without the love and support of my mother, Siv, and father, Gunnar Jonsson (1929–2008), my father- and mother-in-law, David and Phyllis Albritton, and my wife, Vicky Albritton, this book would not exist. *Utan er, ingenting alls.*

Enlightenment's Frontier

Introduction:
The Enlightenment in the Peat Moss

Sometime in the late summer of 1753, six gentlemen ventured into the watery maze of Flanders Moss on the banks of the river Forth, west of Stirling. In the peat below them, Bronze Age artifacts rested with stumps of long gone forests on a bed of glacial deposits of gravel and clay. But the small company was not hunting archaeological treasure or clues to the geological past. The men had come to observe an experiment in improvement conducted by their kinsman and neighbor Mr. Hugh Graeme of Ardgomery. For a few years, Graeme had carried out a trial in "moss husbandry" that had incurred "the Railery and Ridicule of most of the Country." Though the six visitors had been persuaded to review "these Bogs" against their better judgment, they were greatly surprised by the progress of the trial. The common notion of "improvement" in the eighteenth century signified the process by which land was made profitable through enclosure and cultivation. But Graeme's achievement far surpassed the standards of Lowland experience. He seemed to have discovered the secret to unlocking cornucopian abundance in the midst of a sterile wasteland. Where only the wild plants of the bog had grown before, there were now "large Fields of Fine Barley and Bear, in the Quality of the Pickle exceeding any we have seen this Season." Bear, or six-rowed barley, was the grain of ancient Britain, better adapted to the acidic soils and short growing season than wheat. The visitors estimated the yield to be eight bolls per acre in most plots. There were also potatoes "exceeding good, planted, hoo'd and raised with his small Breast Plough." This New World crop had reached Scotland in the late seventeenth century. Like bear, the potato was eminently suited to the prevailing wet conditions. Breast plows were in wide use across early modern Britain, wherever rural plebeians reclaimed wasteland, from Devon to the Scottish Highlands. In his 1686 survey of Staffordshire, Robert Plot described the breast plow or push plow as a wooden beam "somewhat in the shape of an arrow" pushed by a single man to "cut the turf" in the "Moorelands in the Springtime." Flax afforded a fourth flourishing crop in Graeme's bog, "most wanted in the Country" and the special concern of the linen manufacturers in Perthshire. The visitors noted with astonishment that "moss, ten and twelve Feet deep," could yield "Flax of any Quality . . . coarse or fine." So surprising was this discovery that the six men repeatedly took the trouble to stress the veracity of their findings and the authority of their judgments. "Nothing but seeing with Deliberation" had persuaded them of the efficacy of Graeme's method. Social status underwrote the authority of their experience and field observations: "No Gentleman of any Knowledge in Agriculture, who has seen and considered it, will talk of it as too many do." To be safe, they included samples of flax, barley, and bear straight from Graeme's fields as material evidence to silence any remaining doubters. But beneath this gesture of confidence lay an urgent problem of natural knowledge. What was the true character of the northern climate and soil? Could human ingenuity overcome every natural obstacle, or were there strict limits to the power of improvement?[1]

This book tells the story of how the mountains and peat mosses of Scotland became a laboratory for the Enlightenment. Hugh Graeme's curious method of moss reclamation was part of a wave of different improvement projects between 1750 and 1820, including the veteran colonies of the Annexed Estates, the planned villages of the British Fisheries Society, the larch plantations of the Duke of Atholl, and the Caledonian Canal between Inverness and Fort William.[2] The vagaries of imperial conflict marked the beginning and end of northern improvement. When large-scale military recruitment began in the Highlands during the Seven Years' War (1756–1763), landowners and intellectuals came to see the region as a nursery of martial virtue that had to be carefully protected and cultivated. After the loss of the American colonies in 1783, a more liberal impulse gained the upper hand. Improvers now imagined internal colonization and urbanization in the Highlands as an alternative to the expense of overseas empire. During the French Revolutionary and Napoleonic Wars, the wheel turned once again. The landed interest embraced a loyalist ideology committed to national self-sufficiency and maximum population density. But in the wake of the Battle of Waterloo (1815), this sentimental population politics lost its strategic and economic appeal. By the early 1820s, the Enlightenment patterns of improvement were giving way to systematic clearance and emigration.[3]

In the first part of the book—"A New World in the North"—I chart how an alliance of landowners and natural historians developed a paternalist form of improvement to protect Gaelic tenants and subtenants from the pressures of commercialization during the Seven Years' War. Their economic strategy exploited the resources of the Highlands and Hebrides while preserving the Gaelic population as a military and social bulwark of the landed interest. Linnaean natural history formed one pillar of this strategy. The improvement of the Highlands required precise natural knowledge of northern soils, climate, native plants, and traditions. Scottish naturalists claimed to have discovered a "New World" at the edge of the nation, brimming with natural abundance. The other pillar of improvement was a new kind of population politics. By promoting spade husbandry and wasteland reclamation, improvers sought to soften the impact of agrarian capitalism in the north. Rather than assimilating the region directly to the Lowland model of industry and exchange, they favored an alternative path to modernization that mixed distinct historical stages — commerce and primitive agriculture — into a harmonious hybrid. Here, I break with the received account of crofting society in the Highlands, which sees it as a purely economic adjustment to a seasonal wage economy. Instead, I show that the social structure of crofting society grew directly out of the intellectual debates and experiments of the high Enlightenment in Scotland.[4]

Such an *upland* version of the Enlightenment also sheds new light on the origins of classical political economy by exposing its environmental assumptions. In the second part of the book — "Rival Ecologies" — I explore the competing economic interpretations of the Highland environment. Was the market sufficient to improve the natural order, or did the complexity and fragility of natural systems require the intervention of experts? For David Hume, Adam Smith, and their successors in the classical liberal tradition, nature served as a handmaiden for exchange in a double sense. They looked to the natural world for a model of self-regulating balance that justified their own faith in market exchange. At the same time, they championed the market as the best means of managing the balance of nature. This interpretation of nature was derived from a selective model of development based on the mixed husbandry of lowland regions in Scotland and England. A loose constellation of natural historians, agricultural improvers, and conservative landowners suggested instead that the natural order was too complex or fragile to be left unregulated, particularly on the peripheries of the nation and empire. They stressed the need for careful husbandry of resources and population to achieve social harmony. National or colonial autarky was preferable to free trade in an age of incessant warfare and imperial struggle. At times, they appealed to the state for support, but more often, they favored a strategy of civil cameralism, which entrusted such priorities with voluntary associations and private landlords. The clash between liberal and conservative ecologies of improvement shaped the trajectory of Highland improvement and helped trigger the social disaster that befell the region in the nineteenth century. This conflict also extended outward to the colonies as Scottish political economy and natural history migrated to the peripheries of the empire. The contests over Highland improvement generated rival models of colonial development.[5]

The third and final part of the book — "Stationary Highlands" — considers how the experience of northern improvement gave rise to precocious anxieties about environmental degradation and resource scarcity. In the early stages of development, most observers saw in Highland Scotland an "empty world" filled with cornucopian potential. But over time, expert judgment and political opinion shifted from bullish optimism to resignation on both sides of the political spectrum. At the end of the Enlightenment, a darker vision was gaining ascendancy: the "New World" of the north was not empty but "full."[6] A mixture of demographic, intellectual, and political factors propelled this new pessimism. The old priority of high population growth put increasing pressure on the land. At the same time, large-scale commercial sheep farming began to encroach on the regional economy. Wartime concerns with strategic self-sufficiency focused public attention on marginal soils and population limits. Naturalists and political economists made use of quantitative data to survey resources and populations, making ecological strain legible to the government and civil society. When the high expectations of civil cameralism failed to yield fruit, the hardnosed liberalism of T. R. Malthus gained adherents among landlords and savants. The Highland region now seemed a society on the edge of collapse, burdened with surplus population, exhausted resources, and permanent natural disadvantages. Paradoxically, the fear of limits emerged precisely at the moment when Enlightenment ideology and industrialization began to make sustained economic growth imaginable. This pessimistic turn in Highland development anticipated a major strain of modern environmentalism. The condition of Highland society offered an intimation of the "stationary state." Nineteenth-century economists from Malthus to J. S. Mill were haunted by this idea of permanent physical limits to economic growth. The finite supply of land, they thought, must eventually block all progress. Although such fears proved premature to say the least, they have been revived in recent times by natural scientists and environmentalists who worry that a finite biosphere cannot sustain for long the exponential growth of the global economy.[7]

Yet the case of the Highlands also presents a cautionary tale about the politics of human carrying capacity in a complex social order. This quarrel between pessimists and optimists could not be decisively settled because the arithmetic of land use and demographic strain was inseparable from broader social and political controversies. Here, the Highland improvers and their critics were brushing up against basic problems that have become persistent themes of debate in more recent times. How could natural limits be known or forecast? Who defined these limits and in whose interest? Whose claim to resources and land should be honored? What range of remedies could be imagined and debated?[8]

HISTORIOGRAPHY AND METHODOLOGY

The ties between theory and practice in the Scottish Enlightenment have not escaped scholarly notice. Indeed, some of the best work in the field has considered the institutional implications of improvement by investigating such topics as planned villages, the grain trade, academic patronage, the Scottish militia, and the business of printing. For Highland improvement there is also a rich scholarship of social history. Yet the intellectual history of the Enlightenment and the social history of the Highlands have seldom been directly connected.[9] The aim of this book is to bridge that historiographical gap by taking advantage of new developments in the history of science. Within the orbit of Scottish history, the work of Charles Withers, Matthew Eddy, and Jan Golinski has been particularly important in exploring the emergence of natural history and chemistry as enlightened fields of knowledge.[10] Other scholars have traced the rise of economic botany as a tool of the state in European nations and empires. Lisbet Rausing and Alix Cooper offer striking accounts of how Linnaeus and other cameralist natural historians sought to transform the economies of landlocked Continental nations through internal colonization and global bioprospecting. Many Highland improvers looked to Sweden and other northern nations to learn about the possibilities of improvement in the "boreal" zone. Indeed, the Scottish Enlightenment looks decidedly less liberal and more cameralist once we take into account the chain of events in the Highlands between 1750 and 1820.[11]

Some critics may worry that this concern with the natural sciences risks attenuating the concept of Enlightenment too much. John Robertson has made a powerful case for the essential intellectual unity of the movement. His argument rests on two overlapping definitions. On the one hand, the Enlightenment was the project of "human betterment in *this* world." On the other, it was the prerogative of smaller nations or provinces concerned with their own "backwardness relative to the richer and more powerful nations of Europe." Robertson therefore regards the discipline of political economy as the disciplinary fulcrum of the Enlightenment, since it promised to fulfill both priorities.[12] My wager in this book is that Robertson's argument leaves out a fundamental question. Political economists of every stripe from Jean-François Melon and Sir James Steuart to Adam Smith and T. R. Malthus made assumptions about the fit between economies and environment. How could labor and human ingenuity transform the produce of the land? Were there natural limits to improvement? How did natural advantages shape trade patterns? Yet knowledge of soil, climate, and natural advantages was not some fixed and solid foundation on which the debates of political economy could find a sturdy bottom to rest. On the contrary, eighteenth-century concepts of the natural order were fiercely contested and at times seemed to dissipate into a vertiginous flux. This was perhaps especially the case in nations or colonies at the edges of conventional grain cultivation. Here, the question of natural limits to development raised the discipline of natural history into an economic authority that rivaled political economy. In fact, the boundaries of political economy and natural history were not firmly fixed. There was a steady trade in concepts and models between the nascent and contiguous disciplines. While nineteenth-century economic thought harbored a consuming envy of the formalism and mathematical precision embodied in physics, eighteenth-century political economy looked to an earthier range of natural models, drawing on phenomena in natural history and agricultural improvement such as food chains (homeostatic markets), ungulate irruptions (population dynamics), island limits (trade patterns and population models), coal extraction (depletion rates), and soil fertility (rent). By restoring natural history to its status as the uneasy neighbor of political economy, we also see more clearly why enlightened theorists of improvement, for all their optimism, still worried about physical limits to development. In an age when the revolutionary consequences of industrial production had not yet been fully fathomed, it was much more difficult than it is now to deny that the economy formed a subset of the environment.[13]

A word about methodology may be prudent here. My ambition is to pursue the history of eighteenth-century thought from the "ground up" by insisting on the environmental dimension to the Scottish Enlightenment. This means that my analysis circles back and forth between two complementary perspectives. The first aims to widen the conventional account of political economy. Debates over improvement, trade, and empire owed a great debt to natural history. The defense of exchange in Adam Smith was predicated on a selective interpretation of the environment. Smith and his critics launched rival ecologies of commercial development. But this revision in turn implies that the intellectual history of the Scottish Enlightenment cannot be easily separated from a broader history of experiments, projects, and environmental change. The material effects of agricultural improvement and environmental change often intruded directly on the quarrels of savants. The history of enlightened ideas therefore has to reckon with material phenomena like subsistence crises, deforestation, and ungulate irruptions. Such environmental pressures at the same time enabled and constrained enlightened thought by providing the raw materials for rival interpretations of the natural order.

My final wager is that the story of Highland improvement sheds new light on the origins of modern environmentalism. Scholars like Richard Grove, Donald Worster, Gregory Barton, and Harriet Ritvo have presented a range of contending hypotheses about the rise of green consciousness. One well-worn path runs from the romantic critique of industrialization in Britain and the United States to the creation of the first national parks in these countries. How, such histories ask, did the wilderness become an object of public concern and protection? Another line of scholarship looks to the history of exploration and conservation on the margins of early modern European empires. When and why did environmental degradation become a field of scientific study and resource husbandry a matter of state regulation? A third model considers how the challenge of soil husbandry and practices of communal resource management provided the impetus for early ideals of sustainability. Admittedly, the explanatory force of these alternate models hinges on what definition of environmentalism they adopt. Some scholars stress the centrality of a biocentric perspective, that is, the path by which humans came to value ecosystems for their own sake and to protect the diversity of species. Other historians focus instead on the politics of resource husbandry. When did states begin to manage forests and other lands to further national or imperial power? A third perspective emphasizes the evolution of local and communal practices that sought to ensure the optimal yield of resources over multiple generations.[14]

Historians concerned with the origins of environmentalism have for the most part ignored the legacies of the Scottish Enlightenment.[15] The great exception to this neglect is the seminal work of T. C. Smout. Eighteenth-century attitudes toward nature in Scotland vacillated between economic utility and aesthetic delight, according to Smout. Highland tourism was a crucial force, he argues, in imbuing the natural world with new kinds of sentimental and aesthetic value. But for Smout, aesthetic appreciation did not translate into effective conservationism in Scotland until the twentieth century. The Scottish story is one of precocious sentiment followed by long-delayed political action. Richard Grove and Gregory Barton take note of the Scottish background and training of many naturalists active in colonial conservation efforts, but neither investigates the natural history of the Scottish Enlightenment itself. Other scholars have favored an English rather than Scottish perspective. For example, Donald Worster traces the origin of nineteenth-century American conservationism back to the "Arcadian ecology" of the Reverend Gilbert White of Selborne in Hampshire. Worster pits White's gentle vision of human coexistence with the natural world against the "utilitarian" ambitions of Linnaean botany. The Swedish naturalist forged an "imperial ecology" with the same "managerial and exploitative bias" as the political economy of Adam Smith and T. R. Malthus. Harriet Ritvo also stresses the "sentimental" and English origins of modern environmentalism. The romantic defenders of Thirlmere Water in the Lake District sought to stop Manchester municipality from making a reservoir of the lake in the 1870s. Technocratic expertise clashed with a national British lobby that claimed a "nebulous sense of ownership" of the landscape. For Ritvo, this contest pitted utilitarian calculations against aesthetic and literary values.[16]

For all their virtues, these earlier histories have overlooked one of the enduring themes of modern environmentalism. The Scottish Enlightenment was the crucible for early scientific and economic forecasts about the physical limits to growth. In this respect, conservationist sentiment and aesthetic value were of less importance than the power to quantify the material basis of the economy. Richard Grove has rightly stressed the importance of islands as laboratories of environmental consciousness because physical constraints and ecological fragility were more easily detected on such a limited scale. Yet Grove's account neglects the political and scientific history of the concept of carrying capacity. When and how did concerns about environmental limits give rise to a quantitative investigation of population and resources?[17] In the model presented here, the frontier of the Highland periphery offered the first practical laboratory for this kind of politics. Resource strain and demographic pressure were easily noticeable in the north precisely because of the precariousness of the economic base of the region. Moreover, the rapid growth of cities and manufacturing elsewhere in Britain made the marginal character of the Highland economy even more striking to contemporaries. When the improvement schemes failed to lift the region to a higher stage of development, negative expert judgments began to dominate in public opinion. Instead of delivering cornucopian abundance, the northern frontier now seemed to offer an object lesson in the power of natural limits.[18]

Part I

A New World in the North

1

THE MORAL GEOGRAPHY OF SCOTLAND

When Henry Home, Lord Kames, inherited his brother-in-law's property of Blair Drummond near Stirling in 1766, he was faced with a monumental problem of soil husbandry. At the center of the estate was a bog covering 2,000 acres, with three-fourths belonging to Kames. It had formed on top of the deep alluvial clay soils of the carse lands stretching from the Firth of Forth to the hills above Stirling. Scattered evidence of this submerged soil raised hopes that the removal of the moss would uncover the lost arable beneath it. After some abortive trials, Kames determined that the best way of proceeding would be to dislodge the peat little by little. Digging with spades, the workers removed the heath, bog-moss, bent grass, and tree roots at the bottom, leaving only a six-inch stratum of moss to be burned in the spring to yield fertilizing ashes for the first crop. Canals were cut and a waterwheel was added to aid the removal. This work of environmental engineering was combined with a policy of sentimental population politics. To recruit laborers for the moss excavation, Kames turned to Highlanders in Perthshire who had recently been evicted from their farms. Between 1766 and Kames's death in 1782, 42 tenants were brought in, settling more than 350 acres. By 1793, there were 115 families living on the moss, each with a house and some livestock. Together, they had cleared 300 acres down to the carse, raising as much as sixty bolls of oats per tenant on the recovered clay soils. The moss had turned into a "most useful nursery of laborers; and those very farmers who at first so strongly opposed their settlement, now fly to them as a sure resource for every purpose of agriculture." William Wingate's census of Blair Drummond Moss in 1814 listed a total of 1,287 inhabitants, 264 cattle, 375 poultry, and 168 cats. Presumably, there was also an adequate population of mice.[1]

This chapter reconstructs the world of enlightened improvement that inspired the drainage scheme at Blair Drummond. A good place to begin is the Select Society of Edinburgh, the premier venue for intellectual debates in

Scotland during the Seven Years' War. Here, the savants and literati convened to discuss the advantages and risks of commercialization.[2] The judge James Burnett, Lord Monboddo (from 1767), and Presbyterian minister Robert Wallace took the side of the skeptics, warning that improvement without restraint might hurt the social fabric and depopulate the Scottish countryside. The answer, they thought, was to promote a mode of husbandry that maximized the number of people working the land. This intellectual agenda carried over into the newly established Board for the Annexed Estates, a government body set up to manage the confiscated properties of Jacobite rebels. Henry Home, Lord Kames served on the board just before he came into his inheritance. Kames's good friend and client the naturalist John Walker was hired to survey the Annexed Estates and other parts of the northwest. Through this mixture of debate, field work, and estate management, Scottish savants, landowners, and politicians came to see spade husbandry as a counterweight to the social costs associated with conventional forms of agricultural improvement. They also began to develop a practical arithmetic that sought to calculate the measure of minimal subsistence among plebeians. Spade husbandry and potato cultivation were means of maximizing the size of the Highland population in an era of growing military recruitment.

A COMPOSITE NATION

Geographic accident made the Scottish Highlands a laboratory of the Scottish Enlightenment. The central problem of classical political economy, how a rich and a poor country might prosper together, divided not just Scotland from England and other more prosperous nations but also Scotland from itself.[3] The Scottish Enlightenment flourished in a small country that combined two distinct societies: in the north—marginal soil, fractured terrain, Gaelic-speaking people, cattle droving, and an unbroken military tradition; in the central Lowlands—arable fields, easy communications, and an Anglophone community with a long urban history. In a traumatic blow, Highland troops under the Jacobite Prince Charles Edward Stuart overran the Lowlands in the great rebellion of 1745–46. Though the northern army was soon destroyed at the Battle of Culloden, the experience of defeat left a certain mark on the character of Lowland Scottish thought. Soon after the rebellion, Scottish elites in alliance with the British government embarked on a venture of internal colonization to pacify the north once and for all. The Highlands became a colony of the Lowlands where enlightened ideas were tested in practical projects of improvement. Ironically, the defeat of the Highland rebels also paved the way for the idealization of Gaelic culture and the use of Gaelic-speaking soldiers as the highly regarded shock troops of the empire. Just as the social structures of clan society were crumbling, the romance of the Highland tradition gained cultural potency. Between 1756 and 1815, the Highland region offered the most important recruitment zone for the British army out of all proportion to its population.[4]

This question of the Enlightenment in the Highlands may help explain a vexed problem of Scottish intellectual history. Why did the liberal current of classical political economy give way to militaristic loyalism and Malthusian pessimism at the end of the eighteenth century? The hypothesis of this chapter is that a strong conservative tendency was present already at the epicenter of enlightened debate in the 1750s. The challenge of Highland improvement led a group of savants and politicians to formulate a path of development distinct from the better-known intellectual idioms of civic republicanism and classical liberalism, long before the French Revolution. The environmental and ethnic peculiarities of the region were employed to justify a model of improvement based on accommodation rather than assimilation. In contrast, the liberal strategy of David Hume and Adam Smith had no need for special treatment. If the Highlands could not be integrated into the commercial order of the south, then the region must remain an economic backwater of no consequence. But many of the Highland improvers instead gave priority to the social and military aims of the landowning class and the fiscal-military state. The advantage of the Highlands in military recruitment also challenged the basic premise of Scottish civic republicanism. Andrew Fletcher of Saltoun and his followers advocated a national militia to ensure the survival of active citizenship and martial virtue among commercial and polite people. Yet Highland military recruitment seemed to demonstrate that military prowess and commercial society could be combined within a regional division of labor. Lowlanders did not need to cultivate the habits of soldiers when Gaels could do the fighting for them.[5]

In other words, the laboratory of Highland improvement gave rise to rival programs of modernization. In recent years, economic and political historians of various stripes have suggested that states pursued a variety of paths into the modern world. Jeff Horn contrasts the British and French forms of industrialization. Shmuel Eisenstadt has suggested that we must think of modernity itself in plural, as a set of distinct variations rather than a unitary phenomenon. In this context, it is tempting to view the British experience in the eighteenth century as quintessentially liberal compared with that of France and other competitors. But this interpretation exaggerates the liberal character and political homogeneity of British society. Distinct paths appeared not only between nations but also within them. Steve Pincus has proposed that the Glorious Revolution of 1688 saw the clash of two fundamentally opposed programs of state modernization. Against the idea of a hegemonic Whig party, he insists that rival forms of political economy shaped political debate throughout the eighteenth century. This claim for the centrality of the state and political debate is reinforced at least in part by economic historians. Patrick O'Brien, William Ashworth, Prasannan Parthasarathi, and David Ormrod have pressed the central significance of government intervention for the success of Britain's commercial empire and Industrial Revolution. In this model, competing commercial lobbies and political groupings stimulated innovation through a series of policies, including the evolution of the excise, the imposition of import tariffs, and the cultivation of captive colonial markets. Once the manufacturing sector had developed a clear advantage over foreign competitors in a few key industries, liberal views gained in strength, though they failed to capture a stable and hegemonic position.[6]

In the Highland case, strategic concerns compounded the problem of development. State interest in the economy of the region was intermittent and almost always refracted through the lens of military considerations. The most successful lobby in the period was the group of landowner-entrepreneurs that specialized in raising Highland regiments for the Crown.[7] But other improvers steered clear of government involvement, preferring instead to mobilize capital and knowledge through the channels of Scottish civil society. Major cultural and scientific disagreements also shaped the peculiar path of northern improvement. Liberals and conservatives embraced rival views of the natural advantages of the region. The imperative of military recruitment and sentimental population politics competed with a liberal vision of full-scale manufacturing and urbanization.

The conservative version of Highland improvement greatly resembles the type of agrarian transformation charted by Martha Petrusewicz elsewhere in Europe. She points to a common ideal of alternative modernization on the European periphery by comparing elites in Ireland, Poland, and the Kingdom of the Two Sicilies during the period 1820–70. Along these economic margins of the Continent, in civil societies where the nobility dominated public life, landowners rejected the model of modernity associated with industrial England and its concomitant features of "class conflict, popular misery, and unrestrained greed and materialism." To ward off the horrors of Manchester and Birmingham, these elites sought to promote an economy of rural manufactures based on local agricultural produce, around which commerce and free markets were "to grow slowly and gradually." Modest reforms in land tenure, coupled with advances in agricultural science, spread through economic and agricultural improvement societies, were to ensure the social and economic viability of this ideology.[8]

Precisely this anxiety about the social costs of manufacturing modernity was already a pressing topic of debate in the voluntary associations of the Scottish Enlightenment. As early as the Seven Years' War, Edinburgh savants argued the case for alternative modernization in the Select Society. Long before the ideological struggles of the French Revolution, the Highlands became the crucible for a new kind of conservatism intent on balancing the priorities of commerce and tradition. Philosophically, the novelty of this movement lay in its adoption of deliberate anachronism as a proper means of social organization. Clanship, commerce, and the fiscal-military state were all compatible and necessary elements of a greater whole. In the sociological language of the Scottish conjectural historians, this conservatism assumed that social elements from the four stages of history—hunting, pastoralism, agriculture and commerce—could be mixed into a hybrid model of improvement. The stadial history of the skeptical Whig historians thus made possible a new kind of self-conscious anachronism taken up by the defenders of the landed interest.[9]

The peculiar proclivities of the Highland improvers grew out of a larger debate about the social problem of gentlemanly farming. Scottish agriculture was radically transformed in the middle decades of the eighteenth century, catapulting the Scottish economy on to the path of England's commercial agriculture but on a dramatically foreshortened trajectory of decades rather than centuries.[10] This headlong rush provoked questions about the destructive consequences of agrarian capitalism. The lawyer-improvers who attacked feudal vestiges like entail and primogeniture grappled with the possibility that excessive commercialism might threaten the basis of their own authority as landowners. In retrospect, the best known contribution to the debate can be found in book 3 of Adam Smith's *Wealth of Nations*, which sought to redeem the social virtues of agriculture by idealizing the small gentry and tenant farmers. But Smith was a latecomer to the debate: there were many other Scottish participants, including Robert Maxwell, Robert Wallace, Archibald Grant, Adam Dickson, Sir James Steuart, Lord Kames, and Henry Mackenzie. A fierce debate raged over the proper size of farms, the best balance between arable land and pasture, and the fate of dispossessed rural plebeians. How could the landed interest reconstitute itself as a protector of the social order in an age of commercialization and agrarian transformation?[11]

The ideal of paternalist improvement assumed a particularly strong form in the Scottish Highlands. The European discovery of feudalism was here mingled with the romance of Gaelic poetry and clanship. A specific body of economic works arose dedicated explicitly to the Highland problem, beginning with John Walker's 1764 report on the Hebrides, continuing in texts by James Anderson, John Knox, John Sinclair, and others. This hybrid genre blended elements of travel literature, natural history, and political economy. It drew on an eclectic and cosmopolitan mixture of sources, including Roman history, Swedish economic botany, Continental cameralism, and the sociological jurisprudence of Montesquieu. Such intellectual ferment was typical of Edinburgh's Enlightenment.[12]

THE SELECT SOCIETY OF EDINBURGH

Between 1754 and 1764, the Select Society of Edinburgh formed the principal locus of intellectual debate in Scotland. Among its 162 official members were aristocratic politicians, men of letters, clergymen, merchants, and, lawyers. The participating literati included David Hume, Adam Smith, Adam Ferguson, Lord Kames, and Hugh Blair.[13] Socially speaking, the club connected the rising stars of Scottish intellectual life with the agrarian elite of the nation. Hume described it excitedly to a friend as a movement of "national concern." We know from John Robertson that the Select Society debates helped shape the movement for a Scottish militia in the 1760s.[14] Indeed, the club legitimized and diffused new ideas in moral philosophy, political economy, and history to a wide circle in the Scottish elite. But the society was not simply a mouthpiece of inexorable and unhesitant change. Many of the debate topics offered opportunities to discuss the perils associated with improvement and growth. The urban setting that made the club possible was also a fundamental problem to be debated.

The composition of the Select Society mirrored the peculiar character of Edinburgh. The city formed the political, legal, and ecclesiastical center of Scotland with its law courts, banks, university, and General Assembly of the Kirk. Roger Emerson has argued that the Third Duke of Argyll served as a crucial patron for the institutions of the Scottish Enlightenment. In effect, his political control of Scottish patronage also made Edinburgh a magnet for ambitious men of every type. The landowning elite increasingly sought to establish residency in the city for at least part of the year. These absentee landlords mixed business with pleasure, making Edinburgh a place of genteel consumption and conviviality. In the second half of the eighteenth century, the construction of the New Town heightened the allure of the city with its elegant neoclassical design. It gave permanent expression to the alliance between patrician capital and middling professionals that underpinned the power and wealth of

Edinburgh. The law courts, the Kirk, the university, and the medical school provided the landed interest with useful expertise of all kinds. Town agents, estate factors, and surveyors were drawn from these chattering ranks. The Faculty of Advocates in particular played a role in giving shape to the intellectual life of the city while at the same time creating the legal framework for commercial agriculture in the country.[15]

Twenty-five of the 162 members of Select Societies were noblemen with titles or expectations of one. The rest were for the most part "eldest sons of gentlemen, merchants or clerics." Twenty-six served in the army. Eighteen were merchants and bankers. A total of sixty-one were advocates, plus seven writers to the signet. Eighteen members rose to the Court of Session—Scotland's highest civil court. Among them were some of the most active members of the Select Society such as Lord Kames, Lord Monboddo, and David Dalrymple (Lord Hailes). The Presbyterian clergy provided another important contingent, including Hugh Blair, John Walker, and Robert Wallace. Fifteen physicians joined, most prominently William Cullen, Alexander Monro, Joseph Black, and the Regius Keeper of the Botanic Garden John Hope. From the university also came principal William Robertson, Francis Home, and James Russell, among others. These professionals were tied to the Scottish nobility by double social bonds. Not only did they form the service elite of Edinburgh, but they also shared with the nobility the social and economic imperative of landownership. Many of the members in the Select Society owned or could expect to inherit land. But even those who did not often took a strong interest in agricultural improvement. Smith, Walker, Cullen, Wallace, and Hope all wrote or lectured on such questions.[16]

This is not to deny the importance of Glasgow's intellectual life to the Select Society. After lecturing in belles lettres at the University of Edinburgh in the years 1748–51, Adam Smith became a professor of logic and then moral philosophy at Glasgow just as the Select Society was founded. Joseph Black spent the years 1752–55 at the Edinburgh Medical School before returning to his native Glasgow in the period 1755–66. William Cullen came to Edinburgh in 1755 after an unsuccessful bid to teach medicine in Glasgow. Hume, too, entertained ambitions for a professorship at Glasgow. At the highest intellectual level, there was clearly a strong overlap between the two cities in terms of professional opportunity. But the wider member roll seems to indicate a preponderance of Edinburgh professionals together with Lowland landowners who had Edinburgh townhomes. The historian T. C. Smout's contrast between mercantile Glasgow and administrative-agrarian Edinburgh appear to account for this difference. In 1773–74, Edinburgh counted 5.4 percent "Nobles and gentry" as opposed to 1 percent of the same order in Glasgow a decade earlier. In the eastern city 28.8 percent of the population were "professional men" and 12.5 percent were "merchants and manufacturers," whereas in Glasgow the figures were reversed, with 12.3 percent and 30 percent, respectively, in each group. Another contrast involved the religious affiliation of the two cities. Glasgow's mercantile elite supported a conventional and rather rigid Presbyterianism, whereas Edinburgh and the Select Society were home to the Moderate wing of the Kirk. Though too much can be made of Smout's figures, they do seem to explain why the Select Society was formed in Edinburgh rather than Glasgow.[17]

MONBODDO AND WALLACE

Unfortunately, the trail of evidence offers little more than tantalizing glimpses of the recurring issues debated in the Select Society. Because the minutes of the society recorded merely the topics discussed and the member presiding over each "night's entertainment," we cannot know with certainty what sort of arguments were presented, who took an active part, which ideas gained strong support, and whether the society was divided into factions. The cursory accounts of the Select Society by Hume and Carlyle convey a few telling anecdotes but provide no systematic or detailed evidence about the intellectual currents of the club. The *Scots Magazine* in 1755 printed a brief description of the society, noting that it met regularly between six and nine each Wednesday evening from November to August. It also mentioned the principal rules of debate: the preses (presiding officer) of a given meeting would suggest the question to be debated beforehand. Members were permitted to speak three times but under strict time limits. There was a general agreement to avoid delicate topics of theology and political controversy, specifically "such as regard Revealed Religion, or which may give occasion to vent any Principles of Jacobitism."[18]

Given the precarious state of the evidence, what can be said about the intellectual priorities of the Select Society? The questions proposed by its members ranged far and wide, including the merits of paper credit, whether "ancient or modern manners" were preferable "with regard to the condition of women," and "whether the difference of national characters be chiefly owing to the nature of different Climates, or to moral and political causes." John Robertson has rightly suggested that the club supplied an early venue to debate Hume's ideas. Many of the topics seem to reflect Hume's paean to commerce and modern manners. In the face of traditional anxieties about the corrupting effects of wealth, he provided an unapologetic defense of urban society and the world of consumer goods. His *Political Discourses* of 1752 argued that the refinement of the arts was the engine of commercial growth, critical to a process of imitation and innovation that spurred industry in both manufacturing and agriculture. Urban luxury was a foundation for the power and wealth of every modern state. Yet as Robertson notes, Hume's argument may not necessarily have met with enthusiasm in the club. For one thing, the convention of framing debate topics in terms of polar opposites humored traditional anxieties even while it may have aimed to overcome them. The frequent repetition of certain topics also suggests ongoing controversy. In many cases, debates extended over several meetings. On four occasions in 1757 alone the Select Society considered whether commerce and affluence posed a danger to public morality. The idea of luxury provided frequent fodder for discussion; it appears as an explicit topic no fewer than fourteen times during these years. Such recurrence belies any swift and easy triumph for Hume's arguments.[19]

The first great institutional response to the luxury debates in the Select Society was the agitation for a Scottish militia, wherein the clergymen Robert Wallace, Adam Ferguson, and Alexander Carlyle played a decisive part. The topic of the militia first surfaced in the Select Society during the spring and summer of 1755. Initially, the terms of argument seemed to have focused on institutional comparison: "Whether a standing army or a militia properly regulated be most advantageous for Great Britain?" By the following year, the outbreak of the Seven Years' War turned the question of national defense into a practical issue of some urgency. In an unpublished tract, Wallace argued that a militia based on universal military training ought to replace Britain's standing army for financial and military reasons. Ferguson's pamphlet *Reflections Previous to the Establishment of a Militia* expanded the argument to the question of the moral effects of the militia. Ferguson conceived of the militia as an instrument "to mix the military spirit with our civil and commercial policy," though the act of mixing values here involved a balance of forces rather than any actual fusion. The point was not to destroy the desire for wealth but rather to establish some countervailing interest in men. Likewise, the militia introduced an institutional counterweight to the pervasive influence of commerce in everyday life. Across Scotland, the militia would bring together respectable men of every social background to awaken in them a spirit of national defense ("cottagers, day-labourers and servants" were excluded). The Select Society met to discuss this theme in February 1759: "Whether a commercial and military spirit can subsist together in the same nation." In the summer that same year, a French squadron passing through the Hebrides gave further impetus to these worries. By October, a committee of Scottish law lords and advocates including several leading lights in the Select Society drew up a draft bill for a Scottish militia. At one level, the issue could be framed as a simple parity within the Union. Parliament had passed a bill embodying a militia for England in 1757. Why should not Scotland have the same? But equally important was Ferguson's idea of mixing stages. The purpose was to preserve or cultivate a sense of martial spirit in commercial society.[20]

Yet it would be a mistake to see the agitation for the militia as the main argument to emerge from the luxury debates in the Select Society. In fact, some of the strongest advocates of the militia harbored doubts about whether such an institution could resolve the deeper problem. From their perspective, military strength was measured by the state of plebeian bodies and minds rather than the civic spirit of middling merchants or lawyers. Rural recruits were assumed to make the best soldiers. The improver's priority of maximizing rents and profits threatened the agrarian basis of the fiscal-military state by encouraging the dispossession and emigration of the rural poor. The real question of the luxury debate, then, was how to shelter rural plebeians from the forces of agrarian capitalism. Perhaps the most extreme version of this line of argument was promoted by the judge and philosopher James Burnett, Lord Monboddo. The minutes reveal him to be one of the more zealous participants in the Select Society; he was a founding member of the club, elected to the board of presidents for three years in a row, acted as preses more than a dozen times (Hume took the podium only twice), and served repeatedly on the committee charged with formulating new topics of debate. Monboddo was by all accounts a deeply eccentric man, best known to posterity for his quaint obsession with the orang-outang as the missing link between apes and humans. But contemporaries also recognized him as a shrewd jurist, witty conversationalist, and formidable classical scholar. Monboddo's major published works were *Antient Metaphysics* (1771–99) and *Of the Origin and Progress of Languages* (1773–92). In the Select Society, he sponsored debates concerned with paper credit, the corn bounties, luxury, barbarism, and a host of related concerns: "Whether the institution of slavery be advantageous to the free?" "Whether printing has been of advantage to society?" "Whether bounties on the exportation of corn be advantageous to trade and manufactures as well as to agriculture." "Whether is a Nation in a state of barbarity, or a nation of luxury and refined manners the happiest." "Whether Luxury be advantageous to any State?" "Whether the pursuit of Industry and Trade would produce good or bad effects upon the morals of a Nation." "Whether the modern method of improvement by making large farms be not ruinous to the Country?"[21]

Monboddo's questions for the Select Society presaged a number of his scholarly passions. The majority of the fourteen topics that he proposed involved some unflattering contrast between the ancient and modern world. He regarded the growing prosperity of Britain with quaint horror, convinced that the nation and indeed all of Europe would soon collapse into a morass of luxury. He wrote to his friend George Baker in 1782, "Nothing can save us, and indeed I think all Europe from absolute destruction and annihilation, but the study of antient men and antient manners by those who govern us." In his published works from the 1770s and 1780s, he consistently favored the ancients over the moderns with a taste that ran toward extreme primitivism. It is hard to imagine a greater contrast to the bon vivant David Hume than the ascetic Monboddo. To live fully according to the dictates of nature and the ancients, he followed a simple vegetarian diet and a regimen of severe exercise that included an annual trip on horseback from Edinburgh to London even at an advanced age. Monboddo was well known among his contemporaries for his ardent belief that that the diet of modern times was responsible for a radical diminution in the stature of mankind. One of the questions in the Select Society minute book from 1759 seems to bear his signature: "Whither hath mankind decreased in stature strength and virtue during three thousand years?" He enlisted his friend the botanist John Hope (another member of the Select Society) to discover the exact identity of the edible plants *Asphodus* and *Melanchte*, described as the natural food of primitive people in Hesiod and Homer. For Monboddo, the problem of diet was in turn closely tied to an ongoing process of depopulation. He worked for years on an essay about the decline of the British population in modern times, spurred in part by the demographic pessimism of Richard Price and Thomas Percival. Monboddo was struck in particular by the statistical work of Percival, which demonstrated an inordinately higher rate of mortality in the manufacturing town of Manchester compared to the rural village of Menton. Percival and Monboddo both singled out poor air and luxurious living as the main cause of this divergence in death rates.[22]

Predictably, the only modern philosopher Monboddo found favor with was Jean-Jacques Rousseau. He wrote in 1774 that Rousseau alone had the good sense to realize that "the invention of all the arts of civil life" had been "pernicious to mankind." Monboddo's own crusade against technology seems to have begun in the Select Society. The naturalist John Walker recalled an "elaborate speech" made by Monboddo "upon principles highly benevolent and patriotic . . . with much ingenuity and eloquence, that the plough was the most destructive instrument to mankind that ever was invented." Monboddo justified the superiority of the spade over the plow on several counts; it rendered the soil more productive, it introduced methods of gardening into field cultivation, and it "powerfully promote[d] the population of a country." A question in the minute book of the Select Society echoed these sentiments more or less precisely: "Whether the Modern improvements in mechanicks and the multiplying mechanical machines do not tend to the depeopling the world?"[23]

Monboddo returned to the idea of retrograde agriculture in the fifth volume of *Antient Metaphysics*, written after the dangerous dearth of 1795. He extolled the farmer-warriors of the Roman Republic who cultivated the land "with their own hands." Gaul had been conquered "not by the sword only, but likewise by the spade." Monboddo quoted Horace's Ode 3.6: "They were a virile crowd of rustic soldiers, taught to turn the furrow with a Sabine hoe." *Antient Metaphysics* proposed that British cottagers on very modest farms become the principal cultivators of the land in order to boost food production and encourage virtue. Again antiquity provided a model: "A citizen of Rome, in the first ages of their state, lived upon an acre of two of land, which he himself cultivated." Monboddo probably had in mind Pliny the Elder's observation in the *Natural History* that "just over an acre was enough land . . . and no one had more" in the "earliest days of Rome." In a late notebook of preparatory jottings for his unpublished work on the demography of Britain, Monboddo noted that the vitality of the cottager class must determine the size of the general population. They were an "indispensable" breed of servants, day laborers, mechanics, "and what I think of the greatest consequence . . . soldiers." Monboddo boasted that he kept a large number of cottagers on his Kincardineshire estate as a "monument" to the way the land had been populated in "antient times."[24]

No doubt, Monboddo represented an extreme position in the debate over the perils and benefits of commercial society. Yet the worries about luxury that provoked his radical remedies seem to have been widely shared. Preses Dr. Adam Austin asked in December 1755: "Doth the encrease of trade and manufactures naturally tend to promote the happiness of a nation?" The question of population emerged in a host of new questions proposed by the club's committee in July 1758: "Whether the number of People in Great Britain has for these last twenty years been on the Encrease or decline?" "Whether permitting the rich men in any State to have more than one wife, would add to its populousness?" Another topic from the same committee prodded the connection between rural population and military recruitment: "Whether Labourers of the Ground or manufacturers make the best soldiers." Walter Steuart also seemed to follow Monboddo with his topic of February 1760: "Whether in the ancient times of every nation the people were not stronger of body, healthier and longer lived than in late times." Broadly speaking then, these lines of debate connected three major themes: Was luxury a threat to population growth? How could the martial spirit of the nation be preserved in the commercial age? And what were the risks and benefits of agricultural improvement? During the 166 meetings recorded in the minute book, the problem of luxury and anxieties about modern commerce were debated at least fourteen times while the militia issue and related questions of martial prowess was broached eleven times. Finally, the rewards and perils of agricultural improvement were considered no fewer than twenty-four times. In sum, these topics therefore accounted for almost 30 percent of the questions debated.[25]

Among the other members, the Edinburgh clergyman Robert Wallace was perhaps the most sympathetic to Monboddo's views. Wallace's *Dissertation on the Numbers of Mankind in Antient and Modern Times,* published in 1753, inspired a friendly contest with Hume over the tendency of historical demography. Wallace argued that the population of the world had reached its peak in the age of the Roman Republic and Alexander the Great. Under the right circumstances, mankind doubled its size every thirty-three years according to Wallace's "law of procreation" (with six children to each family). A multitude of "moral" causes lay behind the subsequent decline, including overseas colonization, standing armies, "neglect of agriculture," primogeniture, and the "loss of that antient simplicity which had long prevailed." In contrast, the far more numerous population of ancient times had flourished on a "very nearly . . . equal division of the lands, and into such small shares, that they [could] yield little more than what [was] necessary to feed and clothe the labourers in a frugal and simple manner." Whereas a society addicted to fine manufactures required four or five acres per head, a population with simpler taste needed "not one acre for every member of the society." Gaul before the Roman invasion had been a country with this population density. Though Wallace did not suggest that a full-scale return to ancient conditions was possible, he stressed that some of the priorities of ancient governments might yet be viable: "The antients did not neglect trade, but had a greater turn to agriculture; they traded with nations which were not at a great distance, and whose climate better suited their constitutions; but agriculture was their chief employment and they managed it well."[26] Wallace's growing interest in the problem of population seems to have led him away from a more conventional Whig view of progress. Around the rebellion of 1745, Wallace had composed a pamphlet against the Jacobite charge that Scotland had become poorer after the Union with England. On the contrary, he argued, the population and wealth had grown visibly since 1707. While "several Gentlemen and farmers," had evicted the "poorest of the people," small farms were still "nurseries of idleness and a nuisance to the neighborhood." In contrast, poor cottagers who had been dispossessed usually moved to the towns and became useful there. Clearance thus improved the social order in both country and city.[27]

But Wallace's subsequent work, starting with the debate on the trend of the world population, seems to have pushed him away from this "hard" Whig position toward what we might term a "sentimental Tory" priority of guaranteeing a maximum rural population. Wallace's preoccupation with primitive agriculture intensified during the Seven Years' War. After the militia pamphlet of 1756, he produced the polemic *Characteristics of the Present Political State of Great Britain* (1758). This was a scathing social critique of the landed interest cloaked as a patriotic pep talk. The true bulwark of the constitution and the Union were "the robust and hardy commons" "not enervated by the luxury of the Great, but inured to labour." This foundation of national strength had been severely weakened in recent times: "In Scotland we see so many places in this part of the island, that were formerly well peopled, now almost desolate, without house or inhabitants." Farms had been enlarged, arable land turned into pasture, cottagers removed, while the wealthy landowners carried their rental income "out of the country" to spend it in England. Wallace added: "Neither government nor trade ought to be managed with the sole view of procuring vast riches to a few, at the expence of grinding the faces of the poor." In this context, Wallace's militia manuscript appears to be something of an intellectual sideshow. The common thread in Wallace's publications from 1753 was a worry about the effects of commerce on the agrarian order. The call for universal militia conscription merely underlined this deeper problem.[28]

Wallace's social critique reached a still higher pitch at the end of the Seven Years' War. The 1761 utopian tract *Various Prospects of Mankind, Nature, and Providence* proposed a redistribution of land along the lines of an agrarian law. Wallace criticized Rousseau's *Discourse on the Origin of Inequality* for idealizing the savage state and imagined in its place a Platonist utopia where a council of experts managed the division of labor to ensure maximum efficacy. At first glance, the sketch was not only fanciful but also half-hearted since the author retracted his own argument halfway through the book. Even if the earth could be turned into a new Eden, sexual desire and population growth must inevitably destroy the garden from within. Under a "perfect government . . . mankind would increase so prodigiously, that the earth would at last be overstocked and become unable to support its numerous inhabitants." Even the bounty of providence was not inexhaustible. "Limits" had been "set to the fertility of the earth" which "probably could not be much altered without making considerable changes in the solar system." Only "violence and war" would "make room for others to be born." This thought experiment arrived at a long-run model quite similar to the demographic pessimism of two liberal clergymen in the subsequent generation—Joseph Townsend and T. R. Malthus.[29]

Yet certain features of Wallace's imaginary society survived these bleak conclusions to resurface in his next work, A *View of the Internal Policy of Great Britain* (1764). After cycling through the genres of demographic history, wartime polemic, and utopia, Wallace here tried his hand at direct policy advice. The appeal was aimed at the landed interest and specifically Lord Advocate Sir Thomas Miller—a fellow member of the Select Society. Wallace once again focused on the problem of protecting rural inhabitants displaced by estate improvement, and once more, he diverged from Monboddo by rejecting a wholesale retreat to primitive agriculture. Rather, Wallace envisioned an accommodation of surplus population within the framework of commercial land use. His preferred strategy was to devise countervailing pressures against the force of luxury, either through government intervention or paternalist protection. He warned that excessive wealth debilitated the reproductive capacity of the upper orders. Hence, the vital impulse had to come from below: "To increase numbers, you must begin at the lowest of all." Without a hint of irony, Wallace encouraged landlords to raise plebeians as they bred horses, promising that it would be no more difficult and "infinitely more profitable." Gentlemen "of large landed possessions . . . ought to be, the fathers and counselors of society" not just in "national assemblies" but also "in private character." "To increase the number of hardy laborious people is the most important piece of patriotism they can employ themselves about."[30]

Wallace applied a similar logic to the issue of heritable jurisdictions in the Highlands. This feudal form of justice had been a major target of the penal legislation leveled against the region after the rebellion of 1745–46. Wallace applauded the destruction of these archaic vestiges—"too great a power for the public peace"—but noted that their abolition also dissolved the bonds between proprietor and tenants: "When the Lord had a kind of property in and dominion over them, he nursed them with care, for in their number consisted his consequence." The question then was whether such paternalism could be resuscitated on a different footing. Wallace turned to the state for a remedy. Government-sponsored Highland regiments presented proprietors "a means to . . . preserve their population" even after the end of heritable jurisdictions. He added that clan-based recruitment had the further effect of encouraging loyalty and deference in units "formed of neighbours and friends." The introduction of manufacturing villages on estates provided another means of absorbing displaced tenants and cottagers. In Wallace's model, each village would be populated by one hundred dispossessed families, all given equal land. Wallace insisted that such villages must balance the priority of subsistence agriculture against the demands of local manufacturing. To that end, he asked

Lord Advocate Miller to calculate the minimum amount of land necessary "to supply [each] family" employed in village industry with food. The government and the local landlord would then collaborate in introducing the most appropriate form of proto-industry. In other words, within the confines of each manufacturing village, the basic outlines of Wallace's 1761 utopia would be introduced: an agrarian law, minimum subsistence, a life of simplicity, and a division of labor regulated by expertise. While Wallace never endorsed spade husbandry explicitly, his suggestions closely paralleled the plans for crofting settlements on the Annexed Estates during the same period. Lord Advocate Miller was directly involved in the experiment with Highland settlement. Moreover, a decade later, Miller took the lead in a government scheme to monitor and prevent Scottish emigration to America. Wallace's antiluxury polemics thus anticipated the practical population politics of the northern periphery.[31]

A SECOND POLAND

Wallace's ideas were not without critics in the Select Society. Lord Kames—the leading advocate and patron of Smith and Hume—at first favored entail reform rather than the protection of the cottagers as a remedy for the ravages of luxury.[32] Like Wallace, he was appalled by the British defeats in the early phase of the Seven Years' War. In a letter to Sir Gilbert Elliot written in October 1757, he complained bitterly that the nation seemed to have succumbed to "luxury and . . . avarice." "We appear to be a gone people, a ready prey for any bold Invader." This concern fueled his memorandum on the abolition of entail to the lord chancellor Lord Hardwicke in August 1759. After the failure to bring forward a bill on the topic in the previous session of Parliament, Kames and other "publick-spirited People . . . set about a plan that should be more extensive." Entail had indeed been debated repeatedly in the Select Society from 1754 onward. Fearing the opposition of the great landowners of Scotland, however, Kames turned to Hardwicke for support. He warned that "at present a number of Noblemen" were intent on snatching "every parcel of Land that comes to market" securing it by entail to aggrandize their families "till there be not left a single inch of land to be purchased." Such monopoly was "destructive to population." Only in countries where land was "parceled out among many Proprietors" did "skill and industry" afford "bread to a numerous family" in the hands of a "moderate and frugal" proprietor. Excessive wealth at the top also fostered an elite addicted to "foreign luxurys," prone to absenteeism, and accustomed to holding "their inferiors in utter contempt." Without the middling rank of small landowners binding the upper and lower orders together and protecting liberty, all "social duty" was threatened with "extinction." Kames warned that Scotland was well on its way to becoming a two-tiered society of haughty potentates and "Trembling dependants." In the absence of entail reform, the nation might become a second Poland, where the "independency in Electors which is the Cornerstone of the British constitution" would be subverted and poisoned by the influence of "overgrown Potentates." Kames's broadside against entail was followed by a full-scale pamphlet war in the middle of the 1760s between three other members of the Select Society—John Dalrymple, John Swinton, and Patrick Murray. Adam Smith, too, picked up Kames's condemnation of entail in his Glasgow lectures on jurisprudence 1762–63: "This right is not only absurd in the highest degree but is also extremely prejudiciall to the community, as it excludes lands intirely from commerce."[33]

The same concern with market-oriented agriculture led some members of the Select Society to form a separate branch of the club particularly dedicated to rural economy. The *Scots Magazine* printed a list of the branch's debate topics in 1757, only a few of which appear in the minute book of the Select Society itself. Each involved social and economic questions of profound consequence. Were corn lands or grazing of most advantage to the public? "What proportion of the produce of lands should be paid as rent to the master?" What were the proper obligations of tenant farmers to be included in improving leases? What were the "advantages and disadvantages of gentlemen of estate being farmers"? This last question spurred a response by Kames's colleague David Dalrymple (later Lord Hailes), a fellow landowner, judge, and respected antiquarian writer.[34]

Dalrymple's manuscript essay was generally optimistic about the social consequences of agricultural improvement. While he admitted that a greater interest in farming among middling landowners would make many tenant farmers redundant, he also thought that the reclamation of "uncultivated grounds" would "more than compensate for that." Moreover, many farmers condemned to a meager living "which scarce can purchase so many cattle as can drag a plow after them" would "live more comfortably" if they lost their leases and became "hired Servants or Day labourers." "Nay it might be a Question whether removing some of the hands in the Country to the Manufactures in Towns might not be advantageous." In this way, Dalrymple rejected the pessimism of Monboddo and Wallace. Enclosure and farm consolidation would generate sufficient wages for many landless workers, and any surplus hands could go to the towns. But his comment about the possibilities of wasteland cultivation included at least a nod toward spade husbandry insofar as marginal soil was to offer a refuge to the rural poor. Many years afterward,

Dalrymple penned a satirical play in which the poor cottager Slip safeguarded his home against the threat of eviction thanks to his native wit. The essay on gentlemanly farming also tackled another Select Society debate topic: "Whether Labourers of the Ground or Manufacturers make the best Soldiers?" Dalrymple eschewed any distinction among the rank and file between rural and urban recruits: "Being bred to Business does not make Cowards." But at the same time he affirmed that gentlemen farmers were "the surest defence of our Country." Military honor served to guarantee the gentlemanly identity of farming proprietors even as they made maximum profits the guiding principle of their estates.[35]

CANADA AT HOME

Yet Kames and Dalrymple were never unambiguous apologists for agrarian capitalism. Their backing of Lowland improvement came side by side with an active involvement in a state-run project of spade husbandry in the Highlands. In 1761, the two men became commissioners on the Board for the Annexed Estates. This was the most ambitious experiment in government-managed agriculture undertaken anywhere in Britain during the eighteenth century. Thirteen estates scattered across northern Scotland were confiscated from leading Jacobite rebels after the 1745 rising. Initially, the goal was to pacify and civilize the Highlands by means of a mixture of Lowland forms of agriculture and manufactures.[36] A board of commissioners led by Andrew Fletcher, Lord Milton, the lieutenant of the Duke of Argyll, was constituted in 1755 to oversee the Annexed Estates. The group became fully active in 1760 when it began to receive adequate funding. Major activities included the introduction of planned villages and the encouragement of linen manufactures. The board also funded trials in planting, coal prospecting, and botanical inventories. But the beginnings of large-scale recruitment of Highland regiments from 1757 onward complicated the task of the board since the priority of importing a Lowland model of mixed husbandry could not be easily reconciled with the new strategic imperative of the government to maximize the yield of recruits. This contradiction mirrored the intellectual debates of the Select Society about the social costs of agrarian capitalism. Indeed, the debating club and the Board for the Annexed Estates shared a substantial membership. Six members of the Select Society became commissioners of the board from 1755, including MP Gilbert Elliot and the lord present of the Court of Session Robert Dundas of Arniston. Another six served on the board from 1761 onward, including Lord Kames, Dalrymple, John Swinton, and Lord Advocate Miller.[37] Three additional members of the Select

Society were involved as scientific advisers to the board: William Cullen, John Hope, and John Walker. In later decades, Walker became the resident expert on issues of northern agriculture and improvement to the Highland Society of Edinburgh, founded in 1784. Dalrymple and Miller doubled as legal guardians of the great northern estate of Sutherland during the minority of the Countess Elizabeth. Two other prominent figures in the Select Society, George Dempster and William Pulteney, took part in yet another Highland project—the British Fisheries Society, founded in 1786.[38]

Dalrymple and Lord Kames joined the Board for the Annexed Estates with earnest expectations. Kames expressed his gratitude for the appointment with a blend of Roman duty and Scottish sentiment: "'Tis a generous thought to undertake the civilizing so many barbarians; and no man of public spirit or of humanity but must wish to have a hand in it." Dalrymple wrote in his private journal: "1761 August 3, I took my place as one of the Trustees for the annexed estates. I enter upon it with a firm resolution of acting up to the spirit of the annexed law; what success I may have, God knows." The minutes of the board demonstrate that their rhetoric was matched by considerable diligence. Both men were in frequent attendance at board meetings together with fellow Select Society members Lord Stonefield and George Clerk-Maxwell. It was an opportunity for men steeped in the Roman classics to act the part of high-minded conquerors. Sir Gilbert Elliot noted in 1755: "We have opened the Commission for the forfeited estates and flatter ourselves that under our protection a loyal, well policed colony will soon flourish." This rhetoric of internal colonization pervaded the correspondence and minute books of the board. The notion was clearly Roman in pedigree: a state-led enterprise with a strong military orientation, including the pacification of rebels, the construction of strategic roads, and the establishment of settlements for disbanded veterans. Every educated Scot would have been familiar with this process through Tacitus's *Agricola*. The Roman theme was underscored by the geographic circumstances of conquest; this was not a distant overseas colony but a barbaric frontier within the "territorial empire" of Great Britain. John Swinton wrote in his job application to Elliot: "The state of the Highlands is far from being understood. . . . I mean there is really a Canada at Home *si sua bona norunt*." He added, this "is a noble field for a man of any attention, and I own I would wish to be in the Trust that I might be entitled and enabled." Swinton's quotation from Virgil's *Georgics* reveals the agrarian subtext of such a civilizing mission: "O farmers, happy beyond measure, could they but know their blessings."[39]

The fashion for Highland romance inaugurated by James Macpherson (*Fragments of Ancient Poetry*, 1760; *Fingal*, 1762; *Temora*, 1763) likely served as a further inducement for the second generation of commissioners appointed in 1761. Hugh Blair persuaded Lord Kames and Dalrymple to sponsor a tour of Macpherson to collect manuscripts in the Highlands. The aim was to discover the fabled masterpiece of Scottish literature—the poems of Ossian—"recovering our Epic," as Blair put it.[40] In a letter to the bluestocking Elizabeth Montagu, Kames spoke of this literary calling as a patriotic battle against those skeptics (including Hume) who doubted the authenticity of Macpherson's "translations": "Zeal for Ossian, and of the Island in which I was born, made me seriously think of setting about a vindication of that poet as a true historian; and after making many collections from various authors, I have been successful beyond my hope. I have in particular made out, that the manners described by Ossian were the genuine manners of his country." So certain was Kames of his accomplishment that he wrote to Macpherson in order to correct several infelicities of translation and other "imperfections in his edition." Increasingly embroiled in the controversy over Ossian with the English critics, Kames used a good part of the *Sketches of the History of Man* (1774) to launch a broadside on behalf of the Gaelic "Homer." This literary campaign in turn clearly colored his views of Highland improvement, tingeing the civilizing mission with fashionable melancholy. "Compared with their forefathers," he pontificated, "the present highlanders make a very inconsiderable figure." The heroic pastoral stage of history glimpsed in Ossian's poetry, a world of hunters and warriors before the introduction of agriculture, had been lost irrevocably. Kames also took a dim view of the future, predicting that the Gaelic language would become extinct "in a few centuries." Such gloom was entirely in keeping with the dolorous tone of Macpherson's poetry. Yet Kames did not abandon all faith in Highland culture and morals. Remnants of Ossian's spirit lingered in the present. The Gaels retained "to this day a disposition to war, and when disciplined make excellent soldiers, sober, active, and obedient." They were also "eminently hospitable" and entirely "innocent and devoid of malignity." Such sentiments led Lord Kames to the practical question of how to preserve a spirit associated with primitive agriculture in the midst of a new commercial order. Here, he could draw on both the intellectual debates in the Select Society and the administrative challenges he had met with on the Board for the Annexed Estates. Hardheaded population politics went hand in hand with the sentimental idea of Gaelic noble savages.[41]

A basic understanding of the experience of the commissioners can be gleaned from the minute books and papers of the board. The peculiar environmental conditions of the Annexed Estates shaped much of the agenda. In a series of memorials to the board between 1753 and 1755, the Perthshire farmer

Hugh Graeme recommended his own method of "moss husbandry" with a "breast-plow" as the best way of tackling peaty soils and a rainy climate. The minutes of the Board dwelled often on the challenges to conventional Lowland farming, the draining of mosses, the enclosure of plantations, and the most suitable crops. Tenurial organization was also frequently discussed by the commissioners. They favored a cap on tenant farm rentals at twenty pounds. They granted very long leases of forty-one years to tenants deemed to have the means and wherewithal to improve their farms. The rental cap was intended to discourage a larger multi-tenant farm type associated with the influence of clanship. The question of farm size was further complicated by the priority of proto-industrial production. To recruit wage laborers for new manufacturing villages, the commissioners presented the incentive of free cottages with kitchen gardens. Small plots of no more than three acres together with a cow or two were to provide subsistence for each family. Such plebeian families were not expected to keep oxen and a plow. Rather they would cultivate the land with the spade. A third priority linked land with military recruitment and settlement. Toward the end of the Seven Years' War, Lord Milton proposed the introduction of demobilized veterans to the Annexed Estates. The plan was justified by a number of high-minded aims: the "King's Cottagers" were to act as civilizing agents on the estates, offering an example of industry for idle natives, establishing villages in the wilderness, providing skilled labor in fisheries and manufacturing. Such settlements would also provide the government with a standing reserve of soldiers and sailors that could be mobilized in new conflicts. Once again, incentives for settlement included cottages and gardens for spade husbandry ranging between half an acre and three acres. Lord Milton may have been aware of an earlier 1753 proposal for "kitchen gardens" or allotments on the Highland manufacturing stations operated by the Board of Trustees for the Encouragement of Fisheries, Arts, and Manufactures in Scotland (Kames was another member of this other board).[42]

These different pressures—environmental, economic, and military—converged into a policy of preserving and fixing Gaelic plebeians on small units of land around the Annexed Estates. At the end of the Seven Years' War in 1763, the board no longer sought to impose a straightforward case of Lowland commercial agriculture on the region. Instead of assimilation, Milton, Kames, Dalrymple, and the other commissioners pursued a mixed strategy of improvement through accommodation, which prevented the integration of the Highlands into the commercial order of the south. The Board for the Annexed Estates had turned Robert Wallace's plea for an agrarian policy into a full-scale program of population politics. The new croft tenancies for the "King's

Cottagers" were set aside as a reward for the veterans of the Seven Years' War. In essence, they created a surplus population of military plebeians on short-term leases who were dependent on the state for comfort and protection since the land itself was insufficient to provide secure subsistence, let alone farming profits. But such crofts could be created only by confiscating and subdividing land held by others. As Andrew Mackillop notes, the scheme therefore set in motion a domino effect of eviction and subdivision of land across the Annexed Estates.[43]

For the men of the Select Society, this new policy was not devoid of controversy. Dalrymple warned Sir Gilbert Elliot that Milton's plan for settling veterans was at the same time overly ambitious and hopelessly idealistic, poking fun at the idea that rough sailors could serve as paragons of virtue. He also disapproved of Milton's strongman habits on the board: "Honour Swinton's nose grows longer, every day, when he sees with how despotic a hand matters are conducted." Another criticism concerned the question of farm size: Dalrymple wrote in his private journal that the Annexed Estates should be used to reward veterans with "farms of 8–10–12 pound" on "easy" terms. But whatever the cause of his discontent, Dalrymple continued to attend the board meetings diligently as the spade husbandry model was implemented. His attendance dropped off only in the summer of 1765, a full two years after the initial proposal. Given the high rate of absenteeism among other members, such frequent participation might be construed as a form of grudging support for Milton's plan. At any rate, Dalrymple agreed in his private journal that Gaelic fighting spirit must be cultivated by the government. Here, he briefly outlined an alternative mechanism for increasing recruitment yields. Discharged Highland veterans on the Annexed Estates ought to have "a present made them in each county, of a pair of colours taken from the enemy in some Action where they were present." He added: "This mark of military glory to be preserved with them for ever." Reliable quotas required the careful management of native passions: "All Highlanders . . . to enter into . . . service" by satisfying the "two predominant passions" of the natives, "love of military fame and love of gain." The enemy banners would perpetuate "the spirit of glory and emulation."[44]

THE MOSS LAIRDS OF BLAIR DRUMMOND

For Lord Kames, the experience of the Annexed Estates formed the prelude to his own great experiment with "moss husbandry" on the estate of Blair Drummond. Evidently, he took his service as a commissioner very seriously. The board minutes from 1763 to 1766 testify to a nearly perfect attendance record on his part. Moss improvement was a frequent topic of discussion. For example, the board considered the reclamation of a bog near Rannoch that would produce crofts for twenty veterans. Kames also took a strong interest in flax cultivation and linen manufacture. This concern seems to have made him receptive from the start to the strategic function of "kitchen gardens" in securing wage labor for manufacturing villages. In 1759, Kames analyzed a plan for a linen manufacture put forward by the Earl of Breadalbane to the Board of Trustees for the Encouragement of Fisheries, Arts, and Manufactures. To attract flax raisers, he recommended the incentive of a small farm or kitchen garden along with raw materials and tools of work.[45]

Although the projects on the Annexed Estates failed to live up to expectations, Kames applied many of these ideas to the management of his own estate. Over the course of thirty years between the late 1760s and 1790s, the law lord and his son settled hundreds of Highlanders by reclaiming arable land from the moss of Kincardine, just a few miles from Mr. Graeme of Ardgomery's farm. This private initiative supplied an example of successful wasteland culture in the twilight years of the Annexed Estates, ensuring the survival of key ideological elements into the next generation, after Lord Milton's scheme was abandoned. It also provided a practical illustration of the conservative program expounded in James Steuart's *Inquiry into the Principles of Political Oeconomy* from 1767. To counter population decline and to maximize subsistence among rural plebeians, Steuart counseled labor-intensive forms of husbandry. Spade cultivation permitted a larger number of tenants than the labor-saving plow. To a later generation, this dictum of Steuart's political economy would seem a well-established verity. The third edition of the *Encyclopaedia Britannica* hailed the achievement of Lord Kames and his son in 1793 as "the most singular and considerable piece of improvement that has yet been executed in any parish in Scotland." Indeed, the floating of Kincardine moss assumed the character of a brilliant parable for the ideologues of wasteland reclamation. Eulogies included Sir John Sinclair's *Statistical Account of Scotland* (1791–99), John Walker's "Essay on Peat" (1803), James Robertson's *General View of the Agriculture in the County of Perth* (1799), and William Aiton's *Treatise on the Origin, Qualifies and Cultivation of Moss-Earth* (1811). Where the Board for the Annexed Estates had linked the concept of the internal colony to settlements of veterans, Walker, Sinclair, and Aiton loosened its meaning to embrace all areas of peat bogs capable of conversion into arable land, woodland, or pasture. Every settler on such marginal land was a colonist within the empire of moss. In this way, the northern improvers expanded the scale of the project to the Highlands as a whole and defined it along natural rather than military lines, as a feature of the providential economy of peat. From now on, the prospect of internal improvement seemed rooted in the natural order itself.[46]

A crucial factor in the growing popularity of moss husbandry was the purported moral effects of this kind of labor. William Aiton compared the floating of Kincardine moss favorably to the colony of Highlanders David Dale had recruited to his industrial village at Lanark. By settling a group of Highlanders together, entrusting them with long leases, and encouraging hard labor among them, Kames was said to have preserved or regenerated the moral community that bound them together by means common language, dress, and virtues. Strangers to the Lowlands, the Gaels considered "themselves in a manner as one family transported to a foreign land." The isolated and distinct habitat of the peat bog reinforced and reinvigorated their traditional virtues: "From their first settlement to the present day, not a single instance has occurred amongst them of theft, bad neighborhood, or of any other misdemeanor, that required the intervention of the civil magistrate. Nor, however poor in circumstances, has any one of them ever stooped to solicit assistance from the funds of the parish appropriated to that purpose."[47]

Internal colonization created a form of moral reservation, where Gaelic virtues could survive and flourish even in the midst of fundamental agrarian change. The apparent success of Blair Drummond may have played a role in Kames's later efforts to resuscitate the crofting scheme. Andrew Wight's postmortem survey of the Annexed Estates in 1773–74 had brought home the disastrous state of the settlements to the board. After acknowledging the "poor" and "heartless" condition of the colonists in Strelitz and other villages established by the board, Kames recommended a simple remedy: "Let each householder . . . have a kitchen-garden, not less than a quarter of an acre, to be cultivated with the spade." There was little point in pouring further funds into new infant industries or public works: "No better than water spilt on the ground." In the face of rising oatmeal prices, Kames counseled a retreat from the money economy for the colonists. Potatoes, cabbages, and turnips from the kitchen croft could provide sufficient alternative subsistence. The survival of the settlements depended on moral regeneration, and this rebirth from despair would come only from the spade.[48]

THE *CASCHROM* AND THE SPIRIT OF OSSIAN

The practice of spade husbandry had its own conjectural historian. Kames's close ally and colleague in the Select Society the Reverend John Walker was a natural historian of Highland improvement and natural history. Thanks to

Kames, he was appointed in 1764 to survey the agriculture and natural advantages of the Hebrides at the behest of the Annexed Estates. His deep knowledge of the region eventually helped secure for him the professorship in natural history at the University of Edinburgh. In the last two decades of his life, he also served as an acclaimed expert in agricultural improvement for the Highland Society of Edinburgh, a voluntary association that united great and small proprietors throughout the north of Scotland.

It was Walker's "Essay on Peat" of 1803 that commemorated the strange speech of Lord Monboddo in the Select Society against the malice of the plow. Walker wrote about the virtues of the spade himself as early as 1764. But unlike Monboddo, he identified spade husbandry with Gaelic rather than Roman practice. On his first tour of the Hebrides in 1764, Walker found the *caschrom*, the crooked spade of the Gael, wherever agriculture remained "in a very simple uncultivated state." Fashioned from a piece of wood, the "crooked foot" of the caschrom was curved at the end and tipped with a "narrow piece of iron" that served "the purpose of a sock, to penetrate the soil." In the curve of the wood, a peg was fitted to allow the cultivator to use the six-foot spade as a "fulcrum" or "lever" that cut into the soil and turned the turf with "considerable force." Despite the crude simplicity of its design, the spade was highly useful in "cultivating those Rocky Tracts ... inaccessible to the Plough" and among "the numerous small Subtenants, who having no Horse, cannot otherwise get their little Patch of Ground cultivated." On the island of Coll, Walker found the spade in heavy use on plots of land that were "very small" and "equally subdivided" yet "capable of furnishing [the subtenants] with all the necessaries of Life, they seem to have any Demand for." Against the instincts of conventional improvers, Walker recommended the caschrom even in places where the plow was more effective, on account of its "Influence on Population," since it allowed the natives to marry early and feed large families on a minimum of land without the capital needed to own a horse and a plow. Seen from the perspective of the Lowland improver, the toil with the spade no doubt comprised an "ill directed" and even irrational form of labor, yet the peculiar context of Highland development seemed to justify such agrestic heresy. Here, Walker proved a far more tolerant observer than Samuel Johnson, who later dismissed the crooked spade in Skye as irredeemably "incommodious."[49]

Walker was unequivocal about the antiquity of the caschrom in Gaelic tradition. He must have noticed the reference to it in Martin Martin, who mentioned the use of the spade on the Isle of Lewis at the outset of his *Description of the Western Isles of Scotland* in 1703. In Walker's posthumously published *Economical History of the Highlands and Hebrides* (1808), he identified the crooked spade with the most primitive stage of agriculture: "The instruments of agriculture in the Hebrides, are of a very early and unimproved age of the world. They are apparently the same that were used when the art of tillage was first introduced into these countries." By recommending the caschrom for modern use, Walker took the side of prehistory against Lowland agriculture. The Board for the Annexed Estates and private improvers should appropriate elements of ancient tradition in order to encourage the industry and population of the periphery. However, there was a curious commercial twist to Walker's penchant for primitive husbandry. Most implements in the Highlands were made by local blacksmiths. Yet the second half of the eighteenth century saw the beginnings of a commercial market for spade manufacture in Scotland. Ironmongers in Berwick upon Tweed, Glasgow, Dumfries, and Edinburgh produced peat spades and other implements on a significant scale. Commercial availability may have helped open Walker's eyes to the virtues of the technology.[50]

The caschrom also suited Walker's defense of the industrious habits of the Highlanders. The backbreaking labor with the crooked spade was taken as firm evidence of Gaelic vigor and commercial potential. While discussing the physiology of plants with Kames in 1773, Walker offered a neurological justification for the compatibility of hard labor with a northern climate. Like Montesquieu, he postulated that cold air had a bracing effect on the nerves, rendering them denser and therefore less sensitive to pain and pleasure: "It appears to me, that the sensibility of the nerves in the human body, if it does not entirely depend, is at least generally in proportion to the rarity or density of the medium in which they are lodged. The firmer the fiber, the less sensibility; and vice versa. Hence the greater sensibility of mankind in a warm than in a cold climate; greater in an effeminate than a rude age; greater in the female than the male sex; greater in a tender lady than in a robust dairy-made; and greater in the sedentary student than in the active plowman." From this dictum of physiology followed that Gaels were naturally inured to the pain of harsh labor. Such a sleight of hand justified in corporeal terms the primitive forms of exploitation promoted by Walker and Kames, casting an elective affinity among climate, nerves, and the spade. The same medical dogma could also be harnessed to promote military recruitment among the Gaels. Indeed, the heroic labor with the caschrom could be seen as the civilian counterpart to the stamina shown by Highlanders at war. Moreover, the effects of the northern climate guaranteed both *bodily* insensitivity and *mental* acuity, according to Walker. On his 1764 tour, the naturalist found himself "more and more convinced, that the mind of man is to be observed more and more perfect as one moves northwards; that a penetrating air seems to produce penetrating soils, and that wind and weather, the keener they are, appear to give the sharper edge to the human understanding." In this way, economic exploitation and cultural integrity could be compartmentalized neatly. The caschrom was entirely compatible with the spirit of Ossian.[51]

Walker was careful to defend his argument on the basis of utility as much as tradition and physiology. Despite its antiquity, the caschrom was surprisingly effective in the marginal soils of the northwest. According to Martin, the ground on Lewis was dug by large teams of people and then covered with "sea-ware" in a practice called *timiy*, which employed them "daily for some months." This mode of labor produced a great "plenty of corn," in higher quantities than other forms of digging or plowing, albeit at the cost of "great fatigue." Walker reached the same conclusion in the *Economical History*. Where the plow produced ten bolls of bear (the four-rowed barley, *Hordeum vulgare*) on good land, the spade could raise "better than thirteen." In poor soil, "a boll of oats, after the plough, will bring only three bolls, but will produce five after the spade." These estimates have in fact been corroborated by modern research. Analyzing data for returns on seed on the island of Tiree and on the coast of Barrisdale, Robert Dodgshon has established a marked difference between the yield on seed in land worked with the plow and the caschrom. The plow produced rates of 2.2 and 3.5, respectively, for oats and barley on Tiree. Meanwhile, the caschrom and spade effected a return of 5 in the "far more marginal environment" of Barrisdale. Consequently, Dodgshon has proposed that these labor-intensive forms of cultivation were favored over the plow on marginal soils throughout the Highlands and Hebrides during periods of population increase before the age of improvement. In fact, the example of Walker shows that the custom survived the coming of the Enlightenment and was appropriated into his arithmetic of food production.[52]

Walker was not content to rely merely on tradition in making the case for simple agriculture. His report to the Board for the Annexed Estates recognized in no uncertain terms the revolutionary effect of the potato on Gaelic society. This exotic plant had added enormously to the efficacy of spade cultivation in the twenty-five years since its introduction to the Outer Hebrides. Walker noted the vigorous growth of potato crops in lazy beds on Islay. The new security of subsistence was already transforming conditions in the region: "As the Potatoes have spread," he remarked, "all the Highlands, have from this Cause, become sensibly more populous." So bountiful was the harvest even in wasteland soil that this mode of labor in effect released the population from agriculture to other kinds of occupations during parts of the year. Grain crops, in contrast, required an almost "Constant occupation" and still yielded less sustenance. Walker's description demonstrated to the Board for the Annexed Estates not only that the native Gaels were capable of innovation and industry but that the ground, so to speak, was already prepared for the planting of manufactures on the islands. By marrying the traditional custom of caschrom cultivation with the new exotic crop of the potato, the natives had unwittingly created the labor surplus necessary to establish the linen manufactures that Kames and Walker hoped to extend into the north.[53]

In short, Walker's report provided the makings of a hybrid modernity. Taken together, the elements of this new social system—the crooked spade, the potato, and the projected linen manufacture—mixed and jumbled the stages of conjectural history, challenging the notion of a necessary linear progression between primitive agriculture and modern manufacture. The caschrom represented the earliest form of agriculture in its most "uncultivated" state, whereas the lazy bed cultivation of the potato was the outcome of recent ecological exchange, albeit carried out "spontaneously," without the intervention of landlords. Walker's model suggested the possibility of a rural order that could accommodate manufacturing industry without losing the security of agricultural subsistence.

Walker submitted his report on the Hebrides to the Board for the Annexed Estates in 1771, four years after Adam Ferguson's *Essay on the History of Civil Society* (1767) and five years before Adam Smith's *Wealth of Nations* (1776). Though the document went missing soon after, Walker reaffirmed his support for the caschrom in his "Essay on Peat" to the Highland Society of Scotland (1803) and in the posthumous work *Economical History of the Hebrides and Highlands of Scotland*. However brief and crude in comparison with the works of Ferguson or Smith, Walker's text deserves notice for the striking variation it offered on the themes of stadial history and progress. From Walker's caschrom flowed a social order that was supposed to maintain the Gaels in their ancestral land without the perils of rural flight, overseas emigration, or the degeneration of the laborer within the division of mechanical labor. The kinship of Walker's report with the scheme of the King's Cottagers is unmistakable. Together with Kames's moss husbandry at Kincardine, Walker's praise of the caschrom helped sustain and transform the ideology of internal colonization, long after the Annexed Estates experiment had terminated. By placing spade culture within the context of conjectural history, Walker linked the agenda of the Board for the Annexed Estates firmly with the central current of the Scottish Enlightenment.[54]

DUNDAS'S NURSERY

The defense of rural virtue that began with Monboddo and Wallace in the Select Society reached a culmination of sorts in the memorandum on Highland population drafted by the Scottish lord advocate Henry Dundas for William Eden in 1775 at the outset of the American War of Independence. Dundas was the most prominent Scottish politician of the age and the right-hand man of William Pitt the Younger. During his long career, he served as home secretary, first lord of the admiralty and president of the Board of Control. Dundas was just a few years too young to join the Select Society but very much part of the same circles in Edinburgh during the 1760s. He shared with Lord Kames and David Dalrymple a background in law and a double allegiance to the social values of the gentry and the intellectual culture of the Edinburgh literati. Together with his good friend and celebrated author of sentimental novels Henry Mackenzie, Dundas was a member of the Belles Lettres Society in Edinburgh, which functioned as a junior version of the Select Society. The Belles Lettres Society in turn metamorphosed into the Feast of Tabernacles and then the Mirror Club at the end of the 1770s. As John Dwyer and Alexander Murdoch have demonstrated, these circles continued to fret about the problem of luxury long after the demise of the Select Society. Henry Mackenzie's periodicals the *Mirror* and the *Lounger* from the 1770s provide a rich reflection of this concern with the corrupting influence of parvenu wealth and the need to defend rustic simplicity. According to Dwyer and Murdoch, Henry Dundas used the idea of luxury to stir up social anxieties for political gain.[55]

The 1775 memorandum to William Eden illuminates the crucial role of the Highlands in Dundas's paternalist vision, a point neglected by Dwyer and Murdoch. Eden was the under-secretary to the secretary of state for the northern department at this time. The lord justice clerk Thomas Miller (of the Select Society and Annexed Estates) had warned the department about the high levels of emigration from northern Scotland a few years earlier. Miller worried that some Highland counties might become entirely depopulated if no action was taken. In response, the central government began to monitor emigration statistics from customs and local parishes. When Dundas became lord advocate of Scotland in the spring of 1775, he made the issue a top priority. The memorandum began with a withering critique of the punitive legislation that had launched the Annexed Estates experiment. This program to civilize the Highlands had succeeded only too well. It was threatening to "eradicate the spirit of Clanship . . . to a very great degree." Dundas thus echoed Kames's judgment that Gaelic culture was in precipitous decline. To thwart the process, Dundas's memorandum proposed a national project of rescue and revitalization. Although punitive legislation had certainly been necessary in the wake of the 1745 rebellion, it had now lost all relevance. "It is to talk like children to talk of any danger from dissatisfaction in the north." Government policy had yet to acknowledge fully the new reality of the Highlands as a powerhouse of military recruitment. "Highlanders were born to be soldiers," "a set of hardy and brave men" raised in a harsh environment with little economic opportunity. Martial superiority was coupled with surplus population: "There is no doubt that the Highlands produce more inhabitants than are necessary for the local demands of that part of the Country." Clanship gave proprietors "extensive influence" over their people, allowing them to call soldiers "forth into vigorous exertion" "at all times."[56]

Yet the military utility of the region rested on a vulnerable foundation. The spirit of clanship had once fostered a love of population and paternal influence in each proprietor: "He did not conceive money to be the only valuable produce of his Estates but he likeways put a valuation upon what I call a rent in men." Dundas was referring here to ward tenure, the duty of a vassal to provide military service for his feudal superior. Chieftain and tenants were bound together by an extraordinary "bond of union" distinct from that of commercial society. By exiling the leading Jacobite leaders and stimulating a love of gain in the elite, the government had wrecked this kind of feudal paternalism, according to Dundas. Bereft of leadership, the Highland common people had fallen back on emigration as the only remedy.[57]

Dundas's memorandum makes a stark contrast with the harsh words of Adam Smith in book 3 of *The Wealth of Nations*, published the following year. Smith here condemned "the violence of . . . feudal institutions." "In a country which has neither foreign commerce, nor any of the finer manufactures, a great proprietor" had to consume local surplus "in rustick hospitality at home." This kind of generosity enabled him to entertain a "multitude of retainers and dependants" who formed the basis of his private army. The tenant farmers on the estate were kept in the same state of servile subordination without security of tenure or money rents. Both orders derived their subsistence "from his bounty, and . . . good pleasure." Because no central power could stop the feuding of the magnates, "the open country . . . continued to be a scene of violence, rapine, and disorder." Happily, the "silent and insensible operation of foreign commerce and manufactures" gradually brought about the lasting peace that medieval kings had failed to achieve. "For a pair of diamond buckles perhaps, or for something as frivolous and useless," the proprietor "exchanged the maintenance . . . of a thousand men for a year."[58]

For Dundas, precisely such conspicuous consumption and self-interest threatened to destroy the most valuable military recruitment zone in the nation. Some sort of accommodation was necessary to divert disaster. The peculiarities of the region had to be accepted and cultivated, not destroyed. "It ought to be the object of every wise ruler in this country, to cherish and make the proper use of the Highlands of Scotland. Nay I will go further, it is my opinion that even Clanship ought to be cherished." Dundas did not spell out the precise tools of reconstruction in his memorandum. It seems that he developed a plan for Highland policy only piecemeal in the years that followed. But in truth, most of the ideas that he eventually embraced were already available in 1775, thanks to the Select Society and the Board for the Annexed Estates.[59]

Over the next decades, this urge to protect Gaelic culture mushroomed into a series of practical projects. By introducing spade husbandry, potato cultivation, anti-emigration legislation, and overcrowded coastal settlements, Dundas and his allies among the landowners and savants hoped to preserve the Highlands in a state of perpetual loyalty to the landed interest. But after the failure of the Annexed Estates, there was little appetite for state intervention. Instead, voluntary associations in Scottish civil society took the lead, often with the blessing of Dundas himself. This conservative variation on the Scottish Enlightenment comprised a form of sentimental population politics, predicated on the notion that Gaelic people were hardened by a difficult climate and endemic poverty into natural soldiers and loyal subjects of the Crown. Such a defense of rural virtue was in turn the cultural and political consequence of the symbiosis between the fiscal-military state and those proprietors who specialized in providing new recruits for the Highland regiments. During the last four decades of the eighteenth century, crofting gradually became the preferred way for private landowners to maintain a maximum surplus population on their estates for the purpose of military recruitment.[60]

By imagining the Highlands as a separate moral order, Dundas and his associates aimed to balance the urban manufacturing society of the Lowlands against the martial prowess and rural tradition of the north. In 1782, military officers and landlords launched an antiquarian crusade under the banner of the Highland Society of London to restore the right of Scottish Gaels to wear arms and traditional dress. Later priorities also included the preservation of the Gaelic language, a professorship in Gaelic literature, and charity for Highland veterans. They succeeded in overturning the ban in 1783 with the help of Dundas. The following year, Dundas was able to bring a campaign against the Annexed Estates to fruition with the repeal of the 1752 legislation. The thirteen estates were restored to their original owners or surviving descendants. Crucially, Dundas justified this act of privatization as a form of restoration, bringing back the rightful elite to their ancestral duties as leaders and protectors of their clans. Private property was a means to resurrect a traditional form of paternal responsibility. Dundas also helped found the Highland Society of Scotland in 1784 as an interest group for the landowners of Scotland and a vehicle of agricultural improvement and tradition in the north. In 1803, Dundas and Henry Mackenzie collaborated on a bill that effectively banned emigration from the Highlands and Hebrides.[61] All of these measures helped diffuse and strengthen the policy of accommodation first implemented in 1763 by Milton, Dalrymple, and Kames on the Annexed Estates. By this count, it was Wallace, not Hume or Ferguson, who won the great luxury debate of the Select Society.

2

Natural History and Civil Cameralism

On clear days, the herring shoals appeared "near the surface" with a brilliant display of "coruscations that dart[ed] from the diamond, sapphire and emerald." But at night, the loch shimmered like phosphorous where the shoals broke the surface to play. A nocturnal traveler moving across the water might think the sea was on fire.[1]

The Welsh naturalist Thomas Pennant witnessed the dazzling spectacle on Loch Broom during the summer of 1772. To Pennant, the circulation of the shoals seemed to obey the laws of a providential economy. He reported that the herring made a regular migration from the depths of the Arctic Ocean to the seas around the British Isles. The "grand shoal" arrived off the Shetland Isles in June. The "breadth and . . . depth" of the "main body" was such "as to alter the appearance of the very ocean." The herring drove "the water before them with a kind of rippling." This vast army was split into two separate columns at the northern tip of Scotland, appearing on both the west and east coasts. Later in the summer, the herring retreated back to deeper waters and stayed there until November. Flocks of predators marked their coming and going: gulls and gannets in the air, cod and dogfish in the sea. These cycles repeated themselves year in and year out, though the shoals along the western seaboard did not always return to the same sea loch. They were "capricious in their motions" and showed no "invariable attachment to their haunts." Two decades after Pennant's tour, a project to build fishing villages on the west coast foundered in part because the migration of the shoals unaccountably diverted into new and different waters.[2]

For Pennant and other observers, the natural wealth of the Highlands and Hebrides appeared prodigious. Pennant called the migration of herring a "stupendous gift of Providence" to the inhabitants of the British Isles. The Scottish bookseller and promoter of planned villages John Knox revived the old argument that herring was of greater value "than the mines of Mexico and Peru." It was the "natural produce of the West Highlands . . . inexhaustible in number." Yet herring was but one of many resources lauded by improvers. Other improvement schemes focused on flax, larch, rhubarb, dye plants, coal, marble, and lead. In 1764, John Walker reported to Lord Kames from Stornoway on Lewis that he had discovered a "New world," teeming with life and possibilities, every bit as exotic and valuable as James Cook's islands in the South Seas: "I have seen the most fertile lands I ever saw in my life, without cultivation; a people by nature the most acute and sagacious, perfectly idle; the most valuable fisheries, without lines or nets; and in every corner one of the finest harbors that ever nature formed, a beautiful though useful void, as inanimate and unfrequented as those of the *Terra Australis*."[3]

The cornucopian rhetoric and local knowledge of naturalists like Walker, Knox, and Pennant funneled government investment into the region and inspired private projects of landowners and patriotic societies. Yet the influence of natural history is largely absent from the economic history of Highland development. The aim of this chapter is to tell the story of how natural historians claimed a leading role in the internal colonization of northern Scotland. To understand their motives and ambitions, we must place the Scottish voyages of discovery in a Continental context. The taxonomic method and economic botany of the Swedish naturalist Carolus Linnaeus provided a model for many of the Highland schemes. Scottish natural history formed a kind of double exposure, repeating a pattern pioneered in the forests and marshes of Swedish Lapland. In political terms, Highland improvement embodied a hybrid ideology of civil cameralism, which transposed the priorities of self-sufficiency and import substitution from a Continental context of landlocked states into the rich civil society of Enlightenment Scotland.

NATURAL KNOWLEDGE AND ECONOMIC DEVELOPMENT

T. M. Devine has isolated some of the principal economic causes behind the collapse of the Highland economy after 1815. He points to the strong increase in commercialization, beginning by 1760 but intensifying during the French Wars, 1793–1815, which subordinated the Highland periphery tightly to the vagaries of demand from the south while at the same time exposing it to the industrial competition of the Scottish Lowlands and England. These combined pressures encouraged landlords to fall back on the comparative advantage of the region in pastoral husbandry. This turn to sheep farming was in turn predicated on the forcible removal of thousands of tenants from arable land now dedicated to sheep pasture. They were commonly shifted to minimal plots of land with low fertility on the coast known as crofts, whose marginal subsistence was intended to force them into industrious habits and seasonal employment in kelping and fishing. Meanwhile, the domestic boom triggered by the disruption of trade during the French Revolutionary and Napoleonic Wars produced windfall profits for landlords, who eagerly restructured their estates to serve the wartime economy with raw materials. Yet the huge rise in their income was to a large degree wasted on conspicuous consumption and reckless investments outside the regional economy. The scattered attempts to fund alternative sources of employment in the form of infant industries were often destroyed by southern competition. The end result was a massive transformation of Highland society, particularly on the north-west coast and in the islands, which forced tens of thousands from their old settlements to makeshift townships on marginal soils and led to the migration of still larger numbers to the towns of the lowlands and the colonies. Once wartime conditions ended after 1815, the basis for this precarious economy collapsed and even greater emigration ensued.[4]

While Devine's socioeconomic interpretation gives ample weight to impersonal and economic forces, he leaves a crucial part of his story unexamined. Though he admits that "several landlords directly contributed to the malaise of the region themselves," he is content to observe that they simply proved "more interested in extracting profit than in sound investment." The attempts by "some proprietors" to overcome these economic forces with "imaginative schemes" such as "fishing and industrial development" in the end "came to little." Even projects "based on considerable sources of finance" proved incapable of modifying the inexorable trajectory of economic development. Elsewhere, Devine adds the caveat that agrarian change had "intellectual" as well as "material" roots and that the making of the new Highland economy was essentially the product of an "improving ideology." Yet the intellectual substance of this force remains unexamined, as if it were nothing more than a mask for self-interest.[5]

In contrast, this book proceeds on the assumption that ideology and intellectual fashions exercised a considerable influence on the improving strategies pursued by Highland landlords. The business of maximizing profit was hardly a transparent operation to proprietors but involved major uncertainties about technology, markets, state protection, and strategic priorities. Above all, there was controversy over the character of the natural order in the Highlands and Western Isles. Disagreements about the nature of the population and territory among natural historians and improvers generated conflicting economic priorities. How could the imperative of profit be balanced against the value of a large and growing population? To what extent did agrarian patriotism serve as an incentive to or a restraint on the economic schemes of the landed interest? Only by asking questions about the nexus of politics, natural knowledge, and voluntary associations can we understand more fully how the landowning class and its intellectual allies contributed to the disaster that enveloped the regional economy in the nineteenth century. The major element missing from histories of agrarian change in the Highlands is any detailed account of how the motivation of landlords in the period was mediated through the Enlightenment of the Lowlands and the complex array of opportunities envisioned by agrarian patriots. This is the most direct path to understand the force of ideology on its own terms rather than as a mere front for self-interest.

The transformation of the Highlands involved a broad variety of social groups and practices. Internal colonization presupposed a social more than an ethnic boundary. This line separated the landowners participating in a Scottish and British elite culture from their Gaelic-speaking tenants and dependents in the Highlands. The proprietors were by the late eighteenth century firmly bicultural, perhaps more at home in British high society than on their Scottish estates. Absenteeism and conspicuous consumption had taken a firm hold on the Scottish aristocracy and gentry. Indeed, to a considerable degree, the improvement ideology involved not just a search for increasing profits but also a form of political action and cultural consumption, regarded as a vehicle to higher social status within polite society. The bicultural elite sponsored voluntary associations, exchanged seeds, collected literary manuscripts, and conducted lobbying campaigns aimed at the Hanoverian state. The government in turn reciprocated by funding many of the schemes, settling army veterans in planned villages, constructing canals and roads across the region, and granting a royal charter to the British Fisheries Society to foster fishing communities on the west coast of Scotland.[6] While the concerns of the state with national security provided the initial impetus for these campaigns, the authority of the enlightened science conveyed through the agency of voluntary associations like the Highland Society of Scotland set much of the actual agenda for colonization and improvement. Experts in botany, mineralogy, forestry, chemistry, and agriculture conjured up a vision of hidden natural riches and unexploited potential on the Highland periphery. Their knowledge of climate, soils, airs, animals, and plants fueled the optimism about the proper means of managing the territory and population. In the final instance, such confident predictions gave the projects of improvement an air of plausibility, marrying agrarian ideology with the cutting edge of the enlightened sciences.

STRATEGIC SURVEYING

An upsurge of scientific interest in the Highlands began in the 1760s as the Board for the Annexed Estates sponsored a series of tours of the region by natural historians and agricultural writers. While the Reverend Walker explored the Western Isles, the Welsh mining engineer John Williams charted the resources of the Annexed Estates on the mainland between 1763 and 1775. The chemist William Cullen advised the board on the properties of alkali and conducted experiments on weed ashes near Loch Lomond. The engineer James Watt, inventor of the separate condenser for steam engines, made a survey on behalf of the Annexed Estates for the Crinan Canal project. Between 1773 and 1784, the Ormiston farmer Andrew Wight compiled a systematic account of the conditions of Scottish agriculture for the benefit of the board. John Hope, the Regius Keeper of the Botanic Garden in Edinburgh, persuaded the board to sponsor five journeys by his student James Robertson in the years 1767–71 that spanned the region from Arran to the Shetland Isles. But to the great chagrin of Hope and Walker, it was the Englishman John Lightfoot who compiled the first *Flora Scotica*. Lightfoot accompanied Thomas Pennant on his second tour of Scotland in 1772. Lightfoot gained access to John Hope's Herbarium in Edinburgh, as well other "notes and observations" by the Regius Keeper. Most likely, several of Lightfoot's "discoveries" (*Poa alpina, Euphoriba esula, Ranunculus reptans, Betula nana*, and so on) were in fact observations collected earlier by Hope and his students.[7]

These different surveys drove home not only the economic utility of natural knowledge but also the environmental peculiarities of northern Scotland. Unlike estate stewards and surveyors, who operated mostly at the level of individual estates, these naturalists and agricultural improvers were commissioned to provide overarching plans of extraction and growth for the region as a whole.[8] John Hope's memorial to the board on behalf of James Robertson showed the full scope of this vision. Robertson's duties entailed: "1. Accurate descriptions of whatever plant animal or mineral shall come in his way. 2. A distinct account of the soils & of the state of gardening & agriculture in those places he shall visit & some useful hints in relation to the fishing upon the coasts & rivers. 3. An account of the appearances of Lead and other metals. 4. That the Museum in the college of Edinburgh may be speedily increased with the natural productions of this country by the materials he shall bring home if they are allowed to be deposited there." Taxonomic surveys of plants, soils, and minerals were essential to impose order on the natural world. Without the labor of classification, John Walker observed, there could be only "a scene of confusion . . . an inextricable mass of individuals . . . a mere chaos of nameless and undefined beings."⁹

How was the authority of the natural historian expressed? Representative texts like Walker's *Report on the Hebrides,* James Robertson's travel journals, Thomas Pennant's *Tour in Scotland* (1774 and 1776), James Anderson's *Present State of the Hebrides* (1785), and John Lightfoot's *Flora Scotica* (1777) were organized around the interconnected tasks of inventory and exploitation. Sections on local climate, diseases, soil, mineral resources, and the character of indigenous people were followed by advice on the best crops or industries to introduce and the optimal means of managing them. The texts sometimes incorporated wholesale catalogues of native plants, animals, and minerals observed by the author. Such analysis was structured around the narrative of the voyage, taking in the natural history of different regions or islands one at a time. Local informants from the gentry and clergy were acknowledged, but it is difficult to tell whether plebeian sources contributed much, since they were mentioned so seldom. A tendency toward cosmopolitan provincialism was common in these texts. Northern improvers thought in comparative terms about their voyages, though they frequently confined such comparison to other peripheries. They were more likely to trace affinities between northern Scotland and Scandinavia, say, than the Scottish Highlands and the economy of southern England.¹⁰

The heavy use of natural historians by the Board for the Annexed Estates signaled a genuine uncertainty about the future of northern Scotland. No single model of improvement dominated the scene after midcentury. The triumph of sheep farming was by no means a foregone conclusion in 1760 or even 1790. Fisheries, coal deposits, dye plants, naval timber, hemp culture, and many other industries all seemed within the realm of possibility. On a prospecting trip through the Western Highlands in 1770, John Williams discovered a great number of garnets near the farm of Lochknoydart. He marveled that the rocks were "as thick with them, as a plumb cake with courants." If the land could yield such unexpected treasures, what else might expert eyes find?¹¹ This uncertainty was fueled by disagreements among the eighteenth-century natural historians about the malleability of the environment. Extravagant optimism clashed with more cautious views. For some, soil amendments and fertilizers like burnt lime, peat moss, and marl promised to revolutionize the possibilities of land reclamation. For others, experiments in acclimatization seemed to indicate that animals and plants could become habituated to new types of climate. Even the climate itself appeared amenable to improvement. It was commonplace to assume that British forms of agriculture and settlement had altered the climate of North America for the better. The aims of Highland improvement must be understood from within this horizon of contemporary uncertainty and cornucopian hopes, not the environmental science or economic assumptions of posterity.

The dominant role of natural history in Highland improvement was due at least in part to the absence of rival forms of expertise. The major figures in Scottish political economy had relatively little to say about northern developments. True, David Hume's *Political Discourses* from 1752 may be read as a hopeful commentary on the prospects of Highland improvement before the practical schemes had truly begun.[12] But in practice, Hume took little active part in the surveys of the Annexed Estates or any other Highland project. The mature expression of Scottish political economy, Adam Smith's *Wealth of Nations* (1776), dwelled on the Highlands only rarely and almost exclusively as a negative case of poverty and backwardness. Smith showed little enthusiasm for the opportunities of the region and offered no specific remedies to overcome its obstacles, leaving others to explore the particular problems of the Highlands.[13] John Walker clearly benefited from Smith's caution. Walker's posthumous work, *An Economical History of the Hebrides and Highlands of Scotland* (1808), contained a wealth of advice on practical agriculture and natural history but little in the way of Smith's analysis of exchange and history of commerce. The fundamental disagreement between the two forms of economic authority concerned the weight of natural knowledge in economic reasoning. While Smith referred frequently to nature as a moral authority, his concrete discussions of agriculture, climate, and soil tended to be brief and cut from one single mold. This was the ideal of intensive cereal production under the regime of mixed husbandry practiced in England and the Scottish Lowlands. Smith treated it as a universal model of growth that could be extended across the British Empire from New Jersey to Bengal. Nature here served as the benign foundation of exchange: a model of stability and self-regulation. On this assumption, the fundamental problem of economic development consisted in mastering the state rather than the natural order.[14] For Walker, in contrast, the analysis of growth always began with the peculiarities of local ecology. The sections on exchange in Walker's treatise on the economic history of the Highlands were quite eclipsed by the lengthy technical arguments about natural advantages that preceded them. In a private book of aphorisms, Walker dismissed Smith's works as needlessly obscure because they sought to refine "plain thoughts" into "abstract terms." He concluded with a sneer: "This is pedantry." Trade was a simple thing to grasp, whereas the complexity of nature required serious attention. From his first travels in the Hebrides onward, Walker had been alert to the limits of conventional agriculture in northern Scotland and keen to explore alternatives. In addition, Walker was an orthodox adherent of the positive balance of trade and often resorted to an argument for self-sufficiency as the optimal strategy of the nation. Of course, in a very general sense, Smith and Walker agreed on the benign character of the natural world. But Walker did so by recourse to the idea of providential secrets in nature rather than the precept of public virtue from private vice.[15]

NORTHERN TIME TRAVEL

The government sponsorship of natural expertise overlapped with the increasing allure of northern travel in polite society. After Edmund Burke's essay on the sublime and James Macpherson's "discovery" of Gaelic poetry, mountain tourism became all the rage. The output of travel writing about Scotland more than doubled after 1750 compared to the first fifty years of the eighteenth century. There were 113 manuscripts and published texts between 1750 and 1800. This boom intensified in the next fifty years, reaching an additional 279 works by 1850. The vast majority of these texts included significant sections on the Highland region. Among the first literati to cash in on the new fashion were Thomas Pennant, William Gilpin, and Samuel Johnson. Their writings helped elevate the Highland tour to the genteel stature of other circuits like the Peaks of Derbyshire and the Lakes of Cumberland and Westmorland. Moreover, aesthetic appreciation was almost always blended with discourses on natural history, improvement, and antiquarian lore. The new travel books thus helped to bring the technical question of Highland development to the literate public. Pennant's best-selling tours of Scotland repackaged the business of strategic surveying into a form of polite entertainment.[16]

The pleasure of the experience was to a great degree temporal. Highland tours offered a time machine for the adherents of stadial history. Travelers felt themselves moving backward in time the farther into the region they penetrated. The Highlander seemed to them a "contemporary ancestor," in Charles Withers's felicitous phrase. John Walker set the stage for a whole generation of temporal travelers in 1764 when he reported to his patrons on the Board for the Annexed Estates that the inhabitants of the Hebrides were "in almost the same Situation as in the Days of Oscian [sic]."[17] This unique temporal status of northern and western Scotland was compounded by the inclination of the new travelers to assume the guise of projectors, planting imaginary towns and growing fictitious crops. The space of the Highlands seemed to participate in two stages of history at the same time. Most tourists were addicted to prospects, climbing mountains and crossing rivers to survey the landscape and observe its strategic features, exercising the economic as much as the aesthetic imagination. The notion of "prospect" signified both an expansive view and a future laden with promise. In the second sense, the idea was closely linked to the prognosticating powers of the enlightened sciences, which claimed the privilege of detecting the useful in the trivial and the profitable in the neglected. The plausibility of northern improvement came to rest in large part on this mixed rhetorical arsenal provided by conjectural history, "statistical" inquiries, and the natural history of soil and climate.[18]

In the summer of 1772, the rising star of British natural history Sir Joseph Banks organized an expedition to northern Scotland and Iceland. He was accompanied by Carolus Linnaeus's student Daniel Solander and the Scottish physician James Lind. Banks approached the Iceland journey with nearly the same ambition that he had lavished on the South Seas during his voyage with James Cook in 1768–71. His itinerary connected Gaelic Scotland with the world of Old Norse culture and the wider North Atlantic. Banks had settled on the expedition to Iceland after a quarrel with the Admiralty lost him a spot with Captain Cook's second voyage of circumnavigation. The North Atlantic offered a substitute South Pacific: first a ramble through the Hebrides and then onward to the sublime volcanic wasteland of Iceland populated by the descendants of the Vikings. Although the voyage did not produce any publications besides Uno Von Troil's *Letters on Iceland*, Banks did contribute the first learned account of the basalt formations at Fingal's Cave on the island of Staffa to Thomas Pennant's *Tour of Scotland*. He wrote of encountering the Staffa columns at dawn with a rush of wonder: "Compared to this what are the cathedrals." Like Walker and Pennant, Banks was also an admirer of Macpherson's Ossian. He took great pleasure in identifying landmarks from Macpherson's epic and daydreamed of escaping his ship to enjoy the "sweet affection" of Ossian's verses in solitude. He spoke with admiration of the "clannish" ties that bound Gaelic plebeians to their masters and made them far more deferential than English servants.[19]

The Tory lexicographer Samuel Johnson made his circuit with James Boswell from Edinburgh over Inverness to Skye and back via Oban in 1773. Though neither savant was trained in natural history, their accounts dwelled at considerable length on the geographic features of the Highlands and the influence of its natural peculiarities on the inhabitants. Johnson's *Journey to the Western Isles* (1775) ranged over such topics as the degeneration of cattle, the extirpation of native species, island microclimates, afforestation, and kelping. The two travelers had brought a copy of Pennant's first tour with them but found it wanting at times. In general, Johnson was far less sanguine about the prospects of the region than Pennant or Walker. However, this pessimism was linked in turn to a sentimental embrace of the past. Despite his skepticism about the authenticity of Ossian, Johnson relished the chance to "speculate upon the remains of pastoral life." Though he carefully rejected the notion of the Gael as a savage, he observed that the remote situation and difficult environment had kept native society in a state close to the pastoral stage and had preserved a stronger martial spirit than in the south. Without descending into the realm of particular policy, Johnson recommended government action to ameliorate the effects of rack-renting and counter the threat of emigration. Boswell, too, was content to season his *Tour to the Hebrides* (1785) with a sentimental defense of Jacobitism. His argument for the superiority of feudal manners was focused on the authenticity of his own feelings rather than strategies of political or economic retrenchment. He recounted with self-conscious pride in his *Tour* how he wept bitterly on meeting a veteran from the Battle of Culloden. Boswell's main response to Highland improvement thus amounted to a public display of grief. Jacobitism had degenerated into an experience of sentimental tourism.[20]

A third expedition to the Highlands and Hebrides was organized in the summer of 1772. Thomas Pennant equipped a team of assistants, including the English botanist the Reverend John Lightfoot (who would later publish the first *Flora Scotica*), the Gaelic scholar the Reverend John Stuart of Killin, the "servant-painter" Moses Griffiths, and an assortment of fowlers, grooms, and other servants. Pennant was a gentleman naturalist who kept up a correspondence with luminaries like Carolus Linnaeus, Gilbert White of Selborne, Sir Joseph Banks, and J. R. Forster. In the spirit of polite natural history, Pennant's published *Tour in Scotland* mixed aesthetic observations with detailed commentary about husbandry and soil conditions. In his account of Colonsay, Pennant complained that the natives were too poor and too ignorant to take advantage of the secret bounties hidden in the land: "Their poverty prevents them from using the very means Providence has given them of raising a comfortable subsistence. They have a good soil, plenty of limestone, and sufficient quantity of peat. A sea abounding with fish, but their distressed state disables them from cultivating the one, and taking the other." It was the task of the naturalist to bring this desperate situation to the attention of the broader public and mobilize opinion in favor of improvement. Later, Pennant took credit for exciting the wave of public interest in Highland improvement that resulted in the founding of the British Fisheries Society.[21]

For Pennant, the cornucopian promise of the north was necessarily tied to the austere habits of Highland plebeians. To prove his point, he conducted an interview with a ghost. In a solitary chamber in the house of Captain Archibald Campbell on Ardmaddie Bay, Pennant reflected on the events of his voyage through the Hebrides. He imagined himself "gently wafted down the Sound of Mull, bounded on each side by the former dominions, of mighty chieftains; or of heroes immortalized in the verse of Ossian." Working his "busy fancy" into a "species of enthusiasm," Pennant witnessed the apparition of an "ancient warrior," dressed in Gaelic garb, wielding the banned weapons of the target and claymore. But where the poetry about Ossian and Fingal expressed a literary nostalgia for an extinct society, Pennant's ghost embodied vital virtues and a living culture. Hovering in the air before the gentleman naturalist, the apparition excoriated the northern elite, proclaiming that it had sunk deeply into absentee habits, rapacious self-interest, and "degenerate" cosmopolitanism. After the defeat at Culloden, the native "feature and habit [were] changed; the one effeminated, the other become ridiculous by adopting the idle fashions of foreign climes." The ghost begged Pennant to return home, publish his account, and awaken the conscience of the absentee landlords and the public at large. With some modest instruction and economic assistance, the "infant colony" of Gaelic society could be rehabilitated and saved from the disaster of emigration and degeneration.[22]

This rescue operation would bring about a reconciliation of modern commerce and ancient virtue. Pennant encouraged improving landlords to "restore" the "laudable part of the ancient manners" but "eradicate the bad." The key to this act of cultural preservation lay in the nature of the assistance. Any arts introduced among the Highlanders must be "adapted to their climate." Improvers should attempt to introduce only the "coarser manufactures." New industries must harmonize with the simple, harsh conditions of existence in the north. This was the natural basis of Gaelic virtue: extractive industries, simple affections, modest wants, a population bred in a difficult climate. "They require no great matters: a small portion of a raiment; a little meal." "They will not envy you your new luxuries." On such a foundation, the Highlander would submit to military recruitment with cheerful docility. As long as he was assured of some livelihood in his home country and the prospect of returning there after completing his service, he would go "to distant climes . . . [and] sacrifice [his life] in the just cause of the government."[23]

CIVIL CAMERALISM

The time travel of Pennant, Johnson, and Boswell further stimulated the new paternalism that sought to balance the profits of agrarian capitalism against the social and military priorities of the landed interest. After the termination of the Annexed Estates experiment in 1784, Highland improvement shifted into the domain of voluntary associations like the Highland Society of London, founded in 1778, the Highland Society of Edinburgh, created in 1784, and the joint stock company of the British Fisheries Society, launched the following year. The two latter associations in particular offered a new locus for Highland travel and natural history. The tours of James Anderson and the London bookseller John Knox proved critical in promoting the west coast fisheries. Thomas Telford surveyed roads and supervised the Caledonian Canal project under the joint aegis of the House of Commons and the Highland Society of Edinburgh. John Walker, John Williams, and James Headrick found a conduit for their research in the *Prize Essays and Transactions of the Highland Society of Scotland*. Other Highland travelers after 1780 included the missionary John Lanne Buchanan, the astronomer Nevil Maskelyne, the German con artist and jewel thief Rudolph Raspe, the French industrial spy Barthélemy Faujas de Saint-Fond, John Walker's successor as professor of natural history Robert Jameson the geologist, Thomas Garnett, chemist and president of the Edinburgh Society of Natural History, the Forfar gardener George Don, and several students of the botanists John Walker and John Hope, including Francis Buchanan Hamilton and Archibald Menzies.[24]

John Sinclair's *Statistical Account of Scotland* (1791–99) represented the most ambitious attempt to elucidate the natural and social conditions of Scotland during the Enlightenment. This twenty-one-volume work mobilized the Scottish clergy to conduct an anatomy of the Scottish nation at the parish level. A man of prodigious energy but middling intellect, Sinclair proved the right man for the plodding task of collating parish reports. He was helped by such political and intellectual patrons as the Duke of Argyll and Principal William Robertson of Edinburgh University. Historians so far have mined the *Statistical Account* mostly for the rich glimpses of social and economic life that it offers. But Sinclair's twenty-one volumes also offer the most extensive contemporary collection of information regarding the state of the Scottish environment. The printed list of questions for the clergy—*Queries Drawn up for the purpose of elucidating the Natural History and Political State of Scotland*—placed much emphasis on investigating local conditions, ranging over such factors as soil fertility, soil amendments, disease, longevity, wastelands, and crop rotations. Sinclair's questionnaire in fact paralleled the unpublished set of "Queries Concerning the North of Scotland" drawn up by John Walker sometime in the 1780s. They were preceded by a tradition of earlier parochial surveys, including the work of Edward Lhuyd in Wales and the Earl of Buchan for the Antiquarian Society of Scotland. Though the *Statistical Account* relied on a correspondence network rather than the observations of traveling natural historians, Sinclair's questionnaire deliberately followed on the genre of instructions for travelers dating back to Robert Boyle and Robert Sibbald, continued by Carolus Linnaeus, Josiah Tucker, and Leopold Berchtold in the eighteenth century.[25]

The purpose of the *Statistical Account* was to introduce a Continental model of knowledge collection, signaled by the new English word *statistical*. Sinclair cited with approval the dictum of the Prussian reformer Count Ewald Friedrich von Hertzberg that the government did not need to hide any information from its subjects in the age of Enlightenment. Yet it was by no means a quantitative survey in the modern sense. Instead, Sinclair's clergymen compiled a chorographical encyclopedia describing the material and social conditions of each parish, interlaced with scattered quantitative data. In economic terms, Sinclair wanted a "Prussian" economy for Britain. The strategic goal was to achieve self-sufficiency in the food supply and raw materials like wool and hemp for manufacturing through schemes of internal improvement, wasteland colonization, and import substitution. This economic vision was combined with a paternalist population politics. The landed interest should shape and direct society through active intervention, blocking emigration, building planned villages, and establishing model manufactures in the countryside.[26]

Such a fascination with the local and indigenous had been a common fashion in the European republic of letters since the seventeenth century. Paradoxically, the appeal of the local derived in great part from the discovery of the New World and the expansion of overseas trade. The cameralist school of economic discourse recommended that rulers of landlocked states without power to acquire transoceanic colonies should embrace strategies of import substitution and internal colonization as an alternative path to wealth and power. A variety of savants exploited this argument to create a market for their services. At one extreme, alchemists claimed to offer a radical shortcut to mineral wealth. From the alchemists' alembic, bullion would flow without the expense of foreign conquest. Natural historians like Georges-Louis Leclerc Buffon in turn embraced acclimatization as the botanical version of alchemy. Here, too, matter would be transmuted by a skilled operator into something rare and wonderful. But some physicians cautioned against the increase in exotic commodities such as coffee and chocolate. Instead they promoted indigenous substitutes in the name of health, virtue, and a favorable balance of trade. There were a number of successes with imported or indigenous crops that gave an air of plausibility to cameralist schemes, including for example Italian sericulture,

Dutch tobacco cultivation and the introduction of the potato to the Continent. Import substitution thus constituted a rational choice under certain conditions. The strategy of internal development extended to schemes of environmental transformation. In the German lands, the drainage of swamps and reclamation of wastelands laid the foundation for long-term growth. In Denmark, extensive schemes set in motion by the absolutist state may have saved the country from ecological disaster.[27]

Yet Sinclair fused the cameralist goal of self-sufficiency with a liberal critique of the state. In his inaugural speech to the British Wool Society in January 1791, he rejected government intervention in the knowledge economy: "If government engages in any scheme of national improvement, the money allotted for the purpose, is in general improvidently expended; the experiments necessary to be made, are either carelessly tried, or wholly omitted, and when the assistance of the public is withdrawn, the scheme perishes at once." Sinclair instead favored the work of voluntary associations in civil society. "*Information conveyed without the use of force*" was the "great engine" of improvement, in the words of Sinclair's ally Robert Heron. Such a hybrid ideal of governance is best thought of as a *civil* form of cameralism. While the isolated individual lacked the perseverance and capital to succeed, networks of learned and influential men could raise money without waste and diffuse information quickly. The British Wool Society was set up along these lines by Sinclair in 1790. An offshoot of the Highland Society of Scotland, its members included dozens of magnates and gentleman farmers, such as the Duke of Argyll and the Earl of Seaforth. The immediate and technical aim of the British Wool Society was to diversify and refine the sheep breeds of Scotland. This would in turn serve the strategic and long-term purpose of making Britain self-sufficient in fine wool manufacture.[28]

The political ambiguities of civil cameralism also generated contradictions within the project of information gathering. The index in the twenty-first and final volume of the *Statistical Account* was intended to provide a quick overview and comparison of different parishes on a variety of practical questions such as marling, emigration, and enclosure. By educating landowners about natural advantages, Sinclair sought to tailor the methods of improvement to suit specific local conditions. The same principle lay behind Sinclair's other survey writings of the period, the *General Reports on Agriculture* for the Board of Agriculture. Yet such an emphasis on local context confirmed the lack of consensus about the character of the Scottish regions. Because the nine hundred parish reports were presented with a minimum of editorial commentary, the result was by no means without inconsistencies and ambiguities. Some clergymen praised the hand of providence in the localities while others complained bitterly about the "useless gift of nature" hidden in limestone too hard to quarry or coal too deep to excavate. Rather than settling the question of the natural basis of economic development once and for all, the *Statistical Account* instead reinforced the rival views about climate, soil, and other natural advantages that haunted Scottish natural history.[29]

THE TRANSNATIONAL LOCAL

These battles over the order of nature in Enlightenment Scotland were closely connected to the wider European scene. In particular, Highland improvers owed a debt to the Swedish naturalist Carolus Linnaeus. A great many of the savants we have discussed were early adherents and popularizers of Linnaeus's method of classification and economic botany in Britain, including John Walker, John Hope, James Robertson, John Lightfoot, John Stuart of Killin, Sir Joseph Banks, Daniel Solander, and James Anderson. They shared a common faith in the analytical power of Linnaeus's system and its utility as the basis for new ways of mastering the natural world. However, the introduction of the Linnaean method did not follow a single path. British naturalists adopted the new system for widely different varieties of improvement. Such diversity was encouraged by a strong tension within Linnaeus's own works between a moral-medical ideal of autarky and a commercial-botanical strategy for national aggrandizement.

A poor parson's son, Linnaeus rose from obscure and provincial origins to become an ennobled professor at the University of Uppsala and an acclaimed authority across Europe and its colonies. He trained as a physician at Uppsala and then spent a few seminal years in the lecture halls and botanical gardens of Holland. Historians have usually regarded Linnaeus's system of classification as his central and most successful achievement. They note how the system offered a useful and accessible method of grasping the diversity of the natural world, well suited to the encyclopedic temper of the European republic of letters in the Enlightenment. The method consisted in a binomial system of nomenclature, ranking organisms in five principal groups according to class, order, genus, species, and variety. Its general form was conservative, as it built firmly on scholastic tradition. The most innovative aspect of the system concerned the classification of plants. Here, Linnaeus employed a model based on reproductive structure (drawing in part on the previous work of Sébastian Vaillant) in which the number, size, shape, and placement of stamen and pistils determined the genus. The system of sexual classification became the basis of Linnaeus's work *Systema Naturae*, first published in 1735. His simplified method of botanical identification appealed to a wide audience of scholars and amateurs alike, providing important inspiration for the new fashion of botany as a mark of sensibility among cultivated men and women around Europe. Both Rousseau and Goethe were avid followers.[30]

For Linnaeus, such advances in taxonomy were but a means to an economic end. Recently, scholars have begun to shed new light on the political context of Linnaeus's botany. Like many other Swedish savants in the period, Linnaeus's ambitions were shaped by the postimperial condition of the Swedish state and the rise of the protectionist Hat Party in the Swedish Riksdag. After the end of the Great Northern Wars in 1721, Sweden had lost the majority of its Baltic possessions. Together with the engineer Mårten Triewald and the manufacturer Jonas Alströmer, Linnaeus founded the Swedish Academy of Science in 1739 to foster greatness through science rather than war. Like other cameralists, he looked to local resources and indigenous virtue for the sources of national restoration.[31]

Linnaeus's rise to power and influence began in earnest with his expedition into Swedish Lapland in 1732, a two-thousand-mile journey in search of new and valuable plants. After scaling the mountain Vallevare, Linnaeus wrote in his journal: "When I had ascended halfway up the side of it, I thought I had arrived into a new world, and when I arrived at the summit, I did not know, whether I was in Asia or Africa, because the soil, situation and all the plants were unknown to me." Lapland formed a northern frontier where a colonial elite of Swedish administrators and clergymen ruled a majority population of Sami reindeer pastoralists. Lacking both local language skills and a genuine grasp of Sami ethnography, Linnaeus seems to have concocted his own version of native culture for the purpose of self-promotion. This form of northern exoticism permeated the work that cemented his reputation, the *Flora Lapponica* of 1737. The Lapland trip was the first of five voyages of provincial inventory undertaken by Linnaeus. Like John Walker, he saw his travels as a means to discover the providential order within the regions of the nation. The naturalist employed his heightened powers of observation and collection to discover the uses of the local environment. Sometimes, he relied on folk custom; at other moments, he identified resources unknown to natives but evident to the knowledgeable and pious natural historian. Linnaeus observed in the *Flora Oeconomia* (1749), "The final goal of Creation is man. . . . Everything is thus made for the use of man." Such mastery of nature was especially appealing in a poor nation beset by recurring dearth. Hence, Linnaeus's writings on economic botany were frequently occupied with the discovery of edible wild plants such as lyme grass (*Leymus arenarius*) and Iceland moss (*Cetraria islandica*). He linked this humanitarian function of natural history with a moral and economic critique of modern consumption patterns. Tea, coffee, and sugar wreaked havoc with the national health and balance of trade. The habits and traditions of the Sami offered a moral alternative for the Swedish people to emulate. Linnaeus hoped that the alpine or subarctic shrub *Linnaea borealis* could wean his compatriots off their addiction to Chinese tea. Linnaeus's overblown expectations about the Swedish flora were combined with a cult of the northern climate. He believed that the severe climate and poor soils of Lapland had preserved the Sami from the corrupt artifice of urban civilization, which had destroyed the strength and virtue of the Swedes. Lapland was thus the gateway to the Gothic past and national regeneration.[32]

The theory of the natural economy was set out by Linnaeus in the treatise *Oeconomia Naturae* of 1749, a work heavily indebted to British natural theology, particularly the writings of John Ray and William Derham. Linnaeus's treatise described a world of eternal order and static harmony governed by stable proportions, fixed species, regular flows, and cyclical patterns. Each of the three kingdoms of nature—minerals, plants, and animals—underwent the same eternal cycle of "propagation, preservation, and destruction." All species had an "allotted place," and all places had a species to fill it. The Creator had given each animal and plant the proper means to propagate and preserve itself. Competition took place between rather than within species. The whole system formed a minutely graded hierarchy in which each species served as sustenance for another. The hierarchy remained stable because God had fixed the rates of reproduction for each species. The same harmony also extended to the geography and climate zones of the world: "The Creator has apportioned his gifts across the entire world, so that each place has gained a different yet equal advantage in relation to the others."[33]

While Linnaeus's faith in a providential order never faltered, he remained fundamentally ambivalent about the proper function of humankind within the divine economy. Thus the ascetic conception of Sami autarky competed with a very different economic vision. From the 1740s onward, Linnaeus conducted trials in acclimatization in the botanic garden at Uppsala and elsewhere. The hope was to diversify Swedish agriculture with exotic and valuable transplants from southern latitudes. By growing tea, coffee, and other commodities in Swedish gardens and plantations, the nation could benefit from the global economy without the expense of empire or the hazards of trade. In this version of Linnaeus's economic botany, Lapland was to serve as a cash crop colony rather than a model of ascetic virtue. Plantations of nutmeg and saffron would fill the tundra. Whereas Linnaeus's optimism about subarctic spice crops was extraordinary, his interest in Lapland as an internal colony was shared by many fellow savants. The Swedish Academy of Science entertained a variety of proposals about northern improvements from the 1740s onward. Linnaeus himself reported successes with peat moss reclamation and potato culture in his inventory of the province of Dalecarlia (Dalarna). His student Pehr Kalm believed that the climate of Swedish Finland would grow milder as advanced agriculture spread. He claimed that the countries of southern Europe had gone through a similar process in antiquity. Linnaeus agreed that the coniferous forest of the north had a chilling effect on westerly winds and the general pattern of weather. Although Linnaeus never conducted a careful investigation of the Swedish climate, his associate Pehr Wargentin, astronomer and secretary in the Swedish Academy of Sciences, maintained a detailed record of Swedish weather from 1754 until his death in 1783. Wargentin also published comparative studies in the Swedish Academy of Science's journal using meteorological data from Stockholm, Paris, Algiers, and Pondicherry.[34]

These hopes for a miniature empire within the nation were anchored in a theory of biogeography. Though Linnaeus emphasized that the characteristics of species were fixed since Creation, he allowed for a certain plasticity of plants based on habit. This force helped account for the variety of plants and animals generated by domestication and other forms of human selection. It also opened the door to notions of botanical acclimatization. Among the "accidental" causes that fostered change in plants, he listed "climate, soil, heat, winds, change of soil." All of these factors could be manipulated by a skilled gardener: "That varieties are the work of cultivation is clearly shown by *horticulture*, which frequently produces and modifies them." He concluded that a plant therefore might become inured to a northern climate, making it into a new, hardier variety. He did not suggest a causal mechanism to explain the process but was content to insist on its practicability and economic value. Linnaeus simply observed that Sweden already had a share of introduced species that were apparently thriving there, including the mulberry tree. From a theological perspective, Linnaeus's fusion of scripture and natural history made the process a religious necessity. How else could the diffusion of plants from Eden be explained? His *Oratio de telluris habitabilis incremento* of 1744 postulated a story of species migration outward to the different climate zones of the earth. The same unknown mechanism of adaptation might be employed for economic purposes by skilled gardeners and naturalists.[35]

Linnaeus was much preoccupied by the problem of establishing a global network of seed and plant collectors capable of supplying his Uppsala experiments with a continuing flow of valuable specimens. Like his counterparts at

Kew Gardens and the Jardin du Roi, he decided not to rely exclusively on the gift exchange of the international republic of letters since his particular mission of collecting was tied so closely to issues of national security and agricultural espionage. Instead his preferred solution was to groom a generation of *lärjungar* (disciples) to comb the earth at the master's bidding: Pehr Kalm went to North America, Daniel Solander to the South Pacific, Carl Peter Thunberg to Japan, and so forth. Linnaeus's taxonomic innovations—the binomial nomenclature and method of sexual classification—offered a powerful method of connecting periphery and metropole. Local knowledge could be translated into a system of collection with universal reach. Yet these methods proved more durable than the economic aim behind them. Linnaeus's bold global strategy yielded little of profit to the Swedish nation. The trial crops in Uppsala's botanic gardens all failed one after another. Rice, sugar cane, and coffee refused to habituate to the northern climate. By the 1750s, Linnaeus was forced to develop a more cautious theory of acclimatization. He now hypothesized that plants from high altitudes could be transplanted to the Swedish mountains. In particular, he had great hopes for larch plantations. He was also confident that plants from a cold climate such as Tartarian rhubarb could become inured to Swedish winters. This reworking of the theory of acclimatization allowed a sense of optimism to persist. There was no single moment of reckoning to expose the chimera. Even after Linnaeus's death in 1778, the strategy of internal diversification remained intact, offering a spur for new experiments elsewhere.[36]

THE BRITISH RECEPTION OF LINNAEUS

The appeal of Linnaeus's natural history to British savants began with his method. The relative accessibility and simplicity of sexual classification stimulated the growth of a new audience of amateur botanists. British popularizers like Benjamin Stillingfleet and later Erasmus Darwin strengthened this allure by rendering Linnaeus's Latin discourses into polished and entertaining vernacular. The popular turn of natural history in Britain proved a congenial fit with the interest of the landowning elite. Gardening was already a badge of aristocratic status. Botanical collecting became a sign of curiosity and learning among increasing numbers of male and female virtuosi such as Lord Bute and the Duchess of Portland. Adam Smith remarked in *The Wealth of Nations* that there was little profit in the "delightful art" of gardening since "so many rich people" now practiced it "for amusement." Smith taught himself the basics of Linnaean botany as a form of diversion when he was writing his political economy. Landowners also looked to natural history for new tools of estate improvement. It was hardly a coincidence that Stillingfleet and Pulteney both chose to include in their translations different parts of Linnaeus's *Pan Svecicus* from 1749. In this pamphlet, Linnaeus used botanical fieldwork and an early version of binomial nomenclature to suggest a new approach to one of the central problems of agrarian capitalism. By observing the feeding habits of roaming cattle, Linnaeus and his students compiled a list of more than 850 plant species that could serve as alternative forms of fodder. Linnaeus here spoke like a practical farmer about pasture capacity and manure production.[37]

Natural history was quite possibly the "hegemonic" science of late eighteenth-century British elites. But we must not confuse diffusion and popularity with homogeneity of reception. There was little consistency in the appropriation of the new botany by British savants. Local adaptations ranged from the sexually explicit and materialist botany of Erasmus Darwin in the Midlands to the Anglican pastoral of Gilbert White of Selborne, from the cameralism of John Walker's Hebrides to the "neo-mercantilist" strategy of Sir Joseph Banks at Kew Gardens. While we know a good deal about the social circles represented by Darwin, White, and Banks, far less has been said about the peculiar reception of Linnaeus in Scotland. Arguably, Scottish savants felt a closer affinity with the Swedish perspective of Linnaeus than other British naturalists because they shared his preoccupation with the difficulties of improvement on the northern periphery. Though none of the Scottish improvers could be described as a Continental cameralist in a straightforward sense, they were particularly engrossed by the basic themes of Linnaeus's thought, the twin problems of climate and acclimatization. The northern orientation of Linnaean thought was also evident in the first translations of Linnaeus into English. Benjamin Stillingfleet introduced the reading public of Britain to the Linnaean system in 1759 with his blandly titled but often reprinted *Miscellaneous Tracts Relating to Natural History, Husbandry and Physick*. This was a selection of dissertations by Linnaeus and pupils from the *Amoenitates Academicae*. It included Linnaeus's defense of provincial inventory from 1741, "Oration Concerning the Necessity of Traveling in One's Own Country," in which questions of northern improvement played a pivotal role. Linnaeus described the natural riches he had encountered on his domestic journeys, insisting that they were equal or superior to any discoveries overseas. Perhaps his most startling claim was the idea that a northern climate actually accelerated the rate of plant growth. "Where can we have greater opportunities, than in this Sueogothic tract, of considering the intense rigor, and vehemence of winter, the incredible marble-like strength of ice. And yet in this inclement climate grain of all sorts is observed to spring forth sooner, grow quicker, and ripen in less time than in any other part of the world." Providence thus transmuted the conditions of the Arctic tundra into a source of abundance and vitality. Stillingfleet's commentary reinforced this point with further details about the quick development of Lapland grain borrowed from the *Flora Lapponica*. Linnaeus described his northern expedition as a model that supplied vital clues about the neglected biological and cultural diversity of the entire nation: "Lapland alone furnished me some time ago with a hundred rare plants." Who could doubt "that our other provinces conceal in their unfrequented corners other new plants, valuable for use or beauty." While Stillingfleet doubted that there were any new species to be discovered in Britain, he agreed that the economic uses of native plants were much neglected. Richard Pulteney's *General View of the Writings of Linnaeus* of 1781 further stressed the northern orientation of Linnaean natural history by giving an extended account of the Lapland expedition along with glimpses of the significance of Swedish provincial inventory to economic botany. Both Stillingfleet and Pulteney paid close attention to the effects of the northern climate on the Sami population, noting the stamina and austere diet of the natives.[38]

In Scottish circles, this Linnaean project was first taken up by John Walker. As an aspiring young naturalist in search of patronage, Walker wrote to Linnaeus in early 1762 to announce his intention of promoting botany in Scotland and to profess his allegiance to the "sex system." Linnaeus responded warmly and showed particular interest in the prospect of discovering new alpine plants in Scotland. He pushed Walker to compile a proper Scottish flora that could become the guide for botanical acclimatization and the exchange of seed. He advised Walker to record carefully the place and the soil of each plant "in order that they may more easily be cultivated in gardens, while the seeds are being obtained." A few months later, Walker wrote back to report that he had begun a survey of the Scottish mountains. He stressed his attention to altitude, probably in deference to Linnaeus's theory of alpine transplantation. Walker told Linnaeus that he had used the barometer and "geometric mensuration" to relate his plant identifications to the height over the sea. The primary aims of Linnaean natural history were much in evidence in Walker's *Report on the Hebrides* of 1764 and 1771. Although Walker failed to produce the flora Linnaeus had requested, he did include a large number of observations on the natural history of the region. He justified them to Lord Kames and the commissioners for the Annexed Estates as "favorable Opportunities, of turning the Truths of Science to the Purposes of Life." The Hebrides report covered much of the same ground as Linnaeus's provincial inventories. It painted the archipelago as a "National object" unfairly neglected by the public and government. Like Linnaeus, Walker extolled his own endurance and attention in surveying thousands of miles of sea and land. He related the happy effects of a northern climate on plants, quoting Linnaeus's report about the quick maturation of grain in Lapland. He also stressed the benign influence of the climate on the health and longevity of the native Gaels. As Linnaeus had requested, he considered carefully the importance of specific soil types to plant life. He linked the excellent quality of local sheep wool on Oronsay to the sandy soil of its pastures. He touched frequently on the possibility of plant introductions and the problems they involved, particularly the case of flaxseed, which seemed to degenerate in the Western Isles. Walker also discussed the use of local plants as a substitute for expensive or strategic imports, including dye stuff and hemp. Even in the most inhospitable places he found little-known plants that appeared capable of sustaining local improvement. On the mountainous island of Rum, he identified "the *Aira coerulea* of Linnaeus," or purple moor grass, as the linchpin for a new pastoral economy.[39]

To be sure, Walker owed a great debt as well to other British travelers and naturalists. The fascination with the local was by no means a Continental monopoly. When Linnaeus and Walker discussed the possibility of a Scottish flora, they framed it as an attempt to extend the natural theology of John Ray. Walker's Hebrides report also engaged with works such as Sibbald's *Scotia illustrata, sive, Prodromus historiae naturalis* (1684) and Martin's *Description of the Western Isles* (1703). Martin and Sibbald in turn drew on a wider British tradition of chorography and provincial surveys.[40] However, while domestic British works no doubt provided a foil for Walker's schemes, it was the new Swedish botany that imparted them with decisive momentum and authority. Walker's report contained all the signature elements of Linnaean travel: the use of binomial nomenclature and sexual classification, the interest in problems of acclimatization and the effects of climate, the link between climate and native virtue, and the expectation of divine riches in the form of indigenous plants. Walker's contemporaries endorsed this vision. It was the public esteem for economic botany that allowed Walker to obtain the position as professor of natural history at the University of Edinburgh in 1779 against the strong bid of his rival William Smellie, who had made his mark as an anti-Linnaean theorist rather than an expert improver. Lord Kames was a long-standing patron of Walker's work.[41]

TEATIME WITH DR. HOPE

A different variation on Linnaeus's natural history was pursued by John Hope, the Regius Keeper of the Royal Botanic Garden in Edinburgh and professor of botany in the university. Like Walker, Hope was an Edinburgh savant who moved in the central current of the Scottish Enlightenment. He was a founding member of the Select Society as well as the Royal Society of Edinburgh. One measure of his influence in this community was the support he mobilized on behalf of a natural history museum in which the findings of the Highland surveys could be deposited. Hope's 1769 petition was backed by the Edinburgh University principal William Robertson, the physician William Cullen, and the chemists Francis Home and Joseph Black. Hope's strength lay in managing networks and information. Like John Sinclair, John Hope pursued a "civil cameralist" strategy of import substitution that often relied on voluntary associations and informal networks rather than government support. He was no great traveler himself but preferred to delegate the necessary fieldwork to others. As early as 1763, he offered courses about the Linnaean system and arranged annual competitions for his students in order to encourage botanical fieldwork in the Highlands and elsewhere. From the outset, he was keen to expand the botanic garden in Edinburgh along Linnaean lines. A monument to commemorate Linnaeus was quickly erected in the garden after the Swedish naturalist's death. Hope's ambition seems to have been to build a Scottish counterpart to Linnaeus's Uppsala garden, replete with exotic and rare plants from home and abroad. Foreign seed exchange and internal inventory were thus complementary aims. At the same time as Hope organized an inventory of northern Scotland, he was establishing ties with colonial collectors in North America and the West Indies. However, in practice, the two priorities were not easy to harmonize, given scarce funding opportunities and the limited attention span of potential patrons. Hope complained to the Earl of Findlater that British naturalists were all too eager to scour "the woods of America" and discover "every article used in the oeconomy of foreign life," yet had been "absolutely inattentive to the natural productions of our native Country." Hope took particular care in preparing his Highland survey, training a student specifically for the task. He drilled James Robertson in Linnaean nomenclature—"a young man of promising genius tho . . . illiterate"—to become his proxy traveler. After an initial foray to Arran in 1766, Robertson explored the rest of northern Scotland on five trips between 1767 and 1771 organized by Hope and funded by the Board for the Annexed Estates. Robertson's travel journals were conscientiously detailed and full of imaginative suggestions about the economic potential of the periphery. The strong similarities between the reports of Walker and Robertson betray their common debt to Linnaean natural history. As might be expected, Robertson paid particular attention to the hidden uses of native plants, including medicinal herbs, dye stuffs, cattle fodder, and plants suitable for famine relief. Like Linnaeus and Walker before him, Robertson often spoke of folk knowledge in appreciative terms and sought to diffuse it to his learned and polite readers. His reports also contained a large number of observations on the peculiarities of the northern climate, from the spread of plants to the effects of local diseases. By all accounts, Hope was very pleased with the result of the journey. As late as 1784, he recommended that the board sponsor another botanical survey. Yet he did not seek to publish Robertson's reports, except for a brief letter submitted to the *Philosophical Transactions*.[42]

Hope's failure to publish the results of Robertson's journey was probably a consequence of his competing enthusiasm for acclimatization. Like Linnaeus, Hope was torn between his interest in provincial inventory and his expectation that foreign plant introductions might transform the commerce of the nation. At the end of the Seven Years' War, Hope founded the Society for the Importation of Foreign Seeds and Plants, aimed at acclimatizing exotic and valuable plants. He also corresponded with Lord Kames about how to design a winter garden where exotic plants might survive the Scottish winters. The records of the Royal Botanic Garden bear testimony to a very large number of trials with exotics. *Catalogus arborum et fructicum in horto Edinensi crescentium anno 1778* lists many dozens of foreign introductions to the garden, including silver maple, Seville oranges, and St. John's wort from the Canary islands. At least some of these plants and seeds came from Hope's correspondents. His network included overseas collectors such as Alexander Anderson on Saint Vincent and Matthew Guthrie in Saint Petersburg. A primary goal was to obtain medicinal plants capable of thriving in the northern climate and to grow them on a commercial scale. To this end, Hope studied reports by traveling naturalists for clues about the fit between exotic plants and different climate types, including the voyage to North America by Linnaeus's student Pehr Kalm. In practical terms, Hope played an active part in the introduction of Turkish rhododendron to Scotland, esteemed as a cure for arthritic complaints. Another plant of great interest to Hope was the Persian asafetida (*Ferula persica*), which was reputed to have antirheumatic and digestive properties. He also attempted to introduce Chinese hemp (probably *Cannabis chinensis*) into Scotland. Finally, much like Linnaeus, he was keen to break into the Russian monopoly on Tartarian rhubarb (*Rheum palmatum*) and secured a specimen when a Scottish physician brought over rhubarb seeds from Saint Petersburg. Rhubarb was deemed an effective cure of indigestion and therefore an ideal agent against the physiological effects of luxury. For a brief time in the 1780s, rhubarb seemed set to become a major Scottish crop, championed in the Highlands by the Third Duke of Atholl and grown on a large scale by Hope for the Royal Infirmary. At

Hope's death in 1786, a plantation of three thousand rhubarb plants was flourishing near the Royal Botanic Garden.[43]

Hope did not confine his experiments to medicinal plants. Perhaps his most ambitious project was the attempt to grow the true tea bush of China—*Camellia sinensis*—in Scotland. Lettsom's history of tea reported that Linnaeus had managed to grow an inferior variety—the Tsubakki—at Uppsala as early as 1755 (though the real introduction probably took place in 1763). It had been smuggled out of Canton on a Swedish East India Company ship. During his long reign as president of the Royal Society, Sir Joseph Banks was much occupied with the possibility of wresting tea from the jealously guarded Chinese monopoly and diversifying the Indian economy with tea plantations. Hope appears to have preempted Banks in bringing a tea plant back to Britain. A correspondent advised that tea must be transferred to Britain only by stages. Seeds carried out of China should be brought to the Cape of Good Hope and then to Saint Helena, where they ought to be planted in pots protected from the salty foam of the sea. On the journey back through southern latitudes, the tea bush would then gradually grow accustomed to a northern climate. A note by Hope appears to indicate that a successful transfer took place in 1775. According to the catalogue of the Edinburgh botanic garden, true varieties of the Bohea and green tea were growing there in 1778. But the plants must have succumbed to the rigors of the Scottish climate shortly thereafter. When Hope passed away in 1786, James Anderson became the principal promoter of acclimatization and diversification in Scotland. Without the material resources of the Royal Botanical Garden, Anderson concentrated his efforts on the exchange of information through short-lived ventures such as *The Bee* (1790–94) and the British Wool Society. The other principal legacy of Hope's work was the school of devoted students he left behind. Among the students who remained in Britain was Richard Pulteney, the popularizer of the Linnaean method, and James Edward Smith, the founder of the Linnaean Society of London. William Roxburgh and Francis Buchanan Hamilton went to India, George Young to Saint Vincent, and William Wright to Jamaica. While James Anderson carried on the acclimatization tradition in Scotland, many of Hope's students ended up as agents of Sir Joseph Banks's network, serving the empire overseas rather than improving Scotland.[44]

The introduction of Linnaean natural history into the Scottish Enlightenment thus suggested a number of overlapping and conflicting paths of improvement. Internal voyages of discovery and inventory pointed to providential riches hidden within the territory. Northern travel cast a flattering light on the customs and virtues of Gaelic plebeians. At the same time, acclimatization offered the possibility of diversifying Scotland with exotic plants and animals. Even the order of the Scottish climate seemed malleable and subject to improvement. Yet natural history was not merely the source of cornucopian aspirations. Over time, the prospect of transforming the Highlands provoked concerns about the fragility of the natural order. The introduction of the southern Cheviot sheep gave rise to fears that native people and breeds could become extinct. Some naturalists came to believe that the climate itself was subject to adverse human influence. These scientific controversies overlapped with conflicting social and political goals. Was natural history the means to urban liberty or the preservation of ancient customs? Could the transformation of Highland agriculture be reconciled with the priorities of military recruitment and population growth? The civil cameralism of Scottish improvers also clashed with the "neo-mercantilist" objectives of the fiscal-military state. The Duke of Atholl's scheme to make Highland larch the bulwark of the Royal Navy competed with Henry Dundas's initiative to replace English oak with South Asian teak. In the end, the fate of Linnaean natural history and civil cameralism in the Scottish Enlightenment hinged on the outcome of the imperial contest with France. Was northern improvement a legitimate substitute to overseas expansion or merely a temporary surrogate during an interlude of imperial crisis?

3

Improving the Scottish Climate

A sulfurous, dry fog enveloped Europe in the summer of 1783. Bemused observers could stare straight into a noonday sun that the poet William Cowper called nature's "dim and sickly eye." Moving quickly east and south, the strange haze covered the skies of Copenhagen, Paris, London, and Rome. British observers spotted it over England and Scotland after June 19. The Sun, Moon, planets, and stars were all obscured by the haze. To the natural historian Gilbert White, "the sun at noon looked as blank as a clouded moon, and shed a rust-colored . . . light." A stifling heat accompanied the haze. It was the hottest month of July since 1659 in central England. The fog and excessive temperatures persisted upwards of two months over Continental Europe while its flanks drifted into Russia, the Middle East, and perhaps the eastern seaboard of North America. The fog was bitter to the taste, stung the eyes, and vitiated plants with an acidic bite. A Dutch eyewitness saw it destroy the vegetation around the town of Groningen. Leaves withered and turned from their regular green color "to brown, black, grey or white." Similar damage was reported across Europe. People who had been exposed to the fog complained of splitting headaches and respiratory difficulties. Some observers linked it to the outbreak of lethal fevers. Scholars in our own time have estimated that the dry fog raised mortality by 10 percent over the moving fifty-one-year mean for England in the late summer and early fall of 1783. Across the Continent as a whole, victims may have numbered in the tens of thousands.[1]

Yet the strange weather did not seem malign to every observer. In Perthshire near Stirling, John Ramsay of Ochtertyre greeted the fog with pleasure. After the bad harvest season of 1782, the peculiar haze offered a welcome relief: "From the middle of June we had the warmest most growing weather ever known." So confident was Ramsay in the power of good cultivation that he easily found something beneficial in the extraordinary heat and fog. In Ramsay's memoirs, the aberrant weather was assimilated into a larger narrative of dazzling agricultural improvement. Ramsay reduced the sulfurous fog to something familiar and harmless by comparing it with the common sea mist. "There was indeed little sunshine, the ground being covered till far in the day with a thick mist or haar, which moistened the earth and promoted vegetation as copious rains." Other improving landlords like George Dempster similarly welcomed the hot weather and prospect of a decent harvest. James Boswell's estate manager wrote from Auchinleck in Ayrshire on July 12: "This week in General has been very hot, but yesterday and today exceeds, The Air is full of fire we hear thunder at a distenc [sic] almost every day, with heive showers at times here. Every thing grows in a Suprizeing manner."[2]

The dry fog was the result of major tectonic activity in Iceland at the Grimsvotn caldera and Laki volcano in May and June 1783. The main eruption at Laki began on June 8 and continued until February 1784. The fifteen-mile fissure emitted the greatest lava flow in historical times. A quarter of the Icelandic population perished in the aftermath. A gargantuan release of ashes and sulfuric gases drifted downwind into Europe within days. The tulip crop in Holland was badly damaged in late June. Volcanic ashes fell in such large amounts over northern Scotland that they destroyed the crops in Caithness. According to one source, the local population remembered 1783 long afterward as the year of the "ashie." The hot fog and ashes also helped supercharge the atmosphere with condensation. The result was a wave of extremely violent thunderstorms that hit Britain from Aberdeenshire to Devon. While the heavy amount of dust and ashes over Holland and Scotland hinted at a volcanic origin, the cause of the strange weather remained unclear to contemporaries.[3]

The dry fog in the summer of 1783 presents a particularly dramatic illustration of the basic uncertainties permeating eighteenth-century views of weather and climate. The Copenhagen professor Christian Gottlieb Kratzenstein seems to have been the first to connect the dry fog to the Icelandic eruption. In the Anglophone world, Benjamin Franklin ventured the volcanic hypothesis in a letter written to the Newcastle Literary and Philosophical Society in May 1784. Yet he undercut it immediately with an alternative explanation. Perhaps the fog was connected with the effects of a meteor entering the atmosphere. This chapter considers the broader controversies surrounding climate in the age of the Enlightenment. The conventional identification of climate with latitude vied with neo-Hippocratic views that stressed its contingency and complexity. Many natural historians held that human settlement might ameliorate a bad climate. A minority of observers sought to quantify the physical parameters of climate by collecting meteorological data, but most preferred to discuss climate in qualitative terms instead. Interest in species mobility and ecological exchange often trumped concerns with the physical character of the climate. In all of these things, the Scottish Highlands offered a laboratory for rival hypotheses.[4]

MOVING SCOTLAND SOUTHWARD

For the natural historians investigating the Highlands, climate was a fundamental preoccupation. They saw in the force of climate both the source and limit of regional improvement. It constituted the regulating framework for the plant and animal kingdoms of the terraqueous globe, determining the pattern of vegetation and spread of animals across the earth. All generation, preservation, and decay among living species bore the imprint of climate. In James Hutton's words, climate was the "efficient cause of vegetation." Therefore, all sound understanding of agriculture, gardening, and animal breeding must take the natural history of climate into account. In the eighteenth century, enlightened savants liked to imagine the natural order as a divine economy, a self-regulating balance of species and elements, designed by the wise Creator to operate in accordance with laws of nature. This general pattern of orderly design was believed to repeat itself in a myriad of interconnected subsystems. The structure of climatic zones was attributed to the economies of air, water, and soil—the combined influence of regular atmospheric movements, oceanic exhalations, and fermentations of the soil. To grasp the links between these systems, the natural historian needed an understanding of meteorology, hydrography, and geology. The physiology of vegetable and animal economies was a product of acclimatization and habit. For this reason, the force of climate also pervaded the medical, moral, and political economies of the human world.[5]

While the concept of climate penetrated every aspect of eighteenth-century natural history, there was considerable controversy over its precise meaning. Attempts to posit a simple geometric model of climate tended to dissolve into complex contingencies when viewed through a local and historical lens. In Scotland, James Hutton took the side of geometry in his "Theory of Rain," read to the Royal Society of Edinburgh in 1784. He spoke of the "oeconomy of the world," dividing it into three zones—"the torrid region, the temperate, and the frigid." Hutton tried to set forth a systematic and quantitative theory of the relation between latitude, climate, and agriculture in his *Elements of Agriculture*. Yet in the end he had to admit that there was "great variety in the natural temperatures of different places in the same parallels of latitude." The treatise remained unpublished at his death in 1797. Linnaeus in turn originally embraced a latitudinal concept of the distribution of climate zones, based on minimum winter temperatures. His schema divided the world into five climate bands—the Australian, Oriental, Occidental, Mediterranean, and Boreal zones. Linnaeus held that plants possessed an "inherent temperature tolerance range" that destined them for growth in a given band. Later on, Linnaeus abandoned this single-minded emphasis on temperature, recognizing altitude as another crucial variable. He proposed that alpine plants could prosper in mountains anywhere on earth. From this followed that tropical plants grown at high-enough altitudes would transplant easily across different climate zones, even as far north as the Boreal band.[6]

Much of the debate about the physical meaning of climate centered on the differences between the Old and the New World. Why did American and European territories along the same latitude not share the same climate? Georges-Louis Leclerc, Comte de Buffon, famously insisted on the essential difference between the two continents and declared America to be a world of stunted and degenerate natural species. In the 1730s and 1740s, the Anglo-American natural historian Mark Catesby worked out a geometric hypothesis of species variation and climate that tried to explain the divergence. He suggested that American plants and animals underwent a "Gradation of Increase at every Degree of Latitude approaching the Tropick," such that all natural species increased in size the warmer the climate. In the 1770s and 1780s, Benjamin Franklin developed a rival hypothesis about the influence of the Atlantic that aimed to explain the latitudinal discrepancy between the climates of the Old and the New World. He postulated the existence of a great current of warm water flowing out of the West Indies that redistributed heat from the torrid zone of the West Indies to the shores of northwestern Europe.[7]

The difficulties of upholding a strictly geometric notion of climate led many naturalists to the alternative conception of neo-Hippocratic medicine. According to this interpretation, climate exerted its force in local and less regular patterns. More specifically, climate amounted to the sum total of a variety of factors, including latitude, altitude, soil, moisture, atmospheric pressure, vegetation, and human settlement. For example, Lord Kames observed that the land of "Chinese Tartary" in Central Asia was as cold as Iceland even though it occupied the same latitude as France. He explained the discrepancy as the effect of "nitrous soil," high altitude, and the absence of sheltering mountains to the east. Following Hippocrates, many naturalists believed that an analysis of the composition of climate in specific locations could account for the outbreak of disease from foul waters, soils, and airs. Much attention was lavished on the question of how to demarcate any given microclimate. Here, islands made attractive objects of investigation. Natural philosophers promoted the use of the hygrometers to measure the humidity of the atmosphere and eudiometers to assess the oxygen content of the air, by which they hoped to quantify the pattern of dangerous exhalations. More commonly, natural historians in the field employed thermometers and barometers to determine the extent of a given microclimate by measuring its temperature and atmospheric pressure.[8]

While exploring the natural history of the Hebrides and the Highlands, John Walker devised a method of determining altitude by comparing "the degrees of heat at which water would boil, at the same time, and at different elevations." His student James Headrick elaborated on Walker's work, seeking to measure the "medium temperature of a climate, by regular observations, taken at the same place, and at certain hours of the day." Headrick believed that soil temperature provided a key to the variations of local climate, noting distinct differences in measurement among wet, dry, and cultivated soils. In field observations from Arran in the southern Hebrides, he postulated a necessary relation between the intensity of agriculture and the temperature of the soil, which he suggested would in turn modify the local climate in general for the better. Wet soils had an average temperature between 44° and 54° Farenheit, whereas "dry earth" exposed to sunlight ranged between 100° and 120°. Intensive agriculture could raise soil temperature further: "I have known a highly cultivated, and well manured soil, amount to 150°; while the temperature of the atmosphere did not exceed 60°. This shews the powerful effect of draining and cultivating land, in improving the temperature of a climate." Headrick's claim had radical implications for the Highlands. If climate was a local force that could be influenced by the force of agriculture, it followed that microclimates could be altered and managed by human intervention.[9]

Eighteenth-century savants believed that local and regional types of climate could change thanks to the effects not only of cultivation but also of drainage, irrigation, deforestation, or, in some cases, afforestation. If the environmental alterations were done on a large scale, the climate of a whole region could be modified. Many observers believed that the planting of Virginia, and New England had fundamentally transformed the climate of these territories. In this spirit, some doctors and surgeons in tropical colonies favored the "wholesale destruction of scrub and jungle in order to improve ventilation and dispel harmful miasmas." The physician James Lind suggested that Barbados had become healthier with the removal of its tree cover. In the 1830s, James Ranald Martin, a pioneer of Indian medical topography, recommended that twenty thousand square miles of forest ought to be cleared in the Sundarbans. But other savants instead emphasized the benign effect of forest cover. According to François-Jean Chastellux, the preservation of woods and other vegetation helped absorb and neutralize the lethal "mephitical exhalations" of swamps and marshlands.[10]

Such triumphs of improvement had shaped the course of European history as well. For John Campbell, wasteland colonization was also climate amelioration: "both Soils and Climates may in Process of Time be beneficially altered by a vigorous and assiduous Attention to their Improvement." The temperate climate of present-day lowland Britain was an artifact of drainage and deforestation. Moreover, the harshness of the climate in many regions was the result of a decline in cultivation: "The Converse of this Proposition is also true, for in Countries long neglected the Climate becomes unhealthy, and the Soil barren." The correspondent "Nemo" in a travel report to James Anderson's journal *The Bee* invoked the evidence of medieval diet to account for these changes. The "old Saxons, Danes and Britons" consumed far "more flesh, and much less bread, legumes, and fruit than we." Because the character of the national diet corresponded closely to the nature of the climate, this preference suggested that Britain in the Dark Ages had been covered with "endless forests and morasses" and therefore had been "much colder and moister than it is at present." For Edward Gibbon, a simple comparison of the climate of Canada and Germany demonstrated the power of cultivation in ameliorating conditions over the long term. "Canada, at this day, is an exact picture of ancient Germany." Buffon in turn thought that Canada offered a mirror to the climatological past of France. James Hutton agreed that the "climate of a continent" could be "improved." Only the historical force of civilized settlement could account for the discrepancy in climate types along the latitude running through Germany, France, England, and Canada. John Sinclair confirmed the link between drainage, cultivation, and rising temperature in his manual *The Code of Agriculture* (1817).[11]

Some observers believed that they could detect the force of climate change in their own estate management. George Dempster declared to his Danish friend Grimur Thorkelin that the lands between the "56 to the 65 degree of northern latitude" could be rendered as "comfortable" "as it is ten degrees nearer the Equator." Dempster used his Highland estate Skibo in Sutherland to prove the point. Besides potato cultivation and fuel economy, Dempster favored the enclosure of fields by "planting strips of Trees round them." He observed that "the force of the winds and of the Cold [was] so far abated thereby that the Grass within such enclosures [was] often 14 days or 3 weeks sooner fit for pasture than it was formerly." Peaches and apricots thrived in the gardens of Skibo, thanks to concerted "labour and attention." However, Dempster did not expect agriculture to alter the Scottish climate beyond the range of the temperate zone. In this sense, climate bands still remained relatively fixed, even if weather patterns and soil temperatures changed locally.[12]

Hopes of amelioration raised another problem of natural history. What was the original state of the land before improvement? Naturalists diverged in their views of possible changes because they could not agree on the precise character of the unimproved nature of the Scottish climate. Confronted with the complex variety of factors, including the influence of ocean currents, the peculiarities of a northern climate, and the varying conditions of islands, coastal regions, and the alpine interior, they failed to arrive at any sense of common standard or norm. James Anderson characterized the Scottish climate as a whole by comparison with that of England:

> For as England is not only larger in itself, but also approaches much nearer the continent than Scotland does, its climate in some respects more nearly resembles that of a continental country: whereas Scotland, being in itself such a narrow tract of country—so deeply indented by various arms of the sea, and so far disjoined from the main-land, enjoys all the peculiarities of an insular situation in a much higher degree than England. On this account the heat of the summer-season is more moderate in Scotland, and the cold in winter less intense, than in England; so that the variations of heat and cold are far less considerable here than in the southern parts of Britain.

He then went on to describe the peculiarly mild winters of Scotland, contrasted with cases of severe temperatures and heavy snowfall on the Continent or in the north of England. To account for the difference between the coast and the interior in Scotland as well as England, he postulated a principle of variation "in proportion to the height and distance of any place from the sea."[13]

On his 1772 tour with Pennant, John Lightfoot devoted himself mainly to the botanical inventory of the interior of the Highlands. This research was underpinned by certain assumptions about the climate. John Lightwood's *Flora Scotica* insisted on the parallels between the region and northern tracts of wilderness like Lapland and Siberia. He found numerous plants listed in Linnaeus's *Flora Lapponica* and Gmelin's *Flora Sibirica* growing freely in the Highland mountain ranges. In contrast, James Robertson preferred to downplay the importance of altitude and latitude in his botanical surveys, perhaps in an effort to please his sponsors, John Hope and the Board for the Annexed Estates. He minimized the difference between the climate of Nairnshire and that of Edinburgh by locating plants that grew in both locations: "Between Rosmarkie & Tain I found only plants similar to those which grow around Edinburgh, excepting *Draba incana, Saxifraga tridactylites* & *Astragalus uralensis*. As the two former grow plentifully in England, they can hardly be reckoned evidences of the effect of northern climate, unless indeed it shall be said that the *Draba incana*, which inhabits the high grounds in Yorkshire, is here by force of climate made to grow on the low lands. Whatever be in this, I imagine most Botanists would have expected a greater difference between the Flora of Edinburgh & Tain which is two degrees father north."[14]

John Walker's report to the Board for the Annexed Estates stressed the uneven character of the Scottish climate, discussing the distinctive conditions prevailing on different islands in the Hebrides. He provided a vivid depiction of the microclimate of Tiree that linked its benign atmosphere to its low altitude and proximity to warm oceanic currents:

> Tirey, by being so champaign, is much less subject to Rains, than the mountainous Islands, and is remarkable for the mildness of its Climate, which feels no Disturbance, but from the South West Wind. It never suffers any considerable Degree either of Heat or Cold. Its Summers are sufficiently hot, for the Vegetation of all the common Crops of Grain and Grass and the Warmth of its Winters, appears to be greater than that of any other part of Britain, or its adjacent Islands. Being far removed from any considerable Tract of Country, having neither high Land, nor wet Soil and surrounded for a great Extent, by the warm streams of the Ocean, the Cold in Winter, very seldom advances to the freezing Degree. Whole Winters do sometimes pass without Snow, and if it happens to fall, by the same Causes and the warm sandy nature of the Soil, it is quickly dissolved. It may be justly said of Tirey, with regard to Britain, and for the same Reasons, what Caesar observed of Britain, compared to the Continent: *Coelum Gallico temperatius*.

This insular condition allowed for the most remarkable "quick and early crops." The first harvest of bear was "produced ... in 35 Days" and then a second one in barely two months, "the only Instance perhaps known in Britain, of two white Crops, having been reaped off the same Land, in one Season." Yet in the same passage, Walker wavered about the significance of insular microclimates by emphasizing that northern plants generally developed habits of quicker growth than those in more temperate climates. He cited Linnaeus's *Flora Lapponica* for an example of accelerated maturation of common bear, or square barley, in Swedish Lapland.[15]

At the heart of these disagreements was the diverse geography of the Highlands and Western Isles. By deriving an assessment of economic potential from overly general or specific geographic zones, different naturalists proposed a wide variety of often incompatible strategies for improvement. Not infrequently, they also changed their mind about what projects were most likely to succeed. John Walker favored hemp and flax, though later he seems to have prioritized cattle droving and potato cultivation instead. To James Anderson, the mild and even temperatures across the region made sheep farming with Spanish Merinos the most advantageous economic activity, whereas the insular variability in weather and poor soils ruled out flax raising. But by 1790 he had become a champion of the northern Shetland breed instead. For John Lightfoot, the presence of subarctic plants in the mountainous interior suggested that the native population might adapt to a natural economy of modest consumption and indigenous substitutes, along the lines of Linnaeus's Sami. To the Third and Fourth Dukes of Atholl, the inland climate of Perthshire was ideal for plantations of Tartarian rhubarb (*Rheum palmatum*) and Tyrolean larch (*Pinus larix*).[16]

A DECAYING CLIMATE?

Such uncertainty was exacerbated by fears among some observers that the climate was changing for the worse toward the end of the century. The preternatural heat of the summer of 1783 was followed by several seasons of bitter cold. Despite his incorrigible optimism, Ramsay of Ochtertyre recognized that the winter season of 1783 was exceptionally severe. Benjamin Franklin speculated in his letter to the Newcastle Literary and Philosophical Society that the dry fog had lowered the average temperature over Europe and had triggered the harsh winter that succeeded it. Franklin challenged other savants to explore the causal connections between climate variations and volcanic eruptions and meteors. Indeed, he hoped that future events of this sort could be predicted and perhaps anticipated by "such measures as are possible and practicable." Scholars still debate the precise cause behind the cold winter of 1784. One complication here is that the poor weather and near famine of 1782 in the Highlands *preceded* the outbreak of Laki. There is also some uncertainty about whether Laki released sufficient aerosols to have a lasting impact on the European weather pattern. But regardless of the underlying causes, a trend of difficult winters persisted in 1784, 1785, and 1786. The winter season 1788–89 was again severe and protracted. Likewise, the serious dearth of 1795 was preceded by a cold winter. The spring and summer of 1799 were cool and rainy, precipitating another major harvest failure. No wonder, then, if some observers began to fear that the British climate was growing worse.[17]

In Scotland, concerns about adverse climate change appeared in Sinclair's *Statistical Account of Scotland* and the *General Reports* to the Board of Agriculture. While the parish reports offered little in the way of quantitative evidence, let alone systematic or synoptic data, they did convey a general unease about climate change at the level of public opinion and popular memory. Writing in 1793 or perhaps 1794, the Reverend John Grant of Kirkmichael in upland Banffshire insisted that the climate of northern Scotland had grown more inclement in recent decades. Indeed, he claimed that this was common knowledge: "No complaint seems to be more universal over the Highlands." According to popular opinion, the summers had become colder "since the year 1768" and "productive of greater quantities of rain, than was remembered in the same space of time, during any preceding period." Grant himself seemed to believe that the process had begun in the early 1770s. He cited as evidence of deterioration a number of factors: the enlarged beds of rivers, land lost to water erosion, and the reduction in the number of trout. He also observed that migratory birds arrived later in the year and departed earlier than before. Even insects were "less prolific." "The hum of the mountain bee is not so frequently heard." Grant marshaled this evidence to attack a central tenet of enlightened optimism. David Hume and Jean-Baptiste Dubos had it wrong when they asserted "that in ancient times, the seasons were colder than at present." The facts "adduced by these respectable writers" were "too vague and remote to overthrow the experience of feeling." Closer to the coast in Speymouth near Elgin, the clergyman James Gillan agreed that the climate had grown less conducive to agriculture over much of the Highland interior. But he dated the increase of rainfall to 1782 rather than 1768. He also noted that Speymouth's relatively sheltered location protected its crops from the worst damage. William Innerarity in Caputh parish north of Perth provided an "Abstract of the State of the Thermometer at Delvin for 10 Years." This brief register, probably a digest of the weather diary of Margaret Mackenzie of Delvin (kept daily between 1780 and 1805), included high and low temperatures for each month between 1783 and 1792. It also usefully compared Delvin's upland climate with that of Edinburgh. The Delvin temperatures in the winters of 1783 and 1784 were well below the mean toward the end of the period. While the Reverend Innerarity ventured no analysis of the data, he remarked on the increasing frequency of floods in the river Tay during the preceding thirty years. There had been inundations in 1761, 1780, 1789, and 1791. On the other side of the country, in the islands of Eigg and Rum, the Reverend Donald McLean observed that the precipitation over his parish had become heavier in recent years. Like Grant, he invoked popular opinion. "It is remarked by many inhabitants that the seasons are still becoming more and more rainy." Even in the winter, rain rather than snow dominated. The harvest of 1793 had suffered badly. The increasing precipitation made the grain crops "precarious, and of little value."[18]

Some of the county reports to the Board of Agriculture also recorded a deterioration of the climate in northern Scotland. The Reverend James Robertson of Callander suggested a cooling trend in the uplands of Perthshire. He stressed that early forest clearing on the hillsides had resulted in irreversible long-term climate change. Unlike the parish reporters, Robertson dealt with a time scale of centuries rather than decades.

> In northern latitudes, population has been always so rapid and the bounty of nature so scanty, that the cultivation of the ground must have been very early attended to. We have no records of any era in which tillage was not requisite in this country; and the presumption is, that more land was under the plough in remote ages, than in the present times. One thing at least, on this point, is certain, that ground has been formerly cultivated, which is so high, the climate in that latitude now so forbidding and the region of the air so piercingly cold, that no grain we have, could at this day, arrive at any degree of maturity. It is indeed probable that the hills were more easily cleared of wood than the vallies, that they afforded less cover to wild beasts, and that the whole face of the ground, except the summits of the highest mountains, being one continued forest, the climate was more mild and the country warmer, than it shall ever be again, because it cannot be so much wooded.

John Smith recorded a pattern of deterioration in Argyll, too. Hillsides had been cultivated at much higher altitudes in the past, thanks to sheltering forests. Signs of ancient field cultivation in upland landscapes seemed to offer his principal evidence: "It is now a matter of astonishment to the inhabitants of this county to find, in some parts of it, the traces of corn-ridges covered with heath, so high in the hills that no corn could grow there at present." Smith noted that men who died at the turn of the century 1700 could remember a warmer age. In Sinclair's *General View of the Agriculture of the Northern Counties*, a local "gentleman of observation and judgment"—Mr. Millar of Kinchurdy in Cromarty, argued that climate deterioration was more recent. "In his own memory, the climate here has altered to the worse, such as frosty springs, cold summers, and wet harvests, occasioning great failures in crops, especially in farms distant from the sea coast." This was the same time scale employed in the parish reports in the *Statistical Account*. Yet Millar added a crucial caveat based on a longer perspective: "Although, at the same time, he knows it to be a fact consistent with his father's knowledge, that in the year 1688 the harvest was finishing so late as Christmas in the interior of the district; that an inclemency of season continued for ten years afterwards, and a scarcity almost bordering on famine, the boll being at 33s. 4d Sterling." The recent deterioration thus had a precedent in the famine years after the Glorious Revolution. In between lay a period of relatively warmer weather: "In Queen Anne's reign, times became more propitious" once again, "and the climate and seasons improved to such a degree, that the boll came down to 5s Sterling." For Millar, the Scottish climate seemed to have fluctuated in long historical cycles. Periods of deterioration were temporary and reversible. But the precise mechanism behind the cycle was left obscure. Was the downturn the result of anthropogenic or purely natural causes or perhaps a combination of factors? Millar's conjectures of climate history appeared casually in a footnote to Sinclair's book, without further comment.[19]

The absence of systematic quantitative measurements made this controversy over the character of the Scottish climate more difficult to dispel.[20] Sinclair's questionnaire for the *Statistical Account of Scotland* included no direct question regarding the climate and did not ask for any exact temperature data. After all the trouble of organizing a parish-by-parish description of the land and population, it did not occur to Sinclair or his collaborators (including James Headrick) to quantify the fundamentals of climate. As late as the *New Statistical Account* of the 1840s, collection of weather data and temperature ranges was still sporadic rather than mandatory among the contributors. The Highland Society of Scotland also made no attempt to gather information of this sort despite the demonstrable importance of the question of climate to its mission.[21]

Yet such omissions were not necessarily the product of deficient attention in the matter. On the contrary, the neo-Hippocratic idea of local climates may have blocked the path to quantification. The gathering of data to create a composite picture of weather across Scotland made sense only on the assumption that the climate obeyed general laws. To savants of improvement like Headrick and Walker, this was not necessarily so. From their perspective, the qualitative concern with climate on a parish scale in the *Statistical Account* simply conformed to the chorographical ideal of climate as a local force. Of course conditions must differ greatly from one parish to another. Reinforcing this conceptual hurdle was a pragmatic attitude toward agriculture that at times regarded theoretical commitments with indifference, even bordering on suspicion.[22] Such an anti-theoretical stance may have served to discourage a stronger concern with quantification of the climate. The debates over climate were easily overshadowed by an empirical question about the optimal crops for any given soil, in turn a matter for practical experiments and trials rather than the quantitative analysis of weather patterns. Because questions of plant introduction and acclimatization exercised such a strong influence on enlightened agriculture, much of the discussion of climate was diverted to a debate about how to overcome the climate limits through species mobility. Here the natural history of ecological exchange played a pivotal role.

MOBILE SPECIES

In the late Enlightenment, natural historians and agricultural experts proposed a dizzying range of methods to convert nature into capital. Techniques of breeding, hybridization, and grafting promised the creation of novel varieties of animals and plants. Chemical knowledge about the composition of the air and soil types was expected to increase the productivity of the earth through the discovery or invention of natural and artificial fertilizers. Botanical inventories fanned hopes for the discovery of little-known indigenous plants that could serve as import substitutes for raw materials from other climate zones.[23] Above all, the mobility of living species across great geographic distances seemed to supply a means of overcoming boundaries of climate and natural distribution. This involved two possibilities. Species could be transferred within the same climate zone or from one type of climate to another. In the latter case, the specimen had to be given shelter until it was gradually acclimatized to the new conditions. For many improvers, this strategy of transplantation seemed the most promising.

To accomplish the successful transfer of any species required a firm understanding of its "particular nature and oeconomy." In his lectures on natural history at the University of Edinburgh during the 1780s and 1790s, John Walker carefully laid out his views on the topic of plant economies. He was intrigued by the force of habit that he believed pervaded the vegetable kingdom. Walker insisted that acclimatization was identical to a historical process of habituation, inuring plants to new types of soil and air. Discussing certain African flowers brought to hothouses in Holland from the Cape of Good Hope, he noted that these species after a century in Europe had begun to flower at a different period of the year. He also pointed out that "Barley of the same species will grow and ripen in Aleppo and in Scotland in 100 days, and in Lapland in 58 days, but no other of these kinds will grow in other Climates, for the change must have been produced gradually by carrying the Seed from Aleppo to the North." From these observations, Walker concluded that it was "pretty certain that plants, like animals, [will] habituate themselves to the diversities of Climates." Indeed, he predicted that many plants were at present slowly spreading across the globe, into new climate zones. One day, Britain might be producing exotic crops: "I think that rice will in the course of a few Years be produced, in the North of

Europe, for that plant, formerly produced in hot climates in Asia have been gradually accustomed to the change of weather till it has been planted, and is now growing in the North of Germany on the Banks of the Weser, hence it may at least probably be made to grow in Britain." In his 1790 lecture on natural history, Walker told his students that acclimatization was a vital concern for all nations in a "cold and northern" situation, since "most of the valuable and useful plants we possess, have been brought from the warmer climates." Sir John Sinclair concurred in his inaugural address to the Wool Society of Edinburgh in 1791: "Were Great Britain at this moment confined to those particular articles which its soil naturally produced, many of the most valuable productions of its fields, and almost all the productions of its gardens, would never have existed here, and this island could never have been able to have fed one half of its present inhabitants." Sinclair and Walker also extended this axiom to economic zoology, taking an interest in the successful acclimatization of Angora goats and Merino sheep to Swedish latitudes.[24]

Perhaps the true extent of species depended on the perseverance of human industry and expert management rather than any limit set by the natural order. Robert Maxwell, the leading agricultural publicist among Scottish improvers in the first part of the eighteenth century, applied this optimistic conceit to the prospects of Scottish agriculture as early as 1743, in the dedication to the volume of *Transactions* he edited for the Honourable the Society of Improvers in the Knowledge of Agriculture in Scotland:

> It is more profitable for us to make Improvements than Conquests: if it be considered, that, as Natural Historians relate, no Fruit grows originally among us, besides Hips and Haws, Acorns and Pignuts, with others of the like Nature; that our Climate, of itself, and without the Assistance of Art, can make no further Advances towards a Plumb, then to a Sloe, and carried an Apple to no greater Perfection than to a Crab; that our Melons, our Peaches, our Figs, our Appricots and Cherries, are Strangers among us, imported in different Ages, and naturalized in our Gardens; and that they would all degenerate and fall away into the Trash our own Country naturally produces, if they were wholly neglected by the Planter, and left to the Mercy of our Sun and Soil.

Here, the emerging study of biodiversity was conflated with a Promethean definition of agrarian capitalism.[25] The diffusion and variety of animal and plant species to Maxwell demonstrated the transcendent powers of human labor. Even the mundane agricultural order in Scotland was an exotic import, naturalized only by dint of unending industry. Knowledge exchange promised to accelerate the labor of acclimatization. In the Enlightenment, agriculture had ceased to be a haphazard local practice and instead emerged as a national project, governed by the experimental science of natural historians and diffused through patriotic societies, quickening the pace of biological diversification. Maxwell's *Transactions* advocated the naturalization of flax, hemp, saffron, and many other new crops.[26]

In the 1770s, Lord Kames and James Anderson expanded Maxwell's argument, framing it in a language reminiscent of Montesquieu and Smith. Both of them praised the transfer of species as a providential tool to further biodiversity among all nations. Quoting Columnella and other ancients in the *Gentleman Farmer* (second edition 1779), Kames described the profound transformation of European ecology between the Romans and the modern day:

> When Galen the physician lived, the peach was too delicate for the air of Italy. It has been creeping northward slowly; and, even in Britain at present, it is of a good flavour, if artfully cultivated. The cherry tree was brought by Lucullus from the Lesser Asia to Rome, as great rarity; and now it bears good fruit even in Scotland. The blessings of Providence are distributed with an equal hand. Industry will remedy the natural defects of our soil and situation. . . . If wheat, if fruits, if cabbage, if collyflower were confined to their native climates, what would Britain be? Iceland would be not much inferior.

For Anderson, acclimatization served as the material basis of civilizing trade. Although violent conquest had secured the spread of useful plants and animals in antiquity, at the present time, "commerce effects the same salutary purpose in a more gentle and less violent manner. By means of it, many of the fruits and roots of the most distant countries have been naturalized in Europe." Anderson singled out silkworms, potatoes, oranges, rice, and Merino sheep as crucial historical introductions. Like Maxwell, Sinclair, and Walker, he believed that the transfer of species could now be perfected through the supervision and management of experts. The potato in particular was a harbinger of things to come. Though Linnaeus had dismissed the tuber as a close relative of the poisonous nightshade and fit only for pig feed, the Scottish improvers were perfectly confident about its value. The material success of this botanical transplant from the New World rendered other forms of introduction plausible. In this way, the basic crop of spade husbandry supplied a strong rationale for the more exotic schemes of the Scottish projectors.[27]

These developments also created more interest in the historical origins of biodiversity and agriculture. In an unpublished manuscript, Walker speculated about the introduction of grain in the Hebrides. He suggested that only rye, bear, and gray oat had been cultivated in the region before modern times. Norwegian Vikings probably had introduced rye to the Hebrides in the Dark Ages. In *An Economical History of the Hebrides and Highlands of Scotland*, he marveled at the historical adaptation of bear to the Western Isles: "The habit this grain must have acquired by being sown in a country where there is a short summer, in the course of a thousand years, must be remarkable."[28]

Thomas Pennant deepened the time scale by tracing the migration of species from southern continents to northern lands and from the Old to the New World in his *Arctic Zoology*. The aim was to demonstrate how much the pattern of vegetation and the dissemination of animals across the earth owed to the spontaneous mobility of species in prehistory. Like Walker, he imagined that such migration, if sufficiently slow and gradual, allowed the different forms of life to grow habituated to new types of climate.

> Let it not be objected, that animals bred in a southern climate, after the descent of their parents from the ark, would be unable to bear the frost and snow of the rigorous north, before they reached South America, the place of their final destination. It must be considered, that the migration must have been the work of ages; that in the course of their progress each generation grew hardened to the climate it had reached; and that after their arrival in America, they would again be gradually accustomed to warmer and warmer climates, in their removal from north to south, as they had in the reverse, or from south to north.

Pennant and other naturalists also increasingly recognized the possibility of the extirpation of animals and plants in specific regions. Toward the end of the eighteenth century, Erasmus Darwin and Jean-Baptiste Lamarck went one step further, proposing that species not merely underwent migrations but also evolved over time, changing in their essence. Even Linnaeus may have come close to this view in his later years.[29]

John Walker fiercely resisted the notion of evolving plants and animals. If two species could be crossbred to create a new one, then "the Whole Vegetable and Animal Creation, would run into Confusion and Disorder." The infertility of mules preserved the "Order and Regularity" "intended by the wise Creator." All species had been fixed in essence and number since the moment of Creation. Walker also concluded that the animal kingdom was protected by divine mandate: "There is no example of a Species of Animal being intirely lost, though they may be extinguished in a particular Tract of Country." Species loss was always a matter of extirpation rather than extinction. When plants and animals changed habits to accommodate new climate conditions or domestication, they were merely developing into new varieties, a lesser ontological category, in accordance with predetermined divine designs. Walker lectured to his students: "The varieties in the Animal Kingdom proceed no doubt from different Climates, the same Species of Animal indigeneous in Europe, is endowed with very different qualities in North America, where it is remarkable that those of the same species are always less in the New World we know however that Climate and pasture when joined together produce a remarkable change in our Domestic Animals." In a different lecture, he defined varieties as "those beings belonging to any species, differing from it in some triffling circumstances." The cause of such variation was nutrition. It sprang from slow changes wrought by "vitiated sparing nourishment . . . or redundant food." He illustrated the effect by using an observation from his travels: "Open Coleworts carried from the Highlands to some of the fertile Hebrides, and planted in the Gardens, turns to a loose headed cabbage in a few years, and degenerates into a Colewort again if carried back to the barren soil."[30]

These theological injunctions may have contributed to Walker's increasing caution about the prospects of Highland improvement. His posthumous magnum opus *An Economical History of the Hebrides and Highlands of Scotland* (1808) largely abandoned the flirtation with exotic animals and plants in favor of a less ambitious range of possibilities, including cattle breeding, new forms of forage, and northern varieties of oat and barley suitable to the Highland climate. Worries about the decay of plants in poor soils probably set a limit to Walker's expectations for northern acclimatization. He observed that bear (*Hordeum vulgare*) was the best native crop for the "severe climate" and "the only one at present cultivated in the Highlands . . . that deserves to be retained." It was "peculiarly useful in affording a good crop upon land dug with the spade." The only exotic to receive lengthy consideration by Walker at this point was the potato. His 1803 "Essay on Peat" for the Highland Society of Scotland narrowed the prospect of improvement to the reclamation of peat bogs through potato cultivation. The scope of plebeian industry was thus restricted to a narrow band of expectation focused on minimal subsistence and the rough virtues of retrograde agriculture.[31]

THE CLIMATE OF EMPIRE

The role of experts and natural knowledge in Highland improvement was part of a new pattern of increasing government patronage for the sciences from the middle of the eighteenth century onward. Indeed, these Scottish efforts prefigured in important ways the rise of Sir Joseph Banks as the manager of a coordinated policy of ecological imperialism after 1778. Banks shared the ambition of Walker and John Hope to make natural history the master science of improvement. Like them, he thrilled at the possibility of ecological exchange and acclimatization. Banks hoped to lay the proper foundation for the colony of New South Wales in 1788 by carefully stocking it with crops and livestock for the colonists, much as Walker had aimed to manage the ecological tools at the disposal of Highland landlords and tenants in his 1764 report to the Board for the Annexed Estates. But Banks diverged from his Scottish predecessors on one decisive point. Where Walker and Hope favored internal improvement over external colonization, Banks saw natural history as an imperial science. For him, import substitution and crop transfers were tools of diversification overseas rather than the means toward domestic colonization.[32]

Sir Joseph Banks made his mark as a gentleman naturalist with James Cook's first expedition on the *Endeavour* between 1768 and 1771. He cashed in on his fame by occupying the position as the key intermediary between the imperial government and a large, informal network of naturalists extending across Britain and its colonies. John Gascoigne and David Mackay have shown how Banks organized a powerful interest group with considerable influence over imperial policy. He employed a network of collectors and commercial spies (often doubling as colonial gardeners or naval surgeons) who gathered plants and information from around the globe. Kew Gardens under Banks's management became the transfer point for collecting and distributing transplants across the British Empire. From Kew, he attempted to organize a grand strategy of ecological diversification within the empire in order to maximize the economic value of the colonies. The practical method was to select "plants which could be readily transplanted; recommending regions where they might best grow; advising on methods of transporting plants and caring for them at sea; advising on propagating and processing plants" and "maintaining botanical gardens as reception [centers] or way station."[33]

This strategy involved Banks in several ambitious schemes. Perhaps the most spectacular was the venture to transfer the breadfruit tree from Tahiti to the West Indies in order to secure the food supply of the Caribbean slave population after the loss of the American colonies. Despite Captain Bligh's misfortune on the *Bounty*, the transfer did succeed on the second attempt, though the tree never proved vital to the diet of the plantation slaves.[34] Banks also pushed an effort to undermine the Chinese control of tea production by stealing and transplanting tea plants to India. This project was not realized until after Banks's death but proved profitable in the nineteenth century. Yet another endeavor concerned the establishment of a viable convict colony in New South Wales.

To ensure long-term success, Banks masterminded the attempt to establish a "portmanteau biota" of European plants and animals to support the colonists.[35] Only in one major case did Banks seek to import a species directly to Britain. This was the project to introduce and crossbreed the Spanish Merino sheep in order to bolster British wool production. Ironically, the breed was far more successful in New South Wales. Despite Banks's initial disapproval, the Merino was exported to Australia to consolidate its "neo-European" ecology.[36]

Almost all the major agents of Highland improvement in natural history, including Pennant, Hope, Lightfoot, Sinclair, and Anderson, were involved in some capacity as associates and correspondents of Banks's network. The attraction was obvious: Banks could offer vital scientific contacts, financial support, and gainful employment. Yet these cordial relations achieved little in material terms. The meager results of Banks's own northern tour seem to have established a pattern for his fundamentally skeptical view of Highland improvement. What was the Hebridean potato compared to the breadfruit of Tahiti?[37] The talented Scottish naturalists who traveled overseas at his behest, including William Roxburgh and Archibald Menzies, went as emissaries of southern empire, not as Linnaean disciples eager to send home seeds to be acclimatized in Scotland. Banks himself had little patience with Linnaeus's dreams of internal diversification. Why bother with rhubarb in Perthshire or Arctic nutmeg when such species could be cultivated in the East India Company possessions? He treated his Scottish correspondents with civility and warmth, exchanging information when requested, but steered clear of direct involvement in their clubs and projects. At one point in 1783, he briefly assisted John Hope in lobbying the government to boost funding for the Botanic Garden in Edinburgh, giving evidence to secure a grant of three thousand pounds. When Sinclair and Anderson sought to involve him in their Wool Society in 1790, appealing to his well-known fascination with Merino sheep, Banks agreed to part with a guinea in subscription but made sure to note his disagreements with his "Good Friend" Anderson on the limits of northern acclimatization. Not only was he highly doubtful about the fate of the Merino breed in a rainy climate; he also treated the proposed introduction of Shetland sheep to the Scottish mainland with great skepticism. (It seems that Banks at least on this second point was blinded by his own professed "South Country" bias.) Yet curiously, this prejudice did not extend to Iceland. During the Anglo-Danish hostilities of 1807, Banks's interest in Iceland revived, after lying dormant for more than thirty years. For some time afterward, he pondered the possibility of British intervention, ostensibly to prevent famine on the island but perhaps also to make Iceland a colony of the Empire.[38]

The Scottish improvers in turn mirrored Banks's ambivalence. They treated him and his associates with cordial admiration and took advantage of such contacts to gain access to exotic seeds and plants. Yet their enthusiasm about the near periphery and their doubts about the wisdom of overseas expansion precluded closer collaboration. All the same, their own projects derived much of their intrinsic plausibility from Banks's ventures. The fundamental disagreement between Banks and the Scots concerned the particular character of the Highland climate. From Banks's point of view, the natural disadvantages of the region simply could not be overcome. His rejection of the Wool Society agenda was emblematic of a deeper skepticism about the malleability of the northern environment. Among the Highland improvers, such pessimism looked suspiciously like political dogma: Banks had a vested interest in the expansion of empire in the torrid zone and the settlement of distant temperate colonies.

THE EMPIRE WITHIN

In 1785, James Anderson described the empire in America as a "delusive dream" that the nation had only lately begun to escape. This "phantom" had caused Britain to neglect objects of "vast importance" for many decades. "While the most distant parts of the globe have been attentively explored," the nation had ignored its Scottish periphery, even though the Highlands were "much better calculated to encrease the trade, to encourage the manufactures, and to augment the revenues of this nation, than any others that have ever yet been discovered on the globe."[39]

Crucially, Anderson's critique implied that the British Empire rested on a mistaken idea of the natural order. The orthodox view of natural empire enshrined in the Navigation Acts since the middle of the seventeenth century had been given new life by Arthur Young in his *Political Essays* of 1772. Young here proposed that the proper relation between metropole and periphery should be determined by their separation into different climate zones. "To estimate, therefore, the comparative merit of the climate of colonies, it is only necessary to compare it with that of the mother country. If they are the same, or nearly the same, the colony is useless; if entirely different, highly valuable. It is apparent from this remark, that there must be a great difference in value between the English colonies, from variation of climate." Young added to this division of labor another distinction. The temperate climate of Britain would produce necessaries, whereas the hotter temperatures of the colonies must focus on the production of "superfluous commodities" impossible to cultivate at home. Young then enumerated the proper products of the Atlantic colonies. The West

Indies produced coffee, sugar, and rum. From the American South came rice, indigo, cotton, silk, hemp, and flax. The Middle Colonies produced tobacco and iron as well as timber. The northern colonies had poor soils but seas "filled with an inexhaustible treasure in the cod fish." Only tea and spices were not yet available from America, though Young predicted that this would soon change.[40]

Against this imperial order determined by a conventional notion of climate, the northern improvers launched a simple yet devastating critique: What if many of these cash crops could be cultivated in Britain? Already in his 1764 Report to the Board for the Annexed Estates, John Walker had explained how flax and hemp could be made to prosper in many corners of the Hebrides. In the *Tour* of 1772, Thomas Pennant revived the old idea of cultivating tobacco in the Hebrides, especially on the island of Tiree, which seemed "well adapted for the culture of [the crop]." During the American War of Independence, Charles Jackson of Kelso actually succeeded with a trial of tobacco in the Southern Uplands. Meanwhile, John Hope was busy cultivating Chinese tea, rhubarb, and asafetida in the Royal Botanic Garden of Edinburgh. The Third Duke of Atholl also made serious attempts at cultivating Tartarian rhubarb on his Highland estate in Perthshire. The Fourth Duke switched to Tyrolean larch, conceived as a substitute not only for English oak but also for exotic timbers such as South Asian teak. When overseas crops seemed impossible to acclimatize, James Anderson promoted indigenous or northern substitutes, including sugar beets and heather honey for West Indies sugar cane, Silesian milkweed (*Asclepias syriaca*) for Indian cotton, cudbear (a mixture of northern lichen varieties) for southern dye plants, and so forth. During the early 1790s, Anderson's periodical *The Bee* offered a clearing house for ideas of ecological exchange as an alternative to overseas colonization. His anti-imperial ecology found an audience far outside Scotland but also alienated potential supporters at home. While Anderson developed a radical defense of urbanization and manufacturing in the Highlands, his rival John Walker rose to prominence as the expert of the landed interest and the spokesman for a very different vision of internal improvement. It is to the contest between Anderson and Walker that we turn next.[41]

Part II

Rival Ecologies

4

Alternate Highlands

On his first journey through the Hebrides in 1764, John Walker spent seven months looking for God in boggy pastures and windswept uplands. The clergyman naturalist believed that every island contained hidden riches planted there by providence. In the mountains of the Isle of Rum, south of Skye, Walker discovered a "great abundance" of Linnaeus's *Aira coerulea* (*Molinia caerulea*, purple moor grass). This species was far better "suited to [the] climate and soil" of the Scottish uplands than southern kinds of forage plants. It grew wild in large stands almost at the very peak of the hills. If these high meadows were enclosed, Walker thought it might be possible to solve the principal problem of Highland livestock husbandry: how to provide sufficient hay for local cattle. Walker's natural history of local advantages also celebrated the primitive virtue and health associated with a simple diet and a hardy way of life. In another place and time, such ideas might have been little more than amusing reveries, but in Walker's Scotland they found a rapt audience. Landowners were particularly keen on his proposals for a mixed economy in the Highlands and Western Isles centered on potato cultivation, flax raising, kelping, and livestock farming. These hints for northern improvement earned him a place in the firmament of Scottish learning. He was appointed Regius Professor of Natural History at the University of Edinburgh in 1779 and then became the chief naturalist of the Highland Society of Edinburgh.[1]

Walker's conservative natural theology competed with a radically different model of economic development. In the same decade that Walker explored the Western Isles, a tenant farmer in Aberdeenshire began experimenting with a plantation of larch trees on his estate. This was the first project of James Anderson, a brilliant liberal polymath with interests in chemistry, political economy, and agriculture. Anderson, too, found a ready audience for his ideas. He was the intellectual force behind the establishment of the British Fisheries Society and the British Wool Society. His journal *The Bee* became a venue for some of the more radical voices in British publishing. Where Walker's providence promised virtue and health through local knowledge, Anderson pictured the deity as a creature of cosmopolitan exchange. Ecological diversification would pave the way for social and political change. He thought transplanted Merino sheep could provide wool for new manufactures in the Highland interior. On the higher slopes of the mountains, the larch would thrive, yielding turpentine and naval timber. Scottish sugar beets provided a moral substitute to the sugar cane of the slave plantations in the West Indies. On the coast, herring fisheries would foster new towns in the Hebrides and emancipate the Gaelic plebeians from despotic landlords.[2]

These rival visions of economic development competed for support from the government and Scottish civil society. Anderson's liberal scheme of town-building seemed on the verge of success when the British Fisheries Society adopted his plan after the American Revolutionary War. Yet the project was marred by a series of practical problems, including the vexed issue of recruiting settlers. Instead, Walker's conservative model became dominant in the age of the French Revolution. His growing interest in kelp production proved especially well timed. The commercial development of the Highlands and Western Isles was for Walker both a promise and a threat. Whereas Anderson's liberal scheme aimed to maximize the spread of towns and markets in the Highland economy, Walker's conservative perspective favored a moral and geographic division of labor that sought to insulate Highland virtue from at least some of the effects of commercial society. In this balance act, the harsh and difficult environment of the Hebrides was in itself an important endowment. It habituated the common people to a simple life, shielding them from urban luxury and corruption.

PROVIDENTIAL BOTANY

The intellectual path of the Reverend John Walker recapitulates the movement of Highland improvement as a whole between 1760 and 1800. It began with the discovery of a New World and ended in a peat bog. The son of a grammar school rector, Walker was trained to the ministry in the Church of Scotland and eventually rose to become a moderator in the General Assembly of the Kirk but always remained by inclination more a taxonomist than a pastor. The Reverend Walker built an extensive correspondence network with natural historians across Britain and the Continent. In Scotland, his major patrons and contacts included Lord Bute, Lord Kames, and the physician and chemist William Cullen at the Medical School of Edinburgh. A member of Walker's flock grumbled that the minister "spent the week hunting butterflies and made the cure of the souls of his parishioners a bye-job on Sunday." In his correspondence with Carl Linnaeus, the Swedish botanist urged Walker to be the first person to make a botanical survey of the north and west of Scotland. A joint appointment with the Board for the Annexed Estates and the General Assembly of the Church of Scotland permitted him to go on long tours of the Hebrides and Highlands in 1764 and again in 1771. These journeys laid the foundation for Walker's authority as an expert in the natural history and agriculture of the Highlands. Together with John Lightfoot, John Hope, and James Robertson, he pioneered the use of the Linnaean system of classification to chart the region's native species of plants, animals, and minerals.[3]

By all accounts, Lord Kames regarded Walker as his mentor in matters of natural history, particularly in the bewildering matter of plant physiology. Thanks to Kames's patronage, Walker was able to rise in 1779 to the post of professor of natural history at the University of Edinburgh and the Keeper of the Natural History Museum, where he subsequently offered the first regular lectures in natural history from 1782. Although he published relatively little and late in life, many of his opinions probably circulated widely thanks to the courses he taught at the university and through the essays he submitted to the contests of the Highland Society of Edinburgh. Walker also played an important role in the establishment of the Royal Society of Edinburgh and became an active member of the physical section of the institution. He helped sponsor the Natural History Society of Edinburgh in 1782 and the Agricultural Society of Edinburgh in 1790. Among the seven hundred students he taught were leading members of the Scottish gentry as well as a new generation of natural historians and natural philosophers, including Francis Buchanan Hamilton (the surveyor of Mysore and Bengal), Robert Jameson (the Lamarckian geologist), John Playfair (the popularizer of James Hutton's geological theories), and Sir James Edward Smith (the founder of the Linnaean Society of London). By virtue of this work as an expert and teacher, Walker's career formed a bridge between the world of the Select Society and the new voluntary associations that flourished in the 1780s and 1790s.[4]

Walker's authority among landowners and Lowland savants rested on the economic utility associated with natural history. The reports Walker fielded to the Board for the Annexed Estates were shot through with commercial projects and proposals for the diversification of land use. In this sense, Walker was thoroughly committed to the general trend toward "demand management" and commercialization popular among Highland landowners following the Restoration. For Walker, agricultural improvement and natural history were closely allied, subsumed under the greater category of rural economy.[5] "When I first drew out the Plan of my Lectures in natural history, I engrossed in it, the Subjects of Vegetation, Agriculture, the management of cattle, Plantation and Gardening, which comprehended the whole of the *Res Rustica*." In Walker's case, flax may have been the original motive for connecting natural history and agricultural improvement so closely. One of Kames's priorities with the survey of the Hebrides was to assess the possibility of extending the Scottish linen industry from the Lowlands to the islands. Walker's knowledge of plant physiology and acclimatization seemed an ideal instrument to reconnoiter suitable sites for flax raising in the Western Isles.[6]

Every locale had some providential use, no matter how barren in appearance. Only the naturalist was capable of detecting these local prospects for improvements. Like Linnaeus, Walker understood natural theology in economic terms. The pattern of divine design permeating Creation also served to guarantee the natural advantage of even the most remote and humble location. God had provided for the subsistence of his flock in every possible soil and climate. Walker observed in his Report on the Hebrides to the Board for the Annexed Estates: "There is a particular Product for every Country, which its Soil and Climate, and the Situation with Respect to a Market point out. This however, is frequently overlooked or neglected by the inhabitants, and another Product adopted than what nature dictates." It was the gaze of the natural historian that uncovered these hidden riches, revealing the true potential of the periphery. Linnaeus in turn observed in *Species Plantarum* (1753): "The WORLD is the Almighty's theater. . . . We must research these creations by the Creator, which the Highest has linked to our well-being in such a way that we shall not need to miss anything of all the good things we need." Like a new priesthood, natural historians alleviated human suffering by discovering the secret stores of Creation.[7]

Natural historians also noticed the great diversity of species that flourished even in a nutrient-poor habitat. Walker and his colleague John Lightfoot inventoried all the plants that could subsist in peat mosses, including bog myrtle, cranberries, hornworts, sundews, and butterwort. Lightfoot noted that mosses flourished "most in Winter," covering the ground "with a beautiful green carpet" so as to "shelter and preserve the seeds, roots, gems, and embryo plants of many vegetables, which would otherwise perish." Mosses also furnished "materials for birds to build their nests with" as well as "a warm Winter's retreat for some quadrupeds, such as bears, dormice, and the like, and for numberless insects, which are the food of birds and fishes, and these again the food or delight of men." Long before the advent of scientific ecology, Lightfoot and

Walker expressed an appreciation of the beauty and biological function of native flora beyond the bounds of conventional agriculture and gardening. Their accounts treated peat moss as a miniature kingdom governed by its own laws and social relations. The interest in nature's utility here blended with a more general admiration for intricate interdependencies between creatures and plants of only indirect economic value to human beings. Lightfoot's defense of mosses also hinted at an appeal to uncertainty and progress that would become a staple justification for biodiversity in our own time. "MOSSES, by the inconsiderate mind, are generally deem'd an useless or insignificant part of the creation. That they are not is evident only from hence; that He who made them has made nothing in vain, but, on the contrary, has pronounced all his works to be *very good*. Many of their uses we know; that they have many more which we know not, is unquestionable, since there is probably no one thing in the universe of which we can dare to assert that know *all* their uses." Plants with no apparent utility might one day prove profitable. In the fullness of time, purposes would be revealed that the naturalist could not yet imagine.[8]

But the pieties of natural theology could only be revealed through incessant fieldwork. In his Report to the Board for the Annexed Estates, Walker investigated the prevailing conditions of soil fertility, the ratio of arable and pasture land, levels of precipitation, and other characteristics of local climate. Much of the work was guided by the logic of import substitution. Raw materials for Scottish manufactures included talc from Skye for porcelain, kelp for glass manufactures, hemp for the navy, and lead to make pencils. The energy Walker vested in his natural inventories was matched by an orthodox faith in the positive balance of trade. To "entrench our Export" was a primary goal of his political economy.[9]

Walker's patriotism was rooted in literary fashion as much as resource geography. The vogue for Gaelic literature and culture began with the publication of Jerome Stone's Gaelic elegy in the *Scots Magazine* in 1756, and James Macpherson's "translations" of Ossian between 1760 and 1763. Walker opened his Report to the Board for the Annexed Estates by insisting that the population in the Hebrides still belonged to the "pastoral stage of Society." Although there was much hope for progress, it must be conceded that the "Inhabitants, when compared to their Fellow Subjects, with Respect to Arts; are in almost the same Situation as in the Days of Oscian [sic]." In fact, Walker was among the first literati to defend the authenticity of Macpherson's poetry by collecting information about his alleged sources in the Highlands. Like many other travelers, he also sought to discover in situ the Highland locales that best corresponded to the landscapes described in the poems.[10]

Economic botany deepened this notion of the Highlands as a primitive society. Lightfoot's *Flora Scotica* identified hundreds of species of useful native plants on the northern periphery. The fishermen on Skye made their ropes and nets from *Melica caerulea* (purple melic-grass). The roots of *Tormentilla erecta* (*Potentilla erecta*, common tormentil) yielded a tanning agent in Canna, according to Thomas Pennant. *Ligusticum scoticum* (Scotch parsley) served as salad for the poor and a carminative. The stalks of *Utrica dioica* (common nettle) were strong enough to replace hemp. In parts of Europe and Siberia, they were woven into cloth or manufactured into paper. On Mull, *Myrica gale* (bog myrtle) cured the worm in children. On Uist and the mainland, the people used it instead of hops to brew beer. The cones yielded a scum "like bees wax, capable of being made into candles." Lightfoot listed seven economic uses for *Erica cinerea* (fine-leaved heather) in the Western Isles. *Galium verum* (lady's bedstraw) was lauded for its "exceeding fine red Dye" and capacity to bind drift sand. Infused in liquor, the dried roots of the *Orobus tuberosus* (wood pease) repelled hunger and invigorated the mind during Highland travel. The roots of *Potentilla anserina* (wild tansy) tasted much like parsnip and answered on Tiree and Col "in some measure the purposes of bread, they having been known to support the inhabitants for months together." *Lichen islandicus* (Iceland lichen) was ground into powder on Iceland and eaten "as common food, boiling it either in milk or water, or making it into bread." Lightfoot's travel companion Thomas Pennant saw in native plant use the reflection of "rational observation and judicious attention to nature!" Implicit in these catalogues of edible plants, dyes, fiber plants, and medicinal herbs was not only the pious expectation of natural theology but also the social ideal of a labor force content with simple forms of subsistence.[11]

The cultural roots of such primitivism lay partly in the anthropology of autarky articulated by the Skye native Martin Martin (d. 1718). Martin had collected facts and curiosities in the Western Isles on behalf of the Scottish geographer royal Sir Robert Sibbald (1641–1722) and the natural historian and antiquarian Sir Hans Sloane of the Royal Society of London. Drawing on native knowledge of Gaelic culture and language, Martin's *Description of the Western Islands of Scotland* (1703) served as the major guide to the region until Thomas Pennant's tours. The cousin of one clan chief and the tutor of another, Martin moved within an international community of Gaelic soldiers and professionals.[12] Yet rather than analyzing the cultural and geographic agility that characterized his patrician kinsmen, Martin's work singled out and celebrated the ethnic distinctness and physical isolation of the Gaelic lower orders. Borrowing generously from Tacitus's *Germania*, he praised the longevity, health, and temperance of island life, "free from the various convulsions that ordinarily attend luxury." This was a people molded by a nasty climate to brave adversity with industry and ascetic moderation. Martin insisted that "the ignorance of vices [was] more powerful among [them] than all the precepts of philosophy . . . among the Greeks." These were men who knew neither sugar nor cinnamon and slept on "beds of heath" without nightcaps. Such a conflation of Greco-Roman imagery with Gaelic ethnography would have a long life among Martin's readers and imitators.[13]

The double vision of the Highlands owed much to Linnaeus's travels in Lapland. As we have heard, Walker, Robertson, and Lightfoot were all committed to the Swedish botanist's system of classification and the economic priorities embodied in his flora. Indeed, by relying on Linnaeus's *Flora Lapponica* to identify useful or edible Highland plants, their accounts sometimes mixed the cultural legacies and economic prospects of Lapland and northern Scotland.[14] Linnaeus's book dwelled at length on the importance of native botanical knowledge to Sami subsistence. The far north accustomed them to food deemed inedible elsewhere such as unsalted fish, reindeer milk, and native wild plants. It also preserved them from the luxury of modern commerce and made them ignorant of "alcoholic beverages, tobacco, tea, coffee, sugar, silk [and] most spices." Where another observer might have recoiled at debilitating scarcity, Linnaeus saw self-sufficiency and moderation: "The Lapp gets from his Reindeer herd almost all his needs; lives content and happy in his cold and sterile land." This myth in turn helped sustain the moral aspect of Linnaeus's cameralism. The Sami set a virtuous example to the rest of the nation. Only by subduing consumer appetites and denouncing luxury would his compatriots render Sweden truly independent.[15]

Yet the centrality of Lapland to Linnaeus's reputation never matured into a political commitment. The Swedish botanist spent only one summer in the north. Like so many other European social climbers, he took a colonial shortcut to wealth and authority. There was no compelling counterpart to the Scottish politics of population in Linnaeus's thought because he did not think that the Sami needed special protection by the state or civil society (perhaps he would have if he had assigned them a military function). In contrast, Walker's engagement with Highland improvement spanned the entirety of his career, from 1764 to 1803, and was driven by fertile anxieties about the economic and military fate of Scotland. The urgency and consistency of Walker's commitment arose from the ways in which he disturbed and rearranged a mixture of Scottish commonplaces: conjectural history, the fear of Gaelic emigration, and worries about an inverse relation between commerce and martial valor. If history progressed by stages, then was it not inevitable that modern opulence must eclipse pastoral virtues? In practical terms, how could improvement be introduced into the Highlands without provoking emigration and the collapse of the population? Walker's vision of the Highlands sought to resolve this fundamental tension between wealth and virtue by recasting the familiar historical narrative in the form of a moral geography with virtue on the periphery and wealth in the center.

Through the inventory of indigenous substitutes, Walker's enlightened science aimed to bolster traditional forms of "resource management" while adapting them to suit a parallel system of extractive commercial industries. In clan society, the tenant class of tacksmen had served as the managers of natural resources, acting on the principle of communal solidarity—*beathachadh boidheach*—the "comfortable sufficiency for the clan as a whole." These tacksmen allocated the strips of infield and outfield among subtenants, oversaw the use of fertilizer to prevent soil exhaustion, and protected forest stock from grazing and fuel depletion. Now, when economic rationalization demanded the elimination of the tacksman class on the great estates, natural historians like Walker and Lightfoot supplied an alternative mode of "resource management." In collecting information from oral and written sources in Gaelic tradition, these savants aimed to create a store of useful knowledge accessible to the improving landlord and government agents, which could in turn be employed to preserve the plebeian population from both famine and luxury.[16]

This new information economy suggested the possibility of widespread import substitution within British society. The subsistence provided by indigenous plants formed an integral part of the division of labor between southern opulence and northern virtue. By consuming the indigenous riches provided by providence, the plebeian would remain a strong and virtuous laborer amid the opulence expected from new industries without desiring the profits or luxuries of his master. John Hope's student James Robertson wrote of the Orkney cuisine: "Oat-meal, barley, milk, Potatoes & cabbages form the chief articles of Diet, to which the inhabitants of the shores add Fish hung in the sun till they become sour, shell-fish, the flesh & Eggs of Sea-Fowl, the flesh of Seals, Navel Lavers commonly called Slake (*Ulva umbilicalis*) boiled to the consistency of a jelly, & broth made of the Hand Fucus or Dulse (*Fucus palmatus*) with Oatmeal. The simple food however nourishes a race of men deterred by no hardships, appalled by no danger." In other words, these natural historians fostered a double vision of the north. Rather than a sharp transition from traditional "resource management" to the commercial imperatives of "demand management," Walker and his fellow travelers advocated a socially differentiated but economically complementary understanding of Scottish natural resources in which the two systems existed side by side. However, in practice, the more extravagant elements of their economic botany proved redundant. Robertson's Orkney recipes never made it into the enlightened cookbooks. The forward march of the American potato in the north was making the obsession with indigenous flora obsolete even as Walker, Robertson, and Lightfoot were prospecting for useful plants in the mountains.[17]

Peat cutting posed another challenge for resource management. In June 1759, the Board for the Annexed Estates intervened on behalf of the Cromarty proprietor John Gordon of Invergordon, who complained that local inhabitants were abusing their right to take peat from the Moss of Delnie. The Earl of Cromarty had tried to divide the moss in 1739, but no "Decreet arbitral ever followed." Now, the moss was "much destroyed" by "a Number of Fishers and Cottars who Reside upon the Estate of Cromarty." These people cast "large Quantities of peats and Turf . . . for money to the inhabitants of Cromarty and others who have no Moss of their own." The description of resource strain here presumed that only landowners should conduct demand management. Plebeian cottars had no right to exploit commons for market profits. The board's factor at Cromarty endorsed Gordon's petition and asked that the sheriff intervene. It was, he concluded, in the "Interest of all Parties concerned to join in the preservation of the said moss of Delnie."[18]

Many years later, John Walker took up the problem of peat cutting in an essay for the Highland Society of Scotland. "Little attention has hitherto been paid to the manner of working our peat mosses," he noted. "The people are generally allowed to work in them at will; and studying only their own conveniency, they proceed in such an injudicious and hurtful manner, that the mosses come to be demolished and rendered unserviceable." Walker recommended that "all the people who cut peats in a moss, should be made to observe certain rules, that while they serve themselves, they may not injure the interest, either of the landlord or of the community." The solution was to "employ a ground office to superintend the work, and to see those regulations exactly observed; which the proprietor may prescribe." The main rules Walker had in mind concerned the drainage and regeneration of the moss. He insisted that many cases of "exhaustion" were in fact only superficial. The local users had simply cut the moss in "irregular . . . peat pots" without draining it, until they became "pits of standing water." By digging and draining the moss at the same time, it was possible to make much deeper cuts. His second rule was to place soil or turf "at the bottom" of a cut "where the water stagnates." This would allow for the gradual "renovation" of the peat, by preserving "a new grassy surface," which over time allowed for "the formation of a new stratum of peat." These "underfoot peats" would be ready to dig "in the course of 30 or 40 years." Though Walker's view was much too optimistic about the rate of accretion for peat, the example illustrates nicely how natural historians sought to govern the process of resource management in the Scottish Enlightenment.[19]

A WHIG ECOLOGY FOR THE HIGHLANDS

The business of improvement was hardly a conservative monopoly in the Scottish Enlightenment. John Walker's polar opposite here was the Aberdeen agriculturist James Anderson. Anderson is perhaps best known to posterity as an early reader and critic of Adam Smith. John Stuart Mill and Joseph Schumpeter hailed him as the precocious inventor of the theory of rent. But his economic writings were almost always connected with practical schemes and political aims. During the campaign in the mid-1780s to revive the Scottish fisheries, he served as a leading expert witness in the House of Commons. He was also a friend of prominent liberal and republican figures like Jeremy Bentham, the Earl of Buchan, and George Washington. In the early 1790s, Anderson's journal *The Bee* became a major venue for political radicalism. Yet Anderson remains a neglected figure among historians of political thought and political economy. In great part, he has been passed over because his economic and political ideas lie submerged in a much larger body of writings in forestry, natural history, and agriculture. Anderson's 1777 theory of rent is a good case in point. It first appeared as a postscript to a treatise on the history of sheep breeds.[20]

It is tempting to dismiss Anderson's interest in natural history as an eccentric diversion from the sober task of economic analysis. Yet these hybrid pursuits shed much needed light on the neglected connections among classical political economy, natural history, and practical schemes of improvement in the late Enlightenment. Anderson was greatly indebted to Adam Smith's critique of protectionism, but he went beyond Smith by suggesting that natural history held the key to sweeping social transformation. This duality resolves the apparent contradiction of Anderson's writings—why he lodged his theory of rent in a disquisition on Merino sheep. Natural history was for Anderson the primary theater of liberal reform and free trade.

Anderson was the son of a tenant farmer from Hermiston outside Edinburgh. In his youth he studied chemistry under William Cullen. Soon after his Edinburgh studies Anderson married an heiress and became an improving farmer at Monkshill near Aberdeen. But Anderson proved a far better theorist than practitioner of agricultural improvement, much like his English counterpart Arthur

Young. While Anderson spoke warmly of the "spirit of independence" found in "assiduous ... business," he owed much of his success to the patronage of his social superiors, including the Forfarshire laird George Dempster and the radical Earl of Buchan. When he failed to profit from the farming life, he turned instead to the middling profession of publishing. Among his earliest writings were a series of letters on forestry in the *Weekly Magazine or Edinburgh Amusement* in 1771. These included a defense of the utility of diversification and wasteland reclamation through acclimatization. Anderson was particularly fascinated with the central European larch. He praised its properties as a hard timber capable of replacing the oak and exhorted Scottish landowners to plant it on marginal soils at high altitudes as a way of putting their upland estates to profitable use.[21]

Anderson's interest in the environment of the periphery expanded to a scheme for northern industrialization in *Observations on the Means of Exciting a Spirit of National Industry* (1777). The book attacked the long-standing scheme for flax raising and linen manufactures promoted by John Walker and the Board of Trustees for Manufactures. Instead, Anderson favored wool production as a better fit with the Highland climate. He proposed that water-powered woolen mills in the north could compete with the manufactures of Yorkshire. Merino sheep would provide high-quality raw material grown directly in the Highlands. The project hinged on the viability of fine-wool breeds in northern latitudes. Hence, much of the book was occupied with technical arguments about transhumance, medieval wool production, and the relation of wool quality to pasture and climate. Anderson's obsession with the Merino was not uncommon in the late eighteenth century. French and Swedish improvers experimented with fine-wool breeds. Sir Joseph Banks engineered the introduction of the Merino to the south of England in 1791. But for Anderson, the Merino wool was the means to establishing a manufacturing society in the wilderness. "Protect the poor," he wrote. "Raise them from their low estate;— Let them feel what it is to possess. ... Cherish them as the apple of thine eye; and be assured when you do so, you are not fostering an insidious rival, but a brother, who will be ready to share in all." Without new manufactures, he warned, "the liberties of [the] state" would sink "on a tottering foundation."[22]

During the American War of Independence, Anderson's views grew steadily more radical. In 1782 he published a searing indictment of the British Empire entitled *The Interest of Great Britain*. Echoing Adam Smith's rhetoric about the projecting character of empire, Anderson compared the lure of colonial expansion to a "giddy whirl of dissipation." True national wealth was measured in the size of the productive classes, that is, manufacturers and farmers. Emigration to the colonies had acted as a great drain on both. The best cure for such delusions was to turn inward and attend to domestic improvements. Anderson predicted that the days of empire were all but finished: "Part of our external dominions are already gone, which has already induced *some* of the people to turn their attention toward the consideration of our internal resources, the rest are preparing the way for a separation, which at a period, perhaps much nearer than is at present apprehended, must happen."[23]

Despite the radical overtones, Anderson's appeal to internal colonization did not lack an audience in the years after the loss of the American colonies. The middle of the decade saw the birth of two voluntary associations dedicated to improvement in the north of Scotland: the British Fisheries Society, chartered by the Crown in 1786, and the Highland Society of Scotland, founded in 1784 and chartered in 1788. William Pitt the Younger commissioned Anderson to survey the fisheries of the Scottish west coast in 1784. That summer he made a circuit of the Hebrides that became the basis for a lengthy report to the Committee on Fisheries in the House of Commons in 1785. Here, Anderson was making common cause with the Quaker member of Parliament Henry Beaufoy and the Scottish bookseller John Knox. In the spring and summer of 1785, Anderson was examined as an expert witness by the House committee chaired by Beaufoy. Like John Walker, Anderson thus found a ready audience for his hybrid of economic and natural knowledge among leading lobbyists and politicians. His appearance in the Commons was also part of a larger movement toward increasing reliance on expert testimony within the new Select Committee system. British politicians were growing addicted to the appearance of impartial knowledge.[24]

The tour of the west coast formed the core of Anderson's 1785 work, *The Present State of the Hebrides*. The text began with a theoretical and historical disquisition on the causes that had retarded the Scottish west coast fisheries. Chief among them was the phantom lure of empire. The Whig victory for the "Principles of Liberty" in 1688 had proven a false start because the Revolution had also perpetuated the fantasy that overseas possessions were economically beneficial. But the herring fisheries and other domestic improvements now promised to put an end to the mental rot of imperialism. This switch from Merino improvement to fisheries marked a major transition in Anderson's radical ideology. The aim of the herring project was to break the power of the lairds by creating fishing villages that would grow into free towns. While Anderson's earlier treatise on the Merino had criticized the corn bounties and presented a theory of rent, the new book offered a radical meditation on the model of development outlined by Smith in book 3 of *The Wealth of Nations*.[25]

How could a liberal political economist encourage commercial expansion in a land without markets? Anderson turned to history for answers. The oppressed plebeians of the Hebrides must be emancipated in the same way that the serfs of "South Britain" had been freed in the Middle Ages. "By what means was this slavery so gradually and imperceptibly abolished in the State as to have occasioned no political convulsions?" The destruction of feudalism had come about through the founding of towns and the spread of commercial appetites. This peaceful transformation could be reenacted in the Hebrides: "We have every reason to expect the same beneficial effects would now result from a similar plan of conduct." But there was one major obstacle. Smith's model of mutually advantageous trade between country and town was predicated on the existence of an agricultural surplus. This meant that regions where intensive cereal production was possible were more likely to develop advanced commerce. What about places where the soil was too barren to admit of a surplus? Smith had mentioned in passing that a "city, situated near either the sea coasts or the banks of a navigable river" would not be "confined to derive" its subsistence from the immediate hinterland. Anderson's herring scheme expanded on this idea. Perhaps abundant fishing waters could act as a substitute for a rich soil?[26]

Anderson's notion of a "plan of conduct" betrayed a crucial difference with Smith at the level of historical agency. Book 3 of the *Wealth of Nations* characterized growth as a slow procession of homeostatic adjustments: "The progress is frequently so gradual, that, at near periods, the improvement is not only not sensible but . . . there frequently arises a suspicion that the riches and industry of the whole are decaying." In contrast, Anderson anticipated social change on a time scale of decades rather than centuries. Prudent legislators could speed up the slow work of time through the reform of the salt laws and the granting of premiums, which would tempt landowners to part with land and induce poor Highlanders to settle in the new villages.[27] Such judicious use of state power would eventually break up the authority of the landowning class and replace it with a free town population. Anderson had dedicated the *Observations on the Means of Exciting a Spirit of National Industry* to Adam Smith's patron the Duke of Buccleuch. His new book was simply addressed to the Lord Commissioners of the Treasury. Unlike Smith, Anderson also saw some limited need for protectionism in the fisheries. In his parliamentary testimony, he stressed the necessity of subsidies for town building, as well as bounties and premiums for the infant industry. Open competition with the Dutch, the Swedes, and the Danes would become possible only after a transitional phase when the infant industry had matured.[28]

In contrast with Walker's primitivist policy of accommodation, Anderson promoted a brand of internal colonization that was intended to bring the Hebrides fully within the orbit of commercial society. Anderson's interlocutors were Benjamin Franklin and Adam Smith rather than Martin Martin or James Macpherson. He included with his report a map outlining in tantalizing detail an imaginary landscape of new canals and roads across the region. Through the settlements at Ullapool (Wester Ross on the mainland), Tobermory (on Mull), Lochbay (on Skye), and Wick (on the mainland in Caithness), the society would introduce not only houses and harbors for the fishermen but also proper markets and increasing specialization. Anderson's ally John Knox predicted that each village could give employment to a "boat-builder, cooper, net-maker, tanner, blacksmith, mason, house-carpenter, weaver, tailor, shoemaker, butcher, and tallow chandler." Every settlement would also harbor an innkeeper, a schoolmaster, and an apothecary or surgeon. Such a division of labor must go hand in hand with liberal conditions for industry. There could be no "corporations of trades," and the villages would have to refrain from exacting any "fee or entry-money" from new settlers. Both Knox and Anderson insisted that "free towns" required relief from the present taxes on salt, and perhaps also the coal duties, in order to prosper. This combination of trade, specialization, and fiscal exemptions was expected to lift the region from the rude stage of agriculture into the commercial state of society.[29]

The end result of Anderson's parliamentary labors was a Pyrrhic victory for his ideas. Beaufoy's great speech on the fisheries in the House of Commons on July 4 echoed many of Anderson's basic points. It was a national embarrassment that the poor people of the Hebrides suffered while the ocean teemed with an abundant harvest of fish. A labyrinth of well-intentioned yet senseless laws barred the way of the Scottish fisheries. One major obstacle was the onerous salt tax, which severely limited the ability of locals to preserve fish for transportation to distant markets. Above all, the member for Great Yarmouth stressed that legal and economic reform could transform the environment in the most systematic fashion. He compared the natural state of the Highlands with that of the Dutch Republic. Holland had once been a barren wasteland much like the north of Scotland, yet wise laws had made it astonishingly fertile and populous. This was a rousing idea, especially in the wake of an imperial war that had gone disastrously wrong. Beaufoy's bill passed. But Anderson's scathing remarks about the feudal despotism of Highland patricians did little to endear him to the class that controlled the land on which the villages had to be built. Anderson also grew impatient with what he considered the myopic and unprincipled approach of the politicians. While awaiting his first appearance before the committee at the end of April 1785, Anderson vented his irritation to his teacher and friend the physician William Cullen: "As to my own particular business I find Gentlemen desirous of encouraging the fisheries but it will [be] a very difficult thing to make them understand the circumstances that are most essentially necessary. They are in general for adopting a multiplicity of little regulations, which will be of little use."[30] Clearly, Anderson found few politicians sufficiently liberal for his taste. Henry Dundas seemed too busy to grasp the issues. George Dempster was supportive but lacked the requisite influence. To make things worse, Anderson felt badly slighted by Pitt. He accused the minister of inadequately compensating him for the fact-finding mission in the Hebrides. The tension between Anderson's radical principles and the prejudices of his superiors surfaced also during the examination itself. The Third Report of the Fisheries Committee recorded an uneasy exchange between Anderson and the committee in the middle of July 1785. Anderson was pressed repeatedly to acknowledge the benevolent spirit of the landowners toward their tenants and subtenants. His response mixed deference and criticism. He "imagined" that the landlords "in general shew a Spirit of Lenity" but also defiantly noted that "an open market" alone could bring genuine relief to the poor people of the Western Isles. Such radical tendencies alienated crucial allies and patrons. When the British Fisheries Society was founded by Henry Beaufoy and George Dempster with Dundas's help in 1786, Anderson was excluded from the board of directors and his expertise ignored at committee meetings. Indeed, the social aims of the society quickly deviated from Anderson's Whig vision of specialized labor and urban independence, tending instead toward conservative priorities of by-employment and allotments.[31]

Such shoddy treatment merely confirmed Anderson in his beliefs. If anything, his attack on feudalism by way of political economy and natural knowledge intensified in the following decade. He published a pamphlet against the slave trade in 1789 and then a critique of the coal duties in the Hebrides.[32] Anderson's great project in the early 1790s was the journal *The Bee*, which became a major outlet for British radicalism at a time of increasing government repression. One frequent contributor to the journal was Anderson's patron David Steuart Erskine, Lord Buchan, the old Wilkite and supporter of the American Revolution. It was in the pages of *The Bee* that the foremost Scottish radical of the 1790s, James Thomson Callendar, first published his manifesto *The Political Progress of Scotland*. *The Bee* also provided an early venue for Jeremy Bentham to present his idea of the Panopticon.[33] Targets of the liberal journal included the coal duties, salt laws, and the corn bounties. Like Anderson's previous writings, *The Bee* heavily criticized overseas colonies in favor of internal improvement. And once again, Anderson channeled politics through natural history and agriculture. The journal was full of proposals for diversification and ecological exchange that he hoped would transform Scottish agriculture. Politically, Anderson and his collaborators favored the free flow of valuable plants across national and imperial borders. A letter from Anderson to George Washington written in 1793 discussed this imperative. Washington was along with Thomas Jefferson a loyal subscriber to *The Bee*. "Tho' it must be expected that in our attempts to obtain useful productions from one Country with a view to benefit another, we will often find that articles sent to us as valuable turn out to be of little use, we ought not from hence to slacken our endeavour." Anderson then mentioned the benefits of clover, turnips, and potatoes to the British economy. "To obtain one other such article would be a sufficient recompense for thousands of abortive trials. From these Considerations I continue to Collect from all Quarters, to the utmost of my Power, to distribute to others." The letter was accompanied by a packet, containing seeds for Tartarian buckwheat, Tibetan turnips, and a sample of Silesian hemp, among other things. In short, seeds and plants were not secrets of state to be jealously protected but public goods that belonged to all mankind. *The Bee* was meant to serve as clearinghouse for such cosmopolitan exchange.[34]

Environmental transformation was the guiding spirit of Anderson's journal. "I have not a doubt, that [the plants] even of the torrid zone will move towards the poles, and become slowly inured to the climate; that the climate itself will be changed for the better; and that some thousands of years hence reposing under their own olive tree, our posterity may quaff their own wine, and sip their own tea, sweetened with the juice of their own sugar cane." Most frequently *The Bee* celebrated the exchange of plants along northern latitudes, including the transplantation of sugar beets, poppies, madder, larch, and cotton substitutes.[35] In this way, Anderson's journal was reviving and popularizing the many schemes of Regius Keeper John Hope in the Royal Botanic Garden of Edinburgh. Hope had attempted to acclimatize the tea plant, rhubarb, and asafetida among other exotics during the 1770s and early 1780s. The underlying economic aim for Hope and Anderson alike was the dream of bringing the colonies home, by habituating the cash crops to the British nation or finding temperate substitutes in their place. The proposal for sugar beet cultivation was particularly revealing in this regard. If the government refused "to relax the monopoly in favour of the West India islands," *The Bee* suggested that British consumers supply themselves "with sugar from the produce of our own fields." The rhetoric here closely echoed that of *The Present State of the Fisheries*. Just as herring could become the natural basis of liberty for Highland plebeians, the introduction of sugar beets would permit cultivators to bypass the vested interest of the West Indies planters: "Thus might the slave trade be annihilated, even without the intervention of law; and without . . . convulsive struggle . . ." This was abolitionism by ecological means. But the reliance on natural history was also the Achilles' heel of Anderson's political thought. When the diversification experiments failed to deliver lasting material change, their political goals collapsed with them. By the late 1790s, James Anderson abandoned Scotland in favor of London. Though he continued to write about agriculture, he narrowed his focus to conventional mixed husbandry. In a letter to his son, he continued to espouse a fierce "spirit of independence," warning his son against debts and obligations to his superiors. Yet the move from Edinburgh to London marked the end of Anderson's politics of radical transformation.[36]

THE BRITISH FISHERIES SOCIETY

The crisis of the American War served to rejuvenate the rhetoric of internal colonization in Scottish civil society. After the outbreak of the American rebellion in 1775, Lord Kames complained in the *Gentleman Farmer* that "a small share of the money and attention bestowed on raising colonies, would have done wonders at home." He predicted the inevitable secession of the Americans but consoled his readers that agricultural improvement would "amply compensate the loss of these colonies." Unlike overseas expansion, internal prosperity would benefit Britain alone: "Our arts are our own, which we never can be deprived of while industry remains: in the very constitution of our colonies, on the contrary, there are causes of separation, that grow daily more and more efficacious. . . . It is indeed absurd, that a great nation, in the vigor of prosperity and patriotism, can be kept in subjection by a nation not more powerful, enervated by luxury and avarice." The best path to the regeneration of British virtue, Kames thought, went through the establishment of a Scottish "board for improving agriculture." Modeled on the Board of Trustees for Manufactures, it was to include nine members of noted skill and patriotism who would instigate surveys of husbandry at the county level, send out inspectors, offer medals to "rouse emulation in all," issue instructions for farmers, and, most usefully, direct "proper experiments" in agriculture. Kames's proposal came to fruition in 1793, when Sir John Sinclair founded the Board of Agriculture with the support of William Pitt.[37]

Kames's call for a commitment to agricultural improvement was not the only argument for internal colonization to come out of the American crisis. David Young, a Perthshire farmer with ties to the Earl of Kinnoul, recruited more than three hundred subscribers from the gentry and farmers in the region between

Perth, Aberdeen, and Edinburgh to support his book *National Improvements upon Agriculture* (1785). Among them were the Duke of Atholl, the Earl of Breadalbane, Sir William Forbes of Pitsligo, Professor John Anderson at Glasgow University, James Anderson, George Dempster of Dunnichen, and two figures from the Annexed Estates era: John Swinton and John Clerk (the secretary to the Annexed Estates). More than twenty merchants, mostly from Edinburgh and Perth, were also on the list of subscribers. One element of Young's argument targeted urban life. In the spirit of Monboddo and other primitivists, Young warned against the growth of large towns that generally could not sustain their own population. Only small towns and villages were equipped to maintain the nation's birthrates. Hence, it was crucial to maintain a "due proportion" "betwixt the town and country." Like Kames, Young also saw an inverse relation between empire and agricultural improvement. The aim of his proposal was "the raising of new colonies amongst ourselves" to "supply the loss of America." The scheme required the cooperation of the landed order and the government. Young proposed that the military in peacetime should be employed "in improving the waste grounds and muirs throughout Britain." This was a clear echo of Lord Milton's plan for disbanded soldiers on the Annexed Estates. It had been the "custom among the Romans," Young noted, "never to let their armies lie idle." Like Lord Monboddo, he observed that veterans in the Roman legions had been given a "few acres" each to improve with the spade, which kept their minds and bodies "hardy and robust" while stifling dissent and unrest. By constructing "little houses ... with gardens annexed to them" along the coasts, disbanded or disabled sailors could be settled and turned into fishermen. Young saw in these "infant colonies" a universal model that could be extended easily to the civilian population. Reviving the position of Walker and Monboddo, Young thought that spade cultivation boosted moral virtue and birthrates. Kitchen gardens also provided a remedy for the deleterious effects of manufacturing labor. Half an hour of spadework in the morning and afternoon sufficed to maintain the necessary connection of operatives with the soil.[38]

But it was the question of the fisheries rather than spade husbandry that occupied public attention in the immediate aftermath of the American War of Independence. The passage of Beaufoy's bill permitted the formation of a joint stock company that would channel private capital toward the building of planned villages in the Hebrides. The British Fisheries Society won support from a large number of proprietors drawn from both parties, many of them with close personal ties to William Pitt the Younger and Henry Dundas. Among these were the Fifth Duke of Argyll, Earl Gower, Henry Beaufoy, George

Dempster of Dunnichen, William Wilberforce, Neil Malcolm of Poltalloch, Sir John Sinclair of Ulbster, and Sir William Pulteney. By the late spring of 1786, the society had raised subscriptions worth seven thousand pounds from more than a hundred subscribers in Britain at fifty pounds per share. It was further bolstered by an act of Parliament the same year that granted bounties both on the tonnage of herring busses and each barrel of herring caught.[39]

The directors hoped that the new villages would bolster recruitment for the Royal Navy in the Hebrides, prevent Gaelic emigration to America, and make the Highlands a powerhouse of shipping and commerce within the nation and empire. The ideology of the British Fisheries Society was in fact merely the latest incarnation of an age-old obsession with herring fisheries that attributed the rise of Dutch naval and commercial power to the exploitation of this maritime "bullion." George Dempster wrote to his colleague on the board of directors Sir Adam Fergusson: "What is Canada, St Johns or the Bahamas that they should be supported at such an annual expence, while our own coasts are forgotten?" But for other supporters, the establishment of the company would simply serve to diversify the portfolio of a landed class that already held investments both at home and overseas. A sizable portion of the capital of the society, about six thousand pounds, was raised in subscriptions for 138 shares in the company by a contingent of Scots in the East Indies in 1789. Among the sixty-eight subscribers were captains in the Highland regiments, Calcutta merchants, tax collectors, and surgeons. A number of the directors and backers of the society, notably Pulteney and Dempster, had also served in the East India Company. Neil Malcolm, another member of the board, poured his West India fortune into an array of improvement schemes in Scotland. As T. M. Devine and other scholars have noted, returning Scottish nabobs and West Indies plantation owners tended to sink their wealth into landed capital, thus fortifying "the entrenched position of the traditional elites in Scotland rather than [undermining] it." The beneficiaries of overseas empire doubled as advocates of internal colonization.[40]

The long-term aim of the founders of the British Fisheries Society was the urbanization of the northern periphery, rather than the making of a few scattered village communities. George Dempster made a bet with Sir James Riddell that "at least half a dozen Free Towns" would be formed by the society in due course. James Anderson was adamant that the planned communities must be quite large from the outset. The internal colonies of the Annexed Estates had failed because their scale had been too limited. Only full-sized towns could bring true prosperity to the west coast because they alone could provide the sufficient population and market for an advanced division of labor. John Gray agreed that "every projected settlement" should accommodate "the skeleton of a future large city." There was room for "twenty Liverpools" on the west coast. Anderson dismissed worries about urban degeneration as the fanciful fears of "speculative men." The virtues of universal employment and prosperity would compensate for any vices generated by the concentration of population in one place.[41]

However, these high hopes for urban development were dashed in the course of the next decade. A series of unfavorable conjunctures thwarted the aims of the improvers, including the outbreak of war with France in 1793, the unexpected shift of the herring shoals away from the west coast in 1798, and the onset of renewed emigration from the Highlands in 1801. By the first decade of the nineteenth century, Lochbay had all but collapsed and Ullapool was failing to grow in line with official expectations. Tobermory continued to flourish, but this was thanks to commercial activities other than the herring fleet. Solely the station at Wick on the east coast of the mainland in Caithness fulfilled the original expectations of the British Fisheries Society. However, the settlement was too far removed from the Hebrides to be of much benefit to the island economies.[42]

THE QUERIES OF 1787

The British Fisheries project provides an unexpected window on the attitude of landowners in the Highlands and Hebrides to spade husbandry. Anderson's liberal push to nurse new towns and markets ironically seems to have encouraged northern improvers to consider more seriously the conservative alternative. Because fishing was a seasonal activity, the directors of the British Fisheries Society were forced to reckon with the question of by-employments and subsistence. How large an allotment was needed to feed a family? Too small a plot might starve the family, but too much land would create a disincentive to participate in the fisheries. James Anderson and John Knox had shown some awareness of the problem in their original proposals. Knox suggested that an acre or half an acre should be distributed to each house, "whereon to raise vegetables and potatoes; which, with fish at their doors, would form a principal part of their subsistence through the whole year." Likewise, Anderson wanted to grant prospective fishermen a "small spot in each town sufficient for a house and garden" as a perpetual lease (feu). But what had been a relatively marginal question in the promotional work of Knox and Anderson became a major practical concern for the directors of the British Fisheries Society.[43]

On behalf of the board of directors, the Earl of Breadalbane circulated a set of queries to local landowners in February 1787 concerning the incentives necessary to attract settlers. In particular, the third query brought attention to the problem of the precise proportion of land required by each villager. The twenty-seven responses that came in between March and May 1787 were carefully recorded in the minute book of the British Fisheries Society. They ranged over most of the locations contemplated for settlement from Mull and Skye to Ross-shire and included a variety of magnates and lesser proprietors such as the Duke of Argyll, the Duke of Gordon, Lord Stonefield, Archibald Fraser of Lovat, Kenneth Mackenzie of Torridon, Donald Macleod of Geanies, and Hugh Rose of Nigg. The majority of the respondents favored the distribution of small amounts of land to the settlers. Lord Stonefield suggested no more than one acre per fisherman. Sir James Grant of Grant recommended two. Donald Macleod of Geanies promised "a small spot for potherbs and Potatoes to the extent of half an acre to the fishermen." Fraser of Lovat mentioned the distribution of "potatoe ground." Francis Humberstone Mackenzie offered some moorland for his village. The Duke of Argyll (probably via his bailie Colin Campbell) presented a precise quota: "It is computed that betwixt four and five hundred Acres will answer the purposes of each Settlement including the Scite [sic] of the Village—Each Family to have a Cows Grass in Summer—half an acre of Boggy or unimproved Land for potatoes and one sixteenth part of an acre for a garden." Only two of the reports—by James Grant (advocate) and Hugh Rose of Nigg—spoke explicitly of "delving" and spade husbandry, but the other respondents most likely assumed that this was the proper mode of cultivation, given the many references to gardening, kailyards (cabbage gardens), and potatoes, along with the frank admission that the units of land must be strictly limited.[44]

These answers to Breadalbane's queries reveal a serious engagement of landowners with the problem of political economy on the periphery. Virtually all of the respondents recognized that the economic principles of the metropole must be modified to accommodate local peculiarities. Many supplied detailed advice as to how the transition should be effected. This discussion ranged beyond the question of the optimal proportion of land for each settlement to such related issues as the problem of introducing market-oriented conduct among poor people with little experience of such transactions, the difficulty of establishing a distinct division of labor, and the necessity of accommodating tradition and popular expectations during a transitional period. The report by Donald Macleod of Geanies is very revealing in this respect. Macleod began by noting the negative precedent of the Annexed Estates. "There is experience from Lord Kames's benevolent Scheme at the peace 1763 that free houses and acres with boats and tackling are not of themselves a sufficient inducement" to attract settlers. In order to overcome this problem, Macleod suggested that political action on the national level was needed. Parliament must lift the salt and coal duties in the new villages. Such incentives would ensure broad recruitment of skilled labor, attracting not only "fishermen" but also "carpenters, coopers, smiths and other necessary artisans to the stations." Like James Anderson and John Knox, Macleod insisted on establishing a complex division of labor at the outset. It was vital to keep occupations like fishing and curing "separate and distinct." But Macleod was willing to compromise on at least one crucial point. He conceded that market relations could not be unmediated in the "infancy of the undertaking." Instead, the "Society will find it necessary to interpose between the fisherman and the Merchant . . . an Agent." This official undertaker would be "thoroughly versant in the value of the fish" and therefore pay the fishermen with "ready money the whole marketable fish, where landed at a fair and equal price such as the business can afford." Macleod also acknowledged that such intervention would "be attended with an expence" and perhaps "be productive of trouble and even a loss to the Society" but that "great exertions at the commencement of the undertaking" were necessary to ensure "final and ultimate success."[45]

Hugh Rose of Nigg in Ross-shire, the factor for the Countess of Sutherland, tackled the problem of settlement with a specific interest in habits and attachment. He, too, stressed the importance of "proper inducements" for settlers "to betake themselves to live in villages." This was especially pressing on the west coast of Sutherland, where the people were not "all their lives bred fishermen" as they were on the eastern side. How could the society "reconcile them to that mode of life in place of the life they now lead"? Rose followed the general model of demand-oriented growth developed by political economists like David Hume. New forms of consumer desires would alter habits and heighten industry: "It is believed that getting any article a family may want at a very moderate price will induce the Men to fish, and the women to spin in order to come at these articles, and this accommodation ought not be confined to the villagers alone, but should extend to women who might spin yarn even at a distance." Rose's response here expanded on a memorandum he had written on the improvement of the Sutherland estate the previous year. This text had envisioned fishing villages as a part of a wider process of transformation, including the "abolition of personal services," the "improvement of wastelands," and the establishment of "regular markets." Yet the memorandum recognized that the natural disadvantages of the region made conventional husbandry all but impossible "for there are but few places where the plough could be successfully employed." With ten to twenty tenants to each farm, the common people practiced "delving" "with a spade or foot plow which they term *Cascromb* . . . a crooked stick having a particular bend shot with iron." The tool allowed them to cultivate crops of potatoes and grain on their small fields. In the summer, they retired to the shielings in the mountains with their sheep and goats until harvest time in August. This form of husbandry raised a sufficient amount of food to support the inhabitants "thro the year" at least in "good seasons." But Rose also stressed that the common people were "fond of money and therefore" turned to fishing in the summer when the herring shoals appeared. Moreover, the strenuous labor demanded by spade husbandry indicated a propensity for industry that could be directed toward other kinds of employment. Indeed, Rose proposed that spade cultivation might provide the means by which the settlers could "reconcile" to the new "mode of life" in the fishing villages. He recommended that the society rent "one, two or three . . . farms adjoining to each village" to create a "Common" for settlers where they could graze their livestock and improve the land "by Delving." In this way, they could accommodate elements of their traditional life with the new realities of the fishing village and still be "pretty much on the footing" they were used to from the old communities. A similar notion was put forward by the advocate James Grant. "To induce, . . . the people to settle in villages, a prospect of subsistence must be afforded them." Like Rose, he observed that the "Highlanders . . . are not Manufacturers and are not inured to any species of constant or unremitting labor." Continuity in diet was a powerful incentive for settlement. "In order then to induce them to settle in villages, that species of Food which they have been accustomed to live on, must in some measure be secured to them." Such a diet of milk and potatoes in turn involved the keeping of a cow and small potato ground for each family.[46]

A few of the respondents framed the problem of attachment in terms of coercion rather than reconciliation. Alexander Maclean of Coll pushed this line of argument to a harsh conclusion. The fundamental problem in the Highlands, according to Maclean, was that all forms of occupation were "carried on by people who are possessed of lands and who only make the fishing etc a mere temporary object or casualty." Such people "will not easily be persuaded to renounce their possessions to follow a business with which they are but very imperfectly if at all acquainted." In fact, they preferred leisure over work as long as they could draw a meager livelihood from the land. Maclean defined this preference in terms of an irrational attachment: "Their sole attention is in a manner fix'd to the produce of the Earth, their sole object of pursuit is to get a Farm, and a patch of ground however small is infinitely prefer'd to every other mode of gaining a Livelihood." So strong was this bond that schemes of inducements tended to be self-subverting: "Tradesmen of all description are not to be got without procuring farms for them." Yet "no sooner this is procured than they become farmers solely and they give up their trade." Logically then, the introduction of a division of labor required an act of coercion to succeed in a conservative agrarian country. Men must forcibly be separated from the subsistence of the land: "If the inhabitants of those Countrys can procure the bare necessarys of life by their labour from the grounds they possess, their ambition leads them to no farther effort." What class of people could be pushed off the land? Benjamin Dunbar in Caithness proposed that the society should target only the poor class of farmers. He described how north coast fishing was carried out by substantial farmers who refused to give up their land. "No inducement will be sufficient to prevail on these amphibious beings to quit their Cottage and Farm to go always to the sea, and depend solely for their livelihood on its produce." This double commitment led to neglect of both farms and fisheries. Whereas the "smaller sort of Possessor, whose Farms give them less to do, altho' they might be prevail'd upon to take a House in the Village," were too poor to afford "boats, netts or afford House rent."[47]

The problem of subsistence could also be posed in terms of labor time. How much work per day or month did a given unit of land require? The trick was to find the precise balance between conflicting priorities. John Mackenzie's report from March 1787 criticized John Knox's estimate of half an acre per fisher as overly generous. Mackenzie preferred an eighth of an acre, "for the cultivation of more would engross too much of their time in spring the best season for the Cod and Ling fishings." Though he rejected Anderson's unit of one sixteenth of an acre as too small, Mackenzie endorsed Anderson's idea that fishermen and "mechanicks" should be distinguished by different amounts of land. The mechanic class ought to have a fourth of an acre to raise vegetables, since "their time would be more beneficially employed" that way. Larger units of land would also bind artisans to the ground in the villages, making them less willing to emigrate.[48]

These responses did not fail to make an impression on the directors of the British Fisheries Society. In May 1788, they decided to include a garden with each house at Ullapool. The directors stipulated that the "breadth of the Lot for the Kail Yard" could not "exceed the length of the house." In addition they resolved "that to all Settlers of the Description above mentioned, it will be expedient to allow a right of Summer Pasturage at the rate of a Cows grass to each family." This decision in effect made spade husbandry the social foundation of subsistence at Ullapool. But this was not simply a matter of attracting new settlers. The policy was also the most cost effective policy when capital expenditure mounted alarmingly. John Knox's pamphlet of 1786 had estimated the cost of a planned village with thirty-six houses at two thousand pounds. In practice, the settlement at Ullapool swallowed more than nine thousand pounds in the first eight years of development between 1788 and 1796. As the funds became depleted, spade husbandry seemed the only option left to pursue.[49]

THE HIGHLAND SOCIETY OF SCOTLAND

When the project of the British Fisheries Society faltered, the Highland Society of Edinburgh (renamed the Highland Society of Scotland in 1787) took the lead in northern improvement. This institutional shift also marked the victory of John Walker's strategy over the liberal vision of James Anderson. Though Walker did not become an official member of the Highland Society until 1794, he served as a consultant on major technical questions of Highland improvement, including kelp burning, livestock grazing, and peat reclamation.[50]

The first official meeting of the Highland Society was held in Edinburgh during the winter of 1784. Early on, the energy of the directors was centered on the task of acquiring a royal charter and a parliamentary grant. In 1785, the society counted 128 members. By 1803 it had risen to 750. There were two general meetings a year and a committee of directors that met more regularly. A mixture of Edinburgh advocates and landowners dominated among the founding members. Two leading figures in the first generation were the kinsmen Sir James Grant of Grant and his brother-in-law Henry Mackenzie. Grant was an improving laird with a penchant for planned villages. He established Grantown on Spey in 1765–66 and Lewistown in 1769. Mackenzie was the secretary of Henry Dundas, an Exchequer official, as well as the fêted author of the *Man of Feeling* and other novels of sensibility. Mackenzie served as the editor of the society's *Transactions* as well as an ordinary or extraordinary director throughout the era of the Napoleonic Wars. The club also enjoyed the strong support of the leading agrarian magnates in Scotland. The Fifth Duke of Argyll assumed the post as the first president, presiding over the society until 1806. Other grandees included Elizabeth, Countess of Sutherland, Lord Seaforth of Lewis, the Eighth Earl of Moray, and the Fourth Earl of Breadalbane. The "viceroy" of Scotland, Henry Dundas, was made an honorary member in 1786. In the second tier of membership were a mixture of military men, gentry, and urban professionals, including army colonels such as Archibald McNeill of Colonsay, the professor of anatomy Dr. Alexander Munro, and David Ramsay, the publisher of the *Edinburgh Evening Courant*.[51]

In the founding declaration, the Highland Society of Scotland took on a wide-ranging mission. It set out to collect information about the territory and population, to promote agriculture and manufactures, and to safeguard the culture of the Highlands. This agenda revived the improving priorities of the Annexed Estates while expanding them to embrace the entire region and, most notably, to include the explicit task of preserving Gaelic literature.

1. An inquiry into the present state of the Highlands and Islands of Scotland, and the condition of their inhabitants.
2. An inquiry into the means of their improvement, by establishing towns and villages—by facilitating Communication through different parts of the Highlands and Scotland, by Roads and Bridges—advancing Agriculture, and extending Fisheries—introducing useful Trades and Manufactures—and, by an exertion to unite the efforts of the Proprietors, and call the attention of Government, towards the encouragement and prosecution of these beneficial purposes.
3. The Society shall also pay a proper attention to the preservation of the Language, Poetry and music of the Highlands.

Because the society lacked the financial muscle to intervene in the Highland economy on a large scale, it opted to pursue these ends by virtue of a formal system of honors, medals, and the circulation of useful information. This was the strategy of patriotic emulation favored by voluntary associations throughout the eighteenth century. Landowners and tenants would be roused from the slumbers of tradition and indolence by premiums, essay contests, and other forms of competition in civil society. This pursuit of honor through merit was believed to trigger a chain reaction of admiration and imitation in the public. As Adam Smith observed in *The Theory of Moral Sentiments*, it was easier to sympathize with delight than distress. Improvement, in other words, was supposed to spread like a form of sympathetic contagion through cycles of emulation. This was probably why the committee of directors paid such careful attention to the design of the medal for the society's contests. They settled on John Clerk of Eldin's image of a "Highlander in his proper dress and arms presenting himself before the Genius of Scotland" with "his Flocks and Herds, his Fishing Vessels and Implements of Husbandry." It included the motto *"semper armis nunc et industria"* (always armed and now industrious) expressing the double role expected from the natives: "The Highlanders who have long been useful to their Country by their valor and military Talents are now desirous of cultivating also the arts of peace and of benefiting it also by their industry."[52]

Kelping was an early preoccupation of the Highland Society. The burning of seaweed produced alkaline ashes that were employed in English soap and glass manufacture. The market for Scottish kelp was growing dramatically in the last decades of the eighteenth century. During the American War of Independence, the price stood at eight pounds per ton. It rose to twenty pounds a ton in 1810 before collapsing after the end of the Napoleonic Wars in 1815. Strictly speaking, kelping was a "manufacture" in only the most rudimentary sense of the word. Seaweed was harvested with sickles or hooks from rocks in standing water. After drying, the kelp was burned with peat until the alkaline ashes were ready to be collected for transport to the south. The whole business was in the hand of a few merchants who preferred to deal with leading proprietors. In legal terms, seaweed belonged to the owner of the land where it was collected. These landlords paid tenants a pittance for the labor and pocketed the difference.[53]

John Walker won the highest honor of the society, the gold medal of ten guineas, with his essay on kelp in 1788. He identified four species of sea wrack and tangle (*Fucus vesiculosus*, *F. nodosus*, *F. serratus*, and *F. digitatus*) particularly appropriate for kelp burning. He also recommended actual kelp plantations to increase the yield. Proprietors should grow these plants on rocks deliberately placed along shallow beaches. Walker recognized that Scottish kelp was viable only if the rival sources of alkali in the form of foreign potashes and barilla (soda ash) were burdened with high duties. Kelping could be sustained only on "patriotic" grounds, as a protected import substitute; otherwise it would be "impaired, or annihilated." In response, the directors sought to enlist Joseph Black to analyze the composition of the Scottish seaweed and pronounce whether it could substantially improved in quality, but the chemist politely declined the assignment. He had in fact dismissed Scottish kelp as wholly inferior to Spanish barilla two years earlier. Since Black would not help, John Sinclair recommended a new form of kelp kiln to burn high-grade alkali designed by the soap manufacturer Thomas Jameson of Leith. Jameson's trial was a distant forerunner of a later series of chemical experiments funded by the society to prop up Scottish kelp against foreign competition after Spanish barilla returned to the British market.[54]

In 1789, the society received a large injection of funds thanks to the political maneuvering of Henry Dundas and the Duke of Argyll. This money was in fact a vestige of the Annexed Estates money, paid out to the society in the form of a grant of three thousand pounds. That same year, George Dempster persuaded the directors to grant premiums in support of essays on wasteland cultivation, highland planting, and planned villages. Gold medals were offered for the best plan for inland villages and premiums of five pounds each to the first three pioneers in every new settlement (a total of £140 for the year 1790). In the winter of 1790, John Walker announced a "course of Lectures on agriculture and other agrestic subjects," to the members of the society, noting that a great deal of the course would consider "Rural Improvements of the Highland Countries." Later that year, the directors endorsed a scheme by James Anderson and John Sinclair to protect the Shetland sheep breed from extirpation.[55]

In short, at the outset of the French Revolution, the Highland Society had become a platform to promote a new mixed economy in northern Scotland. The model combined sheep and cattle farms in the interior together with kelping industry along the coasts. Premiums for wasteland reclamation were granted from 1791. At first the society recommended the use of capital-intense lime or shell marl as fertilizer; later it favored the cheaper manure of seaweed together with potato husbandry, cultivated either with plow or spade. From 1795, a premium was presented by the society to the tenant in the Western Isles who brought in the largest area of moss or muirland. In 1798–99, the society established a contest for essays on the conversion of peat moss into manure.[56] A sign that this was a concerted campaign came when John Walker persuaded the directors of the Highland Society in 1792 to reward a gold medal to Lord Kames's son George Drummond. Walker noted in his nomination that the successful conversion of Blair Drummond moss into arable land had permitted the resettlement of nearly six hundred Gaels who had been "forced to abandon the high parts of Perthshire . . . on account of sheep farming." To Walker and the directors, the example of Blair Drummond presented a model for "Highland proprietors" everywhere to emulate. The Highland Society thus embraced and revived the original ideology of spade husbandry pioneered by Walker and Kames in the aftermath of the Seven Years' War. A strategy of resettlement and peat reclamation seemed the best means of accommodating surplus population in the age of improvement.[57]

5

Rival Ecologies of Global Commerce

When the French naturalist and industrial spy Bartélemy Faujas de Saint-Fond came to Edinburgh in the fall of 1782, Adam Smith took him to a piping contest. Apparently, Smith wished to conduct an impromptu experiment in sensibility. The moral philosopher was curious to see how his French visitor would react to a form of music he had never heard before. He must have been pleased with the results. In his travel account, Faujas de Saint-Fond described with considerable surprise and revulsion the effects of the bagpipe on his nerves. "I confess that at first I could not distinguish either air or design in the music." He was aware merely of the "convulsive motions" of the piper as he marched "backward and forward with great rapidity" and a "warlike countenance." Only gradually could Faujas de Saint-Fond discern any semblance of melody in the confounded noise made by the piper. Yet he could not help but notice at the same time the animated and sympathetic response of the patrician crowd assembled. During the third part of the performance—a mournful air— several of the "beautiful Scotch ladies" wept with pleasure at the sweet melancholy of the music. But even this show of emotion could not move the French observer to any heights of affection: "The music and the instrument constantly reminded me of a bear's dance." Sadly, Faujas de Saint-Fond made no comment about Smith's reaction. One scholar speculates that the invitation was in fact a cruel prank on Smith's part. Certainly, Smith's attitude toward Highland culture was decidedly cool. In the campaigns of northern improvement, he remained conspicuously above the fray. Indeed, he seems to have crossed the Highland line only once in his life, during a 1759 trip to the Duke of Argyll's home at Inveraray. Smith's letter about the visit contains no kind words about the charms of the scenery or native customs, only a sharp complaint about the "very expensive Inn" he was forced to stay at while awaiting the duke's return. Like Faujas de Saint-Fond at the piping contest, Smith turned a cold eye on the spectacle of Highland improvement.[1]

How can we account for the silence of this leading figure of the Scottish Enlightenment on the subject of Gaelic Scotland? If we take in the entire corpus of Smith's writings and correspondence, the political economist made only passing mention of such topics as Macpherson's Ossian, the martial character of the Gael, and the poverty of Highland society. On the direct question of Highland improvement, the main evidence about Smith's views consists of a brief passage on the herring bounties in the third edition of *The Wealth of Nations* (1784) and two short letters written in 1786 and 1787 to Henry Beaufoy, the Quaker abolitionist and director of the British Fisheries Society. These late fragments paint a vivid picture of Smith's skepticism about such projects yet do not fully explain his silence on a topic so pressing for large portions of Scottish civil society. Why did the economic development of the Highlands not figure as a major topic of inquiry in the *Wealth of Nations*? This admittedly raises thorny methodological questions. An argument about omissions may easily ascend into airy realms of speculation. Fortunately, we can find more solid ground for interpretation by turning our attention outward. Smith had a great deal to say about the environment in his analysis of the British economy and the development of the European colonies overseas. By all accounts he was an avid reader of natural history and works of agricultural improvement in this wider context. Turning outward and facing the empire, we can learn how Smith's principles informed his view of the natural world at large to create a liberal ecology of global commerce.

THE POLITICS OF GRASS

The first plant that the Finnish naturalist Pehr Kalm noticed as he set foot in America was a tuft of native grass, a species of the genus *Andropogon*. The sight induced a flash of taxonomic vertigo. How could a single natural historian cope with a whole continent of new species? "Whenever I looked to the ground I found everywhere such plants as I had never seen before. . . . I was seized with terror at the thought of ranging so many new and unknown parts of natural history."[2] While Kalm's moment of confusion perhaps was exaggerated for rhetorical effect, the episode captures the new centrality of natural knowledge in the world of eighteenth-century commerce. Between 1748 and 1751, Kalm surveyed the colonial environment from Philadelphia through New Jersey and then north up the Hudson Valley to Quebec. The naturalist had been sent on a mission of classification and bioprospecting funded by the Swedish state and masterminded by Kalm's teacher Carolus Linnaeus. The taxonomic aim was to extend Linnaeus's new system of binomial classification to North America by collecting plants and gathering local knowledge. Kalm's other priority was to harness nature for the purpose of national improvement. Kalm was among a group of twenty "apostles" [lärljungar] trained by Linnaeus to scour the globe for a harvest of useful plants that would help diversify and enrich the natural wealth of Sweden. But this was not simply some eccentric preoccupation of a small northern nation. When Kalm's travel journal was translated into English in 1770–71, it contributed to a growing interest in Linnaean science among British elites. Other students of Linnaeus were recruited as expert travelers on James Cook's scientific voyages of circumnavigation. After sailing with Cook in 1768–71, Daniel Solander became the trusted collaborator of Sir Joseph Banks, the manager of the imperial plant exchange at Kew Gardens. In Scotland during the 1760s, John Walker and John Hope introduced the Linnaean method as a tool of internal colonization in the Highlands. At the same time, the French gardener André Thouin aimed to diversify and strengthen French agriculture through plant introductions to the royal botanic garden in Paris. His physiocratic correspondent Pierre Poivre pioneered an early form of scientific conservationism on the Isle de France in the Indian Ocean in the years 1768–71. Across Western nations and empires in the second half of the eighteenth century, natural history became a privileged instrument of power to shape the natural order.[3]

For Kalm and Linnaeus, the knowledge of grass offered a crucial foundation for agricultural improvement. Without good cattle fodder, it was impossible to reach the high levels of manure production required to maintain soil fertility in a regime of commercial mixed husbandry. Sown grasses and new fodder plants were indispensable elements of the green revolution that swept across western Europe in the early modern era.[4] As Kalm set out for America, Linnaeus was completing the *Pan Svecicus*, a list of more than 850 indigenous Swedish fodder plants that could serve as livestock grazing. Kalm, too, had been involved for many years with experiments in grass cultivation together with his aristocratic patron Sten Carl Bielke. Before the journey to America, Kalm had collected grasses species in Russia and overseen their introduction to Bielke's Swedish estate Lövsta north of Stockholm.[5] But in America, Kalm discovered little interest in this kind of husbandry. While his investigations yielded a rich inventory of American grasses, he found that European settlers treated the question with indifference. They left their cattle to graze freely in the forest, taking advantage of abundant native annual grasses that allowed the livestock to multiply enormously. Soon the teeming herds destroyed the original food supply and fell into rapid decline, both in numbers and in stature. For Kalm, this conduct was an object lesson in poor husbandry and worse morals. Settlers greedily took advantage of the fertility stored up in "virgin soils" yet refused to replenish the land with manure when it showed signs of exhaustion. This was madness when God had filled the land with useful native plants that could serve as good hay for cattle to increase manure production. But the majority of American farmers appeared blind to the blessings of natural history: "The grain fields, the meadows, the forests, the cattle . . . are [all] treated with equal carelessness." Kalm's condemnation contained a strong political undercurrent. The divine utility of nature required expert management. This interpretation of nature was firmly grounded in the northern European tradition of cameralism, a movement that sought to strengthen the revenue base of landlocked northern states through projects of improvement and internal colonization. After his long journey through British America, Kalm singled out the governor of New France Marquis de La Galissonnière as a paragon of husbandry: "He told me several ways of employing natural history to the purposes of politics and to make a country powerful." By implication, British husbandry in North America would prosper only if experts were elevated to positions of power.[6]

Kalm's cameralist politics of grass was not the only interpretation of colonial husbandry to enter the Enlightenment. Against Kalm's ecology, Adam Smith articulated a liberal view of the problem of American agriculture. Smith relied directly on Kalm's *Travels in North America* for his own account of American agriculture in *The Wealth of Nations* (1776). He agreed with Kalm that the early settlers had adopted wasteful practices. The "great abundance" of land encouraged the proliferation of cattle let loose by farmers who permitted them to range freely to graze on the profusion of native annual grasses growing in North America. After an initial explosion in numbers, the cattle had depleted the pasture grounds by cropping the annual grasses "too early in the spring, before they had time to form their flowers." As a result, the livestock "degenerated sensibly from one generation to another," growing "stunted" much in the way of the "breed which was common all over Scotland thirty of forty years ago." But in contrast with Kalm, Smith was optimistic about the long-term prospects of colonial husbandry. He stressed that Scottish cattle had recovered from the process of degeneration and was "now . . . much mended through the greater part of the low country" because of rising cattle prices and concomitant investments into breeding and forage. Eventually a large market in beef would emerge in North America as well, inclining farmers to take an interest in cultivated grasses and the collection of manure to introduce mixed husbandry of the English sort.[7]

This quarrel over grass and cattle suggests a new way to think about empire and capitalism. In essence, the defense of global commerce pioneered in the Enlightenment was inextricably tied to the improvement of the natural order. But from the outset, the conversion of nature into capital raised a fundamental question of management. Was the market sufficient to order nature, or did the complexity of the natural order require the intervention of environmental expertise? To grasp this problem accurately, we must resist the temptation to conflate natural history with political economy within a single idiom of improvement. Richard Drayton assumes that "over the long eighteenth century . . . the natural sciences and political economy became inflected . . . into an idea of government in the public and cosmopolitan interest." After the end of European empires, this doctrine persisted under a new name as the "enterprise of 'Development' . . . [and] became the idol of economists and politicians of all races and nations."[8] Yet there are good reasons to suspect that this hypothesis of a unitary model of improvement glosses over serious disagreements over the priorities of development among different kinds of experts. "Seeing like a state," to use James Scott's phrase, involved a variety of strategies to make nature legible, not all of which were compatible.

For Adam Smith and his successors in the classical liberal tradition, nature served as a handmaiden for exchange in a double sense. They looked to the natural world for a model of self-regulating balance that justified their faith in market exchange. At the same time, they championed the market as the best means of managing the balance of nature. Technological innovation, resource substitution, and conservation were all dictated by the rise and fall of prices. Against this liberal view, a loose constellation of naturalists, forestry writers, and assorted imperialists suggested that the natural order was too complex or fragile to be left unregulated, particularly on the peripheries of the nation and empire. They, too, favored commercial growth but linked it to priorities of protectionism, including the conservation of forests and strategic resources. Naturalists like Kalm and Linnaeus founded their expertise on a combination of local knowledge and universal taxonomy that appropriated indigenous information into a global vision of climate zones and ecological exchange. They shared with liberal savants a strong interest in winning the patronage of the state to transform their expert judgments into policy and law.

In short, the eighteenth century saw the emergence of two rival ecologies of commerce.[9] This quarrel over expertise pitted two distinct versions of global modernity against each other along environmental lines. It is thus deeply misleading to cast the history of classical liberalism solely in terms of a struggle between "cosmopolitan" defenders of free trade and "economic nationalists," as Istvan Hont and Lisbet Koerner have suggested.[10] The forces of empire and global capitalism inspired not just the defense of free markets but also a dawning awareness of the environmental foundation of imperialism and the ecological costs of development. Where classical liberalism developed from Hume's specie-flow mechanism over Adam Smith's division of labor to T. R. Malthus's population principle and David Ricardo's concept of comparative advantage, natural history followed a trajectory from Linnaeus's universal taxonomy and Pierre Poivre's climate conservation to Sir Joseph Banks's imperial projects of ecological exchange and Alexander von Humboldt's global plant geography.[11]

This chapter proceeds in four parts. The first section discusses the rise of natural history as a global political and economic force in the eighteenth century. I place particular stress on the notion of natural history as a form of expertise peculiarly occupied with correcting perceived disruptions to the "economy of nature." The second section ventures a new interpretation of Adam Smith's *Wealth of Nations* as a seminal liberal perspective on the natural world. The key claim here is that Smith saw a natural fit between markets and the environment. Markets should be trusted because they presented the most effective means of overcoming problems of scarcity and the best incentives for the improvement of nature. It was these assumptions that set classical political economy on a collision course with the priorities of natural historians. The third section brings together the two ecologies in a brief case study of famine relief in India. Natural historians in Bengal favored hydraulic management to secure the food supply. Smithian economists and administrators instead emphasized the freedom of the rice trade on the assumption that famines had political not ecological causes. Where natural historians stressed the instability of the natural world on the periphery, political economists emphasized its properties of self-regulation and internal harmony. The fourth and final part of the chapter brings these themes to bear directly on Smith's attitude toward the Highlands. Here, too, rival ecologies clashed over the best strategy of improvement. James Anderson's plan for the west coast fisheries marked a high point for the liberal approach. Yet Smith's own views of the British Fisheries Society remained deeply skeptical. Where Anderson hoped that the building of towns and the coming of a greater specialization would smash the remnants of feudalism and spread liberty, Smith saw little but vain idealism and foolish projecting. This suspicion of Highland improvement was ultimately rooted in his assumption that the region was naturally barren and condemned to deprivation. To Smith, such endemic poverty had no redeeming features, since he did not attribute to Gaelic culture any higher military or moral value.

NATURAL HISTORY AS A GLOBAL SCIENCE

During the Enlightenment natural historians across Europe claimed expert authority in managing the environment of the nation and empire.

Leading eighteenth-century naturalists such as Georges-Louis Leclerc de Buffon, Linnaeus, and Banks enlisted the state in projects to diversify and bolster national and colonial economies through resource inventories and ecological exchange. A major impetus for this development came from the Swedish botanist Linnaeus's new system of global taxonomy. But as we have seen, there was no necessary connection between Linnaeus's cameralism and his method. Natural history was ideologically ambiguous, attracting civil cameralists, neo-mercantilists, physiocrats, and even republican figures such as Alexander von Humboldt and Thomas Jefferson. Beneath the diversity of political opinion, however, was a common assumption that expertise about natural systems should have a central place in the making of modern polities and economies.[12]

The attempt to shape colonial ecologies in the Enlightenment formed a political afterthought to the vast biological transformation wrought by the Columbian exchange. Ecological transfers of plants, animals, and pathogens between the New World and the Old had reshaped biota in numerous ways on both sides of the Atlantic nations since 1492. In the early stages, most of these global flows were the result of local initiatives or unintended consequences, without direct state intervention. Spain was the first Atlantic power that aspired to coordinate ecological exchange through centralized scientific and bureaucratic procedures of collection in the sixteenth-century institution known as the Casa de la contratación.[13] Yet it was only in the second half of the eighteenth century that natural history became a common tool of European states. Banks used his close ties with the Pitt ministry and the Crown to embark on numerous projects of this sort, including the transfer of cochineal insects to Madras from South America, breadfruit from Tahiti to the West Indies, cotton seeds to the West Indies from India, Chinese tea plants to India, and the introduction of Spanish Merino sheep to England. Many of these schemes proved chimerical. But there were successes. The tea transplantation was accomplished by the middle of the nineteenth century. Another effective transfer was the wholesale exportation of a "portmanteau biota" to Australia. It was Banks who selected the seeds and plants carried out on the First Fleet to the New South Wales settlement in 1788. A government farm served as the entry point for wheat, barley, oranges, apples, hemp, flax, potatoes, and much more. By 1792 the horticultural basis of the settlement had stabilized and could serve as a staging post for further British penetration into the South Pacific. Banks thus laid the groundwork for engineering the environment of New South Wales into a "Neo-Europe."[14]

Another legacy of eighteenth-century natural history was a growing interest in conservation. Linnaeus and other naturalists held that divine providence had organized the natural world in a system of equilibrium between food supply and population, predator and prey, scavenger and carrion. This notion of an "economy of nature" sensitized observers to instances of ecological disturbance. The French naturalist Pierre Poivre pioneered a new form of science-based conservation in the late 1760s on the Isle de France (Mauritius) by postulating a causal link between deforestation and climate change. Poivre warned that clear-cutting would lead to the desiccation of the island in his widely read book *Travels of a Philosopher*, published in multiple editions in French and English. Poivre managed to persuade the governor of Mauritius to enact a series of reforms to protect the remaining forests and take measures to encourage sustainable agriculture within the colony. Similar schemes were set in motion by naturalists elsewhere. Linnaeus's student Anders Sparrman helped shape a conservationist land ethic in the Cape colony after 1785. In early nineteenth-century British India, colonial officials trained in botany managed the first state-run forest preserves. In the Scottish Highlands, the voyages of Linnaean travelers like James Robertson and John Walker in the 1760s and 1770s spurred the birth of Scottish conservationism by encouraging the national myth of a prehistoric Caledonian forest. Here, too, some improvers stressed that afforestation would improve the climate.[15]

At the core of these different schemes was a moral climatology. The balance of nature presupposed a western European ideal of stability and moderation between extremes of arctic cold and equatorial heat. Tropical territories in the "torrid zone" represented a realm of alien excess: teeming biodiversity, spontaneous abundance, debilitating disease, lethal earthquakes and hurricanes. But even the temperate settler colonies in North America confounded metropolitan expectations. Comte de Buffon and William Robertson cast the New World as a topsy-turvy inversion of the European norm, in which plants and animals must degenerate into feeble and diminutive forms. The founding father and naturalist Thomas Jefferson took it upon himself to refute such disparaging views by demonstrating the vitality and large size of American animals. In other words, the debate over American degeneration further reinforced the significance of naturalist expertise and gave impetus to a self-confident "creole" style of natural history.[16]

Behind this controversy loomed fundamental uncertainties about the patterns of climate in space and time. The effects of continents and oceans on weather patterns were only imperfectly grasped. The study of climate up until the last three decades of the eighteenth century favored historical and cultural explanations over systematic quantitative observation. Though early conservationists like Poivre had begun to associate afforestation with beneficial climate effects, other naturalists regarded the temperate climate of northern Europe as an artifact of deforestation, drainage, and general settlement. On the basis of ancient and medieval sources, they posited a history of climate change that oscillated with the rise and fall of civilizations. From this point of view, the accumulated effect of European colonization was expected to alter the climate of the settler colonies over time, at least if their practices were informed by sound and prudent advice from natural historians. When Alexander von Humboldt revolutionized biogeography and climatology with a new quantitative approach to climate zones and plant geography in 1805, he merely reinforced a moral order of nature firmly established by his predecessors. His political essay on New Spain was replete with advice as to how the enlightened state should introduce and manage cash crops in the "torrid zone." The improvement of nature thus followed two main paths: a gradual convergence of temperate climate settlements toward the European norm or the imposition of a rule by experts in cases where the climate was deemed too extreme ever to be fully assimilated.[17]

THE NATURAL PROGRESS OF OPULENCE

Scattered throughout Adam Smith's *Wealth of Nations* (1776) are numerous traces of early modern agriculture and environment, ranging over such topics as plant transfer, potato diet, cattle droving, kitchen gardens, silver mining, and plantation husbandry.[18] At critical points, Smith turned to the natural world in search of ecological warrants to justify his economic concepts. His global vision of commerce was matched by a global understanding of the natural world. Smith's central argument in *The Wealth of Nations* about exchange and labor rested on an environmental substrate. "The land constitutes by far the greatest, the most important, and the most durable part of the wealth of every extensive country." Capital formation followed a hierarchy ordained by "the natural order of things": capital flowed first to "agriculture, afterwards to manufactures, and last of all to foreign commerce."[19] While Smith's general views of agriculture are well known, the prodigious scholarship devoted to the thinker has had surprisingly little to say about the environmental basis of his vision.[20]

Smith shared his liberal notion of nature with a line of thinkers from David Hume to T. R. Malthus. In particular, he owed a debt to the French physiocrats and their insistence that a free grain trade was the foundation of national wealth. But an excessively narrow focus on the French grain debates obscures other dimensions of Smith's thought, including the contribution of natural history to his global vision of exchange and the thriving culture of agricultural improvement in his native Scotland. Tellingly, Smith's first publication, the letter to the *Edinburgh Review* of 1755, introduced not only Jean-Jacques Rousseau's *Discourse on the Origin of Inequality* and Jean Le Rond d'Alembert's *Encyclopédie* to a Scottish audience but also offered some critical remarks about the natural history of Buffon and René-Antoine Ferchault de Réaumur. When Smith retired from his university position to become a tutor for the future Duke of Buccleuch, one of his responsibilities was to give advice on the commercial reorganization and improvement of the Buccleuch estates in the Lowlands. Smith's library contained prominent works in natural history and agricultural improvement such as Pliny's natural history, Linnaeus's *Systema Naturae* (1735), Benjamin Stillingfleet's introduction to the Linnaean system (1759), Poivre's *Voyage d'un philosophe* (1768), and Kalm's *Travels into North America* (1770–71). Smith made explicit references to Pliny, Poivre, Kalm, and Buffon in *The Wealth of Nations*. In fact, during the years when he was finishing the book in the provincial retirement of his native town of Kirkaldy, he devoted serious attention to the study of botany. Among Smith's close friends and associates were several men with strong interests in agricultural improvement and natural history, including the geologist James Hutton, the judge Lord Kames, the chemist Joseph Black, and the physician William Cullen.[21] Finally, Smith seems to have cultivated a professional interest in chemistry and natural history when he became a commissioner of customs in 1778. One of his duties included the evaluation of commodities. Black's correspondence contains an intriguing palimpsest in the form of a letter from Smith and his fellow commissioners Buchanan and Cochrane, requesting information on the value and chemical composition of a sample of vegetable alkali, partially hidden underneath a draft letter by Black. Smith's zealous work as a commissioner of customs reveals the important place of detailed natural knowledge to servants of the imperial state.[22]

Smith's classical liberalism at the same time borrowed from and challenged the authority of natural history. For his analysis of cash crops and colonial agriculture in particular—the engines of early modern imperial expansion—he relied on the travel reports of natural historians. Indeed, it is difficult to imagine Smith's success as an armchair philosopher of commerce without the growth of naturalist networks along the edges of European empires. In disciplinary terms, *The Wealth of Nations* marked a major attempt to legislate the range of natural phenomena that counted as proper objects of economic analysis. Such a challenge presupposed a great deal of space for exchange and confrontation. Disciplinary boundaries had not yet hardened around eighteenth-century fields of knowledge. Instead, Smith found the raw materials for his global vision within the vast middle ground in which moral philosophy, jurisprudence, civil history, and natural history mixed and clashed.

Smith shared with the natural historians a preoccupation with self-regulating properties. Smith's system of course rested on a similar principle of homeostasis between supply and demand. He located the basic prospects of economic growth in the positive feedback loop between pasture and arable, manure production and soil fertility, town and country, manufacturing and agriculture. Political economy and natural history also shared a common recognition of ecological limits. For all his strident optimism, Smith's theory of labor productivity and mutually advantageous trade presupposed a bounded economy. All people were "maintained by the annual produce of the land." "How great soever," this produce could "never be infinite, but must have certain limits." Natural historians in turn nurtured alchemical hopes of coaxing soil and plants into vastly higher rates of productivity, but they did not envision a leap into a mineral energy economy. Both types of expertise emerged within the constraints of the advanced organic economy before the industrial age.[23]

The major disagreement between Smith and the natural historians concerned the resilience and stability of nature. Smith read natural history selectively in order to underscore the benign operation of natural systems across the globe. His concrete discussions of agriculture, climate, and soil tended to assume a relatively simple and orderly world. This environmental stability was the ultimate guarantor of the success of market exchange. The physiocratic motto: "Laissez faire, laissez-passer," was no empty metaphor. Free trade was the only way to let nature follow its own course.[24] In contrast, natural historians assumed a complex and fragile world in which the self-regulating properties of natural systems could be disrupted. To some degree, this perception reflected the European encounter with new climate zones and habitats. In part, it also registered the convulsions of the colonization process, ranging from famine and epidemics to resource depletion and falling biodiversity. For example, Pehr Kalm reported that both cattle and people degenerated perceptibly in the New World. He also insisted that the population of many species of bird and fish had fallen rapidly since European settlement begun there. Yet natural historians were not offering a revolutionary critique of colonialism so much as a call for imperial reform. Their alarm justified a self-serving appeal to natural history as the optimal tool of the colonial state in managing ecosystems on the periphery. Ecological crisis was the engine of such paternalism.[25]

For Smith, environmental differences of climate and soil functioned primarily as justifications for exchange. Drawing on a tradition reaching back to Plutarch, Smith suggested that the distribution of resources and climate zones across the world made trade rational and desirable.²⁶ Was any ordinary consumer prepared to pay for "claret and burgundy" made in Scotland? "By means of glasses, hotbeds, and hotwalls, very good grapes can be raised in Scotland." But the wine made from them would cost thirty times more than French equivalent. Import substitution was irrational when natural disadvantages could be overcome through trade.²⁷ Clearly, Smith's argument ridiculed the experiments of natural historians. His Scottish contemporary John Hope worked very hard to acclimatize valuable plants to the Scottish climate in the Royal Botanic Garden of Edinburgh. His hothouses were crowded with wilting exotics. Smith's justification of exchange dismissed moral climatology as a distraction. The best response to the challenge of natural disadvantage was not to ameliorate the climate or conserve resources but to establish liberal conditions of trade.²⁸ However, Smith was never impervious to the force of ecological exchange. He was clearly aware of the historical process of the Columbian exchange. In the course of his critique of mercantilism, he stressed that tobacco—the cornerstone of Chesapeake agriculture—could be grown just as well in the British Isles and had in fact been a relatively successful domestic crop until the Crown outlawed its cultivation in the seventeenth century. When the Scottish physician Charles Jackson and his farmer allies began trials of tobacco cultivation outside Glasgow during the American Revolutionary War, they turned to Adam Smith for support and asked him to analyze the punitive effects of customs duties on their enterprise.²⁹

Smith's vision of ecological exchange was in fact profoundly subversive. He wrote in *The Wealth of Nations* that "potatoes and maize" were "the two most important improvements which the agriculture of Europe . . . [had] received from the great extension of its commerce and navigation." Whereas the leading cash crops had generated riches only for the merchants and planters protected by the Navigation Acts, these humble crops could bring benefits to the nation as a whole. If the potato "ever [became] . . . the common and favourite vegetable food the people," it would be possible "to maintain a much greater number of people" on lands where grain was now grown. Smith spoke with startling intensity about the wondrous bodies of Irish porters and prostitutes who had been raised exclusively on a diet of potatoes—"the strongest men and the most beautiful women perhaps in the British dominions." In this rather curious way, Smith used ecological exchange to undercut the importance of colonial cash crops in favor of a more demotic vision of Atlantic agriculture. He probably also saw the productivity of potato crops as a form of insurance against the threat of dearth, though he was quick to emphasize that potatoes could not be stored for years in granaries like surplus wheat.³⁰

A fundamental assumption about the abundance of soil fertility underpinned Smith's account of agriculture: "No equal capital puts into motion a greater quantity of productive labour than that of the farmer. . . . In agriculture too nature labours along with man; and though her labour costs no expence, its produce has its value." Livestock and soil fertility constituted an order of creative labor distinct from its human counterpart. Smith's language stressed the relative autonomy of natural fertility, a force that needed little improvement, except to steer it toward a particular social or political aim. There was a strong echo here of physiocratic thinkers like François Quesnay: "Thus the origin, the principle of all expense, and of all wealth, is the fertility of the land."[31] This "free" gift of nature was the source of a continuous surplus that made agriculture superior to manufacturing production. "It is the work of nature which remains after deducting . . . everything which can be regarded as the work of man. It is seldom less than a fourth, and frequently more than a third of the whole produce. No equal quantity of productive labour employed in manufactures can ever occasion so great a reproduction. In them nature does nothing; man does all."[32] Yet Smith's theory was not reductionist in the style of the French physiocrats. Unlike them, he did not disparage manufacturing as a sterile and parasitical sector of the economy. Rather, he regarded growth as a dialectical process, involving the mutually supportive development of urban manufactures and agriculture. Smith laid out the case for such integrated growth in the chapter on the "Natural Progress of Opulence." The lesson of his parable was that economic growth emerged by stages from a process of gradual adjustments and positive feedback.[33]

Smith rooted his parable in a detailed discussion of the relation between agricultural prices, livestock, and crops. Cattle and beef here played the role of civilizing agents. As long as the price of cattle was allowed to fluctuate freely in response to supply and demand, what Smith termed "the obvious and simple system of natural liberty," such fluctuations supplied sufficient incentive for farmers to find more effective and rational forms of land use. The stronger the demand for beef, the more reason farmers had to increase the size of their herds and improve breeds. The demand for beef also encouraged the improvement of pasture land. By introducing and carefully cultivating "artificial grasses" like white clover and lucerne, farmers increased the yield of grazing land, thus feeding larger herds than before. The final decisive effect of a high cattle price was its influence on soil fertility. Before the expansion of cattle herds, farmers relied on town ordure—"night soil"—to increase the productivity of the land. With increasing cattle herds, farms became self-sufficient in manure. Only then could grain-producing fields reach their full capacity in terms of yield. As food production increased, the population grew and with it the division of labor and the opulence of commercial society. Here, Smith introduced the case of Scottish cattle prices before and after the Union of Scotland and England in 1707. Smith linked the question of improvement directly to a defense of free trade and political integration. When the two countries were joined into a unified market, English demand for Scottish beef drove up prices to unprecedented levels. The boost to the droving business in turn laid a new foundation for the improvement of agriculture in the Scottish Lowlands. Indeed, the boom in manure increased the grain production, which fed growing populations in Glasgow and Edinburgh. Beef, dung, and Union were the true engines of progress: without high cattle prices, no surplus manure and no Scottish Enlightenment.[34]

For Smith, the same dynamic relation of cattle, fertility, and improvement applied to the colonial periphery. Here, he turned to Pehr Kalm's natural history of North America for support. As we have seen, Smith agreed with Kalm that the early settlers had adopted wasteful practices but insisted that the problem could be remedied through the spread of efficient markets. It is crucial to notice how Smith's trust in market exchange displaced questions of local knowledge and naturalist expertise. That is, Smith asserted the equivalence of Scottish Lowland and North American husbandry without offering a causal mechanism or empirical evidence to demonstrate this link. The central tension between superabundant land and good husbandry in Kalm's account, a theme that would fuel American debates about agriculture into the nineteenth century and beyond, went unnoticed in Smith's discussion of colonial cattle. Tellingly, the anonymous work *American Husbandry* (1775) carried the consequences of Kalm's critique to their logical conclusion by calling for a botanic garden on the model of the Dutch East India Company in the British colonies.[35] In contrast, Smith made no mention of Kalm's inventory of native grasses or his advice about introducing English perennials. True, Smith noted the significance of artificial grasses in the improvement of British husbandry elsewhere in *The Wealth of Nations*. But if the introduction of new forage plants was the reason for his confidence, he did not bother to make his assumption explicit. Smith simply adopted a universal stadial model of natural growth. This connected logically with his "Greek" ideal of colonization: British settlements overseas should be treated as embryonic metropoles. Given sufficient autonomy of development, they would eventually follow the "natural progress of opulence" to reach the liberty and prosperity of the mother country.[36]

FAMINE RELIEF

The problem of famine relief arguably posed the greatest political challenge to any liberal account of nature. Smith's views on famine policy were shaped by the peculiar circumstances of the English economy in the seventeenth and eighteenth centuries. Apart from some remote pockets of the northern uplands, England had not experienced a widespread famine since the sixteenth century, thanks to increased agricultural production and integrated market systems. The Scottish Lowlands crossed the same threshold after the "lean years" of the 1690s. But a pattern of recurring famine persisted on the Continent and in the colonies. It was in this dual context that bold new arguments for free trade as the best defense against famine gained strength. David Hume and Charles Smith championed a liberal approach after the English dearth of 1756. During the 1760s, the French government swung toward laissez-faire as well, under the influence of Quesnay and other physiocrats. This movement was crowned by the sophisticated liberal critique of famine relief put forward by Smith, A. R. J. Turgot, and Marie-Jean Condorcet between 1770 and 1776.[37] Against popular conspiracy theories of grain hoarding middlemen, Smith insisted that the interest of the domestic grain merchant "and that of the great body of the people" were "even in years of the greatest scarcity, exactly the same." Only free exchange could calibrate the "daily, weekly, and monthly consumption" of the people to a point "proportioned as exactly as possible to the supply of the season." The corn merchant acted as the direct representative of nature, forcing the poor to moderate their consumption when scarcity dictated so, instilling habits of "thrift and good management" among the lower ranks. Conversely, Smith assumed that a corn (wheat) merchant who raised "the price of his corn somewhat higher than the scarcity of the season" required would "suffer the most by this excess of avarice" since he would be left with stock unsold at the end of the shortage. All these arguments shared the presupposition that agricultural mastery of nature was complete and irreversible and, by implication, that the natural order was fundamentally benign. Smith categorically denied that harvest failure might cause a famine in the wheat-growing regions of Europe if free exchange prevailed. "In an extensive corn country, between all the different parts of which there is a free commerce and communication, the scarcity occasioned by the most unfavourable seasons can never be so great as to produce a famine." Smith claimed a historical warrant for his assertion. After careful study of "the history of the dearths and famines ... of Europe," he was certain that "famine has never arisen from any other cause but the violence of government attempting ... to remedy the inconveniencies of a dearth."[38] This historical inference was equally a claim about the natural world. While contemporary natural historians like Poivre worried about climate change and soil erosion, Smith's model assumed a stable and bountiful natural order immune to large-scale disaster, in which cycles of abundance and scarcity followed an essentially moderate path between extremes. In contrast, Edmund Burke, Jeremy Bentham, and T. R. Malthus would take a far more melancholy view of the environment just a generation later, in the aftermath of the 1794–96 dearth. But Smith's assumption about the stability of the natural order made it possible to challenge one of the traditional justifications for the paternalist state: the strategic imperative of the grain police. For centuries, the state had reacted to dearth by regulating the grain trade and maintaining public granaries. Smith's interpretation of nature replaced the moral economy of the paternalist state with ecological stability as the guarantor of free exchange. It is true that Smith granted an exception to the rule in cases of "most urgent necessity." Yet this should probably be understood as an expression of his political pragmatism rather than a recognition that agricultural yield might collapse.[39]

For Smith, the political etiology of famine extended beyond Europe to major food-producing regions around the globe. His main example here was the case of the Bengal famine of 1770. Bengal had been formally annexed by the British in 1765 when the Mughal emperor Shah Alam granted the East India Company the Diwani—the direct administration of land revenues throughout the province. The prosperity of Bengal stemmed from its thriving wet rice agriculture. The eastern Bengal delta had been reclaimed and deforested by cultivators during Mughal rule in the seventeenth century. Government incentives for land reclamation together with the natural irrigation of the seasonal floods in the estuary helped create one of the most fertile agricultural regions in the world. Yet this political ecology was still vulnerable to dearth and famine. Population growth, price fluctuations, and climate oscillations endangered the subsistence of ordinary farmers. To safeguard the social order, the Mughal Empire expended considerable resources on famine relief.[40] After the British annexation of Bengal, the new regime of unregulated revenue extraction diminished the ability of the native population to withstand a subsistence crisis while the old scheme of state-sponsored famine relief was neglected. When drought struck the region in 1769, two consecutive rice harvests failed in December 1769 and March 1770. The famine began in Bihar and then spread to Bengal. The price of rice rose precipitously to a peak of tenfold the regular level. Contemporary estimates of mortality varied greatly since there were no firm population figures for Bengal in the first place. Warren Hastings's 1772 report assessed losses at a third of the inhabitants. In London, the initial newspaper references ranged from six hundred thousand dead to three million. Later statisticians have concluded that the true number may have approached ten million.[41]

News of the disaster provoked a furious response among critics and would-be reformers of the East India Company. The radical *Middlesex Journal* called for a "steady and moderate administration, disinterested Governors, and above all, a suspension of the spirit of avarice and rapine." Smith's reaction was close in spirit. *The Wealth of Nations* used the famine to indict the trading practices of the East India Company. Rice countries were fundamentally similar to the corn countries of Europe, despite the greater vulnerability of the former to drought on account of the higher levels of water required for rice paddy cultivation. "Even in such countries, however, the drought is, perhaps, scarce ever so universal as necessarily to occasion a famine, if the government would allow a free trade." Smith surmised that "improper regulations" and "injudicious restraints imposed by the servants of the East India Company upon the rice trade, contributed, perhaps, to turn [the 1769] dearth into a famine." Elsewhere, Smith reinforced this political characterization of the Bengal famine by suggesting that falling wages among the common people caused by the tyranny and monopoly of the East India Company was a precipitate cause of starvation. He contrasted famine-ridden Bengal dominated by a "mercantile company which oppresses and domineers" to the flourishing agriculture of the North American colonies, where no chartered company monopolized trade. He also underscored the "super-abundance" of rice production, noting that it yielded two or sometimes three crops a year and therefore sustained a much larger population than corn lands.[42] Though Smith's argument was very brief and tempered by caveats, it was absolutely crucial to his case. By eliminating environmental difference from the equation, he was able to defend the establishment of homogenous liberal principles of governance across the empire. This argument from environmental equivalence proved very influential with later administrators and economic writers, as we shall see.

The significance of Smith's position becomes clearer when we compare it to the rival perspective. Ideas of hydraulic management flourished in the wake of the famine. Early examples include the sharp attack on the East India Company appended to Alexander Dow's 1772 edition of the *History of Hindostan* and Henry Pattullo's proposal for reform of the land revenues of Bengal. These works helped pave the way for the passage of the East India Act of 1773, the first attempt to regulate revenue extraction in Bengal. They also sowed the seeds of the Permanent Settlement in 1793.[43] For both Dow and Pattullo, the question of famine relief was central to their vision of a reformed East India Company.

They emphasized that famines brought on by drought were cyclical phenomena in the history of India: "No country has in all ages been more subject to scarcities, and even to famine." Robert Orme reached the same conclusion regarding agriculture in the Carnatic region of India. "Vast reservoirs" were necessary to "supply the defect of rain during the dry season of the year." Only the state could shoulder the high costs of such precautions. Dow and Pattullo in turn stressed the vital role of public granaries as the best resort in times of dearth.[44]

These early proponents of famine relief set a standard for a generation of natural historians in the service of the East India Company. David Arnold has argued that the Bengal famine represents a fundamental rupture in British views of South Asia. It "helped propagate an image of India as a land still subject to the capricious sway of nature and as a society too feeble and fatalistic to fend for itself."[45] Beginning in the middle of the 1780s, the naturalist Banks gained increasing influence within British India. From his headquarters in London, he established a network of colonial experts and botanic gardens, including the Scots Robert Kyd and William Roxburgh in Calcutta as well as their countryman James Anderson in Madras. This movement was part of a wider exodus of Scottish professionals to the East Indies. Roxburgh had been trained by the Regius Keeper in Edinburgh John Hope alongside another Scottish naturalist in India—Francis Buchanan Hamilton. The latter's survey of Mysore explicitly imitated John Sinclair's *Statistical Account of Scotland*. James Anderson of Madras in turn was on friendly terms with James Anderson, the radical Whig who published reports of his endeavors in *The Bee*. These men also enjoyed the political patronage of Governor General Lord Cornwallis and President of the Board of Control Henry Dundas. Meanwhile, allies in Britain like Alexander Dalrymple and Charles Greville publicized their mission in the metropole. Greville stressed the need for "constant superintendance" in order to "avert . . . calamities arising from physical causes." Drought, floods, and other "irregularities of the seasons" caused "perpetual changes in the produce of agriculture" that in turn led to an increased "frequency of revolutions in government" and "variations in the state of population." All political arrangements had to be provisional and flexible. Natural oscillations "must require inevitably a periodical valuation of the laws." The same spirit of pragmatism fueled an explicit critique of Adam Smith penned by Sir Joseph Banks in 1799. Banks complained bitterly of Smith's increasing influence in government circles: "Every page proves him to be absolutely unpractical in the ways of men." Only a fool would trust the "infallibility of [Smith's] maxims."[46]

In practice, the management of British India involved several compatible aims. It conferred on the colonial state a primary obligation to monitor and husband grain and water. A massive public granary was constructed near Patna in 1786. The settlement of 1793 made the Board of Control and directors of the company responsible for the "general superintendence" of river embankments and the collection of "water in tanks or reservoirs during the rainy season." Greville compared the Ganges to the Euphrates, observing that "enlightened conquerors" might have been able to preserve the fertility of Mesopotamia down to the present. Roxburgh oversaw the establishment of a series of water tanks for famine relief in the vicinity of Calcutta in 1791. Though some observers were pessimistic about the possibilities for control. After measuring the tremendous velocity of the Ganges, James Rennell counseled against any project to straighten the river: "Next to earthquakes, perhaps the flood of tropical rivers produces the quickest alterations in the face of the globe."[47]

The hydrological imperative was connected to the necessity of meteorological observation. Thomas Forrest proposed an early theory of monsoon patterns in his 1783 work. James Anderson in turn identified a zone between sixteen and eighteen degrees latitude prone to drought over a thirty-year period. Robert Kyd's survey of the western side of the Hooghly River from 1791 offered a detailed account of the relation between the harvest cycle and local weather patterns. Francis Buchanan Hamilton made careful notes of the use of embankments and water tanks in his survey of Bengal from 1807. In this way, British naturalists began to disaggregate European generalizations about India in favor of a new, more nuanced delineation of plant geography and climate. Politically, such quantification undermined Smith's "Greek" ideal of ecological equivalence between corn lands and rice countries. In the same spirit, naturalists linked climate research to a focus on agricultural diversification. Because the widespread reliance on rice rendered the population particularly vulnerable to crop failure, Kyd, Roxburgh, and Anderson promoted the adoption of alternative foods. Kyd founded the botanic garden of Calcutta in 1786 to serve in part as a research station to promote drought-resistant plants.[48]

Supporters of Smith were slower to mount a defense of free grain markets in Bengal. *The Wealth of Nations* gained wide public recognition only after Smith's death in 1790. At the end of the decade, T. R. Malthus's *Essay on the Principle of Population* pushed the question of famine relief into new territory. Although he parted ways with Smith by emphasizing that deficiencies in the food supply were the true cause of famines, he also asserted that famines constituted an unfortunate but natural check on excess population. However, this callous position was circumscribed by considerable caveats. During the

Napoleonic Wars, Malthus openly defended restrictions on the trade of grain for the sake of national security and social stability. He also acknowledged a basic ecological difference between Bengal and England. Yet despite these gestures toward nuance and particularity, the function of nature in Malthus remained essentially negative. It was not a force to be explored and mastered. The best strategy of famine relief was to discourage early marriage rather than to penetrate the secrets of the monsoon or reestablish Mughal water-management methods. Malthus's fundamental orientation is evident from a set of queries he drafted about India in 1804 for the benefit of his friend James Mackintosh. The long list focused almost exclusively on vital statistics, not questions of environmental conditions.[49]

The rising credibility of political economy was confirmed by the appointment of Malthus to the East India Company training college in Haileybury in 1805. New Scottish administrators like Thomas Munro and Montstuart Elphinestone reinforced this trend. During the famine of 1812 in western India, they adopted a noninterventionist policy in direct conflict with the earlier priorities of public granaries and natural knowledge. They favored a simplistic form of classical political economy that ignored what hints of circumspection and hesitation there were in Malthus and Smith. This stance extended into other realms of colonial administration. Munro rejected state protection of forests in 1815 in favor of free markets in wood fuel and timber, according to Gregory Barton. S. Ambirajan suggests that such vulgar liberalism exerted a hegemonic dominance until the 1860s. But the picture seems far less straightforward if we consider the uneven application of liberal principles and the resistance of environmental expertise to laissez-faire. Irrigation, railways, and forestry were all privileged spaces of state intervention, as Manu Goswami reminds us. Gregory Barton notes that ideas of forest conservation were ascendant in the years 1807–15, 1831, and after 1855. Botanists like Alexander Gibson played a critical role in these efforts. It was Gibson (another Scottish naturalist) who pioneered a new model of scientific empire forestry with his management of the teak forests in Nilambur in south India. J. F. Thomas, an administrator connected to the circles of naturalist-surgeons, led the charge against Smithian famine policy. In response to the devastating Madras famine of 1837–38, Thomas reasserted the ecological difference of the Raj: "Much of the reasoning of Smith appears to me inapplicable to [India], or to any tropical country in an early stage of civilization." For Elizabeth Whitcombe, the Madras famine galvanized a new wave of hydraulic colonialism. Only districts with extensive irrigation were capable of coping with the disaster adequately. Officials concluded that hydraulic infrastructure would present an effective relief measure and invested three million pounds in the Ganges Canal project, which opened in 1854. Famine relief became linked to a new form of expert authority: the canal engineer. Ironically, the push for irrigation generated a series of secondary problems with water logging, the spread of malaria, and the buildup of mineral salts. Indeed, British engineering schemes were fundamentally inadequate and in fact counterproductive at the level of local water management. Colonial administrators sought quick and large-scale technical fixes rather than a precise understanding of how local ecology and social structures were intertwined. Most fundamentally, these men wielded a power unconstrained by democratic accountability and national citizenship. Only after independence did India break the vicious pattern of recurring famine.[50]

SMITH'S HIGHLANDS

When the harvest failed in the Highlands and Hebrides in 1782, "many hundred persons languished and died through the want of sustenance." John Knox reported that the victims were found "dead on the roads, in caverns and amongst thickets where they had taken shelter." This calamity followed on the heels of a prior harvest failure a decade earlier, in 1771–72. Scholars have used grain prices as a proxy for these severe subsistence crises. Both events were marked by an increase of grain prices by more than 50 percent that held steady over the course of a year. Our local knowledge of the 1782 crisis is greatly amplified by John Sinclair's *Statistical Account of Scotland*. Sinclair was so concerned with the event that his queries to the clergymen included a specific request for more information about the dearth. In fact, the effort to provide famine relief in 1782 marked Sinclair's first successful political action in Parliament. Together with George Dempster and Henry Dundas, he mobilized the Fox-North coalition to intervene. In total, the government expended ten thousand pounds in support of the stricken communities. There were also private charity initiatives of various sorts. Local landowners and clergymen seem to have been instrumental in distributing aid to those most in want. On the estate of James Grant of Grant, his kinsman the sentimental author Henry Mackenzie coordinated the response. Mackenzie was also an eyewitness to some of the worst suffering in a remote corner of Banffshire. In the parish of Cabrach, he saw the reapers "shaking off" the "snow on the standing corn" as they cut it. The poor made "a sort of pottage" from churchyard nettles to eat as famine food.[51] Such experiences helped galvanize a new wave of political and social interest in Highland improvement during the aftermath of the famine. After repealing the Disarming Act in 1783, Dundas went on to return the Annexed Estates to their heritors one year later.

A group of lawyers and landowners, including Grant and Mackenzie, founded the Highland Society of Edinburgh in February 1784. Another led by Dempster established the joint stock company of the British Fisheries Society in 1786. Dundas helped both organizations win official recognition.[52]

One searches in vain for any comment by Adam Smith on the famine of 1782 in his works or correspondence. Smith was preparing the final revised version of *The Wealth of Nations* that fall and winter. New additions included arguments "against the corn bounty [and] Herring buss bounty," as well as a "full exposition of the absurdity and hurtfulness of almost all our chartered trading companies." A letter from Smith to Sinclair in October 1782 expresses the stock suspicion of empire so common at the time—the "futility of all distant dominions"—yet does not dwell on the possibility of internal improvement. In Smith's imagination, the Highlands figured only in a negative sense, as a symbol of endemic poverty, poor infrastructure, and lack of specialization. "In the lone houses and very small villages which are scattered about in so desert a country as the Highlands of Scotland, every farmer must be butcher, baker, and brewer for his own family." Without water carriage or good roads, even the rudimentary elements of the division of labor could not emerge in the "remote and inland parts" of the north. Clearly, the north could not be classified as "corn country" in the conventional sense. Exchange was hampered by the mountainous terrain. The region also wanted cheap fuel in the form of coal. Consequently, wages were far lower there than elsewhere in Britain, a mere "three shillings a week." This had been the common wage of Lowland day labor "in the last century." But such poverty did not inhibit marriage or procreation. "A half starved Highland woman frequently bears more than twenty children, while a pampered fine lady is often incapable of bearing any." Instead, high child mortality did the grim work of limiting family size. "It is not uncommon, I have been frequently told, in the Highlands of Scotland for a mother who has borne twenty children not to have two alive." This phenomenon was particularly pronounced in the barracks of the Highland regiments. Smith here drew on conversations with "several officers of great experience." The passing remark suggests that Smith was far from incurious about the state of the north. A letter written in 1787 shows that Smith discussed the state of the Highland economy with at least one northern proprietor—Sir James MacDonald of Skye (albeit it in the period before 1766). In fact, Smith was more than willing to give Highland Scotland a measure of his attention, but only in this restricted and critical sense. The negative examples of Highland poverty appeared in the first few crucial chapters of *The Wealth of Nations* on the power of labor to transform economies.[53]

There are several interlocking explanations for Smith's silence about Highland improvement. One factor here was probably the controversy over Macpherson's Ossian. In the early draft of *The Wealth of Nations* composed shortly before April 1763, Smith used Macpherson's poetry next to that of Homer to discuss the character of primitive society before the division of labor. "What a perfect uniformity of character do we find in all the heroes described by Ossian?" Around the same time, Smith also briefly mentioned "the poems of Ossian" in his lectures on the jurisprudence at the University of Glasgow. In both cases, Smith took Macpherson's poetry as a historical source that accurately portrayed the spirit of the first stage of history. Yet in the 1776 edition of *The Wealth of Nations*, the comment about Ossian had been carefully excised from the famous passages on the porter and philosopher, even though Smith kept much of the language from the early draft. Hume had raised serious doubts about the authenticity of Macpherson's "translation" in the fall of 1763. It is likely that Hume's criticism persuaded Smith to erase what now seemed an embarrassing error in a passage of such rhetorical and conceptual importance.[54]

Another measure of this cooling attitude can be found in Smith's discussion of martial spirit. In his lectures of jurisprudence, the report dated 1766 concluded with ruminations on the corrupting effects of luxury. According to the anonymous student who recorded the lecture, Smith used the case of the Jacobite Rebellion of 1745 to insist that civilians in commercial nations lost their martial character with the progress of civilization. During the uprising, a host of "four or 5 thousand naked unarmed Highlanders took possession of the improved parts of this country without any opposition from the unwarlike inhabitants." Smith blamed this fiasco on the "disadvantages of a commercial spirit." "The minds of men are contracted and rendered incapable of elevation, education is despised or at least neglected, and heroic spirit is almost utterly extinguished." Perhaps there was still an echo of Ossian here, which would mean that Smith only gradually changed his mind about the authenticity of Macpherson's poetry. But in the sections on martial spirit in book 5 of *The Wealth of Nations*, all talk of the Highland rebellion has disappeared. Instead Smith spoke of the personal devotion of the "highland militia" to its chieftains merely as a thing of the past.[55]

Without any appreciation for Gaelic virtue or the military utility of the Highlands, Smith had little reason to worry about the fate of its population. He observed approvingly that the rents of the region had tripled in the past seventy years, thanks to the Union and the increase in cattle prices. In general, Smith's view of the rural poor was distinctly unsentimental. Elsewhere in *The Wealth of Nations*, he noted that the "diminution of the number of cottagers and other small occupiers of land" was "the immediate fore-runner of improvement and better cultivation" everywhere in Europe. "By the removal of the unnecessary mouths ... a greater surplus ... was obtained for the proprietor." In a 1787 letter to Henry Beaufoy, he stressed that the same process was now at work in the Hebrides. The old system of charging low rent for bad land to a numerous population of poor tenants was losing ground. "The number of such small occupiers is now, no doubt, very much diminished." This was presumably in part a consequence of the spread of commercial cattle farming in the north after the Union. Neither here nor in *The Wealth of Nations* did Smith entertain the notion that possession of land promoted the virtue and health of the rural poor. Only by moving to the higher-wage regions in corn lands or towns could they benefit from agricultural improvement. Although Smith did not live to witness the infamous clearances in Sutherland, it seems possible that he would have defended dispossession as the best means to promote the long-term prosperity of Gaelic plebeians.[56]

Perhaps more surprising is that Smith also rejected James Anderson's liberal vision of northern towns and markets, even though the two savants shared a strong antipathy toward government policy in the region. We know that Smith had read at least one of Anderson's earlier works, the letter on amending the Corn Laws in *Observations on the Spirit of Exciting a Spirit of National Industry* (1777). Anderson here disputed Smith's understanding of export bounties on corn as detrimental to domestic production. The argument hinged on whether the price of corn determined the wages of labor. Smith responded by adding a number of clarifications and caveats in the second and third editions of *The Wealth of Nations* (1778 and 1784). He had presumably perused the rest of Anderson's book as well, including the plan for woolen manufactures and Merino sheep in the Highlands. In a 1780 letter Smith praised Anderson as a "very diligent, laborious, honest man." Like Anderson, Smith took an interest in the Scottish fisheries after the end of the American War of Independence. Smith added a section on the herring bounties to the third revised edition of *The Wealth of Nations* (1784). Both men were critical of the ponderous system of bounties put in place by a 1749 act of Parliament. Any positive effects of the bounties were canceled out by onerous duties and other ill-conceived efforts at regulation. Bounties were given in tonnage to encourage the construction of large decked busses, in imitation of the Dutch fisheries. But Smith noted that such encouragement might result in boat building for the sake of capturing government funding rather than efficient yields of fish. Despite the lavish subsidies, the Free British Fisheries Society founded in 1749 had lost most of its capital. Such bounties also discouraged a second kind of small-scale fishing carried out by poor fishermen. Here Smith contrasted the long-distance decked herring busses of the Dutch with the small boats used in the Hebrides and Shetland Isles. The fractured geography of the northwest favored the latter mode of fishing, since "arms of the sea" ran "a considerable way into the land" in so many places.[57]

The major difference of opinion between Anderson and Smith concerned the link between the state and urbanization. In Anderson's 1785 expert testimony in the House of Commons on the question of the west coast fisheries, he called for a transitional period of bounties and premiums before free trade would be possible. But he also insisted that every kind of bounty was bound to be ineffective without more fundamental reforms. The salt and coal duties had to be abolished in order to encourage the formation of villages and towns. In addition, fishermen should receive free land and free herring boats. Smith, too, tempered his call for free trade with certain pragmatic concessions in the 1784 revisions to *The Wealth of Nations*. Bounties could "perhaps . . . be vindicated" if they served the higher purpose of strengthening the "defense of . . . society." Yet his examples were tied to export bounties for specific manufactures like "British-made sail-cloth and gun-powder," not an objective like the long-term development of the Highland periphery. Anderson's argument for state-supported urbanization in fact targeted a blind spot in the model of town-country synergies laid out in book 3 of *The Wealth of Nations*. This account of the positive feedback between agricultural improvement and the emergence of towns elided the political question of how great a role the economic policy of the state played in the early history of urban settlement. Smith's sketch focused on the spontaneous settlement of artificers in corn lands that afforded a natural surplus for nonagricultural labor. He noted as well the importance of tax exemption to trade, granted by the king or a local lord. But he did not discuss the specific role of the state in encouraging settlements in a land without towns, whether the historical founding of the royal burghs of Scotland by David I or the contemporary establishment of fishing villages in the Hebrides.[58] The only comment we have from Smith on the question of Highland settlement can be found in two letters by him to Henry Beaufoy, one of the directors of the British Fisheries Society. Beaufoy's colleague George Dempster had tried to enlist Smith's services at the behest of the company earlier. Yet Smith took an exceedingly cautious view of the long-term prospects of the joint stock company. After expressing the "highest praise" for the "public spirited intentions" of the society, he insisted that the scheme was hopelessly flawed in practice and that the investors would "lose every shilling" of their investments. His principal complaints concerned the high rent charged to the fishermen for their lodgings (thirty shillings per year), the exorbitant interest charged on capital lent to them to buy the utensils of the fishing trade, and the great probability of fraud and mismanagement among the overseers and agents of the society. In short, the British Fisheries Society was a *project* in the derogatory sense of the word: a high-risk venture liable to corruption and practical failure rather than private prudence and public welfare.[59]

These scattered comments by Smith on the state of northern Scotland are remarkable for their relative brevity and their many omissions. There was nothing here on the benefits or risks of Gaelic emigration, sheep farms, military recruitment, and northern agriculture. Even though nearly all of Smith's life as a writer coincided with the first age of Highland improvement schemes between 1760 and 1790, the population politics of the north seems to have exerted no particular influence on his mind in the 1780s. It is also striking how little he concerned himself with the technical questions about natural history and geography that occupied improvers like John Walker, James Anderson, and the founders of the British Fisheries Society. What was the path of migration for the herring shoals through the Hebrides? How could migrants be induced to settle in villages? Were there opportunities for manufacturing in the Highlands? Instead, Smith's notion of improvement ignored such peculiarities in favor of the abstract model of town growth in corn lands. The fascination with local knowledge felt so strongly by Highland improvers and naturalists held little sway over his mind. While James Anderson tried to fuse liberal principles with an attention to the peculiarities of natural history, Smith's liberal ecology moved in the opposite direction. The fit between nature and markets had to have universal appeal. This is the most fundamental reason why Smith has so little to say about the Highlands in *The Wealth of Nations*. Smith was able to stretch his model outward to accommodate New Jersey and Bengal under the norm of English "corn lands," whereas the Highland periphery could be included only as a *negative* phenomenon, a symbol of endemic poverty and the folly of projectors.

6

Larch Autarky

On the edge of the Perthshire Highlands, a new forest sprouted during the French and Napoleonic Wars. The servants of the Duke of Atholl planted several million seedlings of larch in a scheme intended to secure the naval timber supply of the nation into the distant future.[1] This obsession with the virtue of larch timber was a family patrimony—larch had been planted by several generations of Murrays—and also a persistent dream of the Scottish savant James Anderson. The story of the fourth duke John Murray's larch scheme underscores the centrality of forestry to the politics of the natural order in the Scottish Enlightenment. Conservative improvers and naturalists stressed the multiple strategic problems connected with naval timber. Should the nation risk dependence on overseas nations or colonies for strategic supplies? Did naval timber compete with national food production for arable land? Could British landowners be expected to make investments in forest plantations given the slow rate of return? Leading administrators worried that Britain was headed toward a crisis in the timber supply. The 1787 Admiralty survey of woodlands concluded that domestic supply ran dangerously low across the nation. Murray's larch empire was thus a response to multiple pressures. It combined natural expertise and private capital with the priorities of national self-sufficiency in the spirit of civil cameralism. But the duke's efforts were thwarted by a rival Scottish strategy. None other than Henry Dundas, now Lord Melville, commissioned a global survey to identify accessible stands of naval timbers in 1803–4. Where Murray looked inward for a solution, Dundas gambled on South Asian teak. The two strategies were in fact variations on a common theme. Both relied on naturalist expertise to solve a national crisis of resource exhaustion by setting up a timber reserve. In the context of uncertainty and risk brought on by the Napoleonic Wars, Murray's rationale for Highland conservationism was hardly any less rational than the teak strategy. The duke's project foundered not because of any deficiency on the part of the timber but on account of the unfortunate timing of his prototype larch ship, which was completed only at the end of the wars.

PLANTER NATION

When Samuel Johnson and James Boswell made their famous tour of the Scottish Highlands in 1773, they were traveling through one of the least forested regions in Europe. William Roy's military survey of 1747–55 indicated that no more than 4 percent of the land surface of Scotland was covered by woodland. The Englishman Johnson sneered that "few regions have been denuded like this, where many centuries must have passed in waste without the least thought of future supply." Yet Johnson's comment was hardly fair. Indeed, William Roy seems to have underestimated the woodland cover seriously. The true number for the period was likely closer to 8 percent. Scottish landowners and sylviculturists had already begun to take an interest in afforestation by the early decades of the eighteenth century. Among the more spectacular initiatives was that of Archibald Grant of Monymusk, whose men planted as many as two million trees before 1754 in northeast Scotland. In 1775, William Boutcher rallied a sizable portion of the Scottish elite to support his book on how to improve Scottish forestry. No fewer than 441 subscribers pledged to buy one or more copies of *A Treatise on Forest Trees*, including Henry Dundas, David Dalrymple, and many other gentlemen and professionals.[2]

The mission to plant new forests was cast as a peculiarly aristocratic responsibility. Great landowners like the Earl of Haddington regarded tree planting as an act of paternalist foresight that would increase the value of one's patrimony while at the same time serving the wider public. In a similar spirit, the economist James Anderson encouraged the gentry to embrace forestry as a slow but particularly secure form of investment in his 1771 newspaper campaign. Afforestation here represented a practical version of conservative ideology that combined an orientation toward landed investment with an ideal of long-term organic growth. Anderson and his compatriots also emphasized the duty of landowners to plant woods on marginal soils and at high altitudes. Plantations were a means of redeeming wastelands and fulfilling a providential plan of optimal land use within the nation. Trees were civilizing agents that transformed the wilderness into a valuable investment. A similar rhetoric is to be found in the naturalist surveys commissioned by the government on the Annexed Estates. Writing from Stratherig south of Inverness in 1770, the natural historian John Williams observed with "astonishment" that plantations were so generally neglected in the north, especially considering the "great scarcity of large oak timber all over the island." Both "policy" and "private interest . . . should induce all proprietors to the improvement of their woods."[3]

Not everyone was so concerned. Adam Smith composed and published *The Wealth of Nations* during these years. Though he must have been familiar with the priorities of the planters, he tended to regard deforestation as a simple indicator of progress: "In its rude beginnings, the greater part of every country is covered with wood, which is then a mere incumbrance of no value to the landlord, who would gladly give it to any body for the cutting. As agriculture advances, the woods are partly cleared by the progress of tillage, and partly go to decay in consequence of the increased number of cattle." For Smith, the removal of trees was not all that different from the disappearance of cottagers and small tenants. In his dispassionate appraisal, trees could make no special claim on the imagination. The clearing of woods marked the forward march of human civilization. If trees grew too scarce, then men turned to coal for heating. Only once in *The Wealth of Nations* did Smith attribute a strong ideological meaning to timber. While discussing the construction of the New Town of Edinburgh, he observed that there was scarcely "a single stick of Scotch timber" in that entire section of the city. Instead, the wood had come across the sea from Norway and the Baltic region. The Georgian splendor of the New Town, the supreme material expression of the Enlightenment in Scotland, was a token of exchange rather than national autarky. Smith and his successors in the tradition of classical political economy had no patience for arguments about the strategic necessity of conservation. Timber served the same function as grain in *The Wealth of Nations*. Its economic value was shorn of any sentimental and patriotic association with native soil and self-sufficiency in favor of the symbolism of international exchange: peaceful prosperity and mutual advantage.[4]

The question of planting in this way marked a rift much like that of mixed husbandry between the liberal ecology of commerce and the political vision of civil cameralism. Their disagreement centered on the character of the natural order and the public good. Smith saw the timber trade as yet another justification for liberal exchange. Naturalists in contrast worried about the stability of natural economies and the strategic vulnerability of the timber supply. Hence, they argued for the prudence of long-term management of forest resources by the government and eminent landowners. It was a national duty of the most pressing kind. Yet despite the urgent stake, the planting movement was divided by several unresolved ambiguities: What technical solutions could natural history present to solve the problem of growing naval timber, and what precisely was the role of the state in the selection and protection of forest preserves?

LARCH MANIA

Larch was something of a family obsession for the dukes of Atholl. In 1737, the second duke, James Murray laid out Diana's Wilderness, a grove of deciduous trees northeast of Blair Castle along a series of walks centered on a statue of the Roman goddess. Using seeds secured from the Continent (probably the Swiss Alps), he planted two larches in the grove near Banvie Burn. From such ornamental beginnings, he then added more than a thousand trees on the slopes of the estate. The third duke in turn planted a total of 410 acres in the ten years between 1764 and 1774. However, the larch was not yet an overriding priority in Atholl estate management. As a planter, the second duke was above all a garden-maker determined to imitate and rival the English aristocracy with the landscapes and vistas he fashioned around Blair Castle. The third duke, John Murray, recognized the commercial value of the timber, but his hobbyhorse was a different exotic transplant: the medicinal cash crop of the Turkey rhubarb from Central Asia. By the time of his death in 1774, Atholl produced a rich harvest of the precious plant. It was only with his successor the fourth duke that the allure of rhubarb paled in favor of larch.[5]

Meanwhile, the species gained a vocal advocate in the wider world of enlightened natural history. A series of letters on forestry authored by James Anderson under the name Agricola in the *Edinburgh Weekly Amusement* and the *Scots Magazine* in 1771 sang the praise of the larch. These texts introduced the economic potential of larch timber to a broad Scottish audience for the first time. To Anderson, the promotion of the tree was particularly urgent because it so conveniently combined private gain for the landlord with strategic benefit to the nation. This harmony of patriotism and profit became a common creed among northern improvers. Anderson's letter dwelled at length on the superior qualities of the tree, its quick growth and "prodigious height," its ability to thrive in the "poorest soil, and most exposed situation," and, most important, the "exceeding great durability" of larch timber. While the species did not grow exclusively in northern latitudes, it promised to transform North Britain in a fundamental manner. As a high-altitude exotic, the tree could be transplanted without any natural disadvantage to the Scottish Highlands, where the mountains closely resembled the habitat of its native Alps. Anderson noted in his 1777 treatise on Merino acclimatization that the larch had been introduced "between thirty and forty years ago" to Scotland in the form of a greenhouse plant but had quickly become accustomed to the northern climate and was "now known to be one of the most hardy trees that is found on the face of the earth."[6]

These letters on planting, Anderson's first major publication, also introduced to the Scottish public his idea that economic diversification held the key to Highland prosperity. The larch was to be part of a larger economy of mixed forestry, including beech, sugar maple, and different varieties of pine, which would produce not merely timber but also turpentine, rosin, tar, sugar, potash, and bark for British manufactures. One of the letters to the Scottish press explained the practice of burning high-quality potash and how the new Scottish plantations could support this industry, perhaps eventually eclipsing that of North America. Another letter described how the North American sugar maple could be introduced to Scotland to yield a domestic substitute for West Indies sugar cane. As the conflict worsened in the thirteen colonies, Anderson's commitment to internal improvement and import substitution grew still firmer. If but "a thousandth part of the expence which has been bestowed on America" was invested in the regional economy, these manufactures would soon rival the manufacturing wealth of England.[7]

Anderson's promotional campaign for the larch in 1771 was timely. That same year, the House of Commons had appointed a committee to look into the vexing question of the British timber supply. The committee warned that the English oak plantations had been dangerously depleted. The threat was not simply commercial but also strategic. How could the Royal Navy be supported with timber if the forests were near exhaustion? Anderson used this opportune moment to advertise the alpine transplant as an excellent substitute for oak in shipbuilding. He suggested that larch in fact was a superior timber because it was "lighter and more buoyant," as well as "possibly" resistant to "worms in warm climates." Certainly, its growth rate was far better than the oak, up to six times quicker in the right conditions. Anderson insisted that the tree would "merit the attention of every sincere friend to his country, at least so far as to get a fair trial made."[8]

Though the House of Commons soon dropped the issue of the timber supply, the planting of the exotic tree was already under way among private proprietors in Scotland. According to some sources, Lord Kames had brought the first seeds of larch to Scotland in 1734. But the first large-scale attempts with the tree outside the Atholl estates appears to have begun after 1760, at Tulloch in Ross-shire, in Tealing parish in Angus, on the Innes plantations in Moray, and in Kinloch parish in Perthshire. Over the next few decades, the tree caught on with an increasing numbers of proprietors, no doubt encouraged by James Anderson's propaganda. The letters on forestry were reissued in 1777. Anderson also wrote frequently about the economy of the larch in his journal *The Bee*. Among the Scottish larch planters was Anderson's good friend and occasional patron George Dempster, who began stocking his Forfarshire estates with the tree in 1780. When Dempster purchased a second property in Sutherland in 1787, he was especially keen on the larch, in the hope that it might make an import substitute for the Baltic fir timber and turn the Highlands into "the Norway or Sweden of Great Britain."[9]

The feasibility of forestry in the Highland climate provoked a lot of discussion in the transactions of the Highland Society of Scotland and elsewhere. The mining engineer and naturalist John Williams argued that the upland region was too wet for grain but that the heavy rainfall and water-logged soils were "highly conducive to the rapid growth of timber." The Reverend John Smith of Campbelltown added that the archaeological and historical record supported the possibility of plantations. He claimed that a "great Caledonian forest, at one time" had "covered almost the whole of the highest, and bleakest parts" of Scotland. Indeed, "trunks of its gigantic pines, and oaks, are still to be found in every peat moss, almost at the very top of the Grampian hills." The same was true of the Western Isles: "Wherever there is any moss, to preserve them from corruption, we find the remains of trees, which had grown at no remote period. [Martin] Martin describes some of them as covered with wood, where, now, not a bush is seen to grow." Smith agreed with Patrick Neill that the best method of planting on the islands was to group trees closely together, in order to protect them from the pernicious effects of the sea breeze and the salty spray of the ocean. They both pointed to the success of such dense plantations in Argyll as well as in Norway. Neill noted that seedling trees should be searched for in the colder Norwegian climate rather than the "rich and warm beds of Dickson's nurseries at Edinburgh." Larch, ash, and plane could also be reared on the islands, if only they were first acclimatized in local experimental gardens. To strengthen his case, Neill stressed the analogy between the animal and vegetable kingdom: "it being certain that plants resemble animals in becoming gradually habituated to particular climates and soils."[10]

On the question of profits, the Reverend Smith of Campbelltown acknowledged the problem of slow returns. But he stressed the need for landowners to plan for the future: "If they should not live to fell the trees which they plant, their estates are increased in value, and improved in beauty; and that the plantings would almost, at any time, sell for more than would repay them with interest. Plantations, after a few years, would return them a large annual profit, and in the end, be a fortune for their children." Smith also invoked the political arithmetic of Arthur Young, in order to show that profits were less distant than commonly believed. In their opinion, "planting land, even on a lease of 21 years, would be more profitable than any other improvement; as it would give a return of 6 pounds an acre, with no risque, and little expence or trouble." A landlord planting a forest of a hundred acres upon coming of age would "reap more than 60,000 pounds by the time they are 65; and that from poor land, unfit for husbandry." Echoing Anderson, Smith insisted that a stable price was practically guaranteed, given the diverse uses of wood and timber as an import substitute that could provide Britain with domestic supplies of strategic commodities like tar, potash, turpentine, and raw materials for shipbuilding.[11]

THE MAKING OF HMS *ATHOLL*

John Murray, the Fourth Duke of Atholl, seems to have been committed to large-scale timber production from the beginning. In the first years after his succession between 1774 and 1783, 279,000 seedlings were planted. In the following decade, an even larger plantation took shape near Dunkeld. In the posthumous work, *Account of the Larch Plantations on the Estates of Atholl and Dunkeld*, published by the Highland Society of Scotland in 1832, Murray described the larch as ideally suited for a mixed economy of forestry, agriculture, and pasturage, since it thrived in elevated situations so barren that they could sustain no other use. He speculated that the tree might reclaim even the slopes of the highest and most remote peaks, beyond the reach of Scots pine. With a keen eye for the ecology of the tree, the duke noted that larch litter tended to enrich the soil, transforming marginal lands over time into good pasturage (an effect also observed by twentieth-century ecologists). In this way, planting seemed to offer a substitute for the intense and costly operation of wasteland reclamation by paring, burning, and liming. With a patience and system probably unprecedented among other proprietors and planters, the duke conducted a long series of trials on the properties of the timber. His diligently kept journals recorded a wide variety of possible applications, including mill wheels and axles, building material, coppice for tanneries, posts, rails, and bridges. Only after 1810 did the tests of larch as a naval timber begin to predominate. In the earlier period, forestry in Atholl more closely approximated the ideal of diversification in Anderson. Much oak was still planted on the lowland part of the estates for coppice rather than timber, and the trade in oak bark for the tanning industries was a significant source of income to the duke.[12]

The genesis of Atholl's naval project remains obscure, on account of its long gestation. Only by gradual steps did his interest in larch become a firm conviction about its strategic value. Anderson had proposed the idea of larch as a substitute for oak already in 1771. Murray's first attempt at constructing a boat out of larch in 1777 coincided with the reissue of Anderson's forestry letters in book form. In a brief memorandum on his larch experiments, the duke mentions a series of small vessels built from about 1780. Observing these boats on the local rivers, he soon realized that the timber was greatly superior to fir in longevity, requiring repairs only in intervals of ten rather than three years. Then, as the stands of his father and grandfather began to mature, Murray took to building larger vessels such as ferries and fishing boats for his estates until his larch flotilla included nearly two dozen boats. Much like Anderson, Atholl was struck by the "buoyance" of the timber and its durability, especially compared to oak. The sap of the wood appeared wonderfully potent, sealing the timber against rot. In 1794, a letter from the duke made passing mention of Russian warships built from larch. But Murray's decision to promote the naval uses of larch seems to have matured quite slowly. According to the *Account*, he did not enter into negotiations with the Admiralty until 1807, when Napoleon closed down the Baltic to British timber traders. Two years later, Lord Mulgrave and the Navy Board requested a first shipment of two hundred loads of larch. This delivery was employed for repairs of the store ship *Serapis*, "because there was not enough of it to build a whole ship." Curiously, Murray neglected to make use of the Highland Society of Scotland to lobby the government in Edinburgh or London in favor of larch ships, even though he served as the president of the association between 1807 and 1811. Perhaps he thought the heroic scale and potential profits of the scheme would be diminished by collaboration. Only two years after the duke's death did the Highland Society take up the promotion of naval larch.[13]

Within the navy, Atholl's staunchest ally was the fellow Scot John Deas Thomson on the Navy Board, who warmly embraced the goal of timber autarky. Thomson expressed great satisfaction with the repairs on the *Serapis*, sending glowing reports to the duke in 1811. But at this point the strength of France was already in eclipse. The Napoleonic blockade of the Baltic had been lifted, relieving anxieties about British strategic supplies. In 1812, Robert Dundas suspended the larch experiment temporarily. Untroubled, Thomson met the changing circumstances by adopting a long-term perspective. In 1814, when timber imports were once again flowing freely to Britain from abroad, he assured the duke of the need for patience and persistence in their noble aims: "Past experience tells us how much we ought to foster every means by which we can be rendered independent, and of what importance such valuable timber as the larch will one day or other be, for Naval Purposes." Thomson was encouraged by a certain shift in public opinion on the issue. "I begin to think there are some now amongst us, thoroughly convinced ... the Larch has been mentioned in some late [papers], with the credit due to so valuable an article."

Evidently, the duke took this advice to heart. After 1815, he began yet another phase of intense activity, planting "6500 Scotch acres of mountain-ground solely with larch." This new forest, destined to mature long after his death, was intended to secure the future of the empire. The duke remarked that "if one-fourth part of the product of 2,600,000 larches arrive to maturity in seventy-two years, by the time the present century expires, it will supply all the demands required by Great Britain for war or commerce." The decision marked the final gamble in Murray's scheme. Before the navy had commissioned a single larch ship, he was devoting his energies and capital to a monoculture for the sake of the distant future. On the Atholl estates, Anderson's dream of a diverse and advanced Highland economy in the service of the nation was dissolving into an armada of phantom ships.[14]

In May 1816, Thomson and Atholl finally achieved a token victory over the Admiralty. At this point, Sir Robert Sepping and Robert Saunders Dundas had attached themselves to the party of believers. During a meeting with Sepping at the Deptford naval yards, Dundas announced his approval of "the value of the larch timber in a national point of view" and ordered the construction of a "small sloop of war" out of the material. Further consideration produced a more ambitious design in the form of a sixth-rate twenty-eight-gun frigate at 503 tons, baptized the *Atholl*. The ship required the felling of 772 trees in Dunkeld and Blair, at an average age of sixty years. This wood amounted to about two and a half acres of plantation, severely taxing the stock of mature larch built up by the second and third dukes. Sensing the theatrical value of public trials, Murray orchestrated a series of experiments to drive home the viability of the new timber. A fir frigate called *Niemen* was built side by side with the *Atholl* in order to compare the naval properties of Riga fir and Scottish larch over the long term at sea. The duke also funded a brig made in larch built by a private contractor. He tried, unsuccessfully, to press it on the navy as a troop transport. In March 1818, he organized a small-scale trial of the "transverse strength and resilience" of different forms of naval timber. The test brought together a host of larch proponents, including Atholl himself, his nephew Lord James Murray, J. D. Thomson, William Adair, Lord Prudhoe, and others. Six types of wood were tested, including Memel timber, red larch, English oak, and Riga timber. After several no doubt breathless hours of watching planks twist and shatter under pressure, the observers reached a verdict: "On the whole . . . it appears, that Larch is superior to Oak in stiffness, in strength, and, in the power of resisting a body in motion, (called Resilience) and it is inferior to Memel or Riga Timber in stiffness only." Fishing for wider support, the duke had the report of this experiment published the following year for the benefit of the general public.[15]

When the *Atholl* was launched at Woolwich in 1820, the Navy Board estimated the vessel's life span to be six years. This was in fact a far better prospect than the durability of oaken ships of the same size. After a maiden voyage to Madeira, the *Atholl* performed admirably on active duty in Africa and Europe. An examination conducted in 1824, comparing the *Atholl* and an oaken ship, concluded that the former was far more resistant to "nail sickness" than its rival. The iron nails used to fasten the wood of the hull had caused only limited decay in the larch wood. On a new examination in 1827, the larch ship was found to require only minor repairs, while the surveyors recommended that its twin, the *Niemen*, be demolished and broken up on account of the poor state of the Riga fir timber. These rather sensational findings stirred up some forceful support for the duke's position. A year later, an anonymous officer at Portsmouth dockyards who had surveyed both ships declared that Scottish larch comprised a "great national advantage" which promised to relieve Britain from any future dependence on Baltic supplies of fir. The same year, Atholl's friend Sir A. M. Mackenzie went a step further, asserting that it ought to replace oak as the principal naval timber by and large. "I am confirmed in the Duke's opinion, that whenever a sufficient quantity of larch of proper age, and growing on ground suited to it, can be provided, it will in a great measure supersede the use of oak." A full thirteen years after the *Atholl* was launched and two years after the fourth duke's death, a new examination in 1832 found the ship in excellent condition and esteemed the vessel "fit in our opinion to run at least seven years longer." Captain Duncan of the Ordinance Office reckoned "this wood the very thing for our steamers and by and by there will be no other ship of war built, the Growth of Larch is therefore a matter of great national importance and should be encouraged by all means." At the same time, the Highland Society of Scotland finally threw its weight behind the objective of naval larch. Yet despite this public support, the Admiralty did not see fit to make any changes in the timber policy. Inauspiciously, the *Atholl* was refitted to a troopship that year. This descent into obscurity was completed when the vessel was converted into a store ship in 1850. Yet even so the *Atholl* paid off only in 1861. It could at least be said that the ship had confirmed every prediction voiced by the duke about the longevity and durability of larch timber.[16]

TEAK EMPIRE

The political theater of the larch frigate proved ineffectual at the level of naval policy because of its poor timing, but the strategic potential of the timber was perhaps not inferior to the alternatives that defeated it. Murray's best opportunity to capitalize on Highland timber came during the period when Scots occupied the office of the first lord of the Admiralty. Yet Henry Dundas was never seriously interested in larch as a substitute. Why was he so indifferent to Highland naval timber when he backed several other initiatives in Highland improvement? The short answer is that Dundas's appreciation of domestic forestry was undermined by his commitment to imperial rule in South Asia. Highland expertise clashed with a neo-mercantilist version of natural history.

Scottish officials were instrumental in making the problem of the timber supply of the Royal Navy into an urgent political issue for the nation and empire toward the end of the eighteenth century. Such worries had a long prehistory, but poor management by the Navy Board and protracted naval conflict with France conspired to make the situation particularly dire by the time of the American War of Independence. The Scottish captain and administrator Charles Middleton (later Lord Barham) led the charge for reform when he was appointed comptroller of the Royal Navy in 1778. He was outraged to discover that the stores of timber and other vital supplies in the naval dockyards would last only six months. In the wake of the war, he chaired a special committee to survey and reform the naval timber supply. In the eleventh report of the committee issued in 1792, Middleton and his fellow commissioners concluded after the extensive inventory of the English counties that the nation's resources were stretched very thin indeed. They predicted that Britain must soon become "dependent on other Powers for its supply" of naval timber. They also recognized that this strategic vulnerability was in fact the fruit of Britain's commercial success. Growing wealth and population were the ultimate culprits behind deforestation. Middleton and his colleagues dismissed the hopes of liberal observers that rising prices would provide a remedy. Whereas grain markets provided quick signals for landowners to grow more food in times of scarcity, the benefits of forest plantations were so distant that owners "were driven" to other forms of land use, which offered "more immediate" rewards. Market forces alone could not rectify the situation. Instead, the government must take charge. The problem of domestic supply was compounded by the fact that oak competed with wheat for the best land. Without a change in naval policy, British timber plantations might undermine the other strategic necessity of securing adequate "subsistence [for] the people." The eleventh report suggested that the larch tree "was by far the most likely" to resolve this crisis of competing demands on the land, since it could grow in the uplands rather than in grain-producing areas. There were ample precedents for the practical efficacy of larch wood, since the Venetians had used the timber for centuries and the Russian empress had built a fleet of larch ships at Archangel.[17]

Yet as the timber crisis worsened, the Hanoverian state turned outward to the colonies in search of new supplies. The main driver in this shift toward colonial timber was Henry Dundas. Middleton owed much of his success as an administrator to his ties with the Dundas family. The influence also went the other way. It seems that Middleton acted as something of a mentor to Dundas on naval matters. Dundas was promoted treasurer of the Admiralty from 1782, and when Pitt the Younger returned to government in 1804, Dundas became first lord of the Admiralty. After the renewal of war with revolutionary France in 1803, Dundas and Middleton both feared that the strains on the national timber supply might paralyze British naval power. Dundas compiled a large memorandum to Richard Wellesley in July 1804, which contained damning data on the annual timber stores in the royal dockyards between 1775 and 1803. The highest peaks were recorded at the outset of earlier wars in 1778 and 1791, but the count had dropped consistently over the last ten years to reach 31,000 loads of English oak timber and knees in 1803, roughly half of the supplies counted in 1778 or 1791. This amount was supplemented by a very modest number of foreign timber, 1,568 loads in 1802. A "fatal Want" seemed imminent.[18]

In response, the Navy Board conducted the first global inventory of naval timber. This was at the same time a mark of the profound reach of British power and a measure of desperation about metropolitan shortages. Among many different types of wood, special attention was given to European larch, longleaf pine from the United States, and South Asian teak. Long before the survey was completed, Dundas was prejudiced in favor of teak. He wrote to his colleague Wellesley: "It has recently become my duty to examine this subject to the bottom with a view to the practical use of this system—for the state of Oak Timber in Great Britain and the difficulty of finding an equivalent Substitute for it either in Europe or America, joined to our encreasing demands for the Navy, has rendered it a matter of indispensable necessity to look to India for material insistence." Dundas's advisers in the memorandum of 1804 strongly supported the need for colonial forestry as a necessary form of relief. One adviser wrote that the woods of Burma "would ultimately operate as a preventive to our Forests being entirely exhausted." The problem of national exhaustion was thus coupled directly with colonial abundance. Dundas's memorandum referred to "almost inexhaustible" woods of teak in Pegu, near Rangoon. By waiting until 1807 to begin his bid, Atholl missed a crucial window of opportunity. The global survey had included Highland larch but deemed it an inferior form of wood for shipbuilding. A more sustained effort of promotion by Murray at an earlier point might have tempered such prejudice.[19]

However, even if Atholl had managed to mobilize a lobbying campaign at this earlier stage, he would have faced a problem of short-term supply. Lord Melville's overriding concern was the acute crisis of the timber supply amid a war of uncertain outcome (with no Trafalgar yet in sight). His priorities were firmly fixed on discovering mature timber stock ready for use. Atholl could offer him no such thing. The Perthshire larch plantations were intended as a timber reserve for the long-term, a guarantee of imperial hegemony in the far future. The pressures of the acute emergency easily trumped this plan. When Middleton challenged Dundas's prejudice by recommending larch as a timber substitute, he looked to the Russian czar rather than Atholl for supplies. By 1807, the commissioners of Naval Revision were still more concerned with the duke's oak stands than his larch forests as they responded to the duke's request for a survey. Murray's unfortunate lack of timing also obviated his political advantage with Dundas. When he finally approached the Admiralty, Henry Dundas had been removed from service and forced into retirement on his Highland estate at Dunira. The political debt Dundas owed to the duke and his nephew James Murray for their assistance in securing electoral victories since 1790 in Perthshire could no longer be invoked to raise support for Atholl larch. Yet if Atholl's timing was dismal, Melville's policy on the timber issue was certainly shortsighted and biased in favor of overseas colonies from the outset. Even the strain of the Napoleonic blockade failed to convince him of the virtues of strategic autarky in timber. To Dundas, the rivalry with France would be won in the colonies and on the high seas. Rather than looking inward to muster new resources for a prolonged struggle on the Continent, Britain ought to confront France by conquering its overseas possessions. This orientation probably involved a serious misunderstanding of the French economy, because he exaggerated French dependence on colonial supplies while ignoring the "self-contained and self-sufficient" nature of French commerce. In this way, Dundas's vision of French imperial power formed a mirror image of his own strategic prerogatives.[20]

On the question of timber supplies, Dundas leaned on the judgment of James Rennell, the geographer of Asia and correspondent of Sir Joseph Banks, rather than the radical Whig James Anderson. In Dundas's files on teak, we find an extract from Rennell's *Memoirs* complaining about the "unpardonable Negligence we are guilty of in delaying to build Teak Ships of War for the Use of the Indian Seas." For Rennell and Dundas, the central advantage of teak lay in its power to resist the ravages of the tropical climate. It was the optimal ship timber for the empire in the torrid zone. Rennell noted: "Teak Ships of forty Years old and upwards are no uncommon Objects on the India Seas, while an

European Ship is ruined there in five years." Better yet, the wood was equally suited for northern operations. It could easily withstand the low temperatures of a temperate climate: "The East India Company have a Teak Ship on her 4th Voyage at present, which ship has wintered in England; therefore any objections on the Effects of Frost is done away."[21]

During the timber survey of 1804, one of Melville's advisers, John Atkins, fleshed out the policy implications of a tilt to Indian teak and other kinds of wood. Whether ignorant or contemptuous of the larch as a ship timber, Atkins began with the premise that naval reserves in Britain could be grown only in the lowlands and therefore must compete with the priority of food production. Rejecting a second central assumption of Atholl's larch project, Atkins went on to warn Melville against the reliance on British landlords for timber because, he insisted, no individual proprietor could guarantee the stability of supplies over several generations. By this perhaps not entirely inexorable logic, Atkins recommended the teak of the East Indies as the best substitute for English oak. Taking as his standard the current price of east country crown plank at 26 pounds per load, he suggested that teak plank could be obtained within the same range. A number of factors guaranteed "reasonable" costs of extraction. First, Atkins pointed to the king of Ava's territories on the Irrawaddy River as a forest with "inexhaustible" reserves of timber. Second, the actual magnitude of British needs would be kept hidden to the seller. "Much Secresy should be observed to prevent the Natives being aware that your Demand was large." As a safeguard, Atkins added that other forests could be exploited by force should the locals on the Irrawaddy prove unreasonable about the price. To complete this picture of exotic abundance free from the irksome constraints of European markets, Atkins confirmed Rennell's judgment about the preternatural resilience of the wood: "The durability of the Teak from the Experience which has been made far exceeds any other wood which has been hitherto used in ship building. We have instances where the ships have been built upwards of Forty years, and were then in a perfect state." Like Atholl's larch, this teak appeared to resist "nail sickness." Atkins reported seeing a ship "37 years old" whose iron nails were "covered with a lacquered appearance" caused by the "resinous quality of the wood." The sap of teak, he deduced, protected the nails from "corroding . . . as all Iron work in Oak does." Nowhere in his memorandum did Atkins acknowledge the curious parallels between his southern timber and the larch.[22]

Not all of Dundas's reporters shared Atkins's cornucopian view of South Asian forest resources. The naturalist Francis Buchanan Hamilton (a Scottish student of John Walker and John Hope at the University of Edinburgh) supplied much of the empirical basis of Dundas's memorandum. He contrasted the timber wealth of Southeast Asia with the pillaged state of Mysore's teak forests in the south of India. Buchanan Hamilton reported that he had "passed through the whole extent of the country" in the north of Cochin "without seeing one large Teak tree, although on every hill small stunted plants were common." Dundas's nephew Philip Dundas suggested that the Mysore ruler Tipu Sultan had devastated the Indian woods in his bid to build a navy capable of resisting British expansion. "I fear that the consumption has been of late years (in Hyder's and Tippoo's time and since) greater than the means of the Country could afford." Buchanan Hamilton recommended trade with Siam and Cochin-China to compensate for the exhaustion of Mysore. Soon afterward, the directors of the East India Company established a forest committee to canvass the extent of mature teak timber and promptly discovered that easily accessible stands were indeed exhausted. In a "pivotal and innovative" response, the company banned all felling of teak trees without authorization and confiscated "unclaimed lands." Gregory Barton has charted how these fears gave rise to the first systematic efforts of conservation in the British Empire toward the middle of the nineteenth century. But as we have seen, these concerns can be traced back to the crucible of enlightened improvement. Scottish planters, naturalists, and administrators clearly shared a peculiar sensitivity to the problem of exhaustion. They also shared a bold and imaginative approach to overcoming the threat of collapse through schemes of bioprospecting, domestic diversification, and colonial substitution. Murray's bid to recast the material foundations of naval power at home sprang from the same source as Dundas's global survey and promotion of teak.[23]

RATIONAL PROJECTS

By the time Murray at last won permission to build the *Atholl*, the game was lost. In 1810, a year before his death, Henry Dundas issued a final political gesture: a printed broadside in favor of teak from the wilderness of his forced retirement after an impeachment charge ended his public career. He was now residing more or less permanently at his country estate Dunira, just a dozen miles south of Atholl. Among the improvements Dundas introduced to the estate was a nursery for larch and oak. But his pamphlet contained not a single word about the timber despite Atholl's repeated contacts with the Admiralty since 1807. Instead, Dundas stressed the "present scarcity" of domestic timber. Napoleon's blockade had effectively cut off Baltic supplies, forcing "Britain to seek out American timber." But Dundas made it clear that the real alternative to oak was "the teak . . . of India." Thanks to effective imperial control of the South Asian market, he assured the public that it would come at half the cost of English oak. He went on to recommend that naval dockyards be built at Bombay, Pegu, Rangoon, and Cochin to exploit this timber at the source. On grounds of strategic necessity, the Admiralty had already begun to establish a series of dockyards along the Asian coast that year. In a short time, numerous teak ships were commissioned, entrenching Dundas's vision in the naval budget, although the Asian timber never came into widespread use.[24]

The wartime crisis conditions that might have favored Atholl's argument for autarky in naval timber had passed when Robert Dundas agreed to the construction of the *Atholl*. Yet Murray persisted with his own plans and expanded his plantations greatly after 1815. Murray proved unwilling to recognize the new reality of British hegemony, persisting with his projects as if the Napoleonic wars were yet to be fought. His lobbying activity shared something of this inflexible character. Murray never seems to have entertained the thought of petitioning the Admiralty to establish a dockyard in Scotland to eliminate the problem of transportation costs for his larch. He also remained too single-minded to exploit new opportunities. His friend on the Navy Board J. D. Thomson badgered him repeatedly about adapting larch to the new steam technology. Both Isambard Kingdom Brunel and James Watt Jr. approached him with designs for steamboats. Yet apart from a small trial—the steam yacht *Diana*—Atholl remained rigidly attached to his original idea of sailing ships in larch.[25]

A distant and aloof figure in the circles of the Highland improvers, Atholl opted to stay clear not only of the Highland Society but also of powerful independent figures like Sir John Sinclair and George Dempster. Although his vision of Perthshire larch as the basis of strategic autarky came close to widely held ideals of Highland colonization, he rarely made the connection in his appeals. Murray spoke little of the region as a whole, preferring the narrow perspective of his own estates. In so doing, he isolated himself from men who would have been his natural allies. By linking his project so tightly to his own person, Atholl probably paved the way for the rapid collapse of the larch scheme once that bond dissolved.

One final irony haunted Atholl's failed bid. Just a year after he began to lobby the Admiralty, the main supply route of timber to Britain was disrupted. Napoleon managed to stifle the Baltic timber trade through a mixture of diplomacy and blockade in 1808. This ended the British reliance on Scandinavian timber that Smith had celebrated in *The Wealth of Nations*. Instead, British timber merchants began to look west for an alternative. Imports from British North America expanded from 5,000 tons to 417,000 tons between 1805 and

1825. Before this shift, only a small fraction of timber had come across the Atlantic. At the beginning of the 1820s, Canada supplied nearly three quarters of the total timber imports, helped by preferential duties. When Baltic timber became available again, Canadian imports continued to grow. The Napoleonic blockade thus triggered a supply shift from foreign countries to the colonies.[26] This "mass transfer" of raw materials became possible because of British naval control of the North Atlantic. Pax Britannica underwrote the exploitation of ghost acres in the New World. Murray's new push of planting after 1815 seems doubly misconceived in this light. Not only were the wars over but a new imperial import trade was poised to make his hopes for Scottish forestry obsolete. And yet, there is maybe too much hindsight confidence about this conclusion. No one in 1815 or 1825 could have known with certainty that British naval hegemony would last a hundred years. From this perspective, Murray was responding to a growing order of imperial autarky with his own project of national self-sufficiency. Highland larch was perhaps no less rational than the new age of "mass transfer" from New Brunswick.

John Kay, "Three Giants, with a Group of Spectators." Lord Monboddo's head is visible in the background. From *A Series of Original Portraits and Caricature Etchings; With Biographical Sketches and Illustrative Anecdotes* (Edinburgh, 1877).

William Daniell, "Part of the Northern Face of One of the Shiant Isles." From *A Voyage Round Great Britain, Undertaken in the Summer of the Year 1813, and Commencing from the Land's-End, Cornwall, by Richard Ayton; With a Series of Views, Illustrative of the Character and Prominent Features of the Coast, Drawn and Engraved by William Daniell, R.A.* (London, 1814–24).

…ployed at the Fishery. ——

…nce of both Corn and Bear, which this and all the Coasting

…the height of an ordinary Man, particularly Bear which is

…an sixty pecks from sowing one, which however incredible to

…t to be the case by all who reside in it. — but that which would

…ng their Grounds, which they do by a Machine call'd a barscroam

…he figure here prefix'd and thus pushing

…ns the Work like an ebbploughing;

…lage is carryed on throughout all

…a stranger who knew nothing of

…hey would not readily believe so great

…d be done in this way. ——

…want of labouring Tools & other Implements necessary for

…life, for there is neither Tools Mechanic's in all the Country

…ed to no other could be reconciled to their way of labouring.

…is Farm which are no less remarkably fertile than the

…rn yield as luxuriantly; There are several places about

…athing that considerable additions might be made to them

…rloughing such grounds as will admit of it be introduced

…Tenaments or Cot houses for Servants besides the Miller & Herd who

…rceling to another, now living at the remotest Sheeling belonging

…growing thereon; These people all hold of their Landlady

…to the practice of the Country. ——

Detail from "John Home's Survey of Assynt, in 1774," The National Library of Scotland, Edinburgh.

John Kay, "Dr. John Hope, Professor of Botany in the University of Edinburgh."

John Kay, "Rev. John Walker, D.D., Professor of Natural History in the University of Edinburgh."

William Daniell, "Tobermory on the Isle of Mull." One of the villages erected by the British Fisheries Society.

John Kay, "Lord Rockville, Dr. Adam Smith, and Commissioner Brown." From left to right, Alexander Gordon, advocate, Adam Smith, George Brown, commissioner of excise.

William Daniell, "Remains of the Chapel &c., on Inch Kenneth." Inch Kenneth is a small island on the west coast of the Isle of Mull.

Part III

Stationary Highlands

7

COAL EXHAUSTION IN 1789

The prosperity of modern economies rests in no small part on fossil fuel stock. For a long time, pessimists have worried that high rates of fuel consumption will deplete the stock and jeopardize the gains of industrialization. This quintessentially modern anxiety first surfaced at the end of the Scottish Enlightenment. The Welsh mining engineer and naturalist John Williams announced the beginning of peak coal in his 1789 book *The Natural History of the Mineral Kingdom*. Shortly thereafter, the Scottish mining entrepreneur Henry Gray Macnab sought to refute Williams by presenting a precise estimate of extant coal fields in 1793, but his quantitative model merely fanned the flames of controversy rather than laying them to rest. The debate culminated in 1865 with William Stanley Jevons's work *The Coal Question*, which predicted the peak of British coal production within a few decades. This chapter examines the historical origins of these anxieties. Why did Scottish improvers quarrel about peak coal on the eve of the Industrial Revolution?

The mood of political economy and natural history turned sour between Adam Smith's *Wealth of Nations* (1776) and T. R. Malthus's *Essay on the Principle of Population* (1798). Scottish savants and improvers played an important part in giving voice to this new pessimism. Their worries covered a wide register from climate change and extirpation to overpopulation, famine, and coal exhaustion. Some fears were specific to the Highland region. Others concerned the nation as a whole. During the 1780s, the absence of coal in the Highlands emerged as a major problem of regional development. The founders of the British Fisheries Society, George Dempster and Henry Beaufoy, used the evidence of scarcity to argue for the abolition of the onerous duties on shipborne coal in Scotland. Around the same time Dempster drew attention to the spread of commercial sheep farms in the Highlands. He warned the public that the new sheep economy might soon extirpate all human settlements in the Highland interior. But the liberal clergyman Joseph Townsend took the opposite approach, in his dissertation on the poor laws of 1786, by arguing that the Highland region was in fact severely overpopulated. The harsh climate and poor soils simply could not accommodate the prolific fecundity of Gaelic plebeians. Townsend's prognosis of overpopulation in turn helped trigger a debate concerning the food security of Great Britain in the 1790s. The threat of nationwide famine, long dismissed by liberals like Adam Smith, returned with a vengeance during the serious dearth of 1794–96 and 1799–1801. Demographic and ecological strain seemed to push the British economy to the breaking point.

A LAND WITHOUT COAL

John Williams's warning about coal exhaustion was the fruit of an arduous and futile odyssey spanning more than a decade in search of minerals on the Annexed Estates. This long journey was documented in a series of travel reports to the Board for the Annexed Estates between 1763 and 1774. Williams's letters gradually demolished the expectation of a mineral energy basis for Highland improvement. Northern Scotland, the naturalist demonstrated, was a country without substantial coal deposits. Williams's fieldwork in effect offered the reverse of John Walker's natural theology. Instead of finding riches planted by providence in every part of the region, his geological gaze identified permanent scarcity in one location after another.

Williams's work in the Highlands owed more to the discipline of surveying than to the tradition of natural theology. Unlike Walker, Williams had no connection with the Kirk. Originally from a small village in Montgomeryshire, Wales, Williams turned to surveying and mining for a career after completing his parish school education. By the 1740s, he had established himself in Scotland and became involved with William Roy's military survey of the country between 1747 and 1752. During these years, Williams earned a reputation for scrupulous work. His patron George Clerk-Maxwell observed that "several persons" in the profession exaggerated the value of their discoveries so as to engage "Proprietors in Expensive and fruitless Experiments." Yet Clerk-Maxwell had nothing but praise for Williams's "fair and candid account" of the geological evidence as well as his own expenses.[1]

The Board for the Annexed Estates made the discovery of coal and lead a priority for their surveyors. Lead in particular seemed a promising venture. Alexander Murray of Stanhope had opened the Strontian lead mines in 1724. Perhaps similar ores could be found on the Annexed Estates? At a meeting in the summer of 1763 the commissioners allocated 250 pounds for a mineral survey in Perthshire. George Clerk-Maxwell employed John Williams to search "for coal and minerals in the Barony of Stobhall" to the east of Perth. When the borings at Stobhall proved unpromising, Williams was sent north to Cromarty, where he was disappointed once again. But at Brora, on the estate of the Earl of Sutherland, he finally had some luck. Coal had been wrought there intermittently since the sixteenth century. Williams reckoned that the pit could become a large-scale operation with an injection of capital. Lord Kames and the Earl of Sutherland approved a loan of 1,000 pounds for "erecting machinery on precepts to be drawn by the undertaker." It was the board's boldest technological scheme in the far north. But Kames's proposal was not exactly liberal. He carefully fixed the range of the price, probably mindful that Williams's pit would have no competitors in the region. "That the price of the Coal shall not exceed 3d per ctw on the hill nor be below 2 1/2d as shall be determined by two arbiters, one to be named by the undertaker and the other by the Commissioners of the Annexed Estates." With funding in hand, Williams was able to take a lease for the mine, hire experienced colliers, build a harbor for easy export, and even add a steam engine to the operation. The coal was admittedly not of the best quality, but Williams expected that it could be of genuine benefit in burning lime, which would in turn improve soils in neighboring counties. By June 1766 he reported shipping out six hundred bolls of coal for this purpose. Yet he also complained that the local customs officers were harassing him. "I was beginning to sell coals pretty briskly since summer came in, but the custom house officers have put a full stop to my sale all at once, by seizing some boats and refusing to let others load for coasting within the limits of the customhouse, because they had not made a propper entry at Inverness." Legally, all shipborne coal had to pay a duty of five shillings, sixpence per chaldron. But Williams pleaded for an exemption while the business was still in "its infancy." Could the board intervene with the Customs Office? "A little indulgence at first might encourage the work . . . to come to a bearing." He added, more pessimistically, that the coal was probably not "capable to bear such a burden." Given the utility of cheap coal to the "landed interest," perhaps the board could extract a permanent exemption from the Customs Office? Kames had in fact already introduced the issue to the board. In July, a committee was appointed to petition the Treasury and Parliament. It announced that "the State of the Sutherland Coal" was "in danger of being crushed in its infancy by the duty exacted upon Carriage by the Officers of the Customs at the port of Inverness." But no relief was granted. By November that year, the saga took a turn toward dark comedy. The part of the mine Williams was working at Brora turned out to be highly sulfuric and therefore flammable when wet. Williams reported to the board that he had lost about two hundred pounds' worth of small coal this way. "By laying them on the hill to wait sale, they took fire of themselves, & were spoild." The only coal Williams had found in the Highlands was self-combusting! Beset by this and other difficulties, Williams was finally forced to quit Brora in 1769 at the death of the Earl of Sutherland. When Andrew Wight visited the works in 1781, he found the pit deserted.[2]

After Brora, Williams became an itinerant surveyor again for the Annexed Estates. On mission at Stratherig near Inverness in 1770, he painted a vivid portrait of his labors. "Being often in bad quarters, & generally 6 or 7 o'clock, or more before I come in from the hills, in a fever of fatigue, & when I have got some victuals, I generally go imediately to bed." This made it "very inconvenient" for Williams to keep a "Journal monthly" as the Board had requested. He added stoically: "I put down my remarks in the hills." The following year, Williams surveyed the uplands of Perthshire. In 1772, he visited the estate of Cromarty, Forres in Moray, and Kinlochmoydart, west of Inverness. But by June that year, he had to submit his report to the board "lying on the bed," having "overfatigued [himself], and brought on the piles . . . greatly distressed with this footy disorder for three weeks past." Williams did not try to conceal that his peregrinations had yielded few "valuable discoveries." All he could do was to offer "an honest account" of the poverty of the land. The board's expert witness in Edinburgh, John Clerk of Eldin, endorsed Williams's pessimism. In 1773, the fading hopes of the board came to focus on the western side of the Annexed Estates. Williams noted that there was still "reason to expect [that] valuable discoveries may be made in the west highlands, as a great many mineral appearances are seen; of which there is not the least symptom in the north." On George Clerk-Maxwell's advice, he traveled west to search for slate on the Callart estate and lead at Ardsheal. Williams could soon confirm that the Callart estate held "the best, and best colour'd slate in Scotland." It was "so very regular, and cleaves so well, that I am perswaded, slates of any dimensions may be made there." Following an earlier estate plan made by William Morison, he brought up a drain in a deep gully "in order to get into the strata of Slate at some depth." Here, he found that "the beds were grown so firm at last, as we advanced forward, that we could have begun imediately to work slate." He "caused the men [to] cleave and form some few for a trial which answered very well." Williams also observed that a group of Glasgow merchants had already contracted with Mr. Stuart in Ballachulish for a lease on the Laroch quarry with "the intention . . . to carry them all to North America" but that problems of shipping had stalled the scheme. Stuart's Laroch slate had in fact first been wrought in the 1690s. The board controlled the rival quarry on the Callart estate, which Williams thought was ready for immediate work and would employ "some of the vast numbers of superfluous hands, which the country abounds in." At Clerk's prompting, a series of advertisements were placed in the British press to attract private investment to the Ardsheal lead and Callart quarry. Unfortunately, no "adventurers" came forward to claim a lease. Williams's memorial may have helped confirm the reputation of the Ballachulish slate to a wider circle of people, but it did not succeed in establishing a successful quarry on the Annexed Estates. By January 1775, John Clerk of Eldin expressed open concern that the mineral trials had yielded such little fruit. "I am sorry to observe that tho' several Veins have been discovered and proper Trials made yet none of them has made such Appearance, as to induce any further trial in Argyleshire or Inverness-shire." In February the following year, he finally called off Williams's search: "On the whole, I am of opinion, that the Board should be at no further Expence in making Mineral Trials on the Estate of Perth, or indeed as far as I can learn at present, upon any of the Annexed Estates."[3]

Williams had failed to move the government properties in the Highlands toward a new mineral energy regime. If there was some reason in 1763 to hope that northern Scotland contained a considerable endowment of coal, such optimism seemed far less warranted at the end of Williams's odyssey. When the next great wave of Highland improvement commenced in the 1780s, the improvers took as an established point of fact that the region lacked any substantial deposits of coal. John Knox's *Tour Through the Highlands of Scotland, and the Hebride Isles* (1787) compared the coal-rich Lowlands with the fuel poverty of the north in order to attack the heavy duty on coal imposed by the Act of Union. "Those who inhabit the center, which is the most fertile and opulent part of the country, and where coal is found in abundance are in virtue of the treaty, exempted from any duty upon that necessary article." Such injustice left the region most lacking in coal to pay a tax it least could afford: "While those who inhabit the ruggid and barren extremities of the kingdom, where nature has denied coal mines, and to which the expence of water carriage from distant parts, amounts to more than the prime costs of the coals, are burdened with a duty of 5s. 4d. per chaldron." James Anderson repeated the same charge in *The Bee* and his pamphlet on the coal duties in 1792: "In Scotland, the coal countries are divided from those which have none, by stupendous mountains, through which it is impossible to carry coals by means of rivers and canals, as is done through the central counties of England. The sea is in fact the only channel through which weighty commodities can ever be carried from one part of that country to another."[4]

Coal was a central priority to the advocates of the British Fisheries Society because they saw the fuel as a basic precondition of urbanization. The third parliamentary report on the Scottish fisheries (based in part on testimony by

John Knox and James Anderson) made the point explicitly. The "natural progression" of improvement required that people move together into "close Society," but they could only "live comfortably in Towns" if they had "Coals at as moderate a Price as possible." This position was supported by local leaders in the Highlands, including Donald Macleod of Geanies, sheriff of Ross-shire, Archibald Fraser of Lovat (one of the founders of the Highland Society of Edinburgh), and the surveyor for the British Fisheries Society Robert Fraser. All three noted the importance of cheap coal as an "inducement" to attract settlers. The Highland Society of Edinburgh also took coal scarcity to be a central problem of estate improvement. One of its first essay competitions (in 1788–89) asked writers to consider peat as an alternative: "The means of supplying the want of Coal, and providing Fuel on a Highland estate, from its mosses or otherwise, with the smallest loss of time and trouble to the tenants."[5]

Coal was still very much on John Williams's mind during these years. After his survey work with the Annexed Estates had ended, he found a position as an overseer at the Gilmerton colliery outside Edinburgh, where he remained between 1778 and 1791. Evidently, this work left him plenty of time to pursue scholarly projects. Williams printed a proposal to publish a topographical map of the Scottish coal country in 1780. When nothing came out of this scheme, he moved on to propose a guide to mining technology for "Country Gentlemen" and "Coalmasters." One goal of the guide was to provide "the best history that can be procured of deserted works, which may be of singular use in future, when posterity would wish to know if such coals are worth opening and the circumstances which are for, or against it." Perhaps the fiasco at Brora lay behind this concern with reopening old mines. Certainly, Williams had not abandoned his interest in the Highlands. In the middle of the 1780s, he submitted an essay on peat as a substitute for coal in the competition of the Highland Society of Edinburgh. This essay won a medal and was later published in the society's *Transactions*. He also contributed an essay on improving Highland fisheries. But the bulk of his energies in the period were devoted to a great treatise, *The Natural History of the Mineral Kingdom*, which drew together the different strands of his interests into a natural history of coal, an introduction to mining for landowners, an attack on James Hutton's concept of deep time in favor of a biblical chronology for geology, and a polemic about the dangers of coal exhaustion to the British economy.[6]

Williams wrote in the 1787 *Prospectus* that his first aim with the work was to aid "gentlemen of landed property . . . by guarding them against imposition from ignorance or craft." He approached the Highland Society at this time, "requesting . . . aid and countenance" for his book project. Rather ecumenically, he also contacted the radical Whig Earl of Buchan and asked him to circulate copies of the book to his acquaintances: "The first volume will be generally useful to landed proprietors in mineral districts especially and as an aid to such youth as aim of acquiring mineral knowledge." Williams's work constituted a mineralogical counterpart to Denis Diderot's *Encyclopédie* and Adam Smith's *Wealth of Nations*. Guild traditions, trade secrets, and primitive "superstition" were to be banished by making knowledge a public good in the service of the enlightened elite.[7] Yet Williams undercut this conventional liberal perspective by wedding it to a new, darker vision of the natural order. Here, the experience in the Highlands seems to have played an important part. For his arguments and evidence about geological strata, Williams relied heavily on his fieldwork on the Annexed Estates. Williams's patron the Earl of Buchan noted that Williams "had made an extensive mineral survey in the Highlands of Scotland of which he had kept a Journal. From the whole mass of his Journals kept for 30 years Mr. Williams drew up his history of the Mineral Kingdom." For a book about the "immense consequence" of coal to British manufactures and prosperity, this was a curious choice. In the course of his technical argument about stratification, Williams confirmed that northern Scotland held no significant deposits of coal. The only exception was a promising seam near Castle Leod in Strathpeffer, north of Inverness, but Williams was quick to note that extraction costs would eclipse the profits at the current price of coal. His single reference to the pit at Brora concerned the tendency of this kind of coal to conflagration. Williams's account offered a blanket dismissal of the ores beyond Castle Leod: "I have seen a very small quantity of coal in some other parts of the Highlands, in small fissures of the rocks, . . . but none to be compared for quantity to that at Castle Leod." While the discussion of Highland coal was relatively brief, tucked away in the lengthy analysis of stratification—more in the nature of an embarrassed aside than a full confession—Williams in fact made the possibility of permanent scarcity of coal an integral theme of his book. Already in the *Prospectus* of January 1787, he denounced the "pernicious opinion that our coals are inexhaustible." The *Prospectus* promised "some very serious enquiries into the present state of our collieries . . ." Williams was the first major figure in British natural history to ask whether the energy regime of the nation in fact came with an expiration date. Was the predicament of the Highlands a harbinger of Britain's future?[8]

William began his argument with a scathing attack on the delusions of common sense: "I have not the smallest doubt that the generality of the inhabitants of Great Britain believe that our coal mines are inexhaustible." Against this sense of complacency, Williams warned that British consumers during the eighteenth century had depleted half of the coal ever mined in the nation.

What passed for common sense rested on a sloppy understanding of natural resources. "That the fund of coal treasured up in the superficies of the globe, for the accommodation of society, is very great, I readily acknowledge; but that it is inexhaustible, in the proper sense of the word, I deny." Williams employed his authority as a mining engineer, and his experience in prospecting to emphasize the long history of failed attempts to find coal and the precise limits of extant fields. The major coal mines in the vicinity of Newcastle were "considerably wasted." Colliers had been forced lately to dig deeper and deeper, down to 120 fathoms. Even with the help of "fire engines" the costs of extraction were bound to force a great rise in price for consumers "at no very distant period." Meanwhile, consumption was increasing annually, both in the cities and manufactures of the nation. Williams noted the prodigious use of coal in the capital: 600,000 chaldrons per annum, a figure taken from John Campbell's *Political Survey* of 1775 and thus already outdated. "The continual increase of the coal trade, and of the general use of coals, is so great," he warned, "that the one half of all the coals that were ever consumed in this island and exported from it, have been raised within the last eighty years." And since the public consumed "little coals . . . eighty years ago," this was an unnerving reminder of "how rapidly our coals are wasting." In fact, "the first beginning of the use of coal" could be dated to the end of the sixteenth century. On this time scale, the coal economy suddenly looked fragile and evanescent. Rising prices presaged "plain" and "evident" proof of a looming crisis. Williams then asked the reader to imagine the full consequences of this trend. What would happen to the flourishing economy of Britain he asked, if the coal mines were exhausted? "The prosperity and glory of this flourishing and fortunate island are at an end. Our cities and great towns must then become ruinous heaps for want of fuel, and our mines and manufactories must fail from the same cause, and then consequently our commerce must vanish. In short, the commerce, wealth, importance, glory, and happiness of Great Britain will decay and gradually dwindle to nothing, in proportion as our coal and other mines fail; and the future inhabitants of this island must live, like its first inhabitants, by fishing and hunting." Williams's apocalyptic image was remarkable for acknowledging how central coal had become in the British economy as a source of both domestic heating and manufacturing fuel. In contrast, Adam Smith's famous account of productivity in *The Wealth of Nations* was essentially preindustrial and blind to the new importance of mineral energy. Williams's conclusion was equally bold. Only a political solution could halt long-term collapse. "If our coals really are not inexhaustible, the lavish consumpt of them calls aloud for the attention of the Legislature." Williams's reviewer in the *Scots Magazine* couched the dilemma succinctly: "Private advantages cover that important object of public interest with a veil, which, in less than a century, will be torn aside . . . when there will be no remedy." Williams saw a natural world at the mercy of destructive human exploitation. The economic logic of the extractive industry ran counter to any hope of self-regulation within the natural economy. Coal stocks would not regenerate, as his reviewer observed in the *Scots Magazine*. Only political husbandry could temper the effects of exhaustion. But his notion of disaster was not simply a revival of religious apocalypse. Williams's vision of coal exhaustion extrapolated to Britain as a whole the condition of the Highland economy—a land in a "state of nature"—deprived of coal.[9]

Behind Williams's alarm was a dawning consciousness of the historical scale of mineral consumption. Williams accepted a biblical chronology for the history of the world, but he did not assume that coal was a providential gift of inexhaustible proportions. We might say that Williams's scale of "shallow time" encouraged him to recognize that coal could be used up in just a few generations. The anonymous reviewer of the book in the *Scots Magazine* in 1791 made the same point using the model of wood fuel. Coal consumption encouraged deforestation abroad: "The temporary fuel, which does not *grow*, in the bowels of the earth, is now cheaper for them than their charcoal or wood. By using it, they destroy their forests, as we have destroyed ours." But Williams's political solution to the coal crisis was not a wholesale retreat to renewable resources like wood fuel. Instead, he favored a reduction of coal exports to the Continent to maximize the advantage of coal for the British economy over the long term. Unfortunately, this also entailed a reduction in revenue for the state, since coal exports paid a duty. However, collieries in Cape Breton might compensate for the shortfall by generating new revenues. This was a form of neo-mercantilism close in spirit to the South Asian timber strategy of Henry Dundas. Colonial exploitation would supplement a strategy of internal improvement in the metropole.[10]

MOSS EXHAUSTION AND THE COAL DUTIES

The Highlands were hardly deprived of cheap fuel. There were large tracts of peat moss available for extraction. Was this a providential substitute for coal? Peat is the product of waterlogged and acidic conditions that prevent decaying vegetation from fully decomposing. The rock formations of the British uplands tend to be deficient in calcium, making local soils acidic. Such low pH levels combined with an oceanic climate pattern of high rainfall in the west favors the accumulation of peat bogs. Blanket bogs (mire) form in the uplands when soil becomes waterlogged, depleting the oxygen and inhibiting decomposition, favoring anaerobic decay. Raised bogs emerge in the Lowlands as well under similar conditions. On average, blanket bogs grow to a depth of about six to thirteen feet. In this peculiar and difficult environment, a variety of *Sphagnum* bog mosses are among the few species to thrive. These surface plants in turn feed the underlying mire when they decompose, compacting gradually into peat bogs. Over time, the layers of peat tend toward a steady state in which accumulation growth approaches zero when losses at the bottom balance additions on the surface. At present, blanket bogs cover approximately 10 percent of the land surface of Great Britain. The corresponding figure for the eighteenth century is not known but was presumably larger, since the conditions of the Little Ice Age are believed to have promoted the expansion of peat mosses in the British uplands. John Sinclair calculated that the moors, wastes, and bogs of Scotland amounted to approximately 14.2 million (Scottish) acres in 1795.[11]

Peat was highly valued by the population of the British uplands. In a land long denuded of its forests, peat served as a cheap substitute for wood fuel. Since the late Middle Ages, peat cutting had in fact been conducted on a large scale by tenants and landlords across Britain. Although far less potent in energy density than coal, peat was capable of satisfying a diverse range of economic needs. Later, peat cutting became one of the pillars of the crofting system in Highland Scotland and the Hebrides. Fraser Darling calculated that a family had to cut fifteen thousand peats per year to sustain its meager existence. But peat was not necessarily just the fuel of the poor. Historians have shown that peat served as a crucial energy source in the early modern Dutch Republic, sustaining the largest urban economy in seventeenth-century northern Europe. Could local peat deposits serve as an "inducement" to settle Highlanders in villages and towns?[12] For some improvers—notably John Walker and Archibald Cochrane—peat in fact seemed the best tool to prop up the agrarian order in the north. Both of them expected blanket peat bogs to serve as a great frontier for internal colonization and peat moss husbandry. However, they saw in peat a force of rural retrenchment and moral regeneration rather than urban growth. Other observers viewed peat not as a remedy to coal scarcity but an exacerbating problem. To make the case for lower coal duties, critics like James Anderson and Henry Gray Macnab asserted that peat mosses across Scotland were on the brink of exhaustion.

There was a grain of truth to the claim. The problem here was one of access and carriage cost. John Sinclair's *Statistical Account of Scotland* provided a large body of evidence about local shortages. In the first seven volumes alone, there were at least fifty-eight different parish reports warning of severe scarcity of peat. The complaints extended from Orkney to Angus, Perthshire, and Dumfries. Accessibility rather than overall supply was the key problem. The Reverend John Pirie in Lochlee (Angus) observed that the inhabitants in his parish "hitherto ... have been well supplied with peats; but as the mosses in several places upon the low ground, are nearly worn out, their fuel will be obtained with greater difficulty and labor, in a few years hence." High cost of transportation prohibited exploitation of "ecological slack" in the uplands. No doubt, the hills were "in many places covered with inexhaustible moss," but without "tolerable roads," they remained "at present inaccessible." Oddly, none of the reporters were struck by the patent contradiction of declaring the local supply exhausted while pretending that other sources were "inexhaustible." The Reverend Macrae in Glenshiel (Ross) made the same complaint as Pirie. "There are indeed, inexhaustible funds of moss, but so distant, either on the summits, or behind the mountains, and so inaccessible, by reason of the steepness or ruggedness of the mountains, that the most industrious have a difficulty in being supplied." The Reverend John Downie in Urray (Ross) added that the large mosses on "adjacent hills" went mostly unused because of the great distance of carriage on steep roads. There was no work so onerous to the farmers' horses "as the leading of peats." The process of local exhaustion may have been accelerated by the great fashion among improvers in the late eighteenth century to burn lime as a means of improving soil fertility. From Inveraray, the Reverend Paul Fraser reported that many of the poorer fields on the estate of the Duke of Argyll had been greatly "ameliorated ... by the vast quantities of lime annually laid upon it." But he stressed that only the rich could afford such a method of improvement, on account of the "scarcity of the fuel to burn it."[13]

Almost all these parish reports on moss exhaustion complained about the high price of coal and the heavy duty on shipborne coal. James Anderson marveled at the unanimity of complaints, all the more noteworthy since "most of these writers" were "totally unconnected ... unknown to one another;—each of whom wrote in his retired abode, the unbiased dictates of his own mind" about the "occurrences that fell under his own observation." On the whole, Anderson's observation appears just. John Sinclair had presented the clergy with more than 160 questions to answer in his *Queries Drawn up for the Purpose of Elucidating the Natural History and Political State of Scotland*, but the problems of moss exhaustion and high coal duties were broached only indirectly in a question about the type of fuel used in the parish. We seem to be dealing then with a spontaneous and uncoordinated upwelling of popular anger, widely shared by the public across Scotland. The Reverend Clouston of Cross and Burness in Orkney wrote: "Those few who can afford it, partly use coals from

Newcastle, which, by reason of the duty are dear; and therefore, they justly consider the duty as a great hardship." Because coal across Britain was taxed when carried by shipping but not over land, the duty fell very unevenly on the consumers. The poverty-stricken Highlands and Northern Isles paid as high a duty as the inhabitants of London, "while those of the rich counties of Lothian and Fife [were] exempted." A far more equitable system would be to tax coal "a farthing on the cart load, at the coal-pit," according to the Reverend Jeffray in Lochmaben (Dumfries). This would be "little felt, and easier collected," he added, generating "more money to Government than all this duty." The Reverend Lachlan McLachlan of Craignish (Argyll) also argued for a shift of the burden away from coal shipping to "an insignificant duty, laid on at the pit," where it "would be more productive, and less felt." Like Anderson and Williams, he saw cheap fuel as the precondition of Highland development. Without it, "the progress of improvement will be checked, for want of proper materials to burn lime; and manufactures, under this particular disadvantage can never flourish." This political connection between moss exhaustion and coal duties was underlined by economic preference and social bias. Many of the parish reports favored coal as a superior fuel even when moss was still available. Peat was difficult to dry out sufficiently to make it an effective fuel: "The leakiness of climate often destroys all," whereas coal provided better "firing" and did not have to be collected during the labor-intensive summer season.[14]

When the political campaign against the Scottish coal duties reached a climax in 1792 and 1793, these testimonies provided useful ammunition. James Anderson stepped into the fray in late 1792 with a pamphlet and an article in *The Bee*, which sought to take advantage of the discontentment on display in *The Statistical Account* and to harness it for his own radical aims. Anderson diverged from the parish reports by moving beyond the use of coal as a domestic heating source or fuel for burning lime. Instead, he reiterated his old hopes of introducing an advanced urban economy in the Highlands. To tax coal was to banish "manufactures for ever, from innumerable places, which possess, in every other respect, conveniencies for manufactures and for trade, that cannot be equaled in any other part of Europe." The pamphlet on the coal duties marked for Anderson not only an admission that the Highlands lacked an essential resource but a fundamental shift from his 1777 work, *Observations on the Means of Exciting a Spirit of National Industry*. Water and water-driven mills were no longer sufficient to power a future Highland manufacturing economy. Only coal could do so. We might say that the critique of the coal duties carried Anderson conceptually from the mindset of the advanced organic economy into the mineral energy regime, using the terms coined by E. A. Wrigley.[15]

Anderson was joined by Henry Gray Macnab, a medical student at the University of Edinburgh and future mining entrepreneur. Born in Northumberland but a resident of Glasgow and Edinburgh in turn, he was steeped in the same culture of improvement that shaped Williams, Anderson, and Sinclair. Macnab's *Letters Addressed to . . . William Pitt . . .* (1793) urged the abolition of the coal duties to aid improvement in Highland Scotland and elsewhere. Macnab's work supplied a veritable who's who of the Scottish Enlightenment, quoting Adam Smith, John Millar, Lord Kames, David Hume, Thomas Pennant, Sinclair's *Statistical Account*, and John Knox. In making the case for tax relief, Macnab shrewdly appealed to the minister's fondness for liberal political economy: "The observations of your favorite author, Dr. Smith, are very much in point. . . . 'Taxes upon necessaries, by raising the wages of labor, necessarily tend to raise the price of all manufactures, and consequently to diminish the extent of their sale and consumption.'" He also updated Smith's analysis of the town-country dialectic by introducing explicitly into it the political problem of coal. How could agriculture improve in the way suggested by Smith's model if manufacturers had no access to cheap fuel? But Macnab's supple rhetoric hardly made him a classical liberal. He began his screed by siding with Pitt against the "very unreasonable sentiments of Political Reform." Macnab also defended the economic rationality of the cartel governing the Newcastle coal trade, the so-called Limitation of the Vend. On the battle lines between Tory paternalism and radical Whig reform, he stood firm behind Dundas.[16]

Like Anderson, Macnab turned to the *Statistical Account* in order to argue his case for an abolition of the duties. The appendix of the book included lengthy excerpts from fifty-eight reports, spanning the first seven volumes of Sinclair's work. Macnab also used Pennant's 1772 tour to discuss the meager subsistence of the Western Isles and Knox's 1786 treatise on the fisheries to assert that the region lacked coal mines of any consequence. Sinclair's parish reports in turn suggested to Macnab that "the different substitutes for coal are *nearly exhausted*." Without cheap fuel, the native people were condemned to "emigrate, or perish for want of fuel." Macnab thus conjured up an image of population crisis in the Highlands. But this time, emigration followed from a fuel shortage rather than famine or dispossession. In Macnab's argument, cheap coal and peat were as vital to subsistence as food and drink. The coal duties had *caused* the emigration of great numbers of Britons—"even on a moderate calculation, [no] less than 100,000 souls."[17]

The question of coal widened beyond the Highland problem in the fall of 1792 when coal prices spiked in Edinburgh. Anderson's pamphlet reported that coal now sold for a shilling rather than "fivepence per cwt. the usual selling price here, till within a few months past." He attributed the rise in part to "some coal pits on the frith wearing out, or being drowned, or abandoned." Archibald Cochrane also believed that the old collieries on the Firth of Forth were close to exhaustion. But Anderson's chief explanation was that colliers had formed a combination to raise wages. The anonymous author of *Considerations on the Present Scarcity and Dearness of Coals in Scotland* also rejected the notion of dwindling supply of coal. The problem was one of scarce and unruly labor, since the mines themselves were "in a manner inexhaustible." Writing about the same issue, Henry Grey Macnab blamed the coal duties but agreed that the mines themselves were not at fault. Even if one counted only the coal mines that had already been discovered, those alone would not "be exhausted for many ages to come."[18]

It seems to have been this question of Lowland price spikes that pushed Henry Dundas into action. As a sponsor of the British Fisheries Society, he must have been aware of the effect of the coal duties in the Highlands. Though in his speech in Parliament on May 15, he did not bother to mention the north at all. Instead he spoke of the deleterious effects of the coal duties to the "labour of the people in the southern part of Scotland." During the summer months from June to August, manufactures and fisheries were neglected, as "their whole time was employed in procuring fuel from the morasses for the winter." Since the coal duty brought in virtually no revenue anyway, he suggested that it be shifted to a duty on "stills and rectified spirits." This would yield upwards of thirty thousand pounds per year and at the same time prevent the lower orders from the "excessive use of spirituous liquors." John Sinclair seconded the motion. But they encountered resistance from Sir John Henderson and other "owners of coal in Scotland," who delivered a petition against Dundas's bill on June 11. Dundas now spoke again, reminding the members of Parliament that the "enormous price of 12 shilling" for a hundredweight "excluded all the lower rank of people from the use of that indispensably necessary article." He also countered Henderson's petition with a liberal argument. Whereas Scottish coal owners might erroneously hold on to the duty as a protection of their own limited market, he pointed out that Scottish coal after an abolition of the duty might compete in England on more equal terms and upend the monopoly of the English colliers. Here, Dundas made a show of going against his own interest, since "he himself" was "a coal-owner on the firth of Forth." He also emphasized that the end of the duty opened a new market beyond the Forth "to three fourths of Scotland, which never had been open to them before." This was his only oblique reference to Highland improvement. The bill passed shortly afterward. Superficially, the abolition of the coal duty was a triumph for Anderson's liberal views. Yet it was hardly a victory for the Whig ecology underlying his politics. Instead, the reform had unleashed potent new fears about the fragility of the natural order.[19]

THE LOGIC OF EXHAUSTION

A line of warnings about coal exhaustion can be traced from John Williams to William Stanley Jevons. John Sinclair's *Statistical Account of Scotland* forecast severe limits to the Scottish coal fields in 1794. Robert Bald, Scotland's leading mining engineer and "viewer" in the generation after Williams, predicted the exhaustion of Scottish coal in an 1808 work. John Smith, the Gaelic antiquarian, urged renewed efforts of tree planting to the Highland Society of Scotland for the same reason in 1797. It was, he stressed, the only long-term solution to the lack of coal in the Highlands. Merely to lift the coal duties was not sufficient, since "from the incredible quantity of coals now consumed by machineries, some apprehend that at no distant period, coals too may become scarce, and that we ought to have some resource prepared against so great and possible a calamity." John Walker voiced similar worries in his posthumously published essays on natural history (1812). The general "diminution of coal and peat" in Scotland suggested the prudence of adopting alternative sources of fuel, perhaps in the form of fast growing firewood, like the willow tree.[20]

These worries derived much of their force from the underlying conviction that plentiful coal now formed the basis of national prosperity. When William Pitt the Younger sought to impose a new coal tax at the pit in 1784, his proposal triggered a determined opposition. Pitt wanted to shift the burden of the coal duties from coastal shipping to a more equitable tax on all coal, regardless of its origin and mode of transportation. He hoped that such a tax would prop up public revenues in the wake of the disastrous American War of Independence. Yet his modest and reasonable proposal met with a storm of protest. In the House of Commons, Pitt's critics warned that this new tax might unleash national unrest. Walter Stanhope expected a coal tax to cause "such a clamor and noise . . . as never had been occasioned . . . since the Revolution." William Conynghame thought the tax "would prove the annihilation of his country." Coal was not only the key fuel in heating houses but also a crucial energy source in the manufacturing economy. Indeed, Pitt's proposal was a precipitating cause in the formation of the first unified manufacturing lobby of Britain in 1785—the General Chamber of Manufactures. Finding "men's minds so adverse," Pitt withdrew the bill. Yet the question of coal returned to the national scene the following year, when Scottish improvers sought the abolition of the coal duties as part of the scheme to introduce fisheries in the Hebrides. Once again, cheap access to coal was linked to prosperity and industry. This reform encouraged the lobbyists for the Newcastle coal interest to demand a reduction in coal duties for England as well.[21] Another pressing problem in the period was the recurring spiking price of coal in Edinburgh and London. Were the high prices a sign of impending exhaustion? Some observers worried that high fuel prices might trigger social unrest. The situation eventually became so grave that a Select Committee of the House of Commons convened in 1800 to consider the coal trade. It heard a number of expert witnesses on how to reduce corruption and fraud within the coal industry and how to stimulate the exploitation of "inland" sources of supply beyond Newcastle. Even so, the Newcastle cartel — the so-called Limitation of the Vend — persisted for several more decades. The high duties in England also remained in place until 1831.[22]

A quick survey of the political writings of the period between Pitt's failed coal tax and the select committee on the coal trade in 1800 demonstrates that the notion of an infinite coal endowment often served as a rhetorical tool to defend a given policy, whether liberal, radical, or conservative. For example, in the 1787 debate over the Anglo-French trade treaty, the Foxite Whig William Jowett reminded his fellow MPs that Britain possessed an absolute advantage over French manufacturing. Anyone "well acquainted with [the coal] trade" knew that the British mines were "inexhaustible." No matter how large the export of coal to France, they would "last millions of years." With slightly more modesty, William Hutton's *History of Birmingham* (1781) claimed that the coal deposits that had allowed the city to grow and prosper would suffice for five thousand years. During the price spike of 1799–1800, the radical author behind the anonymous pamphlet *Cursory Remarks on Bread and Coal* repeated the populist accusation from 1793: Why should the poor people starve and freeze when providence had ordained that British coal was inexhaustible? The state must intervene to offer a just price for coal and bread in emergencies. These examples from the literature can easily be multiplied.[23]

There was thus some justice to Williams's complaint in 1789 that the public took the persistence of the national coal stocks for granted. The question for Williams and his successors was how to test the size of the coal deposits empirically. The Reverend John Thomson used a geological survey of the Lowland estates of Balgonie and Balbirnie to generalize about the future of extraction in Scotland in his parish report on Markinch for the *Statistical Account of Scotland*. Thomson warned that the coal fields in the Lowlands were generally more limited than landowners assumed. He also reiterated Williams's point about consumption: increasing demand for coal coupled with finite stock "gives reason to apprehend its being totally exhausted." Like Williams, he attacked the misplaced confidence and ill-informed views of the public. Thomson observed that ignorant strangers passing through were apt to exaggerate the extent of fields. Indeed, "the very dikes and interruptions in the bearing of the strata" were liable to increase "the deception." It is possible that he had a contemporary pamphlet about the coal supply of Edinburgh in mind here, which declared that the high price of coal in the capital had nothing to do with a genuine shortage. There was "no possibility," the anonymous author asserted, that the Scottish mines could be exhausted for "many centuries to come." But in reality, Thomson insisted, only one in fifty acres in Fife actually contained coal. . The gaze of the amateur observer tended to extend the line of seams well beyond their actual extent, creating an impression of "almost inexhaustible" deposits. Yet "what he imagined inexhaustible seams, may possibly be entirely wrought out in less than 100 years." Thomson reckoned that the history of common coal use stretched back about two hundred years and intensive extraction to the last fifty. Everywhere in Britain, the coal fields nearest the coast had already been exhausted, and many other collieries operated only at great depth by means of "fire and water engines." He also dismissed the possibility of great new stocks. "There is scarcely a seam ... of any consequence ... which has not been known to exist for half a century." Instead, Thomson estimated that the amount of coal "already wrought" was "at least equal to the quantities yet to work." Britain had, in other words, already reached peak coal. But the government and the public were "lulled into" a false sense of "security" by the concerted deception of the "proprietors." They were led only by "immediate profit" and refused to advertise any long-term limits to this vital national industry.[24]

Similar warnings surfaced in Robert Bald's work *A General View of the Coal Trade of Scotland* and William Buckland's parliamentary testimony. The force of these forecasts rested in part on empirical observations of local exhaustion but also on an idea of permanent scarcity in nature. The concept of coal as a mineral stock rather than a renewable resource had been established centuries earlier. John Baillie poked fun at the notion of regenerating coal deposits in his 1801 history of Newcastle:

> Some of our readers might possibly enquire how, and at what period of time, huge forests have been thrown many hundreds of feet into the bowels of the earth, and become carbonized there; yet the hypothesis affords some consolation to those who consider that according to the rapid manner in which the coals of this neighborhood have lately been dug up, and that, in the same ration, the coals will be completely exhausted in less than two hundred years hence, and so that rich and valuable trade be at an end; but if coals vegetate,

grow like plants, our posterity may have a fresh harvest to commence. Yet alas, we have faint hopes of such a resurrection ever taking place. Coals have been dug in this vicinity six hundred years ago, but no traces of new strata have ever been discerned.

By the late eighteenth century, the reality of finite stocks was driven home by a number of trends. Evidence of local exhaustion was not difficult to find. Already in 1765, the Duke of Bridgewater's engineer James Brindley had written about the exhaustion of collieries near Macclesfield to justify the construction of a new canal to access more distant mines. John Clerk observed that production in some mines along the Firth of Forth was faltering by 1793. Robert Bald, Scotland's leading mining engineer and "viewer" in the generation after Williams, predicted the exhaustion of Scottish coal in an 1808 work. He reported that numerous collieries in Scotland now lay "completely exhausted and silent." Writing again in 1818, Bald remained convinced that the general trend was negative and irreversible. To this palpable sense of ruin was added the assumption that future discoveries were unlikely or limited. No new fields had been developed during the eighteenth century. The shallow deposits were mostly gone already at the end of the seventeenth century. Instead, miners dug deeper in existing collieries, which raised the costs of extraction. Williams observed in the *Natural History of the Mineral Kingdom*: "Some of the coal pits of Newcastle are one hundred and twenty fathoms deep, and they have increased the powers of the fire engine so much, that it may be said it drains a river from that vast depth; but they cannot increase these powers much farther, without a considerable increase in expenses." These writers tended to see the use of steam engines to pump water out of deepening shafts not as a harbinger of utopian technological possibility but rather as clear evidence of diminishing returns due to mounting costs and difficulties of extraction.[25]

QUANTIFYING THE RESERVES

Yet the argument from local evidence and technological pessimism begged a crucial question. To counter the claim of inexhaustible coal, was it possible to establish a model for the exact duration of the British coal fields as a whole? Williams himself had acknowledged the quantitative weakness of his case: "I have no abilities for nice and extensive calculations, or what is called political arithmetic." The first attempt of this sort appears to have been made by the mining entrepreneur Henry Grey Macnab. Against the worries of "timorous minds" about exhaustion, Macnab developed a formula to establish the true scale of British coal reserves. He had two motives for this. The first was to argue that the coal industry suffered not from exhaustion but glut. Because coal was so abundant, the market tended towards excessive supply. Hence, some strictures on supply were necessary in order to prevent the larger collieries from monopolizing the market. Secondly, Macnab blamed the price spikes and suffering of the poor on the excessive tax burden laid upon Newcastle coal. Here too, he used the argument from abundance. Was there "a sufficient quantity of coal in Great Britain to warrant (consistent with sound policy) the free use of this valuable fossil"? Macnab admitted that it "would be very difficult, indeed, to ascertain, with any considerable exactness, the quantity of coal which is unworked in Great Britain." In terms of local Scottish data, he was content to cite some isolated examples from Sinclair's *Statistical Account of Scotland*. But for the Newcastle seams, he hazarded a "calculation on the ground of probability." In this way, Macnab moved away from the cornucopian logic of "infinite" supply to a precise schedule of exhaustion on a time scale beyond all reasonable worry. There was sufficient coal in Great Britain "to supply all our manufactures and domestic demands/ and our foreign exportation, for upwards of twelve hundred years, even upon a much more extensive consumption than has hitherto taken place."[26]

Macnab's model was predicated on four basic assumptions about the Newcastle coal fields. The seams of coal were "equal to a ... bed of fifteen miles by twenty miles"—three hundred square miles total. Each seam was at least four feet thick. Only a sixth of the seam must be excluded as pillars to hold up the tunnels. One cubic yard of coal weighed one ton, or "twenty hundred weights" (the London chalder was estimated at twenty-seven hundred weights). Macnab estimated that each square mile of coal seams contained approximately 3,845,000 tons. Annual consumption of Newcastle coal amounted to 3,100,000 tons. Hence, one square mile of coal field was equivalent to "a year and a quarter" of consumption. For an area of three hundred square miles, the total deposits amounted to 375 years of consumption. Macnab further assumed that consumption would rise by a fourth in the future, thus reducing the total duration of the field to three hundred years. But he then expanded his scope to include additional coal fields near Newcastle as well as the mines on the west coast near Whitehaven. On this count, there were twelve hundred years of coal in the nation. The peak of coal production was not going to arrive anytime soon.[27]

These calculations opened the door for a host of rival conjectures regarding the future of coal. In 1797, John Bailey presented his own estimate in *The General View of the Agriculture of the County of Northumberland*, a survey coauthored with George Culley and published at the behest of Sinclair's Board of Agriculture. This work was followed by competing calculations from Robert Edington, Thomas Thomson, Robert Bakewell, and others. In 1830, the Reverend William Buckland and the Reverend Adam Sedgwick offered expert testimony in Parliament regarding coal exhaustion.[28] In 1834, the leader of the Tory Party and soon to be prime minister Sir Robert Peel took up the side of the pessimists in a House of Commons speech against the abolition of the coal duties. The political economist William Stanley Jevons entered the fray with *The Coal Question* in 1865. On his count, the "average annual rate of growth of our coal consumption [at] 3 1/2 per cent" would exhaust all available reserves of coal in Britain to a depth of four thousand feet within a century. After Jevons, forecasts of resource exhaustion have become a recurring theme in conservationism, from Theodore Roosevelt to the Club of Rome and beyond. The original quarrel between Williams and Macnab lives on in present-day debates between "cornucopians" and "catastrophists."[29]

HUSBANDING THE FUTURE

Was there a remedy for coal exhaustion? Could a collapse be averted? In 1865, Jevons saw no clear alternative to coal fuel and no benefit to greater efficiency in consumption. He was resigned to the notion of British coal stock as a temporary bonanza that should be used up in a rush of glory. It was the "lavish expenditure of our material energy" that had made possible Watt's steam engine, Adam Smith's political economy, and the rise of the middle class. "We have to make the momentous choice between brief but true greatness and longer continued mediocrity." At the end of the age of manufactures was *the stationary state*, the postindustrial society characterized by material decline and moral purity. In T. B. Macaulay's image, made famous by Gustave Doré's 1870 print, visitors would one day survey the ruins of Victorian London: "Some traveler from New Zealand shall, in the midst of a vast solitude, take his stand on a broken arch of London bridge to sketch the ruins of St. Paul's."[30]

For Williams and his generation, the remedy was quite different. Rather than seeing coal exhaustion as a grand show of liberal self-combustion, they tended to view the threat as an incentive for the landed interest to consolidate its control of natural resources. The Board for the Annexed Estates, which employed John Williams on mineral surveys of the Highlands, was dedicated to reforming land use in the region and setting an enlightened example for both proprietors and tenants. Williams's claim to guard "gentlemen of landed property ... against imposition from ignorance or craft" must be read as a project of agrarian enlightenment. By making mineral knowledge public, he wanted to reform the environmental vision of proprietors, protecting it from rent-seeking conmen and short-sighted greed. This involved an element of practical education as well: Williams encouraged "young gentlemen" to seek out the locations he described in order to see for themselves the truth of his assertions. Robert Bald's work on the coal trade followed a similar model. Bald dedicated his work to John Francis Erskine, proprietor of the Alloa collieries (Seventh Earl of Mar in 1824). He praised the writings of another mine owner, Archibald Cochrane, the Earl of Dundonald, as a fellow reformer of the coal trade. Crucially, Dundonald in turn went on to articulate an archconservative critique of urban life and the vices of manufacturing towns. Dundonald exhorted landowners to exercise their moral authority as guardians of the rural order and social stability. In the same spirit, Bald's warning about shortages encouraged every "patriotic statesman" to protect the national deposits of coal from the ravages of short-sighted greed. Likewise, the husbandry of coal recommended by the Reverend John Thomson in Sinclair's *Statistical Account* was part of a larger project of national self-sufficiency and agrarian patriotism.[31]

While these writers shared a common allegiance to the landed interest, they did not agree on a precise policy of conservation. Williams favored limits on exports to Europe together with duties on New World coals. Bald encouraged export duties to block the drain of British coal to the Continent. He hoped that these limitations would help channel Scottish coal to the peripheries of the nation. Like Thomson, he also emphasized that internal improvement, particularly of the Highlands, might offer a means toward greater self-sufficiency. In John Walker's view, the long-term remedy for coal exhaustion was to switch back to renewable kinds of fuel. Fast-growing wood like the willow tree provided the principal firing in parts of England. John Smith, the Gaelic antiquarian, urged the members of the Highland Society of Scotland to renew efforts of tree planting for the same reason. It was, he stressed, the only realistic solution to the lack of coal in the Highlands since so much of the fuel was now consumed by "machineries" in the rest of the island that coal might soon become scarce everywhere. But these differences of opinion were essentially quibbles over means, not a fundamental difference of social allegiance. For all of these observers, the threat of exhaustion served as a clarion call to unite landowners and politicians in unified action.[32]

8

OVERPOPULATION AND EXTIRPATION

In the early phase of Spanish expansion, a "colony of goats"—one male and one female—was introduced to the small island of Juan Fernandez in the eastern Pacific, according to the Reverend Joseph Townsend. The story of this miniature empire appeared in a curious tract on political economy entitled *A Dissertation on the Poor Laws* (1786). In the absence of predators and with lush island grasses to graze, the couple found it easy to obey the first commandment, "till . . . they had replenished their little island." When the population reached the limits of pasture capacity, "the weakest first gave way" so that "plenty was again restored." From this moment on, the goats of Juan Fernandez "fluctuated between happiness and misery . . . according as their numbers were diminished or increased." The population was "never at a stay" but "nearly balancing at all times their quantity of food." It found a "degree of aequipoise" that was only disturbed "from time to time" by the outbreak of disease or the "arrival of some vessel in distress." Such temporary setbacks were quickly endured: "the survivors never failed immediately to meet returning plenty." But Townsend then introduced a second population into his story. When English privateers threatened to make use of the livestock for provisions, the Spanish commanders "resolved on the total extirpation of the goats" and let loose a pair of greyhounds on the island. These dogs quickly multiplied. Only the refuge of high and rocky ground saved the goats from extermination. "None but the most watchful of the dogs" could now eat goat meat. A "new kind of balance" was thus established. "The weakest of both species were among the first to pay the debt to nature." Here, Townsend turned from natural history to political economy. This was not a story told merely to please the reader's thirst for travelers' tales. The material basis of the island's natural economy—the "quantity of food" available—also regulated the number of the human species in every nation. Moreover, the pressures brought by animal instincts—high rates of procreation and ruthless competition for resources—were the same for human populations. Great

Britain was Juan Fernandez writ large. Worst afflicted of all British regions were the Highlands of Scotland. Here the population was precariously close to the limits of subsistence: "The numbers never fail: the supply is constant."[1]

Townsend's *Dissertation* was only one in a long succession of thought experiments about population growth. Benjamin Franklin's essay of 1779 imagined a world wiped clean of all other plants and animals, harboring only a single species. He picked the garden plant fennel to play the protagonist in this scenario. Even the innocuous fennel could become a hegemonic biological force under the right circumstances. Without any apparent sense of irony, the American patriot suggested that a world empty of all other people could "be replenished from one nation only, as for instance, with Englishmen." Powerful images of nature thus intruded on political economy to suggest that biological phenomena and physical limits regulated the basic features of societies. The project of Enlightenment was acquiring a carrying capacity. Townsend's goat island and Franklin's imperial fennel were both taken up by T. R. Malthus in *An Essay on the Principle of Population* (1798, second edition 1803). Malthus's work in turn helped nurture a growing conviction among Scottish proprietors, savants, and politicians that the Scottish Highlands was the nursery of the largest "redundant population" in Britain. This new brand of population politics served to justify a pattern of systematic clearance and assisted emigration from the 1820s onward.[2]

Townsend's story opens a window on two neglected dimensions of the Scottish Enlightenment. What function did islands play in political economy? How did natural histories of biological invasion shape enlightened thought? As we shall see, the models and images suggested by natural history darkened the tenor of political economy considerably in the decades between Smith's *Wealth of Nations* (1776) and Malthus's *Essay on the Principles of Political Economy* (1798). Worries about overpopulation shaped not only the trajectory of demographic pessimism in liberal thought but also more conservative strains of the Scottish Enlightenment. For improvers like George Dempster and Hugh Rose, however, overpopulation was a problem of social change rather than a biological inevitability. They used the notion of extirpation — another concept widespread in natural histories of biological invasion — to explore the danger posed by sheep farming to the future of Gaelic society. But even this optimism was inflected with a new sense of natural limits and demographic pressure. War and dearth made wasteland colonization a national project subject to precise quantitative estimates in the 1790s. What had once appeared an open frontier now increasingly looked like a shrinking margin. Threatened with invasion without and famine within, Britain during the French Revolutionary Wars of the 1790s began to seem a rather small island.

ISLAND STRAINS

In *A Dissertation on the Poor Laws* (1786), the English clergyman Joseph Townsend achieved the dubious distinction of characterizing for the first time the problem of poor relief in terms of the demographic dynamics of colonial livestock. Townsend was the son of an English linen manufacturer. He studied medicine in Edinburgh under William Cullen in the early 1760s and then served briefly in 1769–70 as a chaplain to the Third Duke of Atholl, accompanying him on the Grand Tour. He settled afterward in the vicarage of Pewsey, Wiltshire, where he wrote a great variety of pamphlets and books, ranging over medicine, political economy, and natural history, including an account of his journey to Spain, a Vade Mecum, and a natural history of the Deluge based on his large collection of fossils. He was also an early champion of William Smith's pioneering work to map Britain's geological strata and mineral resources.[3]

A Dissertation on the Poor Laws took direct aim at Scottish agrarian patriotism. Townsend was not impressed with the optimistic arguments for agricultural improvement and wasteland reclamation. Against Lord Kames's assertion that "a nation can scarce be too populous for husbandry," Townsend objected: "but is it not clear, that when all that is fertile has been cultivated to the highest pitch of industry, the progress must of necessity be stopped." Following Benjamin Franklin and Adam Smith, he noted that the American population had doubled every twenty-five years while the European growth rate was slower, doubling once every five hundred years. He then identified two distinct types of demographic traps in which population growth pressed against the "utmost limits" of food production. In China, the population was saved from famine only by the high productivity of rice and the practice of infanticide. In the Highlands, the great flow of emigrants preserved the country from disaster. Even the most severe frugality and unremitting labor could not make the soil of northern Scotland more fertile. At the same time, Townsend downplayed fears of catastrophic collapse in favor of a "soft" model of emigration: "They do not issue forth . . . like swarms from the northern hives of old . . . but like the silent dew, they drop upon the richest pastures." Because the outward movement was so gradual, the population at home could continuously replenish itself without suffering irreversible decline. It is possible that Townsend's notion of a slow and voluntary drain of people was prompted by his experience as a chaplain to the Duke of Atholl. Although the third duke was pursuing commercial improvements of various kinds, including sheep farms, there is no evidence of systematic clearances. On the contrary, the duke's paternalist approach seems to have made him popular with tenants. At his funeral in 1774, a Gaelic lament was performed to express the grief and loyalty of the common people.[4]

Townsend's equanimity ultimately flowed from his faith in the self-regulating character of demographic change. To explain the futility of the English Poor Laws, Townsend turned to natural history. Human behavior mapped directly on the instincts of animals and plants. Metaphorical animals had been used frequently before in political economy. The Marquis de Mirabeau observed in *L'ami des hommes* (1756): "People multiply like rats in a barn, if they have the means to subsist." Smith wrote in *The Wealth of Nations*, "Every species of animals naturally multiplies in proportion to the means of their subsistence, and no species can ever multiply beyond it."[5] But Townsend's model moved beyond such commonplaces to the biological processes observed by natural historians. In the technical terms of modern evolutionary biology, Townsend's "colony of goats" underwent an ungulate irruption. Island environments have allowed population ecologists to analyze the elements of this phenomenon in detail. When herbivores like deer, bison, sheep, cattle, or goats are introduced into conditions of abundant food supply, the population can grow far beyond the number needed to replace it in the next generation. The animals continue to "increase exponentially until they overshoot the capacity of the plant communities to sustain them (the carrying capacity)." This explosion in numbers is then followed by a population crash until the animal population reaches the level of available subsistence. Grasses or other herbs in turn fluctuate depending on the pressure of herbivore consumption. While early modern observers did not possess the technical vocabulary of ecology or evolutionary biology to analyze the process, they were nevertheless quite familiar with the phenomenon. William Robertson described the astonishing multiplication of feral livestock on the great plains of Argentina: "In this rich pasturage, the horses and cattle imported by the Spaniards from Europe have multiplied to a degree which almost exceeds belief." Adam Smith suggested that such explosions in fact were widespread on the frontiers of the New World: "In all new colonies the great quantity of waste land, which can for many years be applied to no other purpose but the feeding of cattle, soon renders them extremely abundant, and in every thing great cheapness is the necessary consequence of great abundance." Not surprisingly, Smith was particularly interested in the effect of ungulate irruptions on prices: "Though all the cattle of the European colonies in America were originally carried from Europe, they soon multiplied so much there, and became of so little value, that even horses were allowed to run wild in the woods without any owner thinking it worthwhile to claim them." Pehr Kalm's famous account of colonial husbandry reported that great numbers of roaming cattle on the American frontier prevented the introduction of good agricultural practice by extirpating the annual grasses. Smith took a more optimistic line than Kalm by stressing that good husbandry would follow automatically as soon as a market in beef emerged in the colonies. The large herds might in fact whet the appetites of settlers for cheap meat and therefore set in motion the process of agricultural improvement on the periphery.[6]

Ungulate irruptions on islands were also well known to early modern observers. In the sixteenth century, Spanish sailors introduced livestock to islands across the Atlantic and Pacific. The hope was to facilitate long-distance travel with such wandering larders of animal protein. Spanish ships would make landfall as needed to resupply. Yet the introduction of new species often led to "wild ecological oscillations." On the island of Porto Santo in the eastern Atlantic, a wayward band of rabbits managed to sabotage the whole enterprise of colonization. A contemporary observer reported that the rabbits had "overspread the land" and devastated the vegetation "so that our men could sow nothing that was not destroyed by them." Eventually, the rabbits forced the human settlers to evacuate completely. Closer to home, tales of rat invasions and rabbit infestations circulated in the Hebrides. The precarious community on the rocky outcrop of North Rona in the Outer Hebrides was destroyed by famine after rats suddenly appeared and consumed all the crops, according to Martin Martin.[7]

Townsend's natural history of the goats on Juan Fernandez claimed the authority of well-known travelers like William Dampier, William Funnell, and Antonio Ulloa. Karl Polanyi long ago revealed the liberty that Townsend had taken with these accounts. The story of the boom in greyhound numbers on Juan Fernandez could not be traced back to any of the sources. This showed that Townsend's "paradigm" was indifferent to questions of evidence. The island functioned merely as a myth of natural capitalism, a way of disconnecting market exchange from its social logic. We can certainly question Townsend's claim to derive moral authority from natural history for his political economy. But we should not dismiss so quickly his genuine interest in ungulate irruption or the historical roots of the phenomenon. We might in fact trace the greyhound example back to an authentic case, albeit in a different decade and ocean. Spanish conquistadors apparently introduced greyhounds to the island of La Palma in the eastern Atlantic in 1591 as a means of controlling a booming population of wild asses. Townsend was not in the business of writing pure fiction so much as compiling selective and synthetic natural history. The same argument also applies to the link between Juan Fernandez and Daniel Defoe's *Robinson Crusoe*. We know that Defoe borrowed the story of Alexander Selkirk's castaway life on Juan Fernandez for his account of Crusoe's self-provisioning. It is clear from the original biography of Selkirk that the goat population of the island furnished his one-man colony with subsistence, clothing, and shelter.[8]

Part of the attraction of the island model was the ease with which it could be integrated into conjectural history. Directly after the discussion of the ungulate irruption, Townsend merged his demographic account with the Scottish theory of stages of development. The island became a forest. Spatial limits were transposed onto a temporal schema. "In the woods, and in the *savage state*, there can be few inhabitants." The upper limit of population was set in each stage by the mode of subsistence: hunting, herds, agriculture, and trade. But even in the forest, there was sufficient ecological slack for the population of savages to grow: "As long as food is plenty they will continue to increase and multiply." Because the shift from one stage to another was driven by this population growth, historical progress was the product of collective agency beyond the power of individual will or reason. Humanity was as much a biological and demographic phenomenon as the goat population on Juan Fernandez. Even at the highest stage, there was no escape from the fundamental dilemma of the limits on the food supply. In this sense, each stage corresponded to an increasingly large island. The strongest members of society lived well while the weak found only precarious subsistence or worse. For Townsend, the model of Juan Fernandez thus scaled up to the level of the nation and perhaps even the planet.[9]

In T. R. Malthus's work, this dark version of island exemplarity provided the conceptual foundation for his famous theory of population growth. By way of a thought experiment about the island of Britain, Malthus suggested in *An Essay on the Principle of Population* that constraints on agricultural productivity imposed permanent limits on the number of inhabitants the nation could sustain. It was possible to imagine agricultural improvement keeping pace with population growth for a generation, but after that the exponential rate of human growth must outpace every improvement in food production. Malthus, too, used the analogy of animal reproduction to capture this relentless drive. "Through the animal and vegetable kingdoms, nature has scattered the seeds of life abroad with the most profuse and liberal hand." The same "law of nature" applied to people as well as animals. A population was first and foremost a biological force occupying a finite physical space. Even if "every acre of land in the island" was transformed into "a garden," there was always a ceiling to growth. Malthus predicted that the moment of crisis was no more than fifty years' distant in Britain. Assuming a population of seven million for the island in the present (it was in fact over ten million in 1801), he allowed that the number could be doubled to fourteen million by 1823 but refused to believe that sufficient subsistence could be found for twenty-eight million in 1848. Although Malthus revised his starting figure to eleven million in the second edition of the *Essay* (1803), he maintained the same dismal ratio between food supply and population growth. Throughout his argument in both editions, Malthus stressed the continuity between the island case and the carrying capacity of the planet. The same limits must logically apply to the "whole earth." Though Malthus admitted that a planetary crisis was unlikely to occur anytime soon with so "many parts of the globe . . . hitherto uncultivated, and almost unoccupied."[10]

For the second edition of the *Essay* in 1803, Malthus tempered his original pessimism by exploring the power of moral restraint to curb sexual instinct. This growing concern with the "preventive check" pushed him toward a geography of overpopulation. Malthus now added a wealth of historical and statistical data to illustrate his thesis. Amid this great profusion of dismal examples, the Scottish Highlands served for Malthus as the worst case of moral failure in the nation, "probably more redundant in population than any other part of Great Britain." To bolster this claim, he compared Charles Webster's 1755 census of Scotland with the information provided by John Sinclair's *Statistical Account of* Scotland and the first nationwide census of 1801. Thanks to these sets of demographic data, Malthus arrived at a quantitative estimate of prevailing population trends. Sinclair's parish-level perspective seemed to Malthus especially persuasive. Demographic strain was most evident in a discrete local population. Malthus used Sinclair's surveys to stress the fecundity of Scottish women (six to seven children per marriage), the great subdivision of land in the Western Isles and parts of the Highlands, the frequent occurrence of famine in the region, particularly the devastation of 1782–83, and the high rates of emigration. Perhaps nowhere in the region was this fecundity in greater evidence than in "the island of Jura," which Malthus found "absolutely overflowing with inhabitants in spite of constant and numerous emigrations." Such a "swarm of people" was useless to the proprietor. Quarff in Shetland was overcome with poverty and distress on account of the great subdivision of land. Few families owned a plow. The mainland, too, was beset with such difficulties. Duthil in Moray witnessed an "extraordinary" birthrate of one birth per twelve inhabitants annually. The village of Callander in Perthshire was full of "naked and starving people."[11]

Though Malthus recognized that human beings had the ability to check the sexual instinct through the force of reason, this distinction made the case of the Highlands especially invidious. Precisely such powers of foresight seemed to be in short supply among plebeian Gaels. Their rates of reproduction resembled more the "constant tendency in all animated life to increase beyond the nourishment provided." It is hardly a coincidence that Malthus added several admiring comments about Townsend's *Dissertation on the Poor Laws* in his second edition of the *Essay*. Townsend's views of Highland sexuality seem to have done a great deal to shape Malthus's understanding of the region. Gaels proliferated like goats. They had become pests in their own country.[12]

ANGLO-SAXONS, NORWAY RATS, AND THE NEW JERSEY PEASE BEETLE

The stark numbers of Scottish historical demography might suggest that Townsend and Malthus were merely recording physical facts. Between 1750 and 1800 the population rose 34 percent in the Scottish Highlands and Western Isles, to reach a total of 300,000. This spurt was followed by further growth of 53 percent between 1800 and 1841. The population explosion was particularly sustained and spectacular in some of the island parishes of the Hebrides. The Isle of Skye increased from 13,000 in 1772 to 23,000 in 1841. Harris, North Uist, and South Uist doubled their population. Tiree's population stood at 1,500 in 1747 but rose to 4,453 in 1831. The social historians Eric Richards and Michael Flinn have concluded that the Highland region "fell into a Malthusian trap" during the late eighteenth century. Yet such demographic reductionism arguably assumes an overly simple relation between environment, society, and population. At the same time that Townsend was applying his brand of natural history to the Scottish Highlands, other improvers began to articulate a social critique of demographic determinism. Could overpopulation have been a function of land use, property relations, and state policy rather than inadequate food production?[13]

Goats and fennel were not the only animals and plant species to enter political economy in the late Enlightenment. Cheviot sheep provided the raw materials for an alternative model of demography. Beginning in the 1760s, more and more Scottish Highland estates converted to sheep farming. Gradually, new sheep breeds spread north and westward. The shift ushered in dizzying increases in rental value. A landlord could double the value of his estate by converting from stocks of cattle to sheep. During the French Revolutionary and Napoleonic Wars, wool prices and rents shot up further. It is estimated that wool prices rose some 250 to 400 percent between 1800 and 1820. Yet these profits came at a steep social cost. The numerous tenants and subtenants who lived on the Highland estates now competed with Cheviot sheep for the best land and attention of the proprietor. A growing number of Scottish savants sought to mobilize public opinion and politicians to protect the human population against dispossession and emigration.[14]

The social problem of sheep farming was articulated in the startling language of "extirpation." In a prescient letter from 1784, the Forfarshire and Sutherland landowner George Dempster warned Henry Dundas that Gaelic people were on the verge of vanishing as a race. Other improvers like Hugh Rose and John Walker seconded this view. The concept of extirpation had been used by Scottish savants such as William Robertson, Lord Kames, and John Millar to explain the disappearance of ancient peoples or populations in overseas colonies. But it was also employed by natural historians in describing processes of biological invasion, environmental degradation, and campaigns of pest management. Since the early part of the century, a great war had been raging across Britain between rival rodents. Once the haunt of the common or black rat, the island now saw growing numbers of Norway or brown rats spread from ships and ports into the interior. By the 1770s, the naturalist Thomas Pennant predicted that the foreign invader was likely to win the war and destroy the native population. Extirpation apparently went hand in hand with commerce and improvement. Would this be the fate of Scottish Gaeldom as well?

To *extirpate* in the concrete silvicultural sense was to clear stumps or pull up roots. But this meaning was frequently extended to the destruction of an entire animal, plant, or human population. It was also applied to the suppression of a heretical belief or a contagious fancy, as in Henry Dundas's complaint that the "spirit" of emigration in the Highlands could not easily be "extirpated." Finally, extirpation might signify the annihilation of a particular elite group or the fall from power of a dynasty.[15]

Enlightenment savants were quite well acquainted with the possibility of murdering entire human populations. The Old Testament provided several examples of tribes and cities destroyed by a vengeful God and his chosen people (for example, in Exodus 23:22). The pagan classics, too, discussed brutal campaigns of depopulation, including the destruction of Melos in Thucydides and Caesar's war against the Helvetii. Hume's *History of England* (volume 1, 1762) described the Anglo-Saxon invasion of Britain as a genocidal event. When the native Britons refused to submit to the Saxons, the invaders adopted a policy of "total extermination" as their "sole expedient for providing a settlement and subsistence to the new planters." Similar violence was recorded by Scottish historians who believed that the ancient Picts had been massacred by invading Scots. Such slaughter continued in the Middle Ages, according to Hume, when the Cathars were destroyed by the Albigensian Crusaders. John Millar in turn noted that the Moors in Granada had been "entirely extirpated" by the Spanish conquerors. Most recently, the history of New World colonization offered evidence of a staggering demographic collapse from epidemics and violence.

William Robertson's *History of America* charted the near depopulation of the two continents after the arrival of European forces. The Abbé Raynal blamed the conquistadors, who, "intoxicated with ... success, ... resolved to extirpate the people they had plundered." Lord Kames instead stressed the appalling mortality of smallpox, which had decimated the Hottentots, Greenlanders, and Laplanders by two-thirds. He predicted that the same disease would soon "extirpate the natives of North America" if its virulence did not abate.[16]

In the Scottish Enlightenment, the question of extirpation acquired an overt political resonance through Hume's attack on the idea of the ancient constitution. In *The History of England*, Hume rejected the notion of an unbroken tradition of English liberty from the Saxons over the Normans to the Glorious Revolution. In order to deny this continuity, Hume pursued a double line. On the one hand, he claimed that the Saxons were a savage and brutal people who lacked genuine freedom. On the other hand, he argued that Saxon society began and ended in a bloodbath. By wiping out the native Britons, the Saxons had blocked the civilizing influence of Roman Britain and the possibility of a strong central state: "As the Saxons exterminated, rather than subdued the ancient inhabitants, they were indeed transplanted into a new territory, but preserved unaltered all their civil and military institutions." Hence, the Saxon government was weak and "justice was commonly very ill administered, [so that] great oppression and violence seem to have prevailed." The majority of the Saxon people did not enjoy "true liberty." Hume continued his attack on the ancient constitution by emphasizing the violent break between the Saxons and the Normans. "It would be difficult," he wrote, "to find in all history a revolution more destructive, or attended with a more complete subjection of the antient inhabitants." In pursuit of political stability, William the Conqueror laid waste to Northumberland, killing a hundred thousand people, and then proceeded to confiscate the estates of the entire Saxon elite. William's "declared intention was to depress or rather entirely extirpate the English gentry."[17]

In natural history, extirpation carried multiple meanings. One was agricultural: extirpation was hailed as a crucial technique of managing livestock, pests, and weeds. Another was historical: "extirpation" here registered changes over time in biodiversity. A third meaning was theological: this version of the concept acted as a conceptual block against the notion of absolute extinction. Where Hume's civil history was punctuated by the convulsions of mass murder, the natural history of animals and plants in the Enlightenment began with an assumption of divine design and balance. At the level of species, naturalists denied the possibility of wholesale extinction until Georges Cuvier published his paper on the comparative anatomy of elephants in 1796. Linnaeus's dissertation on "The Economy of Nature," translated into English by Benjamin Stillingfleet, was typical in this respect. The Swedish botanist observed that even the most ferocious predator could not "destroy whole species." God had "circumscribed" the expansion of every animal and plant "within certain bounds." Predators were fewer in number than the prey they hunted. The proliferation of plants was constrained by herbivores of different kinds. The caterpillar was "formed in order to keep a due proportion between [meadow grasses] and other plants." If God had not designed the caterpillar, these grasses would "increase to that degree, that they exclude all other plants; which would consequently be extirpated, unless this insect sometimes prepared a place for them." Similar arguments were promoted by Linnaeus's Scottish popularizer, John Walker, who also rejected the notion of species extinction in his lectures at the University of Edinburgh. God had fixed the number of species at Creation: "There is no example of a Species of Animal being intirely lost, though they may be extinguished in a particular Tract of Country." Serious disruptions in the divine economy were impossible. This commonplace of orderly interdependence provided a foundation for the liberal thought experiment of Townsend and Malthus.[18]

Yet evidence of environmental degradation and biological invasion presented savants with uncanny variations on Hume's dark civil history. Reports from the New World included not just stories of human depopulation but also the decimation of native species and the intrusion of unwanted pests from the Old World. Linnaeus's disciple Pehr Kalm collected testimony from American settlers to the effect that the abundance of wildlife had dropped greatly in just a generation or two. In one passage we have already discussed, Kalm described the severe impact of free-range grazing on local annual grasses. Other observers worried about insect invasion. During the late 1770s, wheat fields on farms near New York were destroyed by the sudden appearance of a new insect (the gall midge, *Mayetiola destructor*). American naturalists blamed it on the arrival of British troops and called it the Hessian fly. The origin of the insect is shrouded in obscurity; most likely it arrived in North America from western Asia with grain transports via southern Europe. It seems to have been unknown in Britain until this time. In fact, Sir Joseph Banks led a coordinated campaign to block American wheat imports into Britain during the 1780s for fear that the insect might be released there, too.[19]

The biogeography of the British Isles offered plentiful evidence of extirpation in the historical past. Thomas Pennant's *British Zoology* (1768–71) and *Arctic Zoology* (1784–85) recorded more than half a dozen cases of the disappearance or *near* disappearance of native species, including the beaver, wolf, wild boar, bear, and auroch in the first group and the weasel and common rat in the second. Pennant gave more or less exact dates for each extirpation. The wild cattle (*Urus*, or auroch) had vanished around the year 1466. Wolves were not "wholly extirpated" from North Britain until 1680. And so forth. John Walker added to Pennant's list a species of deer, "exterminated . . . three or four hundred years ago," whose horns were still to be found across Scotland. The story of the wild cattle or auroch presented perhaps the clearest case of historical extirpation across Europe. In antiquity, the species had been widespread from Macedonia to Germania, as testified by Pliny, Caesar, and Strabo, among others. In the eighteenth century, wild cattle remained only in the most remote hinterlands of the Continent, in the Lithuanian forests and Carpathian Mountains. Such a drastic fall in the population of a species was not confined to the distant past. Natural historians and agricultural improvers actively promoted the extirpation of predators and weeds. Hugh Rose's memorandum to the Countess of Sutherland on estate improvement encouraged her and other landowners in the county to destroy foxes and eagles as a preliminary step toward commercial pasturage. "A great part of Sutherland is well calculated for feeding moderate stocks of sheep," he observed. But first, all the predators must be removed. Vermin had been "driven from other counties"—"why not extirpate them here also?"[20]

Not every kind of extirpation served an obvious purpose in the natural economy. Pennant's *British Zoology* recorded an ongoing process of biological invasion in his account of the war between the Norway rat (*Rattus norvegius*, brown rat) and the common rat (*Rattus rattus*, black rat). The Norway rat had arrived in Britain only forty years ago but had already "quite extirpated the common kind." Pennant claimed that it had also reached America by way of a ship from Antwerp. Other sources corroborate Pennant's estimate, dating the spread of the species in the New World to the period after 1755. The natural order at home, it seemed, was as much an artifact of colonizing pressures as that of the New World. The Norway rat spread rapidly in Europe and North America from the eighteenth century and today is the dominant species on both continents. While few people in eighteenth-century Britain mourned the disappearance of the wolf from the island, there was no apparent profit or moral lesson in the war between the brown and black rats.[21]

In his unpublished treatise *The Elements of Agriculture*, the naturalist James Hutton wrestled with the problem of diseases and pests that damaged crops. The last few decades had seen several examples on both sides of the Atlantic, including "the destruction occasioned in the West India islands, first from the small ant, and now from the borer," "the infectious disease among the horned cattle in some parts of Europe," Mr. Marshman's turnip caterpillar in Norfolk—and the black caterpillar in Mid-Lothian. (Hutton did not mention the Hessian fly.) Not all these pests were permanent threats. Hutton observed that the fir caterpillar, so destructive in the pine plantations of the Earl of Leven many years ago, was now little heard of, even though it was still manifestly present in Scottish plantings. "There would seem to be a remedy variously contrived in nature against the excessive multiplication of any particular species." But this consolation went only so far. Hutton admitted that nature had offered no cure for other pests. In America, Kalm's beetle had greatly diminished the cultivation of pease in New Jersey. Meanwhile, Old World agriculture was still haunted by the old fashioned scourge of the locust. "This animal no doubt is fit to desolate a province, and to extirpate any species of plant that were peculiar to one country." Since Hutton had no stomach for biblical notions of divine retribution, he resorted to the idea that there were aspects of that natural order which lay beyond human utility: "Partial desolation is required occasionally in nature, and in the extirpation of one species, another which was before oppressed, naturally succeeds." Such was the "system of nature"—"whatever judgment we may pass upon [it]." In such violent changes, there was "no evil in relation to the whole, nor any error in relation to that system; one which has for principle, to sustain a living World."[22]

In theory, the kingdoms of plants and animals were as orderly as James Hutton's geological cycles of soil formation. His "Theory of the Earth" justified uplift and erosion in deep time as the source of soil formation and hence human agriculture. But even Hutton found it difficult to cast the locust as the necessary emissary of agrarian capitalism. Something inhuman seemed to lurk within the structure of the "living World." The reason for the existence of the locust was obvious only to divine intelligence. In practical terms, this meant that ecological exchange was fraught with danger. Diseases might be "introduced unwarily with a freight seed or breed." Hutton repeated the story of Kalm's close call with the pease beetle. On his return to Sweden in August 1751 after the American voyage, Kalm unpacked a paper that contained sweet peas which he had collected in the New World. To his horror, he found "all the peas hollow, and the head of an insect peeping out of each." Some of them "even crept out, in order to try the weather of this new climate." Terrified, Kalm understood "at once" "the whole damage, which my dear country would have suffered, if only two or three of these noxious insects had escaped." With the sangfroid of the expert bug squasher, "he made haste, to shut the paper again" and thus averted an invasion. In hindsight, Kalm reflected that the beetles probably could not have survived the cold winter of Sweden. Yet the general lesson still seemed clear. In

Hutton's words, "the Guardians" of every nation must attend to future threats quickly, using their expertise in natural history to neutralize them, or else "such beginning evils" might "thro ignorance . . . be suffered to increase" and beget a "calamity."[23]

THE SHEEP FRONTIER

Southern sheep breeds first appeared in the Highlands after the middle of the eighteenth century. They made their way north from bridgeheads in Easter Ross, Argyll, and Perthshire. The retired army office Sir John Lockhart Ross of Balnagowan pioneered the removal of tenants in favor of sheep in Easter Ross after 1770. Joseph Townsend's patron the Third Duke of Atholl set up sheep farms near Blair Atholl. Similar changes were also taking place in the parish of Morvern. The first breed to cross the Highland divide seems to have been the Blackfaced kind, originally from the Scottish Borders. It was accompanied by farmers from the same region with the requisite knowledge. This compact black–and–white-colored sheep had been bred to withstand the rigors of outdoor pasture the year round. In contrast, the old native breeds of the Highlands were relatively sensitive to inclement weather and had to be housed indoors at night. Once the Blackfaced sheep had been introduced in the north, they were thus poised to proliferate rapidly and overtake the native kinds. They were equally a threat to Gaelic plebeians, since they generated far more rent then the human tenants. In the 1780s, the spread of the Blackfaced breed was leading to clearances on a "new scale," according to Eric Richards. George Dempster reported to Henry Dundas that 3,000 Highlanders had emigrated in the summer of 1783. Several hundred people migrated from the estate of Macdonnell after a sheep farm was established there. A granddaughter of Macdonnell worried that the entire country would be "converted into a sheep walk." "I fear that the sheep that can be introduced and reared will form in their stead but a sorry defence against our enemies."[24]

By the 1790s, the new breed in fashion was the Cheviot, which combined the hardiness of the Blackfaced with short-cropped wool more suited to the demand of the wool manufactures. When Henry Dundas solicited information on the causes of Highland emigration in 1803, his adviser E. S. Fraser responded with a dismal lesson in sheep geography. He described a veritable invasion of Blackfaced and Cheviot sheep across the entire region:

> All the Braes of Perth, Dumbarton and Argyle adapted to Sheep—the whole west coast from Oban to Loch Broom, in general and great part of Mull—are

under Sheep. In Skye there are some, and more fast introducing. In Lewis they are now introduced. In Inverness Shire—Sheep extend further inland from the West Coast than by a line with Fort Augustus to the South and North boundaries of the shire. In Ross, and Northwards all parts capable of sheep are or will soon be so occupied. I have not a doubt, from what is now passing in the Setts of Great Estates—that the whole race of Highlanders will in a very few years, be extinguished: and the Sheep come down to the East, as well as West, and North Coasts.[25]

George Dempster warned Dundas about the peril of sheep farming as early as November 1784. A long standing MP for the Perth burghs, Dempster was an occasional political ally of Dundas and an early promoter of the British Fisheries Society. As an improver he had been steeped in the agrarian patriotism of the Select Society of Edinburgh and the militia movement. Dempster had voted against the Stamp Act and supported the American colonists in the lead up to the American War. After the 1782 Highland famine, he turned his attention increasingly toward the Highland question. Alarmed by the rising tide of emigration, Dempster had recently taken a trip to the worst-affected areas between Fort William and Inverness. He noted that the structural transformation of the Highland economy was now generating a surplus population. Because landlords were converting so much land for commercial cattle and sheep operations, the remaining arable land was no longer sufficient to feed the plebeians. This trend coincided with rising expectations of Highlanders about better standards of living. If new economic opportunities were not provided, further emigration would be inevitable.

> At present I will only say that I do not believe the people live worse than they did but on the contrary by means of Potatoes rather better. But they are too numerous for the Country in its present state, which if nothing is done to alter it will soon be applied solely to the breeding of sheep and cattle. The people have got ideas of living more comfortably, and believe it easier to effect that elsewhere than at home, and in the present state of the Highlands it [certainly] is so. The remedy seems to me very simple. Towns should be planned along the Western Coasts and in the Islands, lands lotted for the people to [have], and build Houses and make Gardens.[26]

Dempster's argument in the letter to Dundas was the first in a series of analyses of sheep farming put forward between 1784 and 1789 by improvers such as James Anderson, John Knox, Henry Beaufoy, and Hugh Rose. Anderson and Beaufoy took a hard line and endorsed sheep farming without hesitation. For Beaufoy, sheep provided the best means of exploiting the natural advantages of the country. Reason and nature ordained it. After his tour of the Hebrides in 1787, he submitted an essay to Henry Dundas that strongly urged the conversion of the Highlands to a sheep-farming economy (he repeated the same argument in a speech to the directors of the British Fisheries Society): "That system which follows the course of Nature, *and considers a Watery Climate as much more favourable to Pasture than to Corn, obviously draws from the land its largest produce; and whatever system furnished the amplest produce is, on the whole, undoubtedly the best for Britain.*" (It is not clear whether the last part of the sentence was underlined by Beaufoy or Dundas.) In his lecture to the British Fisheries Society, he drove home the political ramifications without any attempt to veil the facts in sentimental language. The "interests of the general population" required that the Highland region should specialize in sheep farming rather than subsistence for the poor inhabitants. James Anderson agreed. In his own report on the state of the Hebrides, Anderson defended the rationality of sheep farming on the same grounds of superior productivity. He mentioned the example of an estate grossly "over-stocked with people." There were thirty-two families totaling almost two hundred people, yet they only brought in thirty-one pounds of rent annually. If the estate was converted to maintain five thousand sheep, a single "shepherd and his dog" could maintain the whole flock. While Anderson admitted that this was an extreme case, he still insisted that "one-tenth part of the present inhabitants [of the Highlands] would be sufficient to perform all the operations there, were their industry properly exerted." For Beaufoy and Anderson then, overpopulation was strictly speaking a question of profitable specialization. Both of them saw new towns as the best remedy to accommodate displaced tenants and cottars. Both spoke briefly of the value of military recruitment in the region but ultimately downplayed this asset in favor of profits from sheep.[27]

Knox's *Tour Through the Highlands* from 1787 also acknowledged the rational motive behind sheep farms. The Highland climate was "particularly unfavourable to agriculture.... The west coast and the Hebride Islands, are generally deluged with rains in the harvest season." Knox observed that "the glens and straths of the interior parts enjoy little sun, and before vegetation is brought to maturity, the weather breaks, the mountains pour down torrents of water upon the lower grounds." These "heavy rains are succeeded by sleet and snow, which keep possession of the heights till the April sun comes round, when the wretched farmer, renews his fruitless toils of the field." Knox added, "Under such a climate, the best years are bad." "Every third year upon an average, is a year of famine." During such episodes of scarcity, the poor, "instead of being able to pay any rent, must be supplied by the laird, his factor, or some trade, with the actual means of existence, till the grounds yield better crops." The Highland climate forced people to depend on the charity of the social elite or find a wage outside agriculture. "Under these circumstances, it need be no matter of surprise, if gentlemen should embrace the tempting offers from sheep farmers." In this way, Knox defined the Highland poor as a surplus population, trapped by a hostile environment at the margin of subsistence.[28]

But Knox at the same time warned that the coming of the sheep threatened to unleash cultural disaster. He reprinted in his tour of Scotland from 1786 a long excerpt from the Highland minister John Smith's *Galic Antiquities*. Smith predicted that the "violent convulsions" which had brought an end to the "feudal system" and introduced commerce to the Highlands would also cause the extinction of Gaelic customs and poetry. The attention of the landlord was now focused on agriculture and industry, not the patronage of the bard: "In twenty years hence, if manners continue to change so fast as they do at present, the faintest traces shall scarcely be found of our ancient tales and poems." This threat of cultural extinction endangered the military prowess of the Highlanders: "To the poems of Ossian we may attribute a good share of that martial spirit and enthusiasm for war, till of late, so remarkable in the islands. This spirit flourished with the poems of Ossian, and, in a great measure, it dies with them." Smith concluded by quoting Macpherson's lines: "Ossian himself is the last of his race, and he too shall soon be no more; for his grey branches are already strewed on all the winds." Knox in turn placed Smith's cultural analysis in a political context and suggested the possibility of redemption. Through the building of towns along the western seaboard, the martial spirit of the Gael could be preserved and harnessed to serve the nation and the empire. A large Gaelic population was a crucial asset that deserved as much recognition as the rental increase made possible by sheep: "The more I considered this subject, the more important it appeared, both to the strength of the empire, and to the welfare of a great body of people."[29]

Hugh Rose's memorandum about the improvement of Sutherland from 1786 used the same poetic rhetoric of a doomed race. When the Gaelic population had been forced out or diminished because of new sheep farms, the loss would be irreversible. "For, let once the natives of these countries be extirpated or dispersed, it is believed that no set of people, whatsoever, from any other quarter of the globe, would be got to inhabit them." Like Dempster and Knox, Rose stressed the military value of the Highlanders. Extirpation undermined national security: "The preservation of the State at large, is surely so much involved . . . . , that it is surprising the public do not take the alarm, so as to restrain, or put a stop to private interest, or avarice, when making such wide strides towards extirpating the human race from these bleak dreary mountains, from whence, in times of national danger, armies were speedily called forth, and legions rapidly completed." Rose's principled stance won him the respect of George Dempster: "[He] knows the way to set this county on its legs and does all the good he can." It was probably Dempster who put Rose's private memorandum into the hands of John Sinclair. Sinclair published it after Rose's death in *The General View of the Agriculture of the Northern Counties and Islands of Scotland* (1795). It is not known whether the Duchess of Sutherland ever read the memorandum. But the great clearances carried out on the Sutherland estate after 1806 were accompanied by a serious effort at resettlement by her husband, the Marquis of Stafford.[30]

Dempster's own views fell somewhere between Anderson and Rose. In a 1789 pamphlet promoting the British Fisheries Society, Dempster predicted that a "great change" was about to occur in the Highland economy, "either for the better or worse." Sheep farming was no doubt economically rational in a short-sighted sense. A whole village could be replaced by "a single unmarried shepherd and a couple of sheep-dogs." Yet if the sheep farming system prevailed, "the total extirpation of the ancient inhabitants of the country" must follow. The liberal justification for rural clearance in Adam Smith and others failed to put a proper value on rural population: "My sentiments on this subject differ from those of many very sensible men, who tell us the times for breeding men are now over, and that men must give way to a more profitable form of production, that formerly a chieftain wanted money, but now men." To exchange a thousand followers for a diamond buckle was a poor trade. Against Smith, Dempster stressed the multiple uses of a large rural population. They could serve not just as soldiers but also as agricultural and manufacturing labor. Elsewhere, Dempster spoke of the hard bodies and high morals of the Highlanders: "Farmers or labourers of the Ground . . . compose the hardiest most virtuous and most usefull part of every state." Gaelic superiority—in the sense of both virtuous poverty and hard martial bodies—was rooted in the peculiar environment of the region. These mental and physical traits would be dispersed and lost to the nation if the Highlanders were forced to migrate. Neither could they be replaced by newcomers. They were a unique breed.[31]

RESCUING THE SHETLAND BREED

A few years after George Dempster's warning that sheep farms were exterminating Gaelic society, his friends and allies John Sinclair and James Anderson launched a campaign to save the Shetland sheep from extinction. Theirs was an economic scheme driven by the commonplace ambition to diversify the nation with new animals and plants. Yet it came wrapped in a rhetoric of patriotic conservation reminiscent of Dempster's social vision. It even echoed the critique of improvement at the heart of conservative population politics. In both projects, the Enlightenment ideal of ecological exchange provoked a nationalist backlash of sorts.

A steady stream of exotic sheep breeds arrived in Leith harbor during these years. John Holroyd, the Earl of Sheffield, sent an assortment of sheep to John Sinclair, including one ram and twelve ewes with varying mixtures of Merino and South Down, as well as eight Herefordshire ewes and a "small and ugly" three-quarter Merino lamb with exceedingly "fine" fleece. Colonel Fullarton received a flock of sheep from Colchis in Georgia. James Anderson witnessed the arrival of a hairless sheep from Madagascar on a Danish East India Company ship. A small number of the Shetland breed were also introduced from the Northern Isles. The Shetland kind was rumored to be among the last of their type, a breed in danger of extinction. Holroyd wrote to Sinclair: "How happens it that the true Shetland fine wool sheep has been in great measure expelled or contaminated by intruders?" Holroyd was a close supporter of Sir Joseph Banks and had been a driving force during the wool bill controversy a decade earlier. With Banks and Arthur Young, he had helped organize the landed interest in favor of free wool exports against the protectionist demands of the wool manufacturers. Holroyd was full of admiration for Banks's long-term strategy of introducing fine wool Merino sheep to Britain. "No experiment has pleased me better," he wrote. Yet now, even Holroyd had to admit that the ideal of boundless ecological exchange appeared to threaten vital national values, both human and natural.[32]

The campaign to save the Shetland breed began with a petition to the Highland Society of Scotland from John Sinclair in the summer of 1790. A committee formed to investigate the problem, including Sinclair, John Clerk of Eldin, and James Anderson. They also received expert advice from two Shetland natives—the Reverend John Morison of Delting and Arthur Nicholson of Lochend—whose "ardour" was "becoming [to] the ancient race of Caledonian patriots." The committee produced a lengthy report that was printed in twelve hundred copies for the benefit of the public. In an appendix, Anderson sketched the civil and natural history of the Shetland sheep. Here, he repeated arguments he had first made in the 1777 book on Merino acclimatization in the Highlands. England had been famous for fine wool breeds in the Middle Ages. But the ban on wool exports in the seventeenth century had stifled the production. Anderson now cast this decline in terms of island biogeography. When coarse wool became dominant, the older breeds were driven to the margins of the nation. "After the most diligent inquiry" Anderson was forced to conclude that "the fine breed of sheep" was "totally and irrecoverably lost *in England*." Though "adulterated remains of it" existed still in the county of Hereford on the Welsh borders, these sheep were "much debased by intermixing." William Marshall had lamented the decline of the Ryeland breed the year before in his *Rural Oeconomy of Gloucestershire*. According to Anderson, this historical process of decline had also penetrated into Scotland. "For more than a century past, the coarse-wool'd sheep have been imperceptibly debasing this breed, under the name of improving it." A few isolated pockets had persisted for some time in remote corners such as the hills of Galloway and mountains of Aberdeenshire. Yet even in the Western Isles, "the furor of improvement has so generally prevailed, that it is believed none of them contain the breed entirely unmixed." Only the most remote island environment—the Shetland Isles—contained a relic of the ancient fine wool breed of Britain. The Shetland sheep were small and slender, black or white in color, with a mixture of hair and wool. But here, too, the old breed was on the "very verge of being irrecoverably lost." "Several attempts to improve" the breed in recent years had debased it and introduced a new, dangerous disease to the stock. In short, Anderson and Sinclair were proposing a last-minute rescue operation of a dying race under the auspices of the Highland Society of Scotland. This was in keeping with the theological framework of eighteenth-century natural history: species were unchanging, but varieties might come and go. Absolute extinction was possible only at the level of the breed.[33]

Islands were crucial to the conservation of the breed. Anderson praised the efforts of French breeders like Le Blanc and D'Aubenton but noted that their "patriotic" efforts were doomed without assistance from nature. The problem arose in the "rutting season," when regular enclosures could not keep different breeds from intermixing and degenerating. "Nature, however, has provided a set of fences perfectly capable of answering this purpose, at no expence to the owner, along the coasts of Scotland, by having scattered these innumerable islands of various sizes, on which any particular breed of sheep may be kept, without trouble or expence." The milder insular climate was also favorable to fine wool. The Wool Committee of the Highland Society specifically solicited proprietors known to own "holms or small islands" fit for the purpose, including Mr. Campbell of Jura, the Earl of Breadalbane, and the Duke of Argyll. Insularity also made it possible to reverse the process of degeneration by eliminating undesirable traits. Inferior specimens of Shetland sheep could be "extirpated" in order to restore the purity of the original stock. Here, Anderson referred to the experiments of the French breeder Le Blanc. "The quality of the wool depends upon the breed, and not upon the soil or climate." Careful selection would ensure that the superior elements survived. Such qualities depended "principally on the male." The best results came in the second and third generations. Hence, fine wool breeding could produce quick returns, both in quality and in quantity. Within ten years, a small flock might multiply to a million heads. A breed that had been on the verge of extinction could be restored: "In how short a space of time 100 rams and 1000 ewes of the best breed, with the assistance of a proper number of ewes of an inferior quality, might replenish the Shetland Islands."[34] The project also required the protection of sheep from natural predators, as Sinclair's surveyor Richard Ker recognized. For any sheep farms in the north, it would be necessary to "extirpate the race of foxes, eagles, and carrion crows, all of which are exceedingly hurtful to a breeding stock." Ker praised the "wise policy of our more ignorant ancestors" who had "succeeded in totally destroying the race of wolves in our Island." He thought it would be easy to effect the same destruction of the fox by means of bounties and traps. Extirpation and conservation were logically tied together.[35]

The Wool Committee's work met with warm acclaim at the general meeting of the Highland Society. Subscribers to the wool report included the major proprietors of the north. A copy was sent to the king. Holroyd responded to the pamphlet with a gift of three Merino sheep and an offer of more for sale. Later in the summer, Sinclair's contacts in the Shetland Isles sent a small flock of Shetland sheep—four rams and six ewes—to Leith harbor, where they were inspected by Anderson and other members of the committee. The flock was then placed for safekeeping on the small island of Inchcolm in the Firth of Forth. The committee proposed premiums to encourage experiments with fine wool breeds among Highland farmers. Meanwhile, Lord Clanranald and the Edinburgh representatives of the Duke of Argyll and Mr. Campbell of Shawfield offered islands in the west where further trials could be conducted. News of the effort to revive the Shetland breed must have spread quickly among the savants in Edinburgh. Both Dr. Joseph Black and James Hutton were present at the September meeting of the committee. Hutton later wrote in his unpublished treatise on agriculture: "We have a small sheep from Shetland, the race of which was like to have been extinguished by their inconsiderate innovations." He speculated that this northern type of wool was far more suited for easy processing than the Spanish Merino. The silky, soft character of its wool was "transcendent" in quality and promised to be "of infinite importance to this manufacturing island."[36]

Buoyed by the strength of public support, Sinclair and Anderson now opted to break out of the Highland Society to form a separate association dedicated solely to the objective of fine wool. The British Wool Society was founded in late January 1791. The directors included the Duke of Argyll, the Earl of Sheffield (John Holroyd), and the lord provost of Edinburgh. Henry Dundas also took an interest in the scheme. Since the original objective of saving the Shetland breed seemed to have succeeded, Sinclair's attention shifted toward broader issues. Both Anderson and Sinclair subscribed to the old-fashioned tenet that high-quality wool production provided the foundation for national prosperity. "No country ever acquired great commercial opulence without carrying the manufacture of wool to a very high degree of perfection." The wool industry was superior to cotton or linen because its raw materials could be produced at home by the landed interest. "Why should we suffer our supply of it to depend on the caprice of a foreign power"? In his rambling inaugural speech to the Wool Society, Sinclair linked wool autarky to national security. Without a "sufficient store of fine wool at home" along with "the naval stores necessary for our fleet," how could Britain claim to be "an Independent, Manufacturing or Maritime Nation"? But Sinclair also showed some understanding of current consumer trends. He noted accurately that the profits for British coarse woolens were falling in the face of competition from cotton. Like Sir Joseph Banks, Sinclair hoped that high-quality wool would help rejuvenate the British wool manufactures. Ecological diversification once again underwrote import substitution and self-sufficiency. Holroyd's gift of Spanish Merino sheep was a step in the right direction. Sinclair contacted the British ambassador in Sweden to discover details about the Swedish island breed on Gotland. Both Sinclair and Anderson were eager to test the possibility of more far-flung transplants, like the Atlas mountain sheep of North Africa and Asian varieties of fine wool. Sinclair at one point contemplated writing a comprehensive natural history of sheep breeds, but it was James Anderson who did the most to publicize exotic sheep breeds in his journal *The Bee*. In 1791, the Wool Society possessed fifteen flocks of sheep, totaling 800 animals, many of them crosses between regional British varieties and foreign breeds like the Merino. More than 550 of these sheep were dispersed to proprietors "all over Scotland." The drive toward diversification may have remedied an embarrassing shortcoming of Shetland wool. The fleece contained a high portion of long "Stichel hairs" that had to be removed one by one at high cost before the fleece was ready for manufacturing use. In their fervor to rescue the breed from extinction, Sinclair and Anderson had overlooked this problem. Only a brief footnote in the original wool report suggested that a hybrid of Merino and Shetland might be necessary to create a fleece that might "answer for broad cloth." This was tried a year or two later with apparent success.[37]

The northern orientation of the great sheep hunt was a sure indication that Anderson and Sinclair—despite Sinclair's protestations to the contrary—worried about the fit between breed and climate. In this spirit, the Wool Society commissioned a survey by the sheep breeder Richard Ker to investigate the diffusion of sheep in northern Scotland. In the spring of 1791, Ker traveled north from Edinburgh to Aberdeen, then along the coast all the way to Caithness and back again via the Central Highlands. Ker emphasized the dearth of sheep on most estates in his report to the Wool Society. He showed little enthusiasm for the old native breed of the Highlands or the coarse wool of Blackfaced sheep from the Southern Uplands. Instead, he recommended that farmers try the white-faced "Tiviot" breed from the Borders.[38]

The dream of the global diversification of Scottish sheep stocks would prove to be the most short-lived of Sinclair's projects. After a mere three years, in 1794 the British Wool Society ceased to convene. But the Shetland wool inquiry and Ker's survey helped settle a point of genuine uncertainty among Highland proprietors. When Sinclair solicited support for the wool scheme in 1790, John Campbell, Fifth Duke of Argyll, responded with polite skepticism. He had already "made several attempts" in the past to introduce "English and Shetland sheep" on his estate with little success. Campbell confessed that he was "not quite so sanguine as many others are, as to the effect that may be produced." He was particularly concerned about the deleterious effects wrought by "Constant wetness of our climate" on the west coast, "so unlike that of Spain or some of Shetland." Nevertheless, he accepted Sinclair's invitation to be a director of the Wool Society in 1791 and made another attempt with new types of sheep. Once again, he was disappointed by the results. "I cannot boast much of the success of the Spanish or Cheviot breed," he reported to Sinclair in January 1792. "The latter kind most of them had lambs, but as the greater part of the Yews are of a very inferior quality, I cannot rear many of them this year, but shall take care to preserve those that are good of their kind." Campbell was also displeased with the single Merino ram he acquired to improve his stock. The ram proved deficient in these "operations" because he had arrived too late in the season.[39]

Argyll's woes remind us that the sheep frontier for all its force and speed was not an automatic process. Dempster's prediction in 1784 that sheep would exterminate the Gaelic race overlooked a basic problem of natural history. Despite the promise of great profits, there was still uncertainty about the long-term viability of high-quality wool breeds in the north of Scotland. Would the climate and soil suit southern types of sheep? Sir Joseph Banks scoffed at the idea of Merino sheep in the north. He also rejected Shetland wool as unfit for manufacturing uses because of the "Stichel hairs" that marred it. Yet the lobbying of Sinclair and Anderson revealed the range of technical options available. The high-profile success of the Shetland sheep rescue in the summer of 1790 demonstrated that fine wool breeds could thrive in the far north. The Wool Committee's proposal to crossbreed Shetland sheep with Merinos offered a solution to the "Stichel" hair problem. Ker's tour the following spring in turn suggested that high-quality wool from the Borders could succeed in the Highlands. "After many enquiries ... and several surveys made ... it was at least ascertained, that a breed of sheep were to be found on the borders of England and Scotland ... which was peculiarly calculated for a hilly or mountainous district." Sinclair seems to have made up his own mind sometime shortly thereafter. In 1792, he expanded his experiment with Hereford sheep on his Caithness estate to include the Cheviot breed, which Ker had endorsed. Another promotional piece by Sinclair in the *Annals of Agriculture* from 1793 observed that Border farmers had already conducted "a variety of experiments" in their own hills to establish the superior hardiness of the Cheviot relative to the Blackfaced breed. The Cheviot provided the best combination of robust physique and high-quality wool fit for manufacturing use. Beyond the technical realm of natural knowledge, Sinclair was also keen to facilitate practical channels of exchange. The *Annals of Agriculture* essay contained addresses for the best breeders in the Borders. The British Wool Society coordinated a transfer of fifty rams and one hundred ewes from the south to Caithness, a journey of 350 miles, Sinclair noted. Once the sheep had safely arrived, they were "divided into small parcels, consisting of a ram and two ewes, among from 40 to 50 different people." By pooling risk and knowledge in this way, Sinclair sought to guarantee the maximum penetration of the new breed in the north.[40]

The timing of these interventions seems to fit well with what we know about the Cheviot breed's history in the north. Eric Richards notes that the frontier of sheep farms crossed beyond the Great Glen only after 1792. Twenty years later, Sinclair boasted with some warrant to the Duke of Northumberland that he had been instrumental in championing the phenomenal spread of the new kind of sheep across the northern Highlands. "The result has been the most satisfactory. Wedders of that sort sell at from 25 to 90 shilling and upwards, and the wool at from 40 shilling ... per stone. It has added above 5000 pounds per annum to the value of the Roxburgh Estates and to the other grander estates, where the Cheviot breed are kept." There were, he noted, six thousand heads of Cheviot on his own estate and another twenty thousand on those of his neighbors in Sutherland and Reay. The date of Sinclair's boast is not without significance. He was writing at the end of December 1812. The Countess of Sutherland had cleared a portion of her estate in 1806–7 to make room for the new livestock. In 1812, her factors had begun planning for a new phase of dispossession. On Whitsunday that year, Assynt tenants were delivered notices that their leases had lapsed and would not be renewed. As Sinclair composed his letter to Northumberland at the end of December, popular resistance was growing in Kildonan. The first few weeks of 1813 saw clashes between local people and the countess's surveyors. This was the beginning of the most intense and notorious phase of removal and resettlement on the estate.[41]

Yet Sinclair never seems to have doubted his basic assumption that sheep and Gaels were compatible. The Highland race could be protected and preserved much as the Shetland breed had been rescued. To prove this point, he devised the most elaborate and ambitious political defense of wasteland reclamation seen in the Enlightenment. Once again, spade husbandry provided the mechanism by which commercial land use and a growing population could be reconciled. But Sinclair went beyond the old model proposed by Lord Monboddo and John Walker by developing a political arithmetic of land use. The aim was to discover the precise measure of marginal soil still available for improvement, not just in the Highlands but across the whole nation.[42]

9

WASTELAND ISLAND

The limits to the British food supply became a pressing political question at the end of the eighteenth century. In the face of widespread dearth in 1795, the House of Commons appointed a Select Committee led by John Sinclair to ascertain how much of the nation's marginal soil could be converted to arable land. Sinclair's report called attention to the rapid growth of London's population and the danger of relying on foreign supplies in wartime. "The lands now in cultivation," Sinclair noted, "have been found, on the average of several years past, inadequate to the consumption of the Kingdom." But for Sinclair, there was no reason for pessimism. "A general inclosure and improvement" of all the wastelands of Britain could satisfy the domestic demand for grain while even allowing the population to expand. In a separate report to the Board of Agriculture, he predicted that internal improvement would add two or three million inhabitants to the nation, "equal to that possessed by the United States of America, when they first erected the standard of independence against the Mother Country." Sinclair's project of internal empire grew seamlessly out of his interest in political arithmetic and Highland improvement. Wasteland colonization offered a model of autarky and agrarian virtue for the nation at large.[1]

In strategic and economic terms, Sinclair's forecast imagined Britain without the benefit of an empire or long-distance trade. This was hardly an outrageous proposition in 1795. After all, Britain had lost the better part of its colonies after the War of American Independence. Then, the radical turn of the French Revolution had provoked a new kind of ideological contest and an unprecedented level of national mobilization. In hindsight, the wars with revolutionary France marked the transition to Pax Britannica and global hegemony. But in 1795 it was far from clear that Britain could win this formidable test of strength. The threat of invasion loomed large. Long-distance trade looked precarious. Sinclair and his allies rightly worried that Britain cut off from Europe and its colonial possessions might become a besieged island rather than a node in a vast trading network.

This chapter explores the origin of Sinclair's political arithmetic in Highland improvement. First, we survey the changing scene of conservative reaction among Sinclair's Scottish allies, including the activities of the Highland Society of Scotland and the chemical project of Archibald Cochrane, the Earl of Dundonald. Then we turn to examine the agitation of Sinclair in Parliament and the Board of Agriculture. These threads converge into a broader thesis about island consciousness. Sinclair developed a political arithmetic of land use to determine the precise measure of marginal soil still available for improvement. His ambition to quantify the environmental limits of the nation preceded the better-known pessimistic political economy of Malthus by several years. Using a modern term, we might say that Sinclair's inventory of muirs and peat mosses aimed to identify and quantify the internal *ghost acres* of Great Britain. What was the amount of wasteland needed "to overcome a production limit which would otherwise have inhibited domestic growth"? Behind this concern lay strong economic and environmental pressures. Ecological strains multiplied because of the rapid British population growth in the second half of the eighteenth century. In the nineteenth century, these limits were overcome thanks to the ghost acres of the colonies and the transition into a new industrial society based on mineral energy and steam power. But like the advent of Pax Britannica, we must be careful not to project the confidence of Victorian industrialists back into the uncertainties of the 1790s. Sinclair's wasteland calculus and Malthus's population principle were rational responses to the limits of British growth in the peculiar context of the French Revolutionary Wars. This green arithmetic of island limits has now become a central preoccupation of modern environmentalists who worry about overpopulation and ecological strain.[2]

THE ABORIGINES OF IMPROVEMENT

In the winter of 1793, the shadow of radical revolution and war provided a convenient refuge from talk of extirpation and clearances in the Highlands. At the general meeting of the Highland Society of Scotland on January 8, eighty-eight members attended, including such dignitaries as the Duke of Gordon, the Earl of Murray, and Lord Adam Gordon, the commander in chief of Scotland. The occasion was a declaration of loyalty to the Crown and the Constitution, against "all Seditious publications and writings, tending to disseminate Leveling and dangerous doctrines, to create jealousy and distrust and to enflame the minds of the people." Henry Erskine, the dean of the Faculty of Advocates, the implacable Foxite critic of Henry Dundas, read out a resolution condemning the "the exertions of evil designing persons" who "threatened to endanger the safety and peace of the Country." True to the "principles of the Revolution Settlement," the members vowed to protect society against all "attacks from Republicans and Levelers." Fear was growing that foreign infiltrators, radical Irishmen, and other troublemakers had come ashore in Scotland to stir up sedition among the lower orders. The members of the society pledged "every assistance . . . to the civil magistrates" and their firm resolution to oppose such treasonous activities, although they also insisted that "the loyalty of the Highlands of Scotland . . . [was] not to be shaken or impaired." All the same, this declaration was translated into Gaelic to be printed and circulated in the north by the "moderators of the Presbyteries." The following years saw more of these proclamations—on the occasion of the attempted assassination of the king, in support of the Highland volunteer force, and against the threat of French invasion.[3]

The transformation of the Highland Society into a loyalist association was accompanied by the entrenchment of the landed order across Britain. Poor harvests caused severe shortages in 1794–96 and 1799–1801. Landowners profited from record rents but were all too aware of the political risks associated with doubling bread prices in a time of war against a revolutionary republic. Though Adam Smith and other liberal writers had made a forceful case for the benefits of an unregulated grain trade, these harvest failures and the specter of wartime trade disruption gave new momentum to arguments for national autarky. Such anxieties in turn attracted projectors who tried to win the attention of the government with their proposals for emergency measures. In London, John Walker's student Thomas Beddoes published an open letter to Prime Minister Pitt that suggested that the distribution of opium to the poor might alleviate their hunger and extend the working day. In Bavaria, Count Rumford concocted watery recipes for the starving masses of Europe, setting the agenda for counterrevolutionary soup kitchens in London and other cities struck by food riots. The physician Ezra Melroe followed Rumford's lead by analyzing the digestive and economic virtues of soup for the respectable poor. His recipes were based on the principles uncovered by William Cullen regarding the nutritious properties of "oil, jelly, mucilage, and sugar." After the dearth of 1794–95, William Wilberforce and other evangelicals founded the Society for the Bettering the Conditions and Increasing the Comforts of the Poor, which promoted allotment gardens for the poor in England. The ownership of an allotment was intended to instill responsibility in landless plebeians while at the same time providing a means of subsistence in times of dearth.[4]

But some worried that opium, soup kitchens, and allotments might not be enough to counter the threat of revolution. In Scotland, Archibald Cochrane, the Ninth Earl of Dundonald, proposed the wholesale evacuation of the manufacturing sector from the cities. Dundonald was the heir to the mines and plantations of Culross Abbey in Fife, which funded a string of his chemical experiments and publications. During the American War of Independence, Dundonald developed a new method of manufacturing tar to protect ships' bottoms. The tar was extracted from coal rather than wood, eliminating the need for strategic dependency on native timber or Scandinavian imports (the Admiralty rejected the method in favor of copper sheathing). He also played a part in the manufacture of synthetic soda from salt in Scotland. Dundonald's 1795 *Treatise, Showing the Intimate Connection That Subsists Between Agriculture and Chemistry* extended this preoccupation with import substitution and chemical autarky into the realm of agriculture. Rising prices of provisions provided an antidote to "the golden dreams of manufactures and of commerce." Only agriculture could guarantee the "permanent . . . prosperity of [the] nation." Because of the sensitivity of manufactures to the "fluctuation in demand" and the "total suspension of trade by war or other causes," laborers were easily tempted by the promise of fundamental "political change." The dense concentration of manufacturing labor in cities also exposed workers to the "dissemination of pernicious doctrines, by a few profligate persons" who planted seeds of sedition among them. Dundonald's remedy was startling but logical. Agriculture should have preference over all "other pursuits." Those "branches of manufacture" deemed "wise to encourage" should "be promoted [solely] in scattered villages, resembling the townships in America." By severing the link between cities and manufacture, "the diseases of the body and the mind would be rendered less contagious." The new policy also recovered the connection between the worker and the soil. By giving each operative a "sufficient extent of ground" "requisite for raising potatoes, and other vegetables cultivated at his leisure by the spade," the worker would find "an agreeable and healthful change to his confined and sedentary occupation."[5]

By the middle of the 1790s, Dundonald's private affairs were in disarray and his patrimony was nearly exhausted from interminable projects. He badly needed to rehabilitate his reputation for patriotism and ingenuity. His treatise addressed fellow "Cultivators of the soil" and "Proprietors of Fens and Mosses" across the British Isles. The bulk of the text was taken up with the analysis of different kinds of fertilizer. He acknowledged debts to the chemistry of Cavendish and Priestley in chapters on air, gases, and the composition of water, but ignored Lavoisier on account of his radical affiliations with the French Revolution. Dundonald's chemical approach was guided by a firm belief in the power of increasing returns. Fertilizer operated on soil by irreversible force through the agent of saline or other substances. The exhaustion of soil was temporary and its recovery always assured. On this count, Dundonald diverged sharply from Adam Smith and the mainstream of agricultural improvers in the eighteenth century, who linked fertility to cattle manure and therefore stipulated a fixed limit to cereal production in the ratio of pasture land to arable soil. By attributing fertility to "numerous" substances in nature, which Dundonald claimed had "escaped the notice" of his predecessors, he promised to expand the potential of agricultural growth manifold.[6]

Peat moss supplied an "inexhaustible" stock of fertilizer from the mosses of Great Britain and Ireland. Dundonald insisted that top soil and peat enriched each other, such that peat could become the fertilizer of soil and vice versa. In economic terms, peat seemed capable of transforming agriculture in a manner as profound as the use of coal in manufacturing. The discovery promised to alter fundamentally the "poor lands in [the] vicinity" of the bogs, bringing the Scottish Highlands into a state of flourishing cultivation. This was environmental engineering on a scale that would dwarf even the achievement of Lord Kames and his son in Blair Drummond moss. From the "irreversible" effects of peat on the topsoil flowed a chain of political consequences. With abundant fertilizer on hand, the proper balance between agriculture and manufacture could be restored. The landed interest would find a new lease of life, grounded in the authority of chemistry and the providential powers of peat. Even the crofters and resettled manufacturing laborers would benefit, as peat was sure to improve the culture of the spade. Dundonald's ultimate aim was self-sufficiency in food and raw materials like timber, hemp, and flax. Instead of relying on the "precarious supply . . . from foreign States," the reclaimed mosses would provide all the "internal products of our Own Island." In an appendix to the treatise, Dundonald extended his vision to the West Indies. Evidently, the regenerated landed order still needed a sugar fix now and then. He calculated that the bulky sugar transports on their way back to the Caribbean had plenty of cargo space for Scottish or Irish peat treated with alkaline salts and dried into a light ballast. Wherever the soils of the West Indian islands showed signs of exhaustion, this peat amendment could regenerate planter profits.[7]

Dundonald's chemical version of agrarian patriotism was part of a flourishing literature on wastelands and population during the French Revolutionary Wars. John Sinclair single-handedly encouraged a great deal of this wave of writings through his work in sponsoring the regional reports for the Board of Agriculture and as the managing editor of the *Statistical Account of Scotland*. Much like Dundonald's treatise, these reports sought to bolster the landed interest with useful information about improvement. Yet the tools of agrarian modernization—enclosure, abolition of commons, sheep farms, and consolidation of tenant holdings—were also identified as the source of rural depopulation, emigration, and the weakening of agrarian virtue. Many writers in the *Statistical Account* observed that the large rural population of cottagers was particularly vulnerable because, unlike tenants and subtenants, they lacked formal leases. The elderly James Burnett, Lord Monboddo, warned in his last writings that the landed order and rural population were declining precipitously because of such processes of tenurial consolidation. Increasing numbers of small tenants were evicted by the gentry while an ever-growing number of medium-sized estates were absorbed into larger properties. At this rate, he predicted, even the gentry would become extinct within sixty years. In their survey of the northern Scottish counties for the Board of Agriculture in 1795, John Sinclair and George Dempster recognized a similar contradiction at the lower level of rural society. Was it possible to improve and enclose farms "while at the same time" preserving "the cottagers, or lower class of tenantry?"[8]

Sinclair's allies also worried about urban degeneration. As rural society deteriorated, cities were growing beyond their natural bounds. The Reverend James Robertson, minister in Callander, disparaged urban workers as "deformed spawn and jail sweepings," who by their vast consumption of agricultural commodities had become parasites on the true wealth of the country. Cities were morally and economically unsustainable. Urban manufactures had increased the population "beyond what the produce of [the] country [could] support." Like Dundonald, Robertson hoped that industrial production could be divorced from its urban context. He pointed to an encouraging development within his own parish. This was the planned village of Callander, the only veteran settlement of the Annexed Estates to succeed and prosper. In the entry on the village for the *Statistical Account*, Robertson described in detail the startling transformation of the parish within the last generation, from an outpost of four families to a thriving rural community with more than a thousand souls. The key to success was to discover and maintain a balance between population growth, agricultural production, and local employment. Without careful management, a surplus population of idle inhabitants might develop, which would vitiate the body politic and give rise to "bad humors" within the healthy constitution of the village. If the size of the village crossed a certain point, corruption set in, destroying the "whole frame" of the community and breeding "despondency" among the settlers. In Robertson's mind, there seemed to be two thresholds for sustainable communities, one derived from population size and the other from the scale of demand: "Whenever the population of any town or village exceeds the industry of the inhabitants, from that moment the place must decline." He added, "When their consumption is greater than their earnings, when their wants are not supplied by their labour, the stock of the society must decrease, and many undue practices must be substituted for the honest means of procuring subsistence." The moral was clear: rural communities could flourish only as long as they were confined to a modest scale and fostered habits of hard work and moderate appetites.[9]

Yet as a large-scale solution to the problem, planned villages were a very expensive proposition. The bitter lesson taught by the experience of the British Fisheries Society seemed to confirm this suspicion. The founder of the Highland Society, Sir James Grant, built Grantown-on-Spey at the cost of £3,000 between 1765 and 1792. Sir John Sinclair's fishing village at Sarclet in Caithness cost £950 to construct in the early nineteenth century. The other side of the problem was the sheer number of rural inhabitants to be accommodated. An impressive 164 villages were established between 1770 and 1799 in Scotland. But even with many dozens of new settlements, how could three hundred thousand Highlanders find new homes? Given the major demands of capital expenditure and the growing size of the population, the northern improvers were forced to consider cheaper paths to rural virtue. Here, Sinclair himself took the lead, in *The General View of the Agriculture of the Northern Counties*. This text was a collaborative effort with George Dempster, covering the counties of Sutherland, Caithness, Ross, and Cromarty, as well as the Northern Isles. Sinclair wrote the chapter on his home county of Caithness while Dempster covered the east coast of Sutherland. Both promoted wasteland cultivation as the best method of absorbing displaced tenants. For Sinclair, this was the particular responsibility of the largest landowners—"the great and rich ought to preserve, on their estates, a numerous race of hardy peasantry"—while the smaller proprietors could not be expected to follow quite as generous a course. He described at some length the introduction of the Cheviot breed of sheep on the upper reaches of his Langwell estate and his attempt to accommodate the poor people who had been evicted. This policy included loans to buy lime and more secure leases. Sinclair's book also contained excerpts from the writings of Hugh Rose, the deceased factor of the Countess of Sutherland, who had drawn up a master plan for the improvement of her property in 1786. In this way, *The General View of the Agriculture of the Northern Counties* provided a blueprint for wasteland colonization, published with the sanction of the Board of Agriculture.[10]

George Dempster had bought the five-thousand-acre estate of Skibo in Sutherland in 1787. Disillusioned with the corruption and inefficacy of Parliament, he retired from the House of Commons to conduct an experiment in private population politics. He advertised for colonists in *The Bee*, promising liberal conditions. The "Constitution of Creech" made all settlers "tenants for life; exempted them from all [feudal] services of every kind; exacted no additional rent," and gave "what ever ground they reclaim from the waste . . . rent free during their lives, and [that of] their Heir . . . on the same conditions." Dempster also introduced a cotton manufacture in the locality, though this proved an ill-fated venture. The idea of Skibo was to establish a settlement large enough to thrive but not so populous as to invite urban corruption. "The country life," he wrote, was the "most probable seat of happiness and health in this world." Though Dempster had been a founding force behind the British Fisheries Society, the Skibo scheme marked a move away from the liberal dream of urbanization. Great cities were rife with disease, vice, and death. London was a "rabbit warren," Edinburgh a "pigsty." He joked with Sinclair that it would take an earthquake or conflagration to make either one orderly and beautiful. In contrast, Highlanders were "a hardy race, bred in fine air, on wholesome food." Livestock metaphors, it seems, were never far from Dempster's mind.[11]

In contrast with Dundonald, Dempster thought lime provided the best method of converting marginal land into pasture or arable land. Although cattle manure was "extremely limited" in quantity, lime was "one of the most universal mineral productions of nature." It "infallibly" increased output, enriching both tenants and landowners. In modern-day terminology, lime gave a temporary jolt to acidic ground, lowering its pH level sufficiently to allow for grass or even grain cultivation. James Headrick observed that lime was "a most mortal enemy to heath." A dose of lime "in a finely powdered state" "easily extirpated" the plant. Headrick explained that heath "abounds in the gallic acid, and grows only upon such soils as are replete with acids: lime, by neutralizing these, robs the plant of its natural food."[12] Reclamation with lime was the capital-intensive prerogative of a proprietor with money to spare. The lime had to be quarried, burned, transported and spread out on the fields. On his Lowland estate Dunnichen in Forfarshire, Dempster began a large-scale drainage project to access deposits of marl sand at the bottom of Restenneth Loch. The inspiration for this scheme came from the Swedish chemist Axel Fredrik Cronstedt, who reckoned that marl could make an effective lime additive for husbandry. Dempster also turned to his old friend the Glasgow chemist Joseph Black for advice: How should the seventy acres of marl in the lake be treated? Should he build an air furnace to burn the marl? The cost of fuel was a major concern. Dempster asked whether peat could be used instead of wood fuel. Black had a ready answer since he had just analyzed the amount of calcareous matter in marl relative to limestone on behalf of a Caithness proprietor. Although marl was certainly weaker in efficacy, Black was confident that it could be spread untreated on Dempster's fields with reasonable effect. But he also suggested a draw kiln design that might allow marl to be burned using peat. Buoyed by such assurances, Dempster proceeded to drain Restenneth Loch. This faith in the chemical basis of reclamation was essential to Dempster's understanding of internal colonization. After a tour of the central Highlands in 1784, he suggested to Henry Dundas that "the capabilities of those Countries as to improvement in agriculture" were "I venture to say *most confidently* beyond all conception. Limestone every where and a milder climate than I could have conceived." Like the natural historians of the age, Dempster was sure that providence had stored nature with hidden riches that could be discovered by the skillful and attentive observer. He wrote to John Sinclair: "I don't know if ever the thought occurd to you, that Lime, and chalk are the Dunghills of a former world, preserved by crystallization, for the use of the present. Our maker, the first of Cooks, Chemists and Confectioners, has more [pickles] than one."[13]

Hugh Rose's view of marginal soil reflected his pessimism about alternative forms of industry. "Experience" had proven that manufactures and fisheries by their "nature" were "fleeting and uncertain benefits, which often [took] their departure from one country and fly to another. Nothing, therefore, ought to be more seriously attended to, than the improvement of waste land." In this respect, the cottagers and crofters of the northern counties were, as Sinclair put it, the "primum mobile" and the "aborigines of improvement in this country." Their labor corresponded to the crucial earliest stage of agriculture, when land was first reclaimed from the wilderness by the early settlers of Scotland. Sinclair and his collaborators recommended that landlords grant wasteland colonists a cottage, some lime and farming implements, and perhaps two or three acres to cultivate. They recommended the spade as the "fittest" "of all instruments . . . for turning up ground in a rocky country, where a plough can do little or nothing, either from a multitude of rocks, or from the earth being so marshy, that cattle cannot pass over it without sinking." Like John Walker, they observed "that one man can turn over more ground with it in a day, than four can do with a common spade." In a curious echo of Dundonald's peat export scheme, Sinclair also suggested that the crooked spade could be of "much service in cultivating the rocky islands of the West Indies, and consequently alleviating the labor of the slaves there." Conversely, wasteland reclamation required as much attention as any colonial venture: "The objects to which I have been under the necessity of attending are numerous; and in fact the plan embraces such a variety of particulars, that it resembles a system calculated for the establishment of a new colony, or the improvement of an extensive province."[14]

The transfer of the population to these new settlements had to be closely monitored and directed: "Instead of having them indiscriminately scattered, they ought to have assigned stations, and fixed boundaries," drawing them "into small colonies," "so as not to . . . encroach upon the landlord or tenant." By concentrating the poor population in firmly delineated zones, Sinclair hoped to solve the problem of use rights. "It is well known," he wrote, that the "only popular objection to the Inclosure of our Wastes" is that, "while unenclosed, a number of cottagers are enabled to keep cows, by means of their common rights." His 1801 pamphlet described how a model cottage of 3 3/4 acres would suffice to feed a family with a cow. Once cottagers understood that they no longer needed use rights for subsistence, enclosure could proceed without popular resistance. Sinclair practiced a version of this method himself on his Langwell estate in Caithness. He offered the five hundred "little farmers" displaced by the Cheviot flock "two Scotch acres of arable land, or at least fit to be made arable" together with a "house and garden." They were then promised contracts for one hundred to three hundred days as day laborers, paid in kind or in money. To Sinclair, this was a wonderful mark of his own generosity: "Thus the cottager, in a manner, received rent from the landlord instead of paying any."[15]

Wasteland cultivation promised to resolve the contradiction between profits and population, sheep and people. Through internal colonization, the most fertile land could be reserved for enclosure and tenurial consolidation while the population was retained on the estate. The chemistry of peat and lime together with spade cultivation provided the technical knowledge needed to implement this new order. Between 1790 and 1830, James Anderson, Christopher Tait, Lord Dundonald, James Headrick, John Walker, William Aiton, Lord Meadowbank, Andrew Steele, and Robert Rennie published essays on wasteland reclamation. Most if not all of them thought that wasteland colonization was the key to the self-sufficiency of Great Britain in food production. In a superficial sense, theirs was an optimistic vision of agricultural potential, frequently presented with a cornucopian rhetoric. Yet implicit in the very notion of wasteland colonization was an unnerving recognition. If self-sufficiency in food stuff was to be the guiding political and social ideal, then the growing population of Great Britain was closing in on the physical limits of the island. By forecasting the amount of wasteland that remained, John Sinclair made the physical limits of growth into a problem of national politics in the 1790s. The optimistic rhetoric could not conceal the logical corollary to his work. Within the foreseeable future, the island of Britain must run out of arable acres.[16]

SINCLAIR'S ARITHMETIC

At the onset of war with France in 1793, Sir John Sinclair persuaded Prime Minister Pitt and Henry Dundas to support the establishment of the Board of Agriculture and Internal Improvement, committed to wasteland reclamation and autarky at the national level. Despite Pitt's appreciation for Adam Smith's political economy, he took a pragmatic view of economic policy during these years of crisis. There were government supplies of grain from abroad in 1795, bounties on potato cultivation in 1796, and a state-sponsored London Flour Company in 1800. With Pitt's blessing, Sinclair became the first president of the board and Arthur Young its secretary. A slew of other British magnates and dignitaries also joined, including the Fifth Duke of Bedford, Lord Winchilsea, Lord Sheffield, and the bishop of Llandaff. Yet the board never received the full support of Pitt's government. Instead, it had to subsist on a rather meager grant of three thousand pounds annually.[17]

Through the Board of Agriculture, Sinclair promoted internal improvement as a strategic imperative for the nation and the landed interest. This policy combined two priorities, both of which bore the mark of Sinclair's cameralist imagination. One goal was to gather quantitative data about every county in Britain and make this information available to all landowners in order to further the exchange of useful knowledge. It was a natural extension of Sinclair's other great enterprise in these years—*The Statistical Account of Scotland*. The mission of compiling each *General Report* was entrusted to an agricultural improver: James Anderson for Aberdeenshire, William Marshall in the central Highlands, John Smith on Argyll, James Robertson in Perthshire, and so on. For Sinclair, these regional surveys, modeled on British and Continental traditions of political arithmetic, promised to reveal a synoptic view of agrarian society. What was the total land area under cultivation? How could food production be expanded? How much of the territory remained waste? Like Francis Bacon, Sinclair regarded knowledge as a direct instrument of power. The mere act of publishing and circulating information about new crops, livestock, or methods of reclamation was supposed to translate into effective practical innovations at the level of estate management.[18]

The second approach of Sinclair's Board of Agriculture to the problem of subsistence was to advocate a general bill of enclosure in Parliament. Sinclair hoped that such an act would eliminate the exorbitant cost of private enclosure bills, estimated by him at eight hundred thousand pounds for the year 1796 alone. General enclosure would also restore the positive balance of trade, stop the bullion drain, lower spending on poor relief, temper "public discontent" over high prices, and, not the least, permanently add to the strength and wealth of the nation. Sinclair lauded Frederick the Great's Prussia as a model for wartime Britain to emulate. Between 1763 and 1783, the Prussian king and his minister Count Hertzberg had expended the equivalent of six million pounds on enclosing commons, encouraging industry by means of premiums, importing useful "domestic animals," "cultivating Wastes," and building cottages for "introducing new settlers." The fruits of this effort were stupendous: the "naturally barren" nation of Prussia had been raised by "unceasing attention to its internal improvement, to be one of the most powerful countries in Europe." But Sinclair's proposal was hardly a carbon copy of Prussian policy. The enclosure act was intended to facilitate private landlord initiative rather than impose government mandates. By leaving agricultural improvement in the hands of the landed interest, it was an expression of civil cameralism rather than autocratic state building.[19]

Even so, Sinclair's campaign failed miserably. Though he drafted bills for the consideration of Parliament on wasteland reclamation and general enclosure in 1796, 1797, 1800, 1807, and 1811–12, none achieved sufficient support. However, the campaign did have one significant political effect in focusing public attention on the arithmetic of land use and population growth. Sinclair provided a rough sketch of wasteland acreage in a May 1793 speech to Parliament: out of 67 million Scots acres of land in Great Britain, only 7 million were "totally incapable of cultivation." About half of the remaining area was properly cultivated, in grain or pasture, but this left upwards of 30 million acres "either completely waste, or under a very defective system of husbandry." If these wastelands could be reclaimed, they might "by fair calculation . . . furnish subsistence to above ten millions of people." This forecast presumed a ratio of 3 acres for each additional person.[20]

The following year in July 1794, Sinclair revised the number of unimproved acres downward to a figure just below 26 million. This new measure was derived by extrapolation from Charles Vancouver's study of Cambridgeshire. Sinclair regarded Vancouver's report to the Board of Agriculture as a model for the rest of the nation and "by far the most minute" of the surveys conducted for the board, since Vancouver had troubled to go "from parish to parish" to obtain "sufficient information, in regard to stock, produce and population." Vancouver had calculated that there were 319,000 acres of fens, commons, and other unimproved land that could be reclaimed in the county. Sinclair multiplied

Vancouver's figure by seventy to arrive at 22.3 million acres on the assumption that the county of Cambridge comprised a seventieth of the landmass of England and Wales. He then suggested an additional "one sixth" acres of wasteland for Great Britain as a whole, giving a total around 25.9 million.[21]

This, however, was not the end of Sinclair's computations. In 1795, he offered a new account of the number of unimproved acres to his colleagues on the Board of Agriculture. This time, he revised the grand total downward again to 22.1 million acres. Moreover, he reversed the proportions of wasteland from the previous report. Now Scotland seemed to possess the vast majority of unimproved land in Britain, nearly two-thirds of the total. The revised numbers were derived from the growing amount of new data coming in from the board's county reports.

England	6,259,470
Wales	1,629,307
Scotland	14,218,224
Total	22,107,001

For the Scottish area of wasteland, more than 9 million acres were associated with counties in the Highlands, from Argyll and Perthshire to Inverness and Ross-shire. Sinclair's arithmetic thus confirmed and revived the notion of the Scottish Highlands as a British frontier. More generally, Sinclair suggested the following broad categories of reclamation:

	No of Acres
Lands incapable of all Improvement	1,000,000
Lands fit to be planted	3,000,000
Lands fit for Upland Pasture	14,000,000
Lands fit for Tillage	3,000,000
Lands capable of being converted into Meadow, or Water Meadow	1,000,000
Total	22,000,000

The rental value for reclamation of upland pasture, arable land, and water meadows would amount to £6.5 million. The total projected value of annual produce, including plantations, equaled £20.7 million. However, Sinclair lowered his forecast of population increase on wastelands to a figure between two and three million inhabitants. The more he contemplated the problem, the smaller the margin for demographic growth became in his model.[22]

Behind Sinclair's attempt to quantify land use lay a different kind of arithmetic: data on the growth of the British population and the long-term trend of the grain trade. The select committee report published in 1796 considered the rising meat consumption in London between 1732 and 1794 as a proxy for the alarming growth of the urban population. In 1794, the Smithfield meat market saw the sale of 109,000 heads of cattle and more than 700,000 sheep. This was an increase by 43 percent and 36 percent, respectively, compared to the numbers for 1732. The change in urban consumption overlapped with a shift toward net imports in grain. A second report by Sinclair's committee investigated this development. It relied on Charles Smith's *Tracts on the Corn Trade* to chart the trend of exports over the period 1746–65, which had carried an average value of £651,000 per annum. In contrast, the period 1777–97 had seen a switch to net imports. The average cost of imports amounted to £600,000 per annum. But the numbers for the recent dearth were far worse.

Paid to foreign countries for Corn imported	1794	£1,983,856
	1795	£1,535,672
	1796	£3,926,484
	Total	£7,446,012

These imports had the added disadvantage of unsettling domestic prices, which were "often high, and always unsteady." Such volatility in turn fomented "public discontent" and made the lives of the poor uncertain and miserable.[23]

Sinclair's committee then investigated the ratio between grain imports and wasteland acreage. What "extent of Land . . . cultivated at home" "would have produced that quantity" "of grain imported"? The report calculated the amount of different grains imported between 1777 and 1797, including beans, oats, peas, rye, wheat, and oatmeal. The number of acres needed domestically to cover the imports depended on the produce per acre of each kind of grain. For wheat it stood at three quarts per acre. Hence, 2,893,589 quarts of wheat required 964,529 acres at home over a period of twenty years. Per annum, the figure was 144,679.45 quarts per year and 48,226.45 acres in Britain. The 1797 report concluded that an extension of the arable land of Great Britain with 148,000 acres would be sufficient to meet the shortfall of all grain imported into the country during the year 1796. In this way, Sinclair's committee delivered a precise measure of the ghost acres needed for food autarky and a quantitative justification of wasteland reclamation.[24]

Sinclair's wasteland arithmetic and campaign for general enclosure provoked a powerful liberal response. Malthus's *Essay on the Principle of Population* (1798) took aim not only at William Godwin's enlightened optimism but also at Sinclair's model of autarky. Malthus wrote in the second edition of the *Essay on the Principle of Population* (1803): "To restore our independence . . . it is evidently not sufficient . . . to cultivate this or that waste, or even to propose a general enclosure bill." He added, "It is not the question, whether by cultivating all our commons, we could raise substantially more corn than at present." The real problem was how the government would cope with explosive population growth over the long term. Famously, Malthus proposed that population expanded according to an exponential ("geometric") rate and that the food supply could only increase much more slowly, according to an arithmetic rate. Sexual instinct constantly threatened to undo the work of improvement. Famine and other positive checks offered the providential means of reducing surplus population. The second and subsequent editions of the *Essay* tempered Malthus's original position to a certain degree, by endorsing preventive checks and the protectionist policy of the Corn Laws. Yet Malthus still insisted that even the most "enlightened system of agriculture" must fail to "keep pace with an unchecked population."[25]

Malthus's gloomy prognostication, once married to the evangelical belief system of the Victorian bourgeoisie, would have a long intellectual afterlife and strong influence on liberal social policy. Much of the appeal of Malthus's political economy derived from its simple mathematical form. His style of prediction relied on the appearance of analytical rigor rather than exhaustive quantitative data. The empirical case for the exponential growth of population rested on Benjamin Franklin's view of American demography. A population could double every twenty-five years if material conditions were altogether favorable. What would happen if the population of Britain were to grow at a colonial American rate? Malthus suggested that the British "science of agriculture" might keep pace the first twenty-five years of growth and allow for a doubling of the present population. Indeed, he praised the "inclosure of commons and waste land" as a sure way of increasing the "food of the country." But after that first stage of growth, production must inevitably lag behind as population quadrupled. Malthus's argument thus paralleled the pessimistic view of coal consumption. By expanding the temporal horizon beyond present consumption, he sought to show that the current trend was unsustainable in the long term. For the sake of logical consistency, he repeated the same thought experiment for the planet as a whole. The forecast demonstrated that even global growth was constrained by natural limits in the long run. All nations and all empires would sooner or later succumb to the stationary state when the finite supply of land put an end to progress.[26]

ECOLOGICAL STRAIN AND BOTTLENECK PANICS

The rival forecasts of Sinclair and Malthus were expressions of a wider phenomenon of bottleneck panic. This concern with resource exhaustion extended from grain to timber, coal, peat, and hemp. Charles Middleton surveyed the British timber reserves for the Admiralty in 1792. John Williams predicted coal exhaustion in 1789. Henry Gray Macnab warned about moss exhaustion in 1793 by compiling the complaints in Sinclair's *Statistical Account*. These forecasts helped foster a new political arithmetic of environmental limits. Coal stocks were quantified by Macnab and his critics. The Admiralty collated data on national timber stores and surveyed naval timber across the globe. The secretary of state for Home Affairs began to collect statistics on English cereal production in 1795. The dearth of 1795 also inspired Frederick Morton Eden's social survey *The State of the Poor* (1797). A more rigorous parochial survey of the grain harvest was undertaken in 1801, following the precedent of Sinclair's *Statistical Account*. The same year, the British government conducted the first national census of the population. Multiple forms of environmental strain thus became legible to the servants of the state and concerned citizens.[27]

The investigation of population pressure was hardly a new field of inquiry in the 1790s. William Petty and John Graunt pioneered the quantitative study of population in political and medical arithmetic during the Restoration. Worries about overpopulation had haunted English observers in the first half of the seventeenth century. Nehemiah Grew's memorandum to Queen Anne in 1706 offered an estimate of how much the population of Great Britain could be increased through the cultivation of wastelands. Across the Channel, Richard Cantillon calculated the minimum unit of land required to maintain a family in France and England (1.5 *arpents* in the south of France to 4–5 in England). Using similar measures, a number of early modern savants tried to predict the greatest number of inhabitants possible for the world as a whole. Antonie van Leeuwenhoek took the population density of Holland as a model for the maximum population of the planet in a 1679 letter to the Royal Society. Assuming that Holland contained 120 people per square kilometer, he argued for a potential world population of 13.3 billion people. In a private notebook dated 1695–1700, Gregory King suggested a grand total of 6.2 billion inhabitants.[28]

Sinclair's wastelands calculus differed from these earlier thought experiments and ventures in political arithmetic by dint of its ecological and political context. The loss of the American colonies in 1783 gave new force to the argument that agricultural improvement at home should have priority over costly overseas colonies. A sequence of bad harvests in 1794–96 and 1799–1801 confirmed the worst fears of the internal improvers. In 1793, domestic stocks of grain reached a critical low just as war began with France. Would Britain now become dependent on cereal imports to feed its population? At the same time, forecasts of shortages in fuel and naval timber suggested that exhaustion might be a more general phenomenon. While Williams's prediction of coal exhaustion proved grossly premature in hindsight, there were plausible reasons for contemporaries to worry about the full extent of remaining stocks, as we have seen. Such economic and environmental fears mingled with broader concerns about the threat of French radical ideology. Political repression and loyalist reaction dominated the public sphere. Meanwhile, French forces were mobilized to strike at the British Isles in 1796–98 and 1803–5. This invasion threat was succeeded by the Continental blockade from the autumn of 1806. The ensuing disruption of the Baltic trade revived concerns about both timber and hemp imports. No wonder, then, if agrarian patriotism developed an inward-looking orientation preoccupied with domestic improvement and autarky.[29]

Such fears of exhaustion reflected at least in part an underlying ecological bottleneck. E. A. Wrigley's idea of "energy revolution" provides a neo-Malthusian interpretation of the 1790s crisis. On the revisionist assumption that the Industrial Revolution did not transform the British economy until the middle of the nineteenth century, Wrigley suggests that late eighteenth-century society was pressing up against basic ecological limits. "It is difficult," Wrigley observes, "to overstate the severity of the challenge posed by the rapidity of population growth between . . . 1780 and 1840 when viewed in terms of the limitations of an organic economy in a land long settled." The growing population put increasing pressure on soil with competing priorities of "food, clothing, lodging and firing." For Wrigley, it was only the move from the organic economy based on photosynthesis to an industrial mineral energy economy that solved the problem long-term. He gives the coal consumption in 1800 as 11.2 million acres of woodland, or 35 percent of the total land surface in England and Wales. Setting aside that much land to grow wood fuel "would have been quite impractical," especially when one considers the doubling population and "many other competing uses" of land. Once Britain achieved a comparative advantage in industrial production, it could exchange manufactured goods for food imports. Joseph Hume's put the case baldly in his speech on the Corn

Laws in 1833: "There was a limit to the cultivation of land; but there was no limit to the increased employment of hands in manufacturers, save a want of demand."[30]

The growth of the British economy relied not just on internal coal stock but also on external "ghost acres." Brinley Thomas characterizes the period 1750–1800 in British history as an incipient Malthusian crisis with population growing faster than the food supply. For Thomas, it was Irish grain imports that made urban expansion in Britain possible. Kenneth Pomeranz also depicts the condition of late eighteenth-century Britain in terms of an ecological bottleneck. The price of wheat was rising sharply. Benefit from markets in grain had already been exploited fully. At the same time, shortages of naval timber, charcoal, bar iron, and fiber crops became acute. In Pomeranz's model, Britain found a way out of this state of diminishing returns only through the ecological relief provided by overseas colonization and trade. Ralph Davis has calculated that Britain's timber imports more than tripled in value between 1784–86 and 1804–6. They had increased tenfold by 1854–56. James Belich, too, notes that metropolitan agricultural production in the early nineteenth century "barely kept up with population growth." Grain, meat, timber, and wool from the new settler colonies provided the resources needed to sustain urban development in Great Britain. The revival of large-scale emigration from the metropole at the end of the Napoleonic Wars provided another measure of ecological relief. In all these accounts, the escape from the traditional economy into the industrial economy required the supplement of colonial resources to succeed.[31]

While these economic and environmental historians provide us with the material framework necessary to understand the exhaustion fears of the 1790s, they also obscure the political stakes of that moment. What happened when ecological strain became a subject of state intervention and debate? How was resource strain experienced? Who defined these natural limits and in whose interest? What range of remedies was proposed? As we have seen, improvers and politicians embraced competing prospects of emigration, internal colonization, or foreign conquest. Once we consider the politics of ecological strain, we also need to restrict our temporal horizon, to avoid the bias of hindsight. This means taking the uncertainties and perceptions of the 1790s seriously. Industrialization and settler colonies may have provided the long-term solution, but these remedies were not clearly perceived at the time. Indeed, internal self-sufficiency and wasteland colonization seemed far more rational priorities to many politicians and improvers. In their circles, emigration and overseas empire were denounced as a wasteful drain on precious national resources.

Just after the turn of the century, the Highlands became the locus for a debate about overpopulation and autarky. Alarm over Gaelic emigration in 1802–3 provoked a new clash between the rival ecologies of development. On the liberal side, Lord Selkirk and the *Edinburgh Review* stressed the natural limits of growth in the region and the need for free migration to relieve the pressure of population on scarce resources. Among conservative and radical polemicists alike, Highland colonization of wastelands promised the best remedy for the strain brought on by warfare and population growth. James Headrick—Presbyterian preacher, chemist, and assistant to Sir John Sinclair's *Statistical Account*—presented a simple and succinct defense of autarky for the Highland Society of Scotland in 1803. Once the Highland economy had been fully developed, it would render foreign trade and empire redundant. "When these resources are called into action, Britain will become a world, able to contend with another world in arms."[32]

10

"A Stationary Condition for Ever"

The long campaign to colonize the Highlands reached a final crisis point just after the turn of the century. An immediate cause was the Treaty of Amiens between Britain and France from 1801 to 1803. This brief interlude of peace acted as a vent for discontent and ambition in Highland society, encouraging the first great wave of emigration since 1793. Much of it seems to have been voluntary. The old tacksman class within Gaelic society, once the managerial linchpin of the agrarian system, was gradually made obsolete by commercial pressures. These tacksman families now took flight and went west by selling off their assets in cattle.[1] Leading figures in the Highland Society reacted to the news with alarm. Authentic reports of departures quickly ballooned into wild rumors of demographic collapse. To prevent a disaster from occurring, Henry Dundas and the Lord Advocate Charles Hope coordinated the most ambitious attempt at state intervention in Highland affairs since the era of the Annexed Estates.

The 1803 crisis at the same time revived and transformed the Enlightenment quarrel about the natural order in the Highlands. It provoked a clash of rival ecologies every bit as momentous as the battle waged between Tory improvers and the followers of Adam Smith over the management of Bengal. On the right, Henry Mackenzie, John Walker, and their allies defended the idea of internal colonization and state intervention. Like John Sinclair, they saw the Highlands as a wasteland frontier that could ensure British military might and self-sufficiency. On the liberal side, a new pessimism was gaining strength among the Whigs at the *Edinburgh Review*, T. R. Malthus, and Thomas Douglas, Fifth Earl of Selkirk. James Anderson's plan for Highland urbanization and manufacturing gave way to a diagnosis of chronic overpopulation. Lord Selkirk's mixture of political economy and colonial promotion combined principles drawn from Smith and Malthus into a defense of voluntary emigration as a "salutary drain."

The rival ecologies of the Enlightenment also open a new window on the history of environmental thought. Earlier historians of conservationism have tended to gloss over the quarrel between experts and markets. Donald Worster distinguishes between "Arcadian" and "imperial" ecologies, while T. C. Smout tracks the separation of "use" from "delight" in attitudes toward the environment.[2] But the utilitarian or "imperial" approach to nature contained a sharp internal division between those who favored expert management of the environment and those who saw prices and markets as the best guides to optimal use. Moreover, both sides grew increasingly concerned about the fit between society and nature in the late eighteenth century. New techniques of quantification and prediction supplied data about demographic growth and environmental strain. Naturalists and agricultural improvers from John Walker and John Sinclair to William Aiton and Robert Brown explored the limits of soil and climate. Liberal observers in turn warned about the natural constraints to growth set by population growth and the food supply. They began to think of peripheries like the Scottish Highlands as regions plagued by "redundant population." Such zones were concrete versions of the "stationary state," incapable of further improvement and a chilling reminder of the physical limits to growth. Though neither conservative naturalists nor liberal political economists valued nature for its own sake, these rival ecologies articulated notions of economic and demographic vulnerability that have become central components of modern environmentalism. The case of the Highlands was followed by other warning examples intended to demonstrate the possibility of stagnation or collapse, from the American West to Easter Island.[3]

THE MAN OF FEELING RETURNS

When groups of Highlanders began to depart from the Hebrides and the west coast bound for Nova Scotia in 1801, the Highland Society of Scotland mobilized a special committee whose members included Sir John Sinclair, Henry Mackenzie, and the lord advocate of Scotland. Their task was to offer counsel to Henry Dundas regarding the causes of emigration and to appeal to Parliament for assistance. Rumors circulated at the time that upwards of twenty thousand Gaels were on the move and planned to emigrate. Dundas was at this stage secretary of state for war as well as the first lord of the Admiralty. As in the timber crisis of 1803–4, he followed a course of state intervention aided by expert opinion. The minister and his allies found a clever way to curtail emigration without prohibiting it outright. The 1803 Passenger Vessels Act stipulated that all emigrant ships must conform to very exacting and expensive standards of comfort for passengers. British ships were permitted only one passenger for every five tons (including crew). Provisions had to last twelve weeks, including a generous helping of half a pound of meat per day for each passenger. In this way, an argument made on humanitarian grounds effectively disrupted the thriving conveyance business without violating the principle of free movement within the empire. Dundas also introduced a government-funded project of road and canal building into the heart of the Highlands. This political interventionism was underwritten by the social commitment of the Highland Society to a system of spade husbandry designed to retain the Highlanders in their native land.[4]

The moment of crisis came too late for many in the older generation of improvers. John Walker had gone blind, and his health was in rapid decline. His main contribution was an extended essay for the Highland society on the virtues of peat moss reclamation. James Anderson seems to have grown disillusioned with Scottish circles after a quarrel with John Sinclair over the invention of a new method of drainage. Anderson retired in 1797 to Isleworth in Middlesex, where he began publishing a new periodical entitled *Recreations in Agriculture, Natural History, Arts and Miscellaneous Subjects* that abandoned the northern focus of *The Bee*. He responded to the great stir of 1803 only with a short missive pleading for the abolition of the salt duties. Other key figures in Highland improvements were still active but failed to intervene effectively in the debate surrounding the crisis of 1803. John Sinclair fell ill in late 1802 and remained indisposed throughout the next year. George Dempster expressed deep concern about the spread of sheep farms but did not participate in the Highland Society meetings during the years of crisis. In the end, the task of advising Henry Dundas was left to a different circle, led by his right-hand man Henry Mackenzie.[5]

This was a curious twist to Mackenzie's dual career in literature and improvement. Thirty years earlier, his best-selling novel *The Man of Feeling* (1771) had painted a vivid scene of pastoral paternalism. While traveling back from London to his country estate, Mackenzie's protagonist, Harley, encountered a bedraggled vagrant who turned out to be the beggared tenant and soldier Edwards, an old family friend. After hearing the story of how Edwards had lost his lease, Harley granted him a cottage and a garden. "The house upon this farm was indeed little better than a hut," but the "situation . . . was pleasant," and the old soldier, "assisted by the beneficence of Harley, set about improving its neatness and convenience." With the gentleman's help, Edwards "staked out a piece of the green" to make a garden. "It was a scene of tranquil virtue." What had been a sentimental fancy in 1771 became a full-fledged program of state intervention in 1803. Predictably, the edges of humanitarianism hardened in the transfer from fiction to the reality of Highland agrarian politics, yet the moral urgency articulated in *The Man of Feeling* remained a recognizable force driving the new policy.[6]

Henry Dundas's correspondence from the winter and spring of 1803 contains a series of proposals and recommendations that straddle the divide between political economy and sentimental literature. The principal contributions included Henry Mackenzie's memorandum, the report on emigration compiled by the Highland Society of Scotland one year earlier, and the report of E. S. Fraser of Reelig, customs commissioner and close ally of Lord Seaforth of Lewis. An anonymous manuscript on emigration policy dated March 1803 was likely addressed to Henry Dundas as well. Finally, the second volume of the *Transactions* from the Highland Society of Scotland, edited by Mackenzie and published the same year, also contained a number of schemes for improvement, including John Walker's last essay on peat moss and a defense of Highland industrialization by James Headrick. These texts shared a common rhetoric of ethnic apocalypse. The race of the Gaels was on the verge of extinction, thanks to the operation of conveyance agents and the spread of sheep farms. The anonymous author of the "The State of Emigration in 1803" insisted that the conventional rationale of political economists could not apply in this situation. "Mere speculative reasoners" failed to "mark the physical or moral distinctions among mankind" in their calculations. Even "the best political economists such as Adam Smith" did not appreciate the "exceptions necessary" to the calculus of "money rent." In the case of the Highlanders, the "comparative value of the population with a view to national defense" necessarily trumped the concern with landlord profit. In the same spirit, the committee on emigration from the Highland Society of Scotland defined its primary aim as the "enlargement of the population of the Highlands" rather than the "encrease of the Wealth of Proprietors." The strategic value of the Gael was predicated on "physical or moral" peculiarity. The martial virtues of the Highlander were said to be rooted in unique particulars of environment and tradition, making the Gaelic population unique and irreplaceable. By removing the people from the ancestral land through emigration, these virtues would be lost—hence the rhetoric of extirpation and the case for state intervention.[7]

E. S. Fraser observed that the "the very coasts and mountains [the Highlanders] inhabit, impress their hardy character on the natives; and their pursuits, their recreations, their occupations, among these, give energy and force to their mind and body." But such virtues were powerless to stem the tide of sheep. "I have not a doubt, from what is now passing in the Setts of Great Estates—that the whole race of Highlanders will in a very few years, be extinguished: and the Sheep come down to the East, as well as West, and North Coast." He traced the origins of this process to the Act of Union of 1707, when "the mixture of the Nations" "became more intimate." After the failed rebellion of 1745, the growth of commerce hastened "the dispersion of the Highlanders." In the present moment of crisis, economic interest seemed likely to "annihilate the genuine stock." But Fraser here switched from an environmental definition of ethnicity to the language of bloodlines, perhaps borrowed from the natural history of livestock breeding. Because martial valor was a feature of racial stock, there was some hope that "the blood of our ancient peasantry" would not "wholly stagnate, in the veins of their descendants, even in cities and villages."[8]

Ironically, these worries about the extinction of a warrior race emerged after the heyday of Highland military recruitment. Because of the massive scale of mobilization during the Napoleonic Wars, the Highland population could no longer satisfy the demands of the British army. The British state turned elsewhere for recruits, away from the proprietary and rural model of raising regiments on the basis of landlord influence. Though the myth of the Gael as a martial race would continue to grow, the actual importance of the Highlander in the British forces was quickly fading. In a sign of the times, Henry Mackenzie and the Highland Society of Scotland had established the Royal Highland Edinburgh Volunteers in 1797. But Mackenzie and Dundas's other advisers still castigated urban plebeians as inferior military material. The argument about racial extinction conveniently justified the persistence of a privileged role for Highland proprietors in the military labor market.[9]

In all of this, Henry Mackenzie proved a staunch and influential ally of Dundas. He, too, regarded the anti-emigration measure as a means of preserving or reviving the bonds of the Highland community at this moment of crisis. In a memorandum to Dundas written in March 1803, Mackenzie described the fundamental cause behind the current wave of emigration in terms of the disintegration of the moral bonds between landowners and tenants. In previous decades, profitable new breeds of sheep had been introduced from the south country by proprietors in search of higher rents. Gradually, sheep had come to replace the human population of the Highland interior. The hunger for profit was destroying old ties of affection: "It tends evidently to dissolve all Connection between the great landed Proprietors and the Body of the people; it turns the Domains of the latter into a mere Chattel, productive only of so much Money to the proprietor, without influence of attachment even from the few inhabitants who occupy them." The present crisis was precipitated by a mixture of commercial pressures, population growth, and radical agitation. Mackenzie noted that "the manners and the feelings of the people" were "entirely changed from those of former times" as rents had tripled and the population had outpaced any "openings for Industry" and subsistence. Conveyance agents lured many to America. Meanwhile, Jacobin agitators moved through the country and subverted the stability of the rural order with their seditious doctrines. But above all, the new commercial spirit had "loosen[ed] the Ties between the Proprietors of the soil and its Inhabitants or Cultivators." With higher rents and greater profits, the landowners had become estranged from their "Native Districts" and removed to the "Society and Dissipation of the Great Cities," where happiness was measured by "an Increase of Luxury." Mackenzie's diagnosis failed to mention that he himself was a member of this estranged elite. He had grown up on the edge of the Highlands in Nairn near Inverness and married into the prominent Highland family of Sir James Grant of Grant. Mackenzie was much more a creature of Edinburgh than the north. In this sense, he embodied the very attrition of traditional values among country gentlemen across Britain which he now sought to undo.[10]

Mackenzie endorsed the conclusion of his fellow members of the Highland Society regarding emigration. Although an outright ban was inopportune, forceful positive measures were much needed. The Gaelic minority was too valuable as a military resource to be left unprotected from commercial forces. The government should provide public works to generate alternative forms of employment in the face of sheep farming and rental pressures. Mackenzie here praised the private initiatives of the president of the Highland Society, the Duke of Argyll. "Sheep farming [had been] early introduced" on the duke's southern estates, but the "inhabitants whom it displaced found comfortable settlements in the towns of Campbeltown, Rothsay, and Greenoch." Indeed, this coastal population had grown numerous enough to compensate any drain on the rural community. Displaced Gaels were profitably employed in coarse manufactures and the fisheries. For Mackenzie, this was the solution Dundas ought to pursue in other parts of the north. If he could persuade private landlords to cooperate with the government, public works and private initiatives might reinforce each other. Significantly, Mackenzie did not favor the conversion of rural tenants into townspeople without caveats. The new villages were to retain a strong agricultural dimension, which would serve the dual purpose of attracting Gaelic settlers in the first place and then help preserve the rural basis of Gaelic tradition: "Perhaps the more those partake of the Nature of their former Country Occupations, by allowing to the Settlers a certain Portion of ground along with the Sites of their Houses, the more they are likely to attract Inhabitants, and to keep those Inhabitants free from that Dissipation and Immorality which numerous and merely Mechanical Establishments are apt to produce." Each villager would continue to cultivate a patch of ground, for the purpose of subsistence as well as the moral effects of agricultural labor. This was the minimalist pastoral of *The Man of Feeling*, recast as a large-scale project of cultural preservation. Mackenzie's proposal reaffirmed the moral division of labor between Lowland industrial towns and Highland villages that had first been articulated in the circles of the Select Society half a century ago. By pairing village employment and subsistence agriculture, Mackenzie hoped to inoculate the northern population against the dissipation of urban life and the moral degradation associated with manufacturing production. There was more than an echo here of the agenda first set forth by Wallace, Kames, and Walker in the days of the Annexed Estates. Mackenzie's vision also recalled Pennant's interview with the ghostly chieftain in the *Tour in Scotland and Voyage to the Hebrides*, 1772: "They require no great matters: a small portion of a raiment; a little meal.... They will not envy you your new luxuries."[11]

Such notions were put into practice on Loch Tayside in Perthshire by the Fourth Earl of Breadalbane, a leading member of the Highland Society. At the request of the civil engineer Thomas Telford, he produced a brief memorandum about crofting in February 1803, meant to be included in Telford's report to Parliament. Very likely, the 1787 queries about spade husbandry and minimum subsistence circulated by the British Fisheries Society helped inspire the experiment. Breadalbane had served as the deputy governor of the British Fisheries Society and toured the settlements of the society in 1791 together with its secretary Robert Fraser. The two travelers had concluded that the western coast could contain "almost any addition" of population, thanks to the abundant resources of the sea. Breadalbane's settlement at Loch Tayside was a wager that crofting tenure could also thrive in the Highland interior. After careful surveys of the land, he had divided the farms into "small Lotts" and introduced improving leases with "moderate rents." Here he was following the laconic advice of his factor John Campbell: "The sides of Loch [T]ay in general, were never intended by nature for the Plow, even tho the local situation and climate were better than they are." The factor had pushed for sheep farms, but Breadalbane instead preferred a maximum population. "I have besides detached farms in proper situations for a numerous race of Crofters answering to the description in England of *cottagers* with a Cows grass, keep for it winter and summer and some crop—formerly these crofters were a burden on the tenants—in short it is wonderful the effect the above system has produced on the Industry of the People." Breadalbane boasted that the "population of the district ... on the sides of Loch Tay [was] very great, perhaps not to be equalled, considering its extent to any country district in Great Britain." His factor had warned about the surplus of people and cattle on the estate a few years earlier: "The very appearance of the country, which every harvest is eat up and bared in such a manner that there is not a morsel of grass left for any animal whatever, declare it." Now, Breadalbane sought to use the high population density of the district to command the government's attention. The earl had succeeded in raising new battalions for his Regiment of Fencibles a few years earlier at the request of Henry Dundas. But he complained to Telford that the military men were "rather a disadvantage." He asked for government assistance to ensure "work and subsistence for the supernumerary population."[12]

In the years following the emigration panic, the Highland Society of Scotland undertook a mixture of literary and military initiatives that mirrored and amplified Mackenzie's view of the Highlands as a bastion of rural virtue. A continued interest in preserving Gaelic culture was interspersed with wartime campaigns to increase military recruitment. Between 1797 and 1807, John Sinclair led the society's effort to organize and publish a "scholarly" edition of James Macpherson's works, an idea first ventured by Mackenzie. In the aftermath of the 1803 crisis, Sinclair also approached Sir James Grant and Henry Dundas with a proposal to establish a Highland Legion, consisting of four thousand recruits from several regions in the north. The Gaels made the best soldiers because they possessed "naturally a strong Military Spirit, and from their habits of Life, [were] peculiarly well calculated to undergo the hardships of War." Dundas himself offered a paean to the glory of the Highland regiments at the well-attended "extraordinary special" general meeting of the Highland Society in July 1803. With a nod to Ossian, he insisted that the courage of mountain troops was peculiarly animated by "the recollection of the fame of their ancestors." Dundas justified the public expenditures in the region, including the construction of the Caledonian Canal, as a prudent investment that would secure the military strength of the Highlands over the long term. At the same general meeting in 1803, Henry Mackenzie proposed that the Highland Society employ some of its funds as bounties to encourage Highlanders to enlist rather than to emigrate. Such a nudge would awake "the natural disposition of Scottish Highlanders" toward war, he suggested. Advertisements were placed in the newspapers promising two pounds per head for the first one hundred men to enlist. Though the resources devoted were relatively small, the use of a voluntary association as an instrument of military recruitment reflected Mackenzie's belief that a partnership between civil society and the state was best suited to steer Highland development.[13]

PEAT FRONTIER

Wasteland colonization, peat moss, and autarky were closely intertwined in the natural histories sanctioned by the Highland Society during these crisis years. The chemist and preacher James Headrick penned a visionary plan for Highland colonization in 1801. Headrick had served as an assistant of John Sinclair in the 1790s for *The Statistical Account of Scotland* and later became the minister in George Dempster's Angus parish of Dunnichen. Around the turn of the century, he traveled frequently in northern Scotland, surveying the coast up to Loch Broom as well as the islands of Lewis and Arran. Like Sinclair, he maintained that Cheviot sheep were compatible with a large population if marginal soils and alternatives to agriculture were fully exploited. His 1801 sketch of the future economy, published in the second volume of the *Prize Essays and Transactions of the Highland Society*, scrutinized the prospects of wasteland reclamation, herring fisheries, wool manufactures, hemp cultivation, and bar iron. The lack of coal was no permanent limit to development, Headrick suggested, since peat and water mills could fuel industrial development just as well. Like Sinclair, he rejected the agrarian protectionism of the Corn Laws in favor of bounties on wasteland improvement. The growing dependency on foreign corn imports was a serious liability in such dangerous times and tended merely to "stimulate the agriculture of nations who have manifested no very friendly disposition towards us." He also echoed another idea of Sinclair's, that Britain could become self-sufficient in hemp for the Royal Navy by fertilizing Highland soils with peat ashes and seaweed. Headrick's essay was particularly concerned with the worrying news of a northern confederacy between Sweden, Denmark, and Prussia. Throughout the eighteenth century, Great Britain had depended on the Baltic countries "for the raw materials of our fleets." At a moment when the European allies of Britain were toppling one after another and the country stood increasingly isolated against Napoleon's France, Highland wastelands would restore national power and make Britain a "world" unto itself.[14]

It was widely recognized that the possibility of wasteland improvement hinged on the question of the natural history and chemical composition of peat moss. A fifty-pound premium had been offered by the Highland Society in 1799 for the best chemical advice on the conversion of peaty soil into manure. Despite his ailing health, John Walker rose to the occasion and produced a lengthy essay for the *Prize Essays and Transactions of the Highland Society*. In a letter to his friend the chemist Joseph Black, Walker explained that the essay was designed for wide consumption by "Country Gentlemen and intelligent farmers" and therefore eschewed "as much as possible, all the Technical Terms in Natural History and Chemistry." The piece earned the professor a medal in plate and was given pride of place as the first essay in the second volume of the *Transactions* shortly before his death in December 1803. The society found Walker's piece important enough to delay publication of the transactions until the naturalist had finished his revisions. Completed and published at the height of the emigration panic, 1802–3, the essay linked the politics of population once again to the authority of natural knowledge. This time, peat chemistry justified the image of Gaeldom as a New World. While the succession of earlier improvement schemes—flax raising, planned villages, and herring fisheries—had proved frustratingly difficult and slow in execution, the idea of a peat frontier offered a new, fresh direction for the naturalist's imagination, even here at the end of Walker's life.[15]

Walker's last exertion provided a distillation of his long-standing concerns, ranging across the familiar themes of internal colonization, Linnaean inventory, indigenous substitution, medical topography, and spade culture. He began the essay by considering the chemical composition of peat moss. Contrary to common opinion, he found peat bogs a healthy environment and marveled at the purifying properties of moss in water. Even though this "dark brown infusion" was stagnant "during the heats of summer," it remained "perfectly sweet" where torpid water elsewhere by necessity grew putrid. Captain James Cook had discovered this antiseptic quality of peat infusions during his circumnavigation and made good use of such water to maintain his crew in health. The same properties also made peat mosses ideal for the watering of flax to separate the lint from the reed. From these observations, Walker suggested a chemical explanation for the health and vigor of the Highlanders. Whereas stagnant water without peat inevitably bred miasma in the carse countries and fenlands of the plains, the "neighboring uplands" were exempted from contagion. Among the "moors and mosses" of the Highlands, putrid fever, intermittent fever, and putrid soar throat were all unknown. Evidently, moss water had a "powerful influence in preserving vegetable and animal substances from corruption," whether animate or inanimate. The same "bitumen" which preserved peat "from the ultimate stage of putrefaction" also "rendered [it] capable of preserving other bodies." Without arriving at a decisive chemical analysis, Walker's investigation recast the terms of Martin Martin's medical topography of the Gael, shifting the focus from cold air and insularity to the antiseptic character of peat.[16]

Next, Walker turned to the fertility of peat mosses. His approach was more circumspect and cautious than the pronouncements of Dundonald, perhaps conditioned by the habits of the botanical taxonomist rather than the chemical projector. The essay compiled a typology of seven kinds of peat and an inventory of species native to these habitats. While he affirmed the widespread belief that peat bogs had their origin in decaying timber from ancient woods, he also hinted at the succession of plants necessary for the formation of peat. Among the eighty-four "most copious and important Plants" identified by Walker's inventory, more than a dozen were rated as useful in John Lightfoot's *Flora Scotica*. In Walker's opinion, the best prospects consisted in managing indigenous grasses like *Aira coerulea* (*Molinia caerulea*, purple moor grass) to harvest hay or in introducing "exotic cultivated plants" such as turnips, beans, Friesland oats, and potatoes. The affinity of potatoes and peat led Walker to the question of lazy bed agriculture. He had noticed the practice on Islay and elsewhere already during the tour of 1764. This form of cultivation raised a "bed" perhaps six feet wide, composed of layers of seaweed and peat moss, with trenches on both sides to drain off water. Walker noted that the Irish had grown large crops of potatoes in lazy beds on bogs for many years. He found several virtues in this system. The labor of the spade in "the soft peat" was "very inconsiderable" by comparison with other forms of digging. It also produced a superior quality and quantity of potatoes. Even gentlemen ought to cultivate them with the spade rather than the plow for this reason. Because the lazy bed destroyed the heather and "matted turf" underneath it by putrefying them at a rapid rate, Walker recommended the practice as the "first and most effectual method of culture in reclaiming many sorts of wild land." Once "completely rotted," the underlying moss was supposed to become a fertilizer in its own right, superior to the ashes produced by burning the top layer.[17]

Several things stand out in this account. First, Walker used his expertise to describe and promote labor practices on the merit of their practical utility rather than their social origin or intellectual pedigree. Even Irish plebeians possessed knowledge worthy of appropriating and emulating among Scottish gentlemen. Second, Walker was here setting out an elaborate justification for the practice of potato cultivation in lazy beds to the members of the Highland Society. In this way, his expertise gave a scientific imprimatur to the ecological and economic basis of the crofting system. Third, Walker described lazy beds as the first step in an extended process of wasteland reclamation. Once the mossy soil underneath had rotted, the ground would be ready for different crops. This meant that a landlord could claim to be engaged in the long-term improvement of the soil even as he was establishing a coastal proletariat.

To any proprietor still uncertain about the merits of spade cultivation, Walker urged the case of Blair Drummond moss. Every Highland landowner ought to follow Lord Kames's example and gather a "colony" of "moss tenants" to settle peat bogs on his estate. These settlers would at the same time advance their own interest, improve the value of the property, and increase the food supply of the nation. Moss labor was particularly suited for the poorest class of people, since it required "no stock, no cattle, nor any implement but [the] spade." This manner of living was "highly conducive to the population of the country" by encouraging marriage among "the lower people." It also presented "an eligible settlement to country tradesmen just beginning in the world." For all these ranks, "such an opportunity" must banish "all thoughts of emigration . . . especially . . . in the Highlands." Peat cultivation was an act of public spirit for estate managers: "This is a domestic conquest, far preferable to one of a foreign nature. If this is not patriotism, one may be at a loss to know what patriotism is. The achievements of a warrior in the field, may have a more dazzling appearance, but they cannot, in the eye of reason, be accounted equal to this." Walker thus adapted the ideology of internal colonization to the simplest mode of subsistence available in the Highlands. By arguing that mosses were colonies, he turned spade labor and crofting communities into heroic outposts on an internal peat frontier. The moral prescriptions of cameralism and enlightened science here became conflated with the exploitative order of proto-industrialization. After nearly forty years of northern surveys and improvement schemes, Walker had arrived at the minimal version of alternative modernity: a Highlander growing potatoes in a peat bog.[18]

The fashion for peat moss improvement seems to have reached a peak during the first decade of the nineteenth century. After Walker's essay, the Highland Society of Scotland supported similar works by the Reverend Robert Rennie, John Naismith, and William Aiton. The society also expanded its support for practical forms of wasteland reclamation and spade labor. By 1811, Aiton could document several dozen projects of "moss improvement" from Lancashire to Caithness. An Ayrshire notary of humble origins, Aiton had a contagious fascination with all things to do with peat, which earned him a far-flung network of social contacts among landowners. John Sinclair put his extensive address book at Aiton's disposal, providing introductions and information. Aiton visited a large number of estates in order to verify the practical power of moss husbandry. These were not the "fanciful speculations" of an "enthusiast" but careful observations from the field. For Aiton, moss had a host of economic uses—as fuel, manure, rough pasture, plantation, and "soil with culture." His treatise drew a great deal of its argument from Walker's essay while expanding the scope and detail, providing numerous practical examples, and tying peat mosses to the history of the Scottish climate. In Aiton's account, peat moss was the product of a long process of deforestation. Like a number of other observers, he assumed that tree logs and roots buried in the peat offered evidence of this origin. Blair Drummond moss was full of "innumerable trees" cut down by the Romans. "This extensive vale had, in former ages, been covered with growing wood, part of 'Sylva Caledonia,' mentioned by Tacitus." The loss of woodland and spread of blanket bogs had degraded the climate through the accumulation of moist peat, which had a chilling effect on both soil and air. While peat itself was not "alive" in any proper sense according to Aiton, it still accumulated over time through the ongoing absorption of water and formation of sphagnum on its surface.[19]

But this history of degradation was not irreversible. Aiton promoted afforestation and drainage as methods of reclamation. "Where the deep fen, or dark morass now lies, / Tall trees may grow, and richest verdure rise." Aiton observed that fir trees grew spontaneously even in peat eight feet deep. "In the wonderful economy of nature, trees as well as grasses, are provided for almost in every kind of climate, soil and situation." In thin layers of peat where roots could reach the bottom, every species of tree was possible. But for the deeper mosses, it was necessary to cut drains "four or five feet deep" before trees of "aquatic kind" could flourish there. The next, more ambitious step was to drain the moss completely and convert it into soil. If the soil below was superior, then Kames's method of removing the top layer of peat was preferable. In other cases, the Irish lazy bed method offered the most cost-effective means of husbandry by allowing peat itself to be cultivated. Taken together, these different methods promised to extend the arable land and ameliorate the Scottish climate in both Highlands and Lowlands. Such environmental engineering offered a grandiose justification for the poverty and back-breaking labor of crofting settlements. Spade husbandry would slowly alter the climate of the nation over time.[20]

For the second and much enlarged edition of Aiton's book in 1811, he added a highly polemical concluding section. Napoleon's Continental System, established in 1806, and the British counterblockade—the "Orders in Council" of 1807, gave new urgency to the task of wasteland reclamation. This strategy was all the more important since the last thirty years had witnessed a succession of alarming dearths and increasing dependency on imports. Aiton feared that a repeat of the 1782 and 1799 harvest failures in the current condition of blockade and economic isolation might prove fatal to the future of Britain as a "free and independent nation." The old policy of using manufacturing exports to buy food from "foreign countries" was no longer sustainable. Instead, the government must turn inward and encourage the improvement of peat moss. Aiton cited Sinclair's 1795 data on the proportion of wasteland per Scottish county. But he was convinced that some of the reports had grossly underestimated the acreage covered by peat. Drawing on his own knowledge of Lanarkshire, he was ready to double if not triple the official figure of 42,000 acres. In Perthshire, he thought the number should be tripled, to a number close to 3.9 million acres.[21]

Once again, Lord Kames figured as the paragon of northern improvement. Aiton compared Blair Drummond to the "cotton mill colony" of David Dale at Lanark, observing that Kames's project was of far greater significance "in a national point of view." "No species of labor in which mankind were ever employed can be more conducive to health, or less exposed to the contamination of vice, than the improvement of moss soil." He added to Walker's antiseptic effect of peat a sexual and social critique of urban labor. Manufactures broke the spirit and bodies of their laborers, whereas moss husbandry engendered "strong, healthy, and robust" offspring. "None was ever better calculated to increase population, and the means of supporting that increase." During a visit to Manchester, Aiton had witnessed this stark contrast with his own eyes. After examining Mr. Roscoe's peat colony at Chatt Moss, Aiton traveled the short distance into the city and was shocked by the squalor of the manufacturing district. "I saw thousands of poor unhealthy dissipated beings . . . disease and debility were perceptible in many faces." A few days later, riots broke out to confirm Aiton's impression of contaminated morals. In contrast, even the lowliest farm laborer was attached by strong bonds to his master. For Aiton, this translated into a general "attachment to Government." "But a mechanic in the cotton trade, is a mere article of commerce, bought and sold, several times every year their wages are changed, sometimes every week." No bonds of sentiment could survive in such an inhuman and unstable environment. "Several hundreds of them are slaves to one man, or one company, who though their profits are sometimes enormous, can give no security for continuing their people in pay even for a month." He added ominously, "If a Revolution does not meliorate their condition, it can scarcely make it worse."[22]

DRAINING MEN

The liberal *Edinburgh Review* launched a frontal assault on the idea of the internal frontier in April 1804. The occasion for the attack on peat husbandry was the publication of the second volume of the Highland Society's *Prize Essays and Transactions*. Clearly, this was a tempting target for the newly founded Whig journal. The anonymous reviewer agreed with Walker and other observers that the peculiarities of the region required detailed knowledge of local climate and soils. "This district of the empire differs in so many material points from every other" that an external model of improvement drawn from other regions must be "inapplicable" or "prejudicial." But he assumed a far more pessimistic position than Walker and the Highland Society regarding the nature of the northern climate. The cool summers and early autumns with hard winds and rain made "arable husbandry" very difficult. Walker's suggestion that a native crop like bear or a foreign introduction such as Tartarian oats could offer the basis for a viable northern mode of agriculture was therefore dubious. Indeed, the reviewer ridiculed Walker's notion of a basic climatological equivalence between northern Scotland and Norway or Russia. It was "absurd to imagine that seed corn brought from Norway would ripen in as short space of time in the Highlands, as it did in its native country." Walker was nothing but an armchair naturalist. "The Doctor appears to have derived most of his information from books." He was the kind of natural historian who read rather than observed. On the subject of peat husbandry, the reviewer was equally skeptical. He alleged that Walker's chemical knowledge was badly dated: "The reverend author appears to have been well acquainted with chemistry as it existed in the middle of the last century." But even the best new chemistry could not alter the fact that peat agriculture was obviously mistaken since "arable husbandry" was improper for the region. Peat was more properly used as a fuel, not a soil.[23]

This attack on Walker's natural expertise was part of a broader critique of the priorities of the Highland Society. The same anonymous reviewer accused the landed interest in the Highlands of encouraging risky experiments without appropriate knowledge. "We are . . . surprised that, in the two volumes which the Highland Society have published, there is only one very short and unsatisfactory paper on the obstacles to improvement in the Highlands." The attachment of the elite to Gaelic culture was wrongheaded if not perverse. In fact, "an attention to the preservation of the language, poetry, and music of the Highlands, we consider as in a great degree incompatible with the introduction of improvement." Cultural assimilation was a prerequisite for all future progress. "Every method . . . ought to be taken to identify the Highlander, in language and manners, with the other inhabitants of the empire." The *Edinburgh Review* thus took aim at the central objection of Mackenzie and Walker to the political economy of David Hume and Adam Smith. By stripping the Highlander of sentimental value, the reviewer sought to bolster the idea of salutary self-interest. Landowners should embrace full-scale commercialization and not settle for the half-measures prompted by nostalgic memories of clanship. "The landed interest ought certainly to consider the increase of rent . . . as a sufficient compensation for the loss of their feudal honors, power, and attendance."[24] At times, the *Edinburgh Review* seemed to reflect James Anderson's 1777 work *Observations on the Means of Exciting a Spirit of National Industry*. The reviewer faulted the essayists in the *Prize Essays and Transactions* for having so little to say about sheep farming. He argued that wool production might serve as the first step toward a manufacturing economy in the Highlands. Fuel was readily available in the form of "immense quantities of peat, and the powerful waterfalls that abound in all quarters, [which] would support machinery at little expense." Perhaps "charred peat" might serve to produce pig iron or even steel, as James Headrick had suggested. The spread of sheep farms augured a rise in population: manufacturing wages would provide "employment for many more people than the Highlands now contain." This meant more secure subsistence—not through the naturalist's assortment of famine foods but by securing greater purchasing power for the poor. "Under the sheep husbandry, the Highlands would produce subsistence for at least four times as many human beings as they now maintain."[25]

Yet only a year later, the journal presented a much more pessimistic assessment of northern improvement. Gone was the heroic vision of Highland industry from Anderson and Headrick. Instead, the reviewer—none other than Francis Horner—the founder and editor of the *Edinburgh Review*—dismissed both cereal cultivation and manufacturing as feasible options. "The climate of the Highlands is adverse to the production of grain; and that mountainous region contains few mines that can attract knots of population." The gloom of John Williams's surveys hangs thick over Horner's essay. The Highlands were "entirely destitute of coals" and could therefore not be expected to foster "the settlement of manufactures." Conditions of climate, soil, and fuel scarcity preordained the region to be a grazing country. Price and rent offered unequivocal evidence about the *natural* function of the region: "The rapid and continual progress which this system is making, the great profits that have been reaped, and the increased rate of rents, sufficiently prove how well it is adapted to the natural circumstances of the Highlands." Grazing without manufacturing employment necessarily involved a process of depopulation: "Such a revolution . . . in the system of landed property, must be accompanied by an entire change in the distribution of the inhabitants." "The race of cottars" would gradually be pushed into the "manufacturing districts" in the south. Meanwhile, the tenant farmers "with some amount of capital" might use their funds to immigrate to cheap lands in the British colonies. Horner here quoted Smith's dictum about depopulation and progress: "The diminution of cottagers, and other small occupiers of land, has, in every part of Europe, been the immediate forerunner of improvement and better cultivation."[26]

Horner's piece was a review of Thomas Douglas's work *Observations on the Present State of the Highlands* (1805). Though little read by historians of economic thought today, Selkirk's book was much discussed at the time and quite innovative in its attempt to accommodate the political economy of Smith and Malthus within an imperial framework. A liberal principle of mobility provided Selkirk with his departure point. The tenant farmer class in the Highlands favored the option of emigration over manufacturing work at home. It was their right to "carry their capital and labor to the best market they [could] find." Yet such a principle posed a strategic conundrum to Selkirk, who combined his liberalism with a firm support of the empire. Could the flow of labor and capital be directed away from the United States to British North America? Selkirk's book was not simply a theoretical exercise but also a record of his concrete efforts to promote Scottish emigration during the truce with France. In direct defiance of the Highland Society, Selkirk managed to plant eight hundred Highlanders on Prince Edward Island in 1803. Afterward, he went on to promote settlements at Baldoon and Red River in Ontario.[27]

Selkirk's defense of emigration rested on a hydraulic model of the Highland economy. For many years, "a silent but continuous migration towards the great centers of manufacturing" had taken place in those districts of the southern Highlands where sheep farming had first been established. Like Townsend's "silent dew," this demographic "drain" was not only economically necessary but also completely benign. When sheep farms crowded out traditional employments, the excess population had to be dissipated. In the 1803 edition of *An Essay on the Principle of Population*, Malthus alluded repeatedly to the Scottish Highlands as a region with a "redundant population." *Observations on the Present State of the Highlands* expanded this observation into a sustained commentary on the liberal conditions of development. "In every civilized country," Selkirk noted, the owners of large estates reduced their labor costs to the most efficient level, getting rid of "superfluous mouths." This shifted the balance of population away from the country to urban centers. Surplus produce was no longer consumed on the spot but exported to the cities. While Hume and Smith had proposed a schematic version of this model many decades earlier, Selkirk applied the notion explicitly to the Highlands. In a rural country, the profit of the landowner should govern land use and regional specialization. "By this test," the mountainous north of Scotland was suited only for livestock grazing. Hence, the population must be greatly reduced, especially in the rainy climate on the west coast, better suited for sheep than grain. No relief from local manufacturing employment could be expected. The country was "entirely destitute of coals" and had only a few mines of "little consequence." Although peat offered a substitute fuel, it was difficult to gather in a rainy climate and could not match coal in value or utility. Better access to markets could not overcome this basic obstacle. Selkirk had no patience with the Caledonian Canal scheme.[28]

The island of Skye offered a concrete laboratory for Selkirk's argument. He noted that the seven parishes on Skye had seen sustained emigration after 1770 amounting to 4,000 people. He reckoned that a further 8,000 inhabitants had moved to the Lowlands. Yet the demographic data supplied by Webster in 1755 and Sinclair's *Statistical Account* in 1794 indicated that the population had recovered fully from this "drain." It had grown from 11,252 inhabitants in 1755 to 14,470 in the early 1790s. Indeed, when he took into account the total number of migrants born on the island, the population seemed to have *doubled* in the intervening years. To Selkirk, this was a powerful demonstration of the essential truth of Malthus's theory. The Skye data confirmed that "the natural tendency of population to increase" would quickly compensate for the losses induced by emigration. Elsewhere, Selkirk noted the tendency of the cottar class to constantly push against the limits of subsistence even in a moment of profound crisis. Those who remained after the coming of the sheep farms and the commercial consolidation of estates fell "into the station of laborers . . . and other subordinate employments, multiplying till every blank is filled up." This thought led Selkirk to a darker lesson about the physical limits to development. He invited his critics to consider the return of all migrants to the island from their new homes in America and the Lowlands. Would the "wildest declaimer against emigration pretend to say, that it could afford support of employment to them all?" No, there were firm limits to population. Without a natural "drain," demographic growth would bring disaster. Skye thus served as a *Scottish* variation on the island logic of Joseph Townsend's ungulate irruption. The experience of Skye also seemed to confirm Malthus's thought experiment about the *island* of Britain. What would happen when "every acre" of the nation was cultivated like a "garden"? By confronting the problem of growth in northern Scotland, Selkirk brushed against the possibility of the stationary state, much as the search for Highland coal had driven John Williams to conceptualize the possibility of peak coal in Britain.[29]

A specter haunted Selkirk's political economy. Despite his penchant for describing economic change in terms of inevitable natural processes, he recognized that the new order in the Highlands provoked popular resistance. On his tour of the Highlands in 1792, Selkirk had been an eyewitness to the Bliadhna Nan Caorach—the Year of the Sheep—when popular riots against sheep farming swept eastern Ross-shire. Southern graziers had recently brought the new system across the Great Glen. In the summer of 1792, local tenants clashed with two sheep farming brothers by the name of Cameron on the farm of Kildermorie over grazing rights. There were incursions of cattle into land that the Camerons sought to reserve for their herds of sheep. On July 31, a group of two hundred carried out a coordinated protest across the area. Sheep from as far north as Lairg in Sutherland were collected and driven south. Eventually, the herd numbered many thousands. The popular leader Wallace later described the campaign as an attempt to "extirpate all the vipers." But the local gentry organized a counterattack. With the aid of soldiers, they rounded up the expelled sheep and arrested twelve protesters. Though order was quickly restored, Selkirk was struck by the force of popular resentment. "They had for many days the entire command of the country; and it was not from want of opportunity that few acts of pillage or personal violence were committed." He went on to note that there was "scarcely any part of the Highlands that [had] not in its turn been in a state of irritation as great as that of Ross-shire in 1792." Fortunately, the nation had been saved from more serious unrest by the fact that the "new system of management had advanced" only in a "gradual manner" so that discontentment burned unevenly and dissipated when popular leaders left for America (Selkirk seems to have assumed that only tacksmen were capable of organized rebellion). But if this "salutary drain" was suddenly stopped, then northern Scotland might erupt in a cataclysm as dangerous as the Irish rising of 1798. For Selkirk, the Year of the Sheep confirmed the peril of any ban on emigration.[30]

The scheme to settle Prince Edward Island with Highlanders was directed specifically at the tenant farmer class. These were the people with sufficient capital to pay for their own voyage across the Atlantic. They had resolved to emigrate voluntarily and only needed an incentive to settle in British North America rather than the United States. Selkirk offered land in Prince Edward Island not as a permanent gift but on credit to be repaid within three or four years. This emphasis on capital and credit precluded members of the cottar class from Selkirk's attention. Though he called for government support, he was not promoting assisted emigration in the sense of subsidized travel and land for the plebeian masses. He was even less interested in coerced migration. The settlement of New South Wales figured only as a negative model in his argument. He shared with Adam Smith a strong concern with the problem of commercial habits. How could one foster industry and prudence in Highlanders? Charity and coercion only interfered with the development of improving habits. Like Smith, he thought the strategy of the British Fisheries Society basically wrongheaded. Even the most "trifling possession" of land distracted Highlanders from specialization. The habitual attachment to subsistence farming among

Highlanders was so deeply rooted that only "the stimulus of absolute necessity" could "bring them to a life of regular and persevering industry." The proviso to grant pastures and gardens at low rent to settlers allowed them a "sufficient resource" to neglect the fisheries with impunity. This explained why the villages of Tobermory and Stein, on which "very large sums of money [had] been expended, [were] scarcely possessed of a fishing boat, their inhabitants . . . sunk in inactivity."[31]

But Selkirk also went beyond Smith to embrace a different conception of habit. Despite his strong critique of the Highland Society, he incorporated a certain measure of paternalism into his liberal vision. There was little doubt in his mind that the days of the warlike Highlands had passed. The old pattern of attachment between common people and landowners could not be regenerated. "We must go back to the seven-years war to find these regiments in their original purity, formed entirely on the feudal principle." Changing social conditions made the extinction of this military spirit all but inevitable: "A few years more must, in all probability, complete the change in the agricultural system of the Highlands, and bury in oblivion every circumstance that distinguishes the Highlands, as a nursery of soldiers, from the rest of the kingdom." Yet the organized exodus to Prince Edward Island might preserve "a portion of the antient spirit." The collective resettlement of whole communities to new villages and towns in British North America would create a new social basis for martial virtue. Economically, any surviving "feudal" element in the colonial settlements would be entirely innocuous since it could not interfere with the profit motive of a larger landowning class. The difficult conditions of frontier settlement would at the same time encourage a spirit of self-reliance while preserving the "peculiarities of customs and language" inherited from the old country.[32]

This flirtation with Highland romance did no damage to Selkirk's credentials as a liberal savant. Malthus himself was full of admiration for his work. In the appendix to the third edition of *An Essay on the Principle of Population* (1806), Malthus praised Selkirk's "lucid and masterly observations on the present state of the Highlands" and happily endorsed his analysis of the "causes and probable consequences of emigration." Selkirk's work in fact seems to have moved Malthus to rethink his position on emigration. In the 1803 edition of the *Essay*, he had expressed strong skepticism about the relief afforded by emigration. At best, it was only a "partial and temporary expedient" to solve the problem of population. After reading Selkirk, he accepted that "peculiar circumstances" sometimes favored the voluntary outflow of migrants that Selkirk had investigated. Though Malthus still regarded the Highland case rather as the exception than the rule, he condoned the right of the tacksman class to migrate, noting that it was "the duty and interest of governments to facilitate emigration." A decade later, in the fourth edition of the *Essay* (1817), Malthus reaffirmed the importance of emigration as the "only real relief" available when a demographic boom was succeeded by a slump in employment. Once again, he recommended the subject to the "attention of the government." His position shifted further in the following decade, when Malthus advised Undersecretary for War and the Colonies R. J. Wilmot-Horton and gave official testimony to the Select Committee on Emigration. Over time, he seems to have accepted the benefits of government assistance for emigrants, at least in moments of social crisis when population overshot opportunities for employment at home.[33]

Malthus was not alone in his praise. Selkirk's book met with a warm reaction in the press. The *Farmer's Magazine, Annual Review, Agricultural Magazine,* and *Scots Magazine* all joined the *Edinburgh Review* in welcoming a liberal perspective on emigration. Circulating libraries in Scotland were quick to include the book among its select titles. The book went to a second, slightly expanded edition the following year. Nathaniel Atcheson used Selkirk's argument to lobby for more support for British North America. J. C. Loudon incorporated Selkirk's defense of regional specialization into his pamphlet on agricultural rent. Even a hostile critic like James Gordon, writing in the *Edinburgh Chronicle and Herald,* was forced to admit that Selkirk's book enjoyed "extensive popularity." He suggested that Selkirk had benefited greatly from the renewal of war with France in 1803. "The almost romantic story of the settlement of his infant colony" was well calculated to "excite lively emotions of admiration" in an age of anxious, imperial rivalry with France. Selkirk's obvious affinity with Smith and Malthus probably played some part in lending the work public significance. "To those among whom the principles of Dr. Adam Smith and the more recent illustrations of Mr. Malthus are familiar," the *Monthly Review* observed, "the volume presents not a tenet that is questionable, nor a paragraph that is obscure." Selkirk's publisher, Constable, ran an advertisement citing Francis Horner on the pathbreaking achievement of Selkirk's book. It shed fresh light, he noted, "on one of the most intricate parts of the science of oeconomy, that in which the theory of wealth and the theory of population are examined in connexion."[34]

SELKIRK'S CRITICS

Not everyone was so exuberant. Three critics published longer attacks on Selkirk's work. Robert Brown, sheriff-substitute in western Inverness-shire and factor for Lord Clanranald, wrote *Strictures and Remarks on the Earl of Selkirk's*

Observations on the Present State of the Highlands of Scotland (1806). The missives of James Gordon to the Edinburgh press were gathered in *Eight Letters on the Subject of the Earl of Selkirk's Pamphlet on Highland Emigration* . . . (1806). Finally, an anonymous improver contributed *Remarks on the Earl of Selkirk's Observations on the Present State of the Highlands of Scotland, with a View of the Causes and Probable Consequences of Emigration* (1806). All three critics used the well-worn rhetoric of hidden natural advantages and domestic colonization. James Gordon mocked Selkirk's cursory familiarity with local conditions. "Lord Selkirk, I understand, was only one day in Tobermory, and that a very bad one, insomuch, that his Lordship was mostly confined to his house." From such cavalier disregard for the peculiarities of the Highlands flowed the grossly erroneous assumption that "soil and climate" — "nature herself" — were opposed to the "extension of Highland tillage." This misunderstanding marred "the basis of all his reasoning." "This as an abstract and fundamental proposition, I deny." There were still "uncultivated tracts, both vast and numerous," where crops could be grown. The climate, too, was much better than Selkirk supposed. An unbiased observer would find it equal to a great "portion of the cultivated districts of Scotland." Brown in turn argued for diversified agriculture by discussing the feeding habits of livestock. "As sheep always prefer upland pasture, and never descend to the low ground except during storms of snow," these tracts at the bottom of the valleys tended to become overrun with "heath or brushwood" until they could "yield very little assistance" even to the sheep. The anonymous third critic raised the same objection about the natural history of the Highlands. Was sheep farming really the only viable option? "Does the climate and situation of the country present no other means of making it productive?" Why did Selkirk dismiss the alternative strategies of wasteland colonization, fisheries, and manufactures? James Gordon wondered why he was so confident about the prospect of "remote colonization" in Nova Scotia yet downcast about "the very mention of improvement in his own country?" If Highlanders on Prince Edward Island could "overpower the strongest obstacles of nature," then why could they not do so at home?[35]

These three pamphlets offered little in the way of precise and technical analysis of agriculture and natural history, unlike Walker and Aiton. Yet they were remarkable in mounting a self-conscious attack on the environmental assumptions of classical political economy. Selkirk's liberal interpretation served to raise a new awareness in his critics about the political stakes involved in defining the limits of the environment and population growth. A major aspect of this critique was the rejection of simplistic generalization. Brown, Gordon, and their anonymous colleague pitted local knowledge and environmental diversity against the sweeping abstraction of political economy. Gordon ridiculed the vacuous elegance behind Selkirk's ideal of rigid specialization. The idea of "banishing agriculture entirely from the Highlands" while at the same time "dismissing pasturage wholly from the plains of England" was certainly "extremely ingenious in theory." But "the visions of theory" did "not always accommodate the homely circumstances of vulgar practice." Every ordinary farmer would "inform the Noble Lord, that though the relative proportions of arable and grass land must doubtless vary in different places, still his convenience depends on the union, not on the separation of the two."[36]

This critique of Selkirk produced a familiar twist. A good portion of Brown's book was taken up by a description of the increasing popularity of spade husbandry among landowners on the west coast, including Lord Macdonald in Boisdale and North Uist, Mr. Hume of Harris, Lord Seaforth in Lewis, Macdonald in Mull, and Brown's own employer, Lord Clanranald. Brown reported that this trend had started in the North Highlands "about ten or twelve years ago" but was already "becoming universal." For Brown, the new "crofting system" (perhaps the first recorded use of the term) presented a natural fit with the feeding habits of sheep. Landlords found it profitable to carve out crofts from tracts of "low . . . arable ground, or a flat of dead moss" not needed for grazing. He expected that the new government-sponsored network of roads would open up many pockets of arable ground in the interior to cultivation. He also testified to a revolution in local habits. Once listless creatures dozing by the peat fire who subsisted on cattle blood and whey, the crofters were now "active" and "industrious" inhabitants of comfortable cottages built from stone and lime, with "the luxury of glass" in their windows. "Even in the most remote of the Western Isles, the current wages of a laborer are 1s. 6d per day." In this way, Brown reversed the social bias of Selkirk's approach. For him, it was the cottars who represented the most important element of the Highland population. The abolition of the tacksman class was a necessary step toward both demographic growth and greater rental values. The new owner of the Stein estate on Skye had banished the tacksmen and created a cluster of crofts in place of the failed village settlement introduced there by the British Fisheries Society. According to Brown, the crofts had increased profits on rents by 6 or 7 percent.[37]

Brown admitted that there was a convenient fit between spade husbandry and the kelping industry. His account of the origin and diffusion of crofting coincided rather neatly with the geography and chronology of the latter. Brown's employer, Lord Clanranald, drew great profits from kelping on his estate and certainly had an interest in maximizing the availability of seasonal labor. Yet Brown's book included an unvarnished account of the kind of work involved.

"Let any man conceive, how a laboring man in the south, or other parts of the kingdom, would relish to go out, at the ebb of the sea, to his middle in salt water, to cut the ware, and continue during the flood up to the neck in that element, dragging ashore the ware which he had previously separated from the rocks; and from that extreme, be obliged to go and suspend himself over the burning, or the working of the fluid materials of a kelp-kiln." The harsh conditions of such labor justified another attack on Selkirk. "The making of kelp is a dirty and disagreeable employment, and must, if the present race of people were to leave the country, be given up altogether." But Brown was more than a lobbyist for a sectional interest. Kelping was not a central factor in shaping the original ideology of spade husbandry, as we have seen. Brown himself clearly acknowledged this wider horizon when he analyzed the opportunities for crofting in the *interior* of the Highlands.[38]

In fact, the debate over Selkirk's proposal encouraged a more pointed consideration of the general concept of overpopulation. Who defined the natural constraints to demographic growth and for what end? Malthus and Selkirk had both warned that the Highland population was close to its physical limits. Without a "salutary drain" of people through migration, the future looked grim. Selkirk warned that "absolute famine" was a growing threat. Even if the region eluded the worst-case scenario, the poor must cope with the "utmost distress" when they could no longer find land or employment. To escape starvation, they would have to avoid the "burthen of rearing a family." In contrast, Selkirk's critics deployed the idea of the stationary state precisely in order to reject such pessimism. Brown agreed that the number of inhabitants in each nation was limited by "the means of subsistence, procured by labor." Population growth could continue "until all the land" of the country was "reduced to the highest state of garden culture." Only certain "districts in China, and Japan" seemed to have arrived at this advanced stage. If Scotland suffered from a redundant population, it was the consequence of weak policy and the stranglehold of custom, not the limits of nature. For Gordon, the problem of Scotland's "superpopulation" could be solved by new employment afforded by the fisheries. This was a political rather than a natural question because it required the abolition of the salt laws. It was also a problem of habit since Gaels would have to be weaned off their attachment to the land and learn to fish for an occupation. But both obstacles could be overcome gradually. Brown proposed that the "Highlands and Isles, like America," were still in a "state of infancy, where the cultivated land is not brought to yield half the value it might do." He, too, expected fisheries and agriculture to sustain a much larger population over time. The main threat to the economy was the possibility of mass emigration.

He warned that "it would require, at least, a century to fill up the chasm, while all the improvements now going on must be at a stand." The most categorical critique of Selkirk came from the anonymous author behind the third pamphlet. Turning the overpopulation argument on its head, the writer insisted that large-scale emigration would plunge northern Scotland into a permanent state of inertia. When the majority of the population had vanished and the "supplies of the necessaries of life" had to be imported "from a great distance," rents would become stagnant, arable land would "yield an inferior produce," and the "fleeces of its flocks must be sent out of it for the purpose of being manufactured." Even pestilence or famine allowed a population to rebound. When sheep took over, depopulation would arrest all growth permanently. "This condemn[ed] [the region] to a stationary condition for ever." Permanent stagnation was not the effect of natural limits but the consequence of bad policy, producing an artificially arrested economy.[39]

This quarrel between Selkirk and his critics was part of a broader debate on the precise relation between population and land in the wake of Malthus's *Essay*. Arthur Young's pamphlet *The Question of Scarcity Plainly Stated* (1800) recommended half-acre potato allotments (with additional pasturage for a cow or two) as an insurance against future dearth for families with three children or more. John Sinclair followed suit with the aptly titled *Observations on the Means of Enabling a Cottager to Keep a Cow* (1801). The essay calculated that three acres would provide sufficient subsistence for a family of six. John Walker contributed a *Memorial Concerning the Present Scarcity of Grain in Scotland* (1801), in which he contrasted the nutritional value of an acre of pasturage to an acre of potatoes. A middling crop of potatoes produced "about fifty bolls" or the equivalent "daily allowance of 6lbs of potatoes for ten men through the whole year." A switch to a potato diet was "more wholesome" and "better able to support mankind in health and strength" than any "grain, meat, or . . . food whatever." Malthus in turn took up the question of spade husbandry directly in the 1803 edition of the *Essay*. He warned that Young's proposal would have worse effects even than the Poor Laws, since allotments must encourage a population far "beyond the demand for labor." The quarrel persisted for several decades to come. In later editions of the *Essay*, Malthus turned his attention to Richard Owen's radical version of spade husbandry. *The Report to the County of Lanark* (1821) envisioned plebeian allotments as a form of unemployment insurance. But Owen's blueprint for reform also marked the outer limits of "potato utopianism." His Tory counterpart William Cobbett worried that the potato in fact undermined the possibility of a stable and secure rural order. Gone were Adam Smith's beautiful Irish porters and prostitutes, bred exclusively on a diet of potatoes. Cereal production was the guarantor of medium-size farms. The potato crop increasingly became identified with pauperism rather than social insurance, particularly after the great Irish famine of 1845.[40]

THE AFTERMATH

The crisis of 1803 produced a new, sharper division between the rival ecologies of the Highlands. Tory projects dominated in the short term, but the appeal of Malthus and Selkirk grew among landowners and estate factors looking to vindicate large-scale eviction. During the Highland famine of 1847, leading administrators involved in the crisis followed a strict Malthusian formula. Only in the final two decades of the century did crofter agitation and romantic Highlandism trump the notion of salutary clearance. The basic problem of Highland development was identical to the dilemma of colonial management on the peripheries of the empire. Were profits and prices the best guide to the natural order? Or did the optimal use of the environment require state regulation and expert management? Questions of subsistence were crucial to governance in both South Asia and the Highlands. Yet differences in ideology shaped the horizons of acceptable policy. Compared to the authority of the colonial state in South Asia, power in the Highlands was far more dispersed among landowners. When the state proved unwilling to intercede on the behalf of the Highland crofters, civil society played a mitigating role in Scotland. The Lowland public showed at least intermittent sympathy for the plight of the Highland community, despite perceptions of racial difference. Even at the height of the Highland food crisis in 1847, crop failure never degenerated into mass death. Eviction and emigration were the culturally permissible remedies for overpopulation sanctioned by the Scottish elite.[41]

The clash of rival ecologies was full of unintended consequences and pyrrhic victories. The case of the Caledonian Canal provides a sad illustration of these contingencies. This was the largest injection of public funds into the Highland economy hitherto seen. Thomas Telford had originally suggested a public expense of £50,000 annually over seven years. Completed in 1822, after eighteen years of construction, the canal finally cost an astonishing £912,000, more than half of which was paid by the government (£470,000). In fact, the price tag for the Caledonian Canal nearly eclipsed Sinclair's grandiose 1803 plan for the "domestic colonization" of Scotland, which had budgeted what had at the time seemed an impossible sum of £501,500 for canal engineering and other schemes. The idea of a water link between the North Sea and the Irish Sea between Inverness and Fort William had been broached a generation earlier when the Board for the Annexed Estates commissioned a preliminary survey in 1773. During the emigration crisis, the canal project was revived as part of the public works scheme set in motion to halt Highland emigration. William Jessop and Telford surveyed the sixty-mile line between Fort William and Inverness in 1801–2. They ventured a state-of-the-art design for the canal, including more than twenty locks and the use of steam engines to pump out excess water during construction. Strategic considerations were decisive. The new canal would allow Liverpool and Dublin ships quicker access to the Baltic and German ports without "running the Gauntlet in the British Channel" or risking the "dangerous Navigation" of the Pentland Firth. Besides protecting civilian shipping from French privateers, it would also permit naval squadrons to transfer smoothly from the North Sea to the Irish Sea or bring troops to Ireland from Fort George. The depth and width of canal and locks were set to accommodate a thirty-two-gun frigate.[42]

The pivotal figure in the Caledonian Canal scheme was the Eskdale native Thomas Telford. During the 1790s, he had acquired a national reputation for innovative design in canal and bridge building. The thousand-foot cast-iron aqueduct over the Dee at Pontcysyllte was perhaps his greatest achievement. But Telford was also closely involved with the British Fisheries Society from the spring of 1790 onward, surveying its settlements and suggesting improvements to buildings and docks. This commitment to Highland engineering continued for the rest of his life. In political terms, Telford sympathized strongly with the policy of intervention. After surveying the region in the fall of 1802, he collaborated with Henry Mackenzie and the Highland Society on a strategic plan for new infrastructure. He also contacted his old employer in the British Fisheries Society the Earl of Breadalbane. Telford was especially keen on the "judicious proportion of sheep, black cattle and cultivation" he had noticed along the road between Killin and Kenmore at Loch Tay. This was an ideal of diversified land use quite close to that of John Walker and Robert Brown. Breadalbane responded with the memorandum on the virtues of crofting tenure and the necessity of government intervention to accommodate the "supernumerary population" on his estate. Telford's second report to Parliament followed a similar line. The preservation of the Highland population in its native country was a top priority for the nation. Telford's principle of intervention was quite expansive: "Interference of Government should extend only to the removing [of] Obstacles, and affording Conveniencies, which are of a Nature not easily to be surmounted by Individuals, or any Body of Men who can be brought to act together . . . and where it is evident that by removing those Obstacles . . . the Exertion of Individuals will be greatly facilitated, so as to promote the general Good of the

Empire." For Telford, this principle justified government support of both Highland infrastructure and fisheries. His report saw Breadalbane's Loch Tay settlements as the optimal hybrid of commercial profit and high population density. Telford assumed that the wool price would peak at a level that would still allow for cattle herding and a large native population. The valleys would then contain a *natural* division of labor: "The Farms will be subdivided, and a proportion of Black Cattle and Cultivation be introduced in the lower Grounds in the Vallies, while the upper Parts of the Hills continue to be pastured with Sheep."[43]

At first blush, it might seem odd to label the Caledonian Canal a Tory project. None other than Adam Smith praised the extension of canals and roads as "the greatest of all improvements." New infrastructure encouraged liberty by breaking down the "natural" monopolies of local landlords, forcing them to contend with a market of "rival commodities." Smith connected the problem of infrastructure directly to the pitiful state of forestry in the Highlands. "For want of roads and water-carriage," only the bark could profitably be extracted and the timber was "left to rot upon the ground." But Smith also forcefully argued against public support for infrastructure elsewhere in *The Wealth of Nations*. The great canal through Languedoc—Canal du Midi—which connected the Mediterranean with the Atlantic, had cost the French state the equivalent of nine hundred thousand pounds. Yet the toll to maintain it was farmed out to the engineer Pierre-Paul Riquet, who "dissipated" the revenue "in ornamental and unnecessary expences, while the most essential parts of the work were allowed to go to ruin." For Smith, the involvement of the state automatically carried a risk of misappropriation. Once the government became habituated to a steady stream of revenue, it was likely that the addiction might last indefinitely. The case of the French post roads also demonstrated to Smith that public revenue tended to go to a few symbolic objects of high visibility and prestige, whereas "little works" of greater cumulative importance were neglected. Only in China and Hindustan, where the revenue derived almost exclusively from land, were the prospects for state management of infrastructure more auspicious. Smith's many reasons for caution perhaps explain the skepticism of later liberal writers regarding the Caledonian Canal. Indeed, the *Edinburgh Review* maintained a deafening silence on the subject. Selkirk's *Observations on the Present State of the Highlands* did broach the question but took an even more pessimistic approach than Smith. He admitted the "great and permanent national utility" of Telford's canal and roads yet in the same breath insisted that they could offer only "temporary relief" and did not change the "essential circumstances of the country."[44]

As it happens, the expense of the canal was all out of proportion to its benefits. In the short term, the scheme yielded employment for a group of three thousand Highlanders recruited from across the region over the period 1804–22. While steam engine pumps were used for the construction of the locks, much of the labor involved in making the cut through layers of moss, sand, and gravel was done with simple spades and picks. Yet when the canal at long last opened in 1822, the expected jolt of commerce never materialized. The end of the Napoleonic Wars also made the military function of the canal obsolete. It was, in T.M. Devine's words, "an engineering marvel but a commercial white elephant." Already suffering from a decline in wool and kelp prices, the Highland economy continued to contract, while waves of emigration and forced evictions reduced its population in the north and west. In 1839, merely 2.5 percent of the shipping around northern Scotland passed through the canal.[45]

The Tories were not alone in winning pyrrhic victories. The spread of Malthusian ideology in the Highlands sowed dragon's teeth. William Young—the factor of the Countess of Sutherland—at first took the view that a large native population was intrinsically valuable. New forms of employment in fisheries and manufactures could easily accommodate all the people moved from the interior to the coast. But Young began to vacillate after the subsistence crisis of 1808. By 1813–14, he had fallen under the influence of Malthus's theory and admitted that emigration might play a role in "thinning" the population. At the same time, Lord Selkirk visited Sutherland to recruit migrants for his new Canadian regiment based in Upper Ontario. Young's successor Patrick Sellar, educated at the University of Edinburgh by Adam Smith's disciple Dugald Stewart, proved a devoted follower of liberal ecology. When the crop failed in the autumn of 1816, he concluded that the interior of Sutherland should be cleared of inhabitants and was fit only for sheep. This was "the year without a summer," when wheat yields fell to a dangerous low point across the West. The likely cause was the eruption of Mount Tambora in Indonesia the previous year. The lingering food crisis in 1816–17 served to harden the attitudes of the proprietors and administrators. Sellar suggested that emigration alone could resolve the situation. If the countess would buy land in Nova Scotia, the surplus population could be shipped off there. During the most active phase of the Sutherland Clearances in 1818–19, a number of dispossessed tenants went to the Cape of Good Hope on an assisted emigration scheme. Sellar used Malthus's law of population to argue that emigration must be followed by a permanent switch to sheep farms. Otherwise the population would simply rebound and the problem would reappear in the next generation.[46]

Selkirk's plea for the right of Highlanders to emigrate bore fruit after his death in 1820. Two years later, the undersecretary for the colonies Wilmot-Horton took up the case for assisted emigration. His parliamentary committee debated the virtues of Upper Canada, Sierra Leone, and New South Wales as receptacles of British emigrants. The fear of radicalism within the establishment in the years of Peterloo and the Cato Street conspiracy no doubt contributed to this sea change. The growing resistance to the Highland clearances may also have had a part. Selkirk's warning about popular resentment toward sheep farming proved prophetic. The government lifted the final humanitarian restrictions on emigration in 1827. Yet as Karen O'Brien points out, the driving ideology of Wilmot-Horton and his allies was a romantic critique of political economy. The Tory government offered state assistance to pay the cost of passage. Emigration had become a new area of state intervention.[47]

The excesses of the Sutherland Clearances served as a rallying point for the opponents of Malthusianism during the course of the nineteenth century. Several generations of critics—from David Stewart of Garth and Hugh Miller to William Thomas Thornton and Alexander Mackenzie—attacked the policy of sheep farming and clearance as a gross mismanagement of human and natural resources. Theirs was an ecology of sufficiency rather than cornucopian abundance. Highland soil and seas could sustain the welfare of a modest native population. On this count, the clearances had gratuitously destroyed thriving settlements nurtured by a mixed economy. In the last few decades of the nineteenth century, the critique gained social urgency and political muscle through the growing pressure of crofter agitation in the Highlands and the compelling precedent of Irish land tenure reform. The liberal Napier commission in 1883 acknowledged the right of remaining crofters to legal restitution. It was, according to Lord Napier, the great "social question . . . still unsolved." Crofters were no longer superfluous people in a marginal land but tenants whose rights must be restored so that the natural advantages of the Highlands could be put to proper use. In the words of Lord Napier: "The Highlanders possess the salubrity of the mountain and the sea, more variety of diet, a large amount of milk and fish, a share of personal property, cows and sheep, the implements of spinning, weaving, fishing, and husbandry. . . . Compared to the people of the city and the south, even the poorest crofters have in ordinary seasons sources of superior welfare." Arguably, it was the idea of sufficiency that enabled the liberal volte face from Malthusianism to land reform. Rights and restitution were meaningful only in the context of an environment capable of sustaining something other than sheep farms.[48]

Conclusion: The Ghosts of the Enlightenment

The hopes for a "New World" in the Highlands were dashed by a cascade of failures. Natural historians were too sanguine about the extent of northern resources and the efficacy of acclimatization. Agriculture failed to ameliorate the Highland climate. The campaign to build towns and villages faltered. Windfall profits from kelp and wool collapsed after the Napoleonic Wars. The Caledonian Canal proved a monumental miscalculation. Already in the closing decades of the eighteenth century, naturalists and political economists had begun to unmake the New World of the north. By running the engine of natural history in reverse, their inventories now revealed physical limits rather than hidden abundance. John Williams predicted national ruin with his startling forecast about coal exhaustion. Joseph Townsend set forth a model of overpopulation through the natural history of island ungulates. George Dempster redefined Gaelic population politics as a race against extirpation. Lord Selkirk and his detractors debated how close Highland society was to the stationary state. These premonitions of disaster were borne out when kelping profits fizzled in the 1820s and landlords began to clear their estates of a population now deemed redundant. Emigration seemed to offer the only relief for a country so deficient in natural advantages. Later in the century, sheep farms were turned into sporting estates and deer forests as the global wool market undercut the Scottish industry. Even the Cheviot herds failed to turn a profit anymore.[1]

These pessimistic and cornucopian views developed in tandem.[2] The natural theology of hidden riches motivated the initial wave of surveys and schemes by John Walker. But it also set in motion John Williams's quixotic prospecting journeys. After Williams, the political arithmetic of coal stock evolved through dueling quantitative estimates. The debate over wasteland colonization followed a similar dynamic. Sinclair mapped the ghost acres available for improvement and autarky in food. Then Malthus quashed Sinclair's vision of autarky by arguing that population growth would outpace every gain in productivity at the margin. In Williams's forecast of coal exhaustion, the optimism of Scottish stadial history was turned on its head. The triumph of the commercial age rested on finite stocks of mineral fuel. Once this transitory abundance had been depleted, Britain would return back to the stage of primitive agriculture. "The future inhabitants of this island must live, like its first inhabitants, by fishing and hunting." Yet Williams's prediction was in turn an expression of the growing strength of the manufacturing economy. The new centrality of mineral energy to mass production made worries about the depletion of coal potent.[3]

Where once the natural world of the north had appeared to promise boundless resources and indefinite growth, the region now delivered a model of stagnation. This picture of the stationary Highlands seemed to confirm empirically the deepest fears of classical political economy—that physical factors of soil fertility and other natural endowments dictated limits to growth that neither labor nor technology could overcome. We can trace this line of thought from Joseph Townsend and T. R. Malthus to John Stuart Mill. Along another path of anxiety, the warning of John Williams about peak coal gave rise to a genre of depletion calculations which culminated in William Stanley Jevons's 1865 work *The Coal Question*. Despite the growing speed and scale of industrialization after 1830, the idea of the stationary state proved surprisingly persistent. Indeed, the concept multiplied to include a broad range of past, present, and future societies. The "cottier system" of Ireland and Highland Scotland were seen as agrarian variations on the theme. China represented a more advanced and ancient version of stagnation. There were also predictions of a postindustrial future for Britain, on the model suggested by John Williams. But Mill and John Ruskin recast the prognosis of decline into a utopian possibility for the arts to triumph over gross materialism. Ruskin dreamed of the "sweet spring-time" for "our children's children . . . when their coals are burnt out, and they begin to understand that coals are not the source of all power Divine and human." The stationary state also moved up and down the spatial scale, from regions to nations and empires. In Malthus's *Essay*, concrete limits to growth were regional in Britain; the Highlands had the most "redundant" population in the island. For Robert Torrens, only overseas emigration could prevent the coming of the stationary state in the nation as a whole. Yet the case of China appeared to show that even a vast empire could succumb to overpopulation. Worse yet, Malthus's original thought experiment predicted a stationary state for the planet, if the human species outpaced aggregate food production. Perversely, the increase of prosperity and population seemed to be moving the world ever closer to the edge.[4]

When industrialization transformed the Western world in the late nineteenth century, these fears finally lost some of their force. The astonishing gains in productivity wildly exceeded anything Williams, Malthus, or Jevons could have imagined. Most economists abandoned the Victorian obsession with the finite supply of land. But the idea of the stationary state found a new lease of life by migrating into other disciplines. Environmentalists Paul Ehrlich, Georg Borgström, and Garrett Hardin raised the specter of overpopulation once more in the postwar era. The Club of Rome commissioned the seminal report on *The Limits to Growth* in 1972. More recently, Johan Rockström and others have proposed a model of nine planetary boundaries to economic development. This approach eschews the question of resource exhaustion in favor of the analysis of anthropogenic pressure on systemic processes at the planetary scale. Among these critical thresholds, anthropogenic climate change poses the greatest immediate threat. So much of the economic prosperity of the past two centuries has relied on the Pandora's box of the mineral energy economy. But it has also turned human beings into a "global geophysical force." Carbon dioxide emissions from the burning of fossil fuels have triggered a process of rapid climate change. These unintended effects of modern energy consumption may linger for tens of thousands of years, longer than the span of recorded history. Against this background of deepening environmental crisis, a growing number of scientists and environmentalists now attack the idea of endless growth as a dangerous delusion. If their predictions are correct, then we will have to face the politics of environmental limits as a species. No doubt, we have come a long way from the New World of John Walker and the stationary Highlands of T. R. Malthus. And yet, the ghosts of the Enlightenment may still return to haunt us.[5]

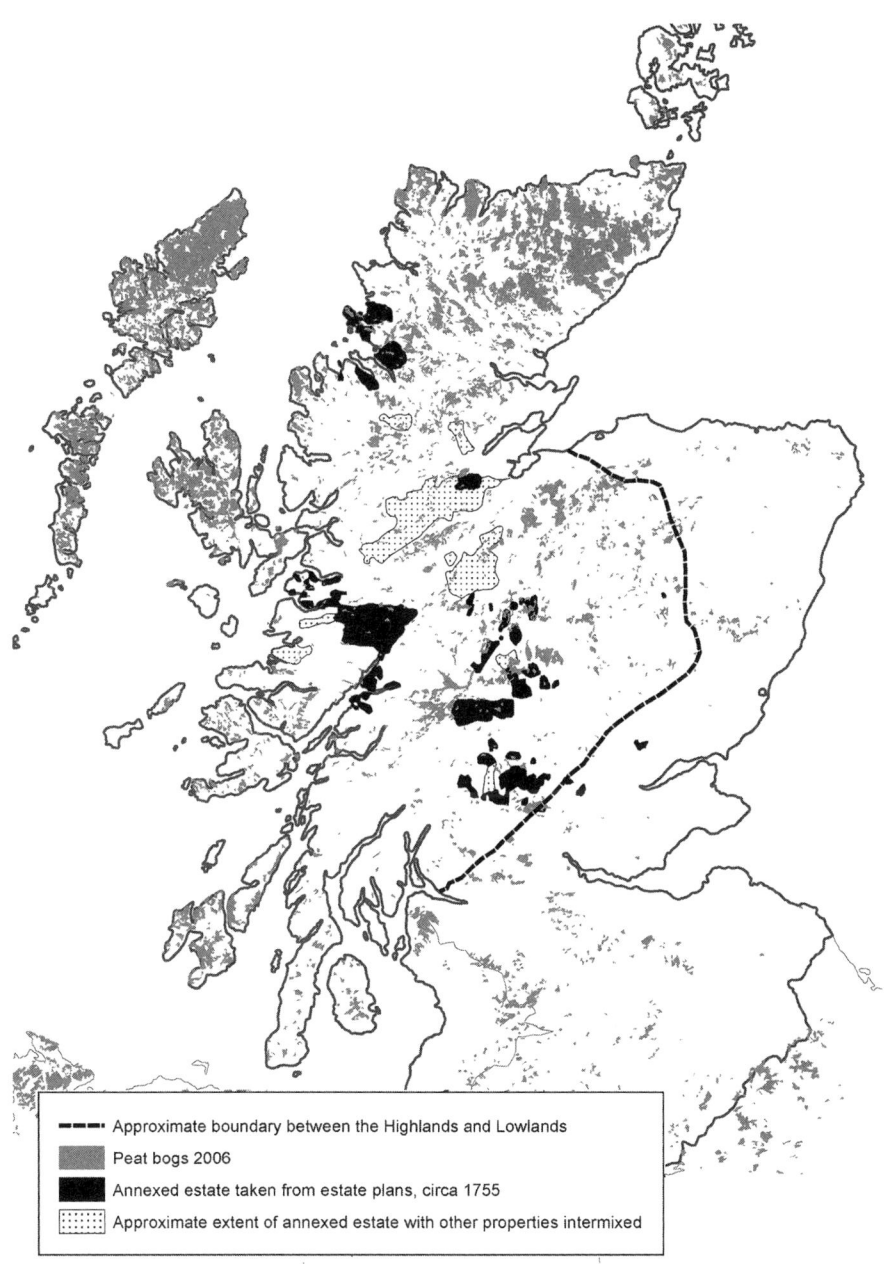

Source: Location and extent of annexed estates adopted from Annette M. Smith, *Jacobite Estates of the Forty-Five* (Edinburgh: John Donald, 1982).

Abbreviations

AHR	*Agricultural History Review*
ANH	*Archives of Natural History*
AUL	Aberdeen University Library, Special Collections
BJHS	*British Journal for the History of Science*
BL	The British Library
BM	Blair Castle Muniments, Blair Atholl
BOD	Bodleian Library, Oxford
DNB	*Oxford Dictionary of National Biography*
EUL	Edinburgh University Library, Special Collections
GUL	Glasgow University Library, Special Collections
HL	The Huntington Library, Los Angeles
KVAH	*Kungliga Vetenskapsakademiens Handlingar*
NA	National Archives, Kew
NAS	National Archives of Scotland (formerly The Scottish Record Office)
NLS	National Library of Scotland
OSA	John Sinclair, ed., *The [Old] Statistical Account of Scotland; Drawn Up from the Ministers of the Different Parishes*, 21 vols. (Edinburgh, 1791–99)
RBG	Library of the Royal Botanic Garden of Edinburgh
THSS	*Prize Essays and Transactions of the Highland Society of Scotland*
WN	Adam Smith, *An Inquiry into the Nature and Causes of the Wealth of Nations*, 2 vols., ed. R. H Campbell, A. S. Skinner, and W. B. Todd (Oxford: Oxford University Press, 1976)

Notes

Introduction

1. "Copy Letter and Memorial to the Trustees of the Linen Manufactories; from Some Gentlemen of Perthshire and Stirling-Shire, October 2, 1753," NLS, MS 17563, 52–53. The six visitors included Thomas Graeme of Duchray, J.P., James Fairfoull of Brandam, J.P., John Buchanan of Glins, J.P., John Campbell of Kilpunt, John Stirling of Garden, George Montgomery-Moir of Leckie, John Callender of Craigforth, J.P., and David Graeme of Meiklewood. On their gentlemanly testimony, see NAS, E728/9/1–2; see also J. G. Harrison, "A Historical Background of Flanders Moss," *Scottish Natural Heritage Commissioned Report No. 002* (ROAME No. F02LG22, 2003), 49–51, 122; and *Oxford English Dictionary*, s.v. "Improve v.²." For the origin of six-rowed barley, see Daniel Zohary and Maria Hopf, *Domestication of Plants in the Old World: The Origin and Spread of Cultivated Plants in West Asia, Europe, and the Nile Valley*, 2nd ed. (Oxford: Clarendon Press, 1994), 55. On the diffusion of the potato, see Redcliffe Salaman, *The History and Social Influence of the Potato*, rev. ed. (Oxford: Oxford University Press, 1985), 344; Martin Rackwitz, *Travels to Terra Incognita: The Scottish Highlands and Hebrides in Early Modern Travellers' Accounts, c. 1600 to 1800* (Munster: Waxmann, 2007) 382; and Robert Dodgshon, *Land and Society in Early Scotland* (Oxford: Clarendon, 1981), 301. For the breast plow, see also "Memorial Anent Improving the Highlanders of Scotland 1753," NLS, 17563, 103; Plot quoted in G. E. Fussell, "The Breast Plough," *Man* 33 (July 1933): 109–14; cf. Robert Maxwell, *Select Transactions of the Honourable the Society of Improver . . .* (Edinburgh, 1743), 53.
2. John Robertson dates the Enlightenment as "the movement which began in the 1740s and ended in the 1790s"; *The Case for the Enlightenment: Scotland and Naples, 1680–1760* (Cambridge: Cambridge University Press, 2005), 8. My own chronology extends the influence of the Enlightenment to the end of the Napoleonic Wars.
3. On the birth of population politics, see Michel Foucault, *Histoire de la sexualité, I: La volonté de savoir* (Paris: Gallimard, 1976), 186–88; and Foucault, *Security, Territory,*

Population: Lectures at the Collège de France, 1977–1978, ed. Michel Senellart (New York: Picador, 2007), 323–28.
4. For the received account of crofting, see Malcolm Gray, *The Highland Economy, 1750–1850* (Edinburgh: Oliver and Boyd, 1956), 71–72, 131–32, 196–99; and James Hunter, *The Making of the Crofting Community* (Edinburgh: John Donald, 1976). My argument builds in part on Andrew Mackillop's discovery that crofting was implemented as a policy by the Board for the Annexed Estates under Lord Milton (Andrew Fletcher); see *"More Fruitful than the Soil": Army, Empire and the Scottish Highlands, 1715–1815* (East Linton, UK: Tuckwell, 2000), 108–27 passim. However, I differ from Mackillop by exploring the roots of crofting more broadly as a product of enlightened debates about the fate of the rural population in an age of improvement. On paternalist rural policies in general, see Christopher A. Bayly, *Imperial Meridian: The British Empire and the World, 1780–1830* (London: Longman, 1989); Nigel Everett, *The Tory View of Landscape* (New Haven: Paul Mellon Center, 1994); and Sarah Lloyd, "Cottage Conversations: Poverty and Manly Independence in Eighteenth-Century England," *Past and Present* 184 (August 2004): 69–108.
5. My aim here is to reconsider the history of the origins of development policy within a wider debate about natural knowledge. For some important earlier contributions to the field, see, e.g., A. E. Youngson, *After the Forty-Five: The Economic Impact on the Highlands* (Edinburgh: Edinburgh University Press, 1973); Richard Drayton, *Nature's Government: Science, Imperial Britain, and the "Improvement of the World"* (Cambridge, MA: Harvard University Press, 2000); Ha Joon Chang, *Kicking Away the Ladder: Development in Historical Perspective* (London: Anthem, 2003); Istvan Hont, *The Jealousy of Trade: International Competition and the Nation-State in Historical Perspective* (Cambridge, MA: Harvard University Press, 2005); Tania Murray Li, *The Will to Improve: Governmentality, Development, and the Practice of Politics* (Durham, NC: Duke University Press, 2007); Gilbert Rise, *The History of Development: From Western Origins to Global Faith*, 3rd ed. (New York: Zed Books, 2011).
6. I borrow the terms *empty* and *full world* from Herman E. Daly, "Uneconomic Growth: Empty-World versus Full-World Economics," in *Sustainable Development: The Challenge of Transition*, ed. Jurgen Schmandt et al. (Cambridge: Cambridge University Press, 2000), 63–77.
7. E. A. Wrigley, *Energy and the English Industrial Revolution* (Cambridge: Cambridge University Press, 2010), 1–2, 50–52; Donella Meadows et al., *Limits to Growth: The 30 Year Update* (White River Junction, VT: Chelsea Green, 2004); Will Steffen, Paul J. Crutzen, and John R. McNeill, "The Anthropocene: Are Humans Now Overwhelming the Great Forces of Nature?" *Ambio: A Journal of the Human Environment* 36 (2007): 614–21; Johan Rockström et al., "Planetary Boundaries: Exploring the Safe Operating Space for Humanity," *Ecology and Society* 14 (2009): 1–33; Tim Jackson, *Prosperity Without Growth: Economics for a Finite Planet* (London: Routledge, 2009); Juliet Schor, *Plenitude: The New Economics of True Wealth* (London: Penguin, 2010); Lester R. Brown, *World on the Edge: How to Prevent Environmental and Economic Collapse* (New York: W. W. Norton, 2011). The full story of how nineteenth-century fears of the stationary state shaped modern environmentalism is a task beyond the scope of this book.

8. Compare Jared Diamond, *Collapse: How Societies Choose to Fail or Succeed* (New York: Penguin, 2005), with the essays in Patricia A. McAnany and Norman Yoffee, *Questioning Collapse: Human Resilience, Ecological Vulnerability, and the Aftermath of Empire* (Cambridge: Cambridge University Press, 2010).
9. T. C. Smout, "The Landowner and the Planned Village," in *Scotland in the Age of Improvement: Essays in Scottish History in the Eighteenth Century*, ed. N. T. Phillipson and Rosalind Mitchison (Edinburgh: Edinburgh University Press, 1970), 73–106; Smout, "The Improvers and the Scottish Environment: Soils, Bogs and Woods," in *Eighteenth Century Scotland: New Perspectives*, ed. T. M. Devine and J. R. Young (East Linton, UK: Tuckwell, 1999), 210–24; Istvan Hont and Michael Ignatieff, "Needs and Justice in the '*Wealth of Nations*,'" in Hont, *Jealousy of Trade*, 1–44; John Robertson, *The Scottish Enlightenment and the Militia Issue* (Edinburgh: John Donald, 1985); Richard Sher, *Church and University in the Scottish Enlightenment: The Moderate Literati of Edinburgh* (Edinburgh: Edinburgh University Press, 1990); Sher, *The Enlightenment and the Book: Scottish Authors and Their Publishers in Eighteenth-Century Britain, Ireland, and America* (Chicago: University of Chicago Press, 2007); Roger Emerson, *Academic Patronage in the Scottish Enlightenment* (Edinburgh: Edinburgh University Press, 2008). For the Highlands, see Rosalind Mitchison, *Agricultural Sir John: The Life of Sir John Sinclair of Ulbster, 1754–1835* (London: Geoffrey Bles, 1962); Youngson, *After the Forty-Five*; Jean Dunlop, *The British Fisheries Society, 1786–1893* (Edinburgh: John Donald, 1978); J. M. Bumsted, *The People's Clearance: Highland Emigration to British North America, 1770–1815* (Edinburgh: Edinburgh University Press, 1982); Eric Richards, *A History of the Highland Clearances*, 2 vols. (London: Croom Helm, 1982, 1985); Peter Womack, *Improvement and Romance: Constructing the Myth of the Highlands* (Houndmills, UK: Macmillan, 1989); T. M. Devine, *Clanship to Crofters' War; The Social Transformation of the Scottish Highlands* (Manchester: Manchester University Press, 1994); and Allan I. Macinnes, *Clanship, Commerce, and the House of Stuart, 1603–1788* (East Linton, UK: Tuckwell, 1996).
10. Steven Shapin, "Property, Patronage, and the Politics of Science: The Founding of the Royal Society of Edinburgh," *BJHS* 7 (1974): 1–41; Shapin, "The Audience for Science in Eighteenth-Century Edinburgh," *History of Science* 12, no. 2 (1974): 95–121; Roger Emerson, "Sir Robert Sibbald, Kt, the Royal Society of Scotland the Origins of the Scottish Enlightenment," *Annals of Science* 45 (1988): 41–72; Emerson, "The Scientific Interests of Archibald Campbell, 1st Earl of Ilay and 3rd Duke of Argyll (1682–1761)," *Annals of Science* 59 (2002): 21–56; Jan Golinski, *Science as Public Culture: Chemistry and Enlightenment in Britain, 1760–1820* (Cambridge: Cambridge University Press, 1992); Golinski, *British Weather and the Climate of Enlightenment* (Chicago: University of Chicago Press, 2007); Charles W. J. Withers, *Geography, Science and National Identity: Scotland Since 1520* (Cambridge: Cambridge University Press, 2001); Withers, "The Rev. Dr. John Walker and the Practice of Natural History in Late Eighteenth Century Scotland," *Archives of Natural History* 18 (1991): 201–20; Withers and Paul Wood, eds., *Science and Medicine in the Scottish Enlightenment* (East Linton, UK: Tuckwell, 2002); Matthew D. Eddy, *The Language of Mineralogy:*

John Walker, *Chemistry, and the Edinburgh Medical School, 1750–1800* (London: Ashgate, 2009); Eddy, "The Aberdeen Agricola: Chemical Principles and Practice in James Anderson's Georgics and Geology," in *New Narratives in Eighteenth-Century Chemistry: Contributions from the First Francis Bacon Workshop, 21–23 April 2005* ed. Lawrence M. Principe, *Archimedes* 18 (2007): 139–56.
11. Alix Cooper, *Inventing the Indigenous: Local Knowledge and Natural History in Early Modern Europe* (Cambridge: Cambridge University Press, 2010); Lisbet Koerner, *Linnaeus: Nature and Nation* (Cambridge, MA: Harvard University Press, 1999).
12. Robertson, *Case for the Enlightenment*, 374–75.
13. The notion of natural history as the privileged economic authority of peripheries is derived in part from Lisbet Koerner's *Linnaeus: Nature and Nation*. The interaction of political economy with natural philosophy, natural history and agricultural treatises has been the subject of a great deal of investigation already; see, e.g., Keith Tribe, *Land, Labour and Economic Discourse* (London: Routledge and Kegan Paul, 1978); Philip Mirowski, *More Heat than Light* (Cambridge: Cambridge University Press, 1989); Catherine Larrère, *L'invention de l'économie au XVIIIe siècle* (Paris: Presses Universitaires de France, 1992); and Margaret Schabas, *The Natural Origins of Economics* (Chicago: University of Chicago Press, 2005). Notice that the classic account of Highland improvement by Youngson, *After the Forty-Five*, dismisses the debates over natural knowledge as the territory of overconfident and foolish projectors (65–66).
14. The first group of scholarship on the British and North American origins of conservationism includes Roderick Nash, *Wilderness and the American Mind* (New Haven: Yale University Press, 1967); Donald Worster, *Nature's Economy: A History of Ecological Ideas*, 2nd ed. (Cambridge: Cambridge University Press, 1994); T. C. Smout, *Nature Contested: Environmental History in Scotland and Northern England Since 1600* (Edinburgh: Edinburgh University Press, 2000); Smout, "The Highlands and the Roots of Green Consciousness, 1750–1990," in *Exploring Environmental History: Selected Essays* (Edinburgh: Edinburgh University Press, 2009); and Harriet Ritvo, *The Dawn of Green: Thirlmere, Manchester, and Modern Environmentalism* (Chicago: University of Chicago Press, 2009). The second group on empire and conservation includes Richard Grove, *Green Imperialism: Colonial Expansion, Tropical Island Edens and the Origins of Environmentalism, 1600–1860* (Cambridge: Cambridge University Press, 1995); Gregory Barton, *Empire Forestry and the Origins of Environmentalism* (Cambridge: Cambridge University Press, 2002); and William Beinart, *The Rise of Conservation in South Africa: Settlers, Livestock and the Environment, 1770–1950* (Oxford: Oxford University Press, 2003). The third group includes Ramachandra Guha, "Radical American Environmentalism and Wilderness Preservation: A Third World Critique," *Environmental Ethics* 11, no. 1 (1989): 71–83; Elinor Ostrom, *Governing the Commons: The Evolution of Institutions for Collective Action* (Cambridge: Cambridge University Press, 1990); Steven Stoll, *Larding the Lean Earth: Soil and Society in Nineteenth-Century America* (New York: Hill and Wang, 2002); Brian Donahue, *The Great Meadow: Farmers and the Land in Colonial Concord* (New Haven: Yale University Press, 2004); and Paul Warde, "The Invention of Sustainability," *Modern Intellectual History* 8 (2011): 153–70.

15. But for a brief overview of classical political economy and environmental thought, see E. Kula, *History of Environmental Economic Thought* (New York: Routledge, 1998), chaps. 2 and 3 passim; and J. E. de Steiguer, *The Origins of Modern Environmental Thought* (Tucson: University of Arizona Press, 2006), 1–10.
16. Smout, *Nature Contested*; Smout, "Highlands and Roots of Green Consciousness"; Grove, *Green Imperialism*, 312, 347; Barton, *Empire Forestry and Origins of Environmentalism*, 47–48; Worster, *Nature's Economy*, 53; Ritvo, *Dawn of Green*, 104.
17. Joel E. Cohen, *How Many People Can the Earth Support?* (New York: W. W. Norton, 1995); Matthew Connelly, *Fatal Misconception: The Struggle to Control World Population* (Cambridge, MA: Harvard University Press, 2008); on Enlightenment arithmetic more generally, see *The Quantifying Spirit in the Eighteenth Century*, ed. Tore Frängsmyr, J. L. Heilbron, and Robin E. Rider (Berkeley: University of California Press, 1990); Andrea Rusnock, *Vital Accounts: Quantifying Health and Population in Eighteenth-Century England and France* (Cambridge: Cambridge University Press, 1992); Lorraine Daston, *Classical Probability in the Enlightenment* (Princeton, NJ: Princeton University Press, 1995); Keith Michael Baker, *Condorcet: From Natural Philosophy to Social Mathematics* (Chicago: University of Chicago Press, 1992); and Ian Hacking, *The Taming of Chance* (Cambridge: Cambridge University Press, 1990).
18. The concept of the northern frontier combines several themes in this book. In environmental terms, the idea of the frontier has been revived to designate a colonial process of ecological transformation by environmental and world historians, often involving boom-and-bust cycles or other oscillations between abundance and scarcity. The concept of the frontier also captures the peculiar intellectual and cultural expectations of contemporary travelers and improvers. Eighteenth-century observers in Scotland routinely spoke of the internal colonization of northern Scotland, comparing Highland improvement to Roman and American forms of frontier expansion or the scientific exploration of other peripheries, including Lapland and the South Seas. Compare Frederick Jackson Turner, *The Frontier in American History* (reprint ed., New York; Dover Publications, 1996); John F. Richards, *Unending Frontier: An Environmental History of the Early Modern World* (Berkeley: University of California Press, 2003); Edmund Burke III and Kenneth Pomeranz, *The Environment and World History* (Berkeley: University of California, 2009); William Cronon, "Landscapes of Abundance and Scarcity," in *Oxford History of the American West*, ed. Clyde A. Milner II, Carol A. O'Connor, and Martha A. Sandweiss (Oxford: Oxford University Press, 1994), 604; James Belich, *Replenishing the Earth: The Settler Revolution and the Rise of the Anglo-World, 1783–1939* (Oxford: Oxford University Press, 2009), 6–7; and Brian Dolan, *Exploring European Frontiers: British Travelers in the Age of Enlightenment* (London: Palgrave Macmillan, 2000).

CHAPTER 1. THE MORAL GEOGRAPHY OF SCOTLAND

1. OSA, 21: app., "Parish of Kincardine," 156–57, 159–61; John Walker, "An Essay on Peat, Containing an Account of Its Origin, of Its Chymical Principles, and General

Properties; Its Properties as a Manure, and as a Manured Soil; The Different Methods of Its Cultivation; Its Usefulness in Plantation and Gardening, and as a Fuel," *THSS*, vol. 2 (Edinburgh, 1803), 101; *Encyclopaedia Britannica*, 3rd ed. (1793), s.v. "Moss, Kincardine"; *OSA* 21: app., 162–66, 173; Andrew Wight, *Present State of Husbandry in Scotland*, 4 vols. (Edinburgh, 1778–84), 1: "Appendix: Improvements by Lord Kames on the Estate of Blair-Drummond," 381–83; James Robertson, *A General View of the Agriculture in the County of Perth; With Observations on the Means of Its Improvement* (Perth, 1799), 251–52, 484–516; NAS, GD1/321, "Census of the Inhabitants of Blair Drummond Moss, 1814," 22 (Wingate's count included both living and deceased "moss lairds").

2. The eighteenth-century term *savant*—a man of learning or science—is particularly apt to describe the identity and authority of these men.

3. Istvan Hont, "The 'Rich Country–Poor Country' Debate in Scottish Classical Political Economy," in *Wealth and Virtue: The Shaping of Political Economy in the Scottish Enlightenment* (Cambridge: Cambridge University Press, 1983); A. J. Youngson, *After the Forty-Five: The Economic Impact on the Scottish Highlands* (Edinburgh: University of Edinburgh Press, 1973); Roger L. Emerson, "The Scottish Contexts for David Hume's Political-Economic Thinking," in *David Hume's Political Economy*, ed. Carl Wennerlind and Margaret Schabas (New York: Routledge, 2008), 10–30.

4. Allan I. Macinnes, *Clanship, Commerce and the House of Stuart, 1603–1788* (East Linton, UK: Tuckwell, 1996); Andrew Mackillop, *"More Fruitful than the Soil": Army, Empire and the Scottish Highlands, 1715–1815* (East Linton, UK: Tuckwell, 2000), 236 (48,000 recruits from 300,000 inhabitants); T. M. Devine, *Clanship to Crofters' War: The Social Transformation of the Scottish Highlands* (Manchester: Manchester University Press, 1994); Devine, *Scotland's Empire, 1600–1815* (London: Penguin, 2003); Hugh Trevor-Roper, "The Invention of Tradition: The Highland Tradition of Scotland," in *The Invention of Tradition*, ed. E. J. Hobsbawm and T. O. Ranger (Oxford: Oxford University Press, 1983); Peter Womack, *Improvement and Romance: Constructing the Myth of the Highlands* (Houndmills, UK: Macmillan, 1989); Eric Richards, "Scotland and the Uses of the Atlantic Empire," in *Strangers Within the Realm: Cultural Margins of the First British Empire*, ed. Bernard Bailyn and Philip D. Morgan (Chapel Hill, NC: University of North Carolina Press, 1991), 67–114.

5. Fania Oz-Salzberger, "The Political Theory of the Scottish Enlightenment," in *The Cambridge Companion to the Scottish Enlightenment*, ed. Alexander Broadie (Cambridge: Cambridge University Press, 2003); Nicholas Phillipson, "Culture and Society in the Eighteenth-Century Province: The Case of Edinburgh and the Scottish Enlightenment," in *The University in Society: Studies in the History of Higher Education*, ed. Lawrence Stone, 2 vols. (Princeton, NJ: Princeton University Press, 1974); Phillipson, "The Scottish Enlightenment," in *The Enlightenment in National Context*, ed. Roy Porter and Mikuláš Teich (Cambridge: Cambridge University Press, 1981); Roger L. Emerson, *Essays on David Hume, Medical Men and the Scottish Enlightenment: Industry, Knowledge and Humanity* (Farnham, UK: Ashgate 2009), 239; Emma Rothschild, *Economic Sentiments: Adam Smith, Condorcet, and the Enlightenment* (Cambridge, MA: Harvard University Press, 2001), 52–64; for a view

that stresses the persistence of the radical Enlightenment in popular politics, see Bob Harris, *The Scottish People and the French Revolution* (London: Pickering and Chatto, 2008), 25–40.

6. For useful definitions of *modernity* and *modernization* along these lines, see Steve Pincus, *1688: The First Modern Revolution* (New Haven: Yale University Press, 2009), 9–10; Jeff Horn et al., *Reconceptualizing the Industrial Revolution* (Cambridge, MA: MIT Press, 2010), 17, 87; Shmuel N. Eisenstadt and Wolfgang Schluchter, "Introduction: Paths of Early Modernities—A Comparative View," *Daedalus* 127, no. 3 (1998): 1–18; Patrick O'Brien et al., "Political Components of the Industrial Revolution: Parliament and the English Cotton Textile Industry, 1660–1774," *Economic History Review*, n.s., 44, no. 3 (1991): 395–423; William Ashworth, "The Intersection of Industry and the State in Eighteenth-Century Britain," in *The Mindful Hand: Inquiry and Invention from the Late Renaissance to Early Industrialisation*, ed. Lissa Robert, Simon Schaffer, and Peter Dear (Amsterdam: Koninklijke Nederlandse Akademie van Wetenschappen, 2007); Prasannan Parthasarathi, *Why Europe Grew Rich and Asia Did Not: Global Economic Divergence, 1650–1850* (Cambridge: Cambridge University Press, 2011); and David Ormrod, *The Rise of Commercial Empires: England and the Netherlands in the Age of Mercantilism, 1650–1770* (Cambridge: Cambridge University Press, 2003).

7. Mackillop, "More Fruitful than the Soil," 64.

8. Martha Petrusewicz, "The Modernization of the European Periphery: Ireland, Poland, and the Two Sicilies, 1820–1870: Parallel and Connected, Distinct and Comparable," in *Comparison and History: Europe in Cross-National Perspective*, ed. Deborah Cohen and Maura O'Connor (New York: Routledge, 2004), 151–52, 159; Arno Mayer, *The Persistence of the Old Regime* (New York: Pantheon, 1981), 12–13.

9. Compare with the concept of "salvage colonialism" in George Steinmetz, *The Devil's Handwriting: Precoloniality and the German Colonial State in Qingdao, Samoa, and Southwest Africa* (Chicago: University of Chicago Press, 2007), 13; contrast my account with J. E. Cookson, "The Napoleonic Wars, Military Scotland and Tory Highlandism in the Early Nineteenth Century," *Scottish History Review* 78, no. 205 (1999): 60–75.

10. T. M. Devine, *The Transformation of Rural Scotland: Social Change and the Agrarian Economy, 1660–1815* (Edinburgh: John Donald, 1994).

11. WN, 1: bk. 3; John Robertson, *The Case for the Enlightenment: Scotland and Naples, 1680–1760* (Cambridge: Cambridge University Press, 2005), 391; R. H. Campbell, "The Scottish Improvers and the Course of Agrarian Change in the Eighteenth Century," in *Comparative Aspects of Scottish and Irish Economic and Social History, 1600–1900*, ed. L. M. Cullen and T. C. Smout (Edinburgh: John Donald, 1977).

12. For the Scottish discovery of feudalism, see Colin Kidd, *Subverting Scotland's Past: Scottish Whig Historians and the Creation of an Anglo-British Identity, 1689–c.1830* (Cambridge: Cambridge University Press, 1993), 129–84 passim; and Eric Hobsbawm, "Scottish Reformers of the Eighteenth Century and Capitalist Agriculture," in *Peasants in History: Essays in Honour of Daniel Thorner*, ed. Eric Hobsbawm et al. (New Delhi: Oxford University Press, 1980).

13. Roger Emerson, "The Social Composition of Enlightened Scotland: The Select Society of Edinburgh, 1754–1764," *Studies on Voltaire and the Eighteenth Century* 114 (1973): 291–329.
14. John Robertson, *The Scottish Enlightenment and the Militia Issue* (Edinburgh: John Donald, 1985), 84–86.
15. Roger Emerson, "The Scientific Interests of Archibald Campbell, 1st Earl of Ilay and 3rd Duke of Argyll (1682–1761)," *Annals of Science* 59 (2002): 21–56; A. J. Youngson, *The Making of Classical Edinburgh*, 2nd ed. (Edinburgh: University of Edinburgh Press, 2003); Stana Nenadic, *Lairds and Luxury: The Highland Gentry in Eighteenth-Century Scotland* (Edinburgh: Birlinn, 2007), 197–203.
16. Emerson, "Social Composition," 292, 301, 303, 308, 310–12; Steven Shapin, "Property, Patronage, and the Politics of Science: The Founding of the Royal Society of Edinburgh," *BJHS* 7 (1974): 4; J. B. Morrell, "The University of Edinburgh in the Late Eighteenth Century: Its Scientific Eminence and Academic Structure," *Isis* 62, no. 2 (1971): 162–63; Roger Emerson, "The Founding of the Edinburgh Medical School," *Journal of the History of Medicine and Allied Sciences* 59, no. 2 (2004): 183–218; Charles Withers, "William Cullen's Agricultural Lectures and Writings and the Development of Agricultural Science in Eighteenth-Century Scotland," *Agricultural History Review* 37, no. 2 (1989): 144–56.
17. On the Edinburgh Enlightenment, see James Buchan, *Capital of the Mind: How Edinburgh Changed the World* (London: John Murray, 2003). For Glasgow, see *The Glasgow Enlightenment*, ed. Andrew Hook and Richard B. Sher (East Linton, UK: Tuckwell, 1995); Roger Emerson and Paul Wood, "Science and Enlightenment in Glasgow, 1690–1802," in *Science and Medicine in the Scottish Enlightenment*, ed. Charles W. J. Withers and Paul Wood (East Linton, UK: Tuckwell, 2002), 110–11; T. C. Smout, *A History of the Scottish People, 1560–1830* (London: Collins, 1969), 381; and Shapin, "Property, Patronage," 3–5.
18. "Book of Rules and Minutes of the Select Society," NLS, Adv 23.1.1, 2 (hereafter cited as BRMSS); Hume, *The Letters of David Hume*, vol. 1, ed. J. Y. T. Greig (Oxford: Clarendon Press, 1995), 219; Alexander Carlyle, *Autobiography of the Rev. Dr. Alexander Carlyle, Minister of Inveresk; Containing Memorials of the Men and Events of His Time* (Boston, 1861), 227, 241; *Scots Magazine* 17 (1755): 126–27.
19. David Hume, *Political Writings*, ed. Knud Haakonsen (Cambridge: Cambridge University Press, 1994), 105–14; Robertson, *Militia Issue*, 85; BRMSS, 19–20, 74–75, 88–89, 101–3 (four times in summer of 1757)115–17, 149–50, 158–59, 167–68; on Hume and creative imitation, see Maxine Berg, "In Pursuit of Luxury: Global History and British Consumer Goods in the Eighteenth Century," *Past and Present* 182 (2004): 85–142.
20. Robertson, *Militia Issue*, 87–91; Adam Ferguson, *Reflections Previous to the Establishment of a Militia* (London, 1756), 132–34.
21. The minute book records Burnett as preses on the following pages (known topic proposed by Burnett indicated by *): 26*, 91, 98*–99* (twice), 103*–5* (twice preses, three topics proposed), 109*, 111*, 118*, 128*, 139*, 141*, 158*, 167*.
22. BRMSS, 80; NLS, MS 24501, ff. 148–49, MS 24554, 99, 110; cf. Richard Price, *Observations on Reversionary Payments . . .* (London, 1771), 237–38.

23. James Burnett, *Of the Origin and Progress of Language*, vol. 1, 2nd ed. (Edinburgh, 1774), 381; Walker, "Essay on Peat," 100; *BRMSS*, 116.
24. James Burnett, *Antient Metaphysics, Volume Fifth: Containing the History of Man; In the Civilized State* (Edinburgh, 1797), 31, 38, 307–8; Pliny the Elder, *Natural History: A Selection*, trans. John Healy (London: Penguin, 1991), 217; Nathan Rosenstein, *Rome at War: Farms, Families, and Death in the Middle Republic* (Chapel Hill: University of North Carolina Press, 2004), 73–74, 231–32nn52–53; NLS, MS 24579, 26.
25. *BRMSS*: debates on luxury and manufacturing: 19–20 (Ramsay, the first topic mentioned in the minutes), 74–45 (three times in a row), 88–89, 101–2 (three times again), 103–4 (Burnett on luxury), 115–17 (twice), 149–50 (Cullen on luxury), 158–59 (Burnett on luxury), 167–68 (Burnett again); debates on the militia and martial spirit: 59–63 (three times), 86–87, 92–93 (twice), 133–35 (martial and commercial spirit, twice), 144–46 (standing army, twice), 156–57 (Taitt on martial and commercial spirit); debates on agriculture: 27–28 (corn laws), 42–44 (entail, twice), 65–66 (entail), 81–82 (Swedish land laws), 99–100 (corn bounties, twice), 100–101 (entail, three times), 118–19 (great or small farms, twice), 120–21 (Irish cattle, twice), 124–25 (land taxes), 134–37 (Irish cattle, twice), 139–40 (large farms, twice), 140–41 (entail), 146–47 (grass), 159–60 (Campbell on stabilizing effect of landed interest), 160–64 (Taitt on landed interest and liberty, twice). All page references here include the date when the topic was proposed and the occasion when it was debated.
26. Robert Wallace, *A Dissertation on the Numbers of Mankind in Antient and Modern Times: In Which the Superior Populousness of Antiquity Is Maintained* (Edinburgh, 1753), 5, 11, 13, 25, 68, 83, 96, 147. For the quarrel with Hume, see Ernest Mossner, *The Forgotten Hume* (New York: Columbia University Press, 1943), 111–17, 127–31.
27. EUL, La II 97/5, Robert Wallace, "An Address to the Jacobites in Scotland . . . ," c. 1745, ff. 29–30.
28. Robert Wallace, *Characteristics of the Present Political State of Great Britain* (London, 1758), 205, 138, 46.
29. Robert Wallace, *Various Prospects of Mankind, Nature, and Providence* (London, 1761), 43, 111, 113–19. Robert Luehrs, "Population and Utopia in the Thought of Robert Wallace," *Eighteenth-Century Studies* 20, no. 3 (1987): 331–33; James Bonar, *Theories of Population from Raleigh to Arthur Young* (New York: Macmillan, 1931).
30. Robert Wallace, *A View of the Internal Policy of Great Britain; In Two Parts; Part I: Of the Alterations in the Constitution, from the Reign of Henry the Seventh . . .* (London, 1764), 284–85, 287.
31. Ibid., 78–79, 287–88; on Miller, see Bernard Bailyn, *Voyagers to the West: A Passage in the Peopling of America on the Eve of the Revolution* (New York: Alfred A. Knopf, 1986), 57–62.
32. On Kames, see Alexander Woodhouselee, *Memoirs of the Life and Writings of the Honorable Henry Home of Kames*, 2 vols. (Edinburgh, 1807); William C. Lehmann, *Henry Home, Lord Kames, and the Scottish Enlightenment* (The Hague: Martinus Nijhoff, 1971); Ian Simpson Ross, *Lord Kames and the Scotland of His Day* (Oxford: Clarendon Press, 1972).

33. NLS, MS 11014, f. 81; BL, Add. Ms. 35449, f. 189, "Considerations upon the State of Scotland with Respect to Entails," ff. 191–93; compare with Hume's characterization of feudal Scotland as a Polish path of development: "That Politics May Be Reduced to a Science," in *David Hume: Essays Moral, Political, and Literary*, ed. E. F. Miller (Indianapolis, IN: Liberty Classics, 1978), 16–18. For a longer discussion of Kames's attack on feudalism, see Kidd, *Subverting Scotland's Past*, 134–35, 140–42, 151, 161–64, 177; on the entail debate, see 163 ff.; cf. Adam Smith, "Report of 1762–3," in *Lectures on Jurisprudence*, ed. R. L. Meek, D. D. Raphael, and P. G. Stein (Oxford: Oxford University Press, 1978), 69–71.
34. *Scots Magazine* 19 (1757): 163–64, 260; note also Dalrymple's role in supplying historical data for Smith's argument about grain prices, cf. Adam Smith, *Correspondence*, vol. 6 of *The Glasgow Edition of the Works and Correspondence of Adam Smith*, ed. Andrew Stewart Skinner (Oxford: Oxford University Press, 1987), 139, 145–50.
35. NLS, MS 25453, ff. 107–12; David Dalrymple, *The Little Freeholder: A Dramatic Entertainment, in Two Acts* (London, 1790).
36. Annette Smith, *The Jacobite Estates of the Forty-Five* (Edinburgh: John Donald, 1982); the Highland survey conducted by representatives of the Church of Scotland reached the same conclusion in 1760. Their key priority was linguistic assimilation through the parish school system; see BOD, MS Top Scotland 2, ff. 41–47.
37. On Cullen's involvement, see NLS, MS 17590, 1762, 42; on military recruitment and the Annexed Estates, see Mackillop, "More Fertile than the Soil"; for a complete list of board members, see Smith, *Jacobite Estates*, 239–41. The members of the Select Society who served on the board include, from 1755: Mansfeld Cardonnel, George Drummond, Robert Dundas, Sir Gilbert Elliott, James Ogilvy (Earl of Findlater and Seafield), and James Ogilvy (Lord Deskford); from 1761: John Campbell, Lord Stonefield, Sir David Dalrymple (Lord Hailes), Henry Home (Lord Kames), Francis Garden (Lord Gardenstone), James Montgomery (Lord Alexander), Sir Thomas Miller (Lord Glenlee), and John Swinton; from 1770: Sir James Adolphus Oughton; and from 1776: David Ross (Lord Ankerville).
38. Smith, *Jacobite Estates*, 32, 44; H. J. Noltie, *John Hope (1725–1786): Alan G. Morton's Memoir of a Scottish Botanist*, new rev. ed. (Edinburgh: Royal Botanic Garden, 2011), 46; Bailyn, *Voyagers to the West*, 57; NLS, MS 25301, f. 188 (Dalrymple and Sutherland); Jean Dunlop, *The British Fisheries Society, 1786–1893* (Edinburgh: John Donald, 1978).
39. NLS, MS 11015, ff. 116 (Kames to Elliot), 82 (Swinton to Elliot), MS 25426, f. 35 (Dalrymple); attendance based on the minute book of the Annexed Estates, 1763–66, NAS, E721/7–9; Elliot quoted in Mackillop, "More Fertile than the Soil," 82; Tacitus, *The Agricola and Germania*, trans. H. Mattingly (London: Penguin, 1970); for George Clerk-Maxwell, see *Transactions of the Royal Society of Edinburgh* 1 (1788): 51–56; on agricultural improvement as an ideology of domination, see Richard Drayton, *Nature's Government: Science, Imperial Britain, and the "Improvement" of the World* (New Haven: Yale University Press, 2000).
40. NLS, MS 25300, f. 76; Hugh Trevor Roper, *The Invention of Scotland: Myth and History* (New Haven: Yale University Press, 2008), 92.

41. Lord Kames to Mrs. Montagu, May 22, 1771, quoted in Woodhouselee, *Memoirs of Kames*, 2:90–91; Lord Kames, *Sketches of the History of Man*, 2 vols. (Edinburgh, 1774), 1:42, 307–8; Robert Wokler, "Apes and Races in the Scottish Enlightenment: Monboddo and Kames on the Nature of Man," in *Philosophy and Science in the Scottish Enlightenment*, ed. Peter Jones (Edinburgh: John Donald, 1988), 152–53.
42. NAS, E728/9; NLS, MS 17563, ff. 102–4 (Graeme), 142–43 (Board of Trustees); Smith, *Jacobite Estates*, 27; Mackillop, "More Fruitful than the Soil," 82, 84, 95.
43. Compare with P. J. Marshall, *The Making and Unmaking of Empires: Britain, India and America, c. 1750–1783* (Cambridge: Cambridge University Press, 2007), 182. The new policy in the Highlands from 1763 could be seen as an internal variation on Marshall's imperial theme of accommodation. I am deeply indebted to Andrew Mackillop for his insistence that Highland crofting had a political rather than economic origin. His work, however, analyzes the activities of the Board for the Annexed Estates in isolation from the intellectual culture of Edinburgh and its debates about feudalism and commerce. For Mackillop's original thesis, see "More Fruitful than the Soil," 90–91, 99.
44. NLS, MS 25426, ff. 35, 169.
45. NAS, E721/8, f. 163 (Rannoch); NAS, GD112/12/1/4/8 (Breadalbane scheme); Kames appears to have been planning a book on agriculture in 1753 or earlier, NLS, MS 10782, 61; *Transactions of the Royal Society of Edinburgh* 1 (1788): 8; Stewart Richards, "Agricultural Science in Higher Education: Problems of Identity in Britain's First Chair of Agriculture, Edinburgh, 1790–c1831," *AHR* 33, no. 1 (1985): 61.
46. *OSA*, 6:493–97, 21:151–81, app., "Parish of Kincardine" [by George Drummond]; EUL, La III 352/1b, 153; Walker, "Essay on Peat"; Alexander Allardyce, ed., *Scotland and Scotsmen in the Eighteenth Century*, 2 vols. (Edinburgh, 1888), 2:537; Christopher Tait, *An Account of the Peat-Mosses of Kincardine and Flanders in Perthshire: From the Transactions of the Royal Society of Edinburgh* (n.p., [1792]); Robertson, *General View of the Agriculture in the County of Perth*, app. 2, 485; Aiton, *A Treatise on the Origin, Qualities, and Cultivation of Moss-Earth . . .* (Air, 1811); James Steuart, *An Inquiry into the Principles of Political Oeconomy* [1767], 2 vols., ed. Andrew S. Skinner (Edinburgh: Oliver and Boyd, 1966), 1:130; cf. *The Agrarian History of England and Wales*, vol. 6: 1750–1850, ed. G. E. Mingay (Cambridge: Cambridge University Press, 1989), 59–64.
47. Walker, "Essay on Peat," 103–5; *OSA*, 21: app., 173–74; Wingate's list includes the origin of at least some of the families on the moss. Out of approximately 140 families or settlers, more than 80 came from the parishes of Lyon, Callander, Breadalbane, and Balquihidder. Other parishes frequently mentioned include Comrie, Strathern, Stirling, and Lochearnside. See NAS, GD1/321, "Census of the Inhabitants of Blair Drummond Moss, 1814," 2–21; Robert Heron, *Observations Made in a Journey Through the Western Counties of Scotland*, 2 vols. (Perth, 1793), 2:443; Aiton, *Treatise on Moss-Earth* 341–42, quoted in T. C. Smout, *Nature Contested: Environmental History in Scotland and Northern England Since 1600* (Edinburgh: Edinburgh University Press, 2000), 20.
48. "Hints, by Lord Kames, to the Commissioners of the Annexed Estates," in Andrew Wight, *Present State of Husbandry in Scotland*, 1:188, 191–92.

49. Walker, "Essay on Peat," 100–101; Walker had joined the club in 1760 so this may give us an approximate date for Monboddo's speech on the assumption that Walker heard it himself; Margaret M. McKay, ed., *The Rev. Dr. John Walker's Report on the Hebrides of 1764 and 1771* (Edinburgh: John Donald, 1980), 35, 43, 101–2, 172, 210–11; Walker, *An Economical History of the Hebrides and Highlands of Scotland*, 2 vols. (Edinburgh, 1808), 1:125–30; I. F. Grant, *Highland Folk Ways* (London: Routledge and Kegan, 1961), 104–6; Samuel Johnson, *A Journey to the Western Islands of Scotland* (London: Penguin, 1984), 89. Walker linked spade cultivation and industry without mention of religion in the Report to the Annexed Estates whereas the report to the General Assembly of the Church of Scotland was replete with scathing references to Papist idleness. See "Dr. John Walker's Report to the Assembly, 1765," *Scots Magazine* 28 (1766): 686.
50. Martin Martin, *A Description of the Western Islands of Scotland Circa 1695 and a Late Voyage to St. Kilda* (Edinburgh: Birlinn, 1999), 14; Walker, *Economical History*, 1:120; cf. McKay's assessment in her introduction to *Walker's Report on the Hebrides*, 15. In supporting cultivation with the caschrom, Walker "was governed by social rather than economic criteria and advocated agricultural techniques to achieve his aims." Alan Gailey and Alexander Fenton, *The Spade in Northern and Atlantic Europe* (Belfast: Ulster Folk Museum, 1970), 190.
51. Walker to Kames, February 18, 1773, quoted in Woodhouselee, *Memoirs*, 2:28; Walker to Kames, August 17, 1764, quoted in Sir William Jardine, ed., *The Naturalist's Library*, vol. 12 (Edinburgh, 1842), 17–50; on the acuteness of northern minds, compare the Scots doctor John Arbuthnot, *An Essay Concerning the Effects of the Air on Human Bodies* (London, 1733); and Christopher Lawrence, "The Nervous System and Society in the Scottish Enlightenment," in *Natural Order: Historical Studies of Scientific Culture*, ed. Barry Barnes and Steven Shapin (London: Sage, 1979).
52. Martin, *Description of the Western Isles*, 14; Walker, *Economical History*, 1:127; Robert Dodgshon, "Budgeting for Survival: Nutrient Flow and Traditional Highland Farming," in *The History of Soils and Field Systems*, ed. S. Foster and T. C. Smout (Aberdeen: Scottish Cultural Press, 1994), 89–90.
53. McKay, *Walker's Report on the Hebrides*, 78, 101–2, 172, 210–11. But note Kames's critique of lazy bed cultivation, *The Gentleman Farmer*, 2nd ed. (Edinburgh, 1779), 390.
54. Matthew Eddy, "Scottish Chemistry, Classification and the Early Mineralogical Career of the 'Ingenious' Rev. Dr. John Walker," *BJHS* 35, no. 4 (2002): 428; McKay, *Walker's Report on the Hebrides*, 10, 15; Walker, *Economical History*, 1:2, 130; EUL, La III 352/6, "A Catalogue of the Books in Natural History with a Few Others Which Belonged to the Late Rev. Dr. Walker, Died January 22 1804." EUL, Dc 1.57–59, "Essays, Transcripts and Other Papers."
55. Michael Fry, *The Dundas Despotism* (Edinburgh: Edinburgh University Press, 1992); David Brown, "The Government of Scotland Under Henry Dundas and William Pitt," *History* 83 (1998): 265–79; John Dwyer and Alexander Murdoch, "Paradigms and Politics: Manners, Morals and the Rise of Henry Dundas, 1770–1784," in *New Perspectives on the Politics and Culture of Early Modern Scotland*, ed. John Dwyer, Roger Mason, and Alexander Murdoch (Edinburgh: PUB, 1982), 238.

56. BL, Add MSS 34412, ff. 352–57.
57. BL, Add MSS 34412, ff. 353–54.
58. WN, 1:414–15, 418–19.
59. BL, Add MSS 34412, f. 354.
60. On private crofting schemes and military recruitment, see Mackillop, "More Fruitful than the Soil," 101.
61. Fry, *Dundas Despotism*, 138–39, 246–48; NLS, Dep 268/1, Dep 268/21, Highland Society of London, "Minute Book, 1783–1792."

Chapter 2. Natural History and Civil Cameralism

1. Thomas Pennant, *A Tour in Scotland and Voyage to the Hebrides, 1772*, ed. Andrew Simmons (Edinburgh: Birlinn, 1998), 324–25; *THSS*, vol. 2 (Edinburgh, 1803), 436.
2. Pennant, *Tour in Scotland, 1772*, 324–25; Pennant, *British Zoology*, 4 vols. (London, 1768–70), 3:286; Jean Dunlop, *The British Fisheries Society, 1786–1893* (Edinburgh: John Donald, 1978), 140–42, 150–51; on the vagaries of herring migration, see *THSS*, 2:435–36.
3. Pennant, *British Zoology*, 3:286; John Knox, *A Tour Through the Highlands of Scotland, and the Hebride Isles, in MDCCLXXXVI* (London, 1787), iii–iv, 26–27; for the "New world," see Walker to Kames, December 10, 1764, EUL, La III 352/1a, f. 11, quoted in Charles W. J. Withers, "The Rev. Dr. John Walker and the Practice of Natural History in Late Eighteenth Century Scotland," *ANH* 18, no. 2 (1991): 208; on the "useless void," see Walker to Kames, August 18, 1764, NAS, GD24/1/564, f. 138, quoted in Charles Withers, "Geography, Natural History and the Eighteenth-Century Enlightenment: Putting the World in Place," *History Workshop Journal* 39 (1995): 137.
4. T. M. Devine, *The Scottish Nation: A History, 1700–2000* (New York: Viking, 1999), 193–95.
5. Devine, *Clanship to Crofters' War: The Social Transformation of the Scottish Highlands* (Manchester: Manchester University Press, 1994), 51; Devine, *The Transformation of Rural Scotland; Social Change and the Agrarian Economy, 1660–1815* (Edinburgh: Edinburgh University Press, 1994), 64–65; Devine, *Scottish Nation*, 189; Devine, "A Conservative People? Scottish Gaeldom in the Age of Improvement," in *Eighteenth Century Scotland; New Perspectives*, ed. T. M. Devine and J. R. Young (East Linton, UK: Tuckwell, 1999), 231–32.
6. Allan Macinnes, *Clanship, Commerce and the House of Stuart, 1603–1788* (East Linton, UK: Tuckwell, 1996), 230; Stana Nenadic, *Lairds and Luxury: The Highland Gentry in Eighteenth-Century Scotland* (Edinburgh: John Donald, 2007).
7. NAS, E727/46/1–49; *DNB*, s.v. "Williams, John"; NLS, MS 5006, "Memorial of Dr. Cullen," 1763; NAS, E730/27/1–7 (Cullen); D. M. Henderson and J. H. Dickson, eds., *A Naturalist in the Highlands: James Robertson, His Life and Travels in Scotland, 1767–1771* (Edinburgh: Scottish Academic Press, 1994); for Watt and the canals, see Annette Smith, *The Jacobite Estates of the Forty-Five* (Edinburgh: John Donald, 1982), 210–11; Wight, *Present State of Husbandry in Scotland*; Harold R. Fletcher and William

H. Brown, *The Royal Botanic Garden Edinburgh, 1670–1970* (Edinburgh: HMSO, 1970), 61–62; NAS, E727/47/1–5, quotation on 1; NAS, E728/43/1; John Lightfoot, *Flora Scotica; or, A Systematic Arrangement, in the Linnaean Method, of the Native Plants of Scotland and the Hebrides*, 2 vols. (London, 1777); Jane K. Bowden, *John Lightfoot: His Work and Travels with a Biographical introduction and a Catalogue of the Lightfoot Herbarium* (Kew: Bentham-Moxon Trust, 1989).

8. Annette Smith discusses the naturalist surveys briefly but does not analyze the strategic function of natural history, *Jacobite Estates*, 31–33; on surveyors and surveys, see 41–42. Devine, *Transformation of Rural Scotland*, 61, 66–70; Macinnes, *Clanship, Commerce*, 220. Note also the role of John Ainslie in the history of Scottish surveys; see Charles Withers, "Geography, Geometry and Mapping in the Scottish Enlightenment," in *Science and Medicine in the Scottish Enlightenment*, ed. Charles Withers and Paul Wood (East Linton, UK: Tuckwell, 2002), 65–68.

9. NAS, E728/43/1; John Walker, *Essays on Natural History and Rural Economy* (Edinburgh, 1812), 327.

10. Margaret M. McKay, ed., *The Rev. Dr. John Walker's Report on the Hebrides of 1764 and 1771* (Edinburgh: John Donald, 1980); James Anderson, *The Present State of the Hebrides and the Western Coasts of Scotland* (Edinburgh, 1785); John Lightfoot, *Flora Scotica; or, A Systematic Arrangement in the Linnaean Method of the Native Plants of Scotland and the Hebrides*, 2nd ed., 2 vols. (London, 1789), 1:xii–xv. For the credibility generated by patrician informants, see Charles W. J. Withers, "Travel and Trust in the Eighteenth Century," in *L'invitation au voyage: Studies in Honor of Peter France*, ed. John Renwick (Oxford: Voltaire Foundation, 2000), 50.

11. NAS, E727/46/27.

12. Roger L. Emerson, "The Scottish Contexts for David Hume's Political-Economic Thinking," in *David Hume's Political Economy*, ed. Carl Wennerlind and Margaret Schabas (New York: Routledge, 2008), 10–30; George Caffentzis, "Civilizing the Highlands: Hume, Money and the Annexing Act," *Historical Reflections / Réflexions historiques* 31, no. 1 (2005): 169–94.

13. WN, 1:96–97; John Robertson, *The Case for the Enlightenment: Scotland and Naples, 1680–1760* (Cambridge: Cambridge University Press, 2005), 390. For further discussion of Smith's views, see chapter 5.

14. WN, 1:240–41, 363–64, 524–26; John Walker, *An Economical History of the Hebrides and Highlands of Scotland*, 2 vols. (Edinburgh, 1808)

15. EUL, Walker Papers, Dc 2.40, Walker, "Occasional Remarks," 110; Dc 2.36, Walker, "Queries Concerning the North of Scotland," 165, 167.

16. Arthur Mitchell, "List of Travels and Tours in Scotland, 1296 to 1900," *Proceedings of the Society of Antiquaries of Scotland* 35 (1900–1901): 431–638.

17. Mackay, *Walker's Report on the Hebrides*, 35; Charles Withers, "The Historical Creation of the Scottish Highlands," in *The Manufacture of Scottish History*, ed. Ian Donnachie and Christopher Whatley (Edinburgh: Polygon, 1992), 147–48; Kathleen Wilson, "Pacific Modernity: Theater, Englishness, and the Arts of Discovery, 1760–1800," in *The Age of Cultural Revolutions: Britain and France, 1750–1820*, ed. Colin Jones and Dror Wahrman (Berkeley: University of California Press, 2002), 89–90; cf.

Johannes Fabian's critique of "allochronism" in *Time and the Other: How Anthropology Makes Its Object* (New York: Columbia University Press, 2002).

18. Womack, *Improvement and Romance*, 62–65. For the meaning of the enlightened prospect, see Charles Withers, "Introduction" to Pennant, *Tour in Scotland, 1772*, xix–xx; and Alan Chalmers, "Scottish Prospects: Thomas Pennant, Samuel Johnson, and the Possibilities of Travel Narrative," in *Historical Boundaries, Narrative Forms: Essays on British Literature in the Long Eighteenth Century in Honor of Everett Zimmerman*, ed. Lorna Clymer, Robert Mayer, and Everett Zimmerman (Newark: University of Delaware Press, 2007).

19. Roy A. Rauschenberg, "The Journal of Joseph Banks's Voyage Up Great Britain's West Coast to Iceland and to the Orkney Isles July to October 1772," *Proceedings of the American Philosophical Society* 117, no. 3 (1973): 186–226, ff. 189–91, 205, 212; *Scots Magazine*, November 1772, 637–38; Edward Duyker, *Nature's Argonaut: Daniel Solander, 1733–1782* (Melbourne: Miegunyah, 1998); Pennant, *Tour in Scotland, 1772*, 255–68; Martin Rudwick, *Bursting the Limits of Time: The Reconstruction of Geohistory in the Age of Revolution* (Chicago: University of Chicago Press, 2005), 77.

20. For mountain tourism, see T. C. Smout, "Tours in the Scottish Highlands from the eighteenth to the twentieth centuries," *Northern Scotland* 5, no. 2 (1983): 99–121; Keith Thomas, *Man and the Natural World: Changing Attitudes in England, 1500–1800* (Oxford: Oxford University Press, 1983), 260–69; and Samuel Johnson and James Boswell, *A Journey to the Western Islands of Scotland and The Journal of a Tour to the Hebrides* (London: Penguin, 1984), 105, 215, 225, 236.

21. Thomas Pennant, *The Literary Life of the late Thomas Pennant* (London, 1793), 15; Pennant, *Tour in Scotland, 1772*, dedication, xxvii–xxviii, 229–30. For the participants in the expedition, see NLS, Adv 29.5.5 I, ff. 20, 25. Pennant testified in the 1785 hearings on the fisheries in Parliament, see *Committee Appointed to Enquire into the State of the British Fisheries, Third Report from the Committee Appointed to Enquire into the State of the British Fisheries . . .* (n.p., 1785), 74–77.

22. Pennant, *Tour in Scotland, 1772*, 364–65, 367–68; John Dwyer, *The Age of the Passions: An Interpretation of Adam Smith and Scottish Enlightenment Culture* (East Linton, UK: Tuckwell, 1998), 151–52 (on nostalgia and ghosts), 164 (on the survival of the sentimental savage *as* the genteel reader); cf. Peter Womack, *Improvement and Romance*, 97–98, 101–9.

23. Pennant, *Tour in Scotland, 1772*, 293–95, 368–69; cf. Dwyer, *Age of the Passions*, 154, on Ossian as a synthesis of ancient virtue and modern sentiment. Thomas Pennant, *Tour in Scotland, 1769* (Chester, 1771), 165–67, includes a list of Gaelic virtues: hospitality, generosity, politeness, curiosity, and decency. See also John Knox, *A View of the British Empire, More Especially Scotland . . .*, 2 vols. (London, 1784), 14–16.

24. For Highland travelers, see *DNB*, including "Industrial Spies." For George Don, see Harold Fletcher and William H. Brown, *The Royal Botanic Garden Edinburgh, 1670–1970*, (Edinburgh: HMSO, 1970), 76–77. On Hope's students, see H. J. Noltie, *John Hope (1725–1786): Alan G. Morton's Memoir of a Scottish Botanist*, new rev. ed. (Edinburgh: Royal Botanic Garden, 2011), 84–93.

25. OSA; John Sinclair, *History of the Origin and Progress of the Statistical Account of Scotland* (Edinburgh, 1798), iv, xi; Edward Lhuyd, *Parochial Queries in Order to a Geographical Dictionary, a Natural History &c. of Wales* ([Oxford?], 1697); Leopold Berchtold, *Essay to Direct and Extent the Inquiries of Patriotic Travellers . . .* (London, 1789); Walker, "Queries Concerning the North of Scotland." Note also the role of Earl Buchan in proposing a parochial survey in 1781; see Charles Withers, "Geography, Geometry and Mapping in the Scottish Enlightenment," in *Science and Medicine in the Scottish Enlightenment*, ed. Charles Withers and Paul Wood (East Linton, UK: Tuckwell, 2002), 64–65.

26. John Sinclair, *Queries Drawn Up for the Purpose of Elucidating the Natural History and Political State of Scotland* (Edinburgh, 1790), 5; Ewald von Herzberg, *Sur la population des états en général et sur celle des états prussiens en particulier* (n.p., [1785]), 30. On Sinclair's use of the German term *Statistik*, see Ian Hacking, *The Taming of Chance* (Cambridge: Cambridge University Press, 1990), 26–28.

27. Andre Wakefield, "Books, Bureaus and the Historiography of Cameralism," *European Journal of Law and Economics* 19 (2005): 311–20; Pamela Smith, *The Business of Alchemy: Science and Culture in the Holy Roman Empire* (Princeton, NJ: Princeton University Press, 1997); Lisbet Koerner, *Linnaeus: Nature and Nation* (Cambridge, MA: Harvard University Press, 1999); Emma Spary, *Utopia's Garden: French Natural History from the Old Regime to the Revolution* (Chicago: University of Chicago Press, 1999); Alix Cooper, *Inventing the Indigenous: Local Knowledge and Natural History in Early Modern Europe* (Cambridge: University of Cambridge Press, 2007), 42–44; Luca Molà, Reinhold C. Mueller, and Claudio Zanier, eds., *La seta in Italia dal Medioevo al Seicento: Dal baco al drappo* (Venice: Marsilio, 2000); H. K. Roessingh, "Tobacco Growing in Holland in the Seventeenth and Eighteenth Centuries: A Case Study of the Innovative Spirit of Dutch Peasants," *Acta Historiae Neerlandicae* 11 (1978): 18–54; Jordan Goodman, *Tobacco in History: The Cultures of Dependence* (London, Routledge, 1993), 142; Tobias Kuster, "500 Jahre kolonialer Rohrzucker—250 Jahre europäischer Rübenzucker," *Vierteljahrschrift für Sozial und Wirtschaftsgeschichte* 85 (1998): 477–512; J. A. Perkins, "The Agricultural Revolution in Germany, 1850–1914," *Journal of European Economic History* 10, no. 1 (1981): 71–118; David Blackbourn, *The Conquest of Nature: Water, Landscape, and the Making of Modern Germany* (New York: W. W. Norton, 2006); Thorkild Kjaergaard, *The Danish Revolution, 1500–1800: An Ecohistorical Interpretation* (Cambridge: Cambridge University Press, 1994).

28. John Sinclair, *Address to the Society for the Improvement of British Wool; Constituted at Edinburgh, on . . . January 31, 1791*, 2nd ed. (London, 1791), iii–iv, 32; Robert Heron, *General View of the Natural Circumstances of Those Isles, Adjacent to the North-West Coast of Scotland, Which Are Distinguished by the Common Name of Hebudae or Hebrides* (Edinburgh, 1794), 99. Sinclair's economic doctrine did not privilege land over labor; see *Essays on Miscellaneous Subjects* (London, 1802), 261–62. Compare "civil cameralism" with James Livesey's definition of civil society as the attempt to "reconstruct the psychology of organic community with the tools of individualist society" in *Civil Society and Empire: Ireland and Scotland in the Eighteenth-Century Atlantic World* (New Haven: Yale University Press, 2009), 14. The Society of Arts,

Manufactures and Commerce (founded 1754) pursued a strategy of self-sufficiency and import substitution that favored raw materials from the colonies instead of the metropole; see Maxine Berg, "In Pursuit of Luxury: Global History and British Consumer Goods in the Eighteenth Century," *Past and Present* 182 (2004): 131, 135–37.
29. For the "useless gift of nature," see OSA, 11:68.
30. Philip R. Sloan, "Natural History, 1670–1802," in *Companion to the History of Modern Science*, ed. Roger C. Olby et al. (London: Routledge, 1990).
31. Sten Lindroth, *Kungliga Svenska Vetenskapsakademiens historia, 1739–1818*, 2 vols. (Uppsala: Almqvist and Wiksell, 1967), 1:1–6; Koerner, *Linnaeus*, 105.
32. Koerner, *Linnaeus*, 60, 92, 114–15, 149; Linnaeus, *Iter Lapponicum*, in *Skrifter af Carl von Linné: Utgifna af. Kungl. Vetenskapsakademien*, vol. 5, ed. Thomas M. Fries (Uppsala: Almqvist and Wiksell, 1913), 106–7; Carl von Linné [Linnaeus], *Dalaresa* (Stockholm: Almqvist and Wiksell, 2004), 65–66; Carl Frängsmyr, *Klimat och karaktär: Naturen och människan i sent svenskt 1700-tal* (Uddevalla: Natur och Kultur, 2000), 135–44; Gunnar Eriksson, *The Atlantic Vision: Olaus Rudbeck and Baroque Science* (Canton, MA: Watson, 1994).
33. "Oeconomia naturae" in Carl von Linné, *Valda smärre skrifter af allmänt naturvetenskapligt innehåll*, ed. Thomas M. Fries (Uppsala: Almqvist and Wiksell, 1906), 12.
34. Pehr Wargentin, "Anmärkningar om climaters skiljeaktighet," *KVAH*, July–September 1757, 165–77; Wargentin, "Anmärkningar om svenska climatet," *KVAH*, October–December 1757, 245–63; Wargntin, "Jämförelser mellan svenska och franska climaterna, samt tvänne andra sydligare," *KVAH*, January–March 1758, 1–15; [Linnaeus], *Dalaresa*, 33, 45; Carl von Linnés, *Lappländska resa* (Stockholm: Natur och kultur, 2004), 28; see also Frängsmyr, *Klimat och karaktär*, 48–51, 54, 96–97.
35. Koerner, *Linnaeus*, 126; James L. Larson, *Interpreting Nature: The Science of Living Form from Linnaeus to Kant* (Baltimore: Johns Hopkins University Press, 1994), ch. 4; Linnaeus, *Philosophia Botanica*, trans. Stephen Freer (Oxford: Oxford University Press, 2003), 115–16.
36. Koerner, *Linnaeus*, 113, 121–22, 126–27; Staffan Müller-Wille, "Nature as a Marketplace: The Political Economy of Linnaean Botany," in *Oeconomies in the Age of Newton: Annual Supplement to Volume 35 History of Political Economy*, ed. Margaret Schabas and Neil De Marchi (Durham, NC: Duke University Press, 2003), 168; on the practice of collecting, see Müller-Wille, *Botanik und Weltweiter Handel; Zur Begründung eines Natürlichen Systems der Pflanzen durch Carl von Linné (1707–78)* (Berlin: Verlag fur Wissenschaft und Bildung, 1999), 157–72.
37. John Gascoigne, *Joseph Banks and the English Enlightenment: Useful Knowledge and Polite Culture* (Cambridge: Cambridge University Press, 2003), 98–107; Frans A. Stafleu, *Linnaeus and the Linnaeans: The Spreading of Their Ideas in Systematic Botany, 1735–1789* (Utrecht: A. Oosthoek's Uitgeversmaatchappij, 1971), 199–240; D. P. Miller, "'My favorite studdys': Lord Bute as Naturalist," in *Lord Bute: Essays in Reinterpretation*, ed. Karl W. Schweizer (Leicester: Pinter, 1988), 213–39; Richard Drayton, *Nature's Government: Science, Imperial Britain, and the "Improvement" of the World* (New Haven: Yale University Press, 2000), 41, 96–97; David Elliston Allen, *The Naturalist in Britain: A Social History* (1976; reprint ed., Princeton, NJ: Princeton

University Press, 1994), 27, 35–44; Erasmus Darwin, *The Botanic Garden: A Poem, in Two Parts* ... (London, 1791); WN, 1:169; E. C. Mossner and J. S. Ross, eds., *The Correspondence of Adam Smith* (Oxford: Oxford University Press, 1977), 252; Koerner, *Linnaeus*, 48–49; Benjamin Stillingfleet, *Miscellaneous Tracts Relating to Natural History, Husbandry, and Physick* ... (London, 1759), 184–201; Richard Pulteney, *A General View of the Writings of Linnaeus* ... (London, 1781), 374–409. Note also James Anderson's endorsement of Linnaeus and the grass inventory of 1749 in *Essays Relating to Agriculture and Rural Affairs*, vol. 2, 2nd ed. (Edinburgh, 1777), app., 351–413.

38. John Pickstone, *Ways of Knowing: A New History of Science, Technology, and Medicine* (Chicago: University of Chicago Press, 2001), 68; Stillingfleet, *Miscellaneous Tracts*, 13, 17; Pulteney, *General View*, 4–13.

39. EUL, La III 352/1a 1–8, 352/1b 91–92; McKay, *Walker's Report on the Hebrides*, 33–35, 129–30, 182–83, 188–89, 198.

40. EUL, La III 352/1a 2–3, 9–10; EUL, Dc 2.36–38 (notes on Sibbald's natural history by Walker); Koerner, *Linnaeus*, 23, 82. For Sibbald's prominence, see R. L. Emerson, "Sir Robert Sibbald Kt, the Royal Society of Scotland and the Origins of the Scottish Enlightenment," *Annals of Science* 45 (1988): 41–72; C. W. J. Withers, "Geography, Science and National Identity in Early Modern Britain: The Case of Scotland and the Work of Sir Robert Sibbald, 1641–1722," *Annals of Science* 53 (1996): 29–73; Vladimir Jankovič, *Reading the Skies: A Cultural History of English Weather* (Chicago: University of Chicago Press, 2000), 78–81; and Koerner, *Linnaeus*, 23, 82.

41. C. W. J. Withers, "Natural Knowledge as Cultural Property: Disputes over the Ownership of Natural History in Late Eighteenth-Century Edinburgh," ANH 19, no. 3 (1992): 293–94.

42. Harold R. Fletcher and William H. Brown, *The Royal Botanic Garden Edinburgh, 1670–1970* (Edinburgh: HMSO, 1970), 57–67; nine letters from Hope to Linnaeus are reprinted in A. G. Morton, *John Hope, 1725–1786, Scottish Botanist* (Edinburgh: Edinburgh Botanic Garden Trust, 1986), 31–35; DNB, s.v. "Hope, John"; NAS, E727/47/1–4, E728/43/1, 3; Henderson and Dickson, *Naturalist in the Highlands*, vii, 2, 9, 12, 93–94, 97, 117; John Hope, "A Letter from John Hope ... to William Watson ... on a Rare Plant Found in the Isle of Skye," *Philosophical Transactions (1683–1775)*, vol. 59 (1769): 241–46; for Hope's networks, see NAS, GD253/144/1/1–8, GD253/144/2/1–8.

43. Roger Emerson, "The Edinburgh Society for the Importation of Foreign Seeds and Plants, 1764–1773," *Eighteenth-Century Life* 7 (1982): 73–95; NAS, GD253/144/3/18 (Kames and the winter garden); John Hope, *Catalogus arborum et fruticum in horto Edinensi crescentium anno 1778* (Edinburgh, 1778), 2, 4, 9; NAS, GD253/144/11/9, /25–26 (Kalm and climate), GD253/145/7/10 (rhododendron), 253/144/13/20–21 (Chinese and Indian hemp), GD253/144/2/1–8 (Asa foetida); John Hope, "Description of a plant yielding Asa foetida. In a letter from John Hope, MD, FRS, to Sir Joseph Banks, Bart, PRS," in *Philosophical Transactions of the Royal Society* (London, 1785), 36–39; NAS, GD253/144/5/1–12 (rhubarb); NAS, GD253/145/14/46–51 (rhubarb); Noltie, *John Hope*, 34; Koerner, *Linnaeus*, 128.

44. NAS, GD253/144/3/25 (notes on tea transfer), GD253/144/7a/90 (notes on tea in 1775); John Coakely Lettsom, *The Natural History of the Tea-Tree, with Observations on the Medical Qualities of Tea, and Effects of Tea-Drinking* (London, 1772), 32; NAS, GD253/146/1/2 (Bohea tree in 1775); Hope, *Catalogus arborum*, 20; Ray Desmond, *The European Discovery of the Indian Flora* (Oxford: Oxford University Press, 1992), 231–33; on Hope's students, see Noltie, *John Hope*, 84–93.

Chapter 3. Improving the Scottish Climate

1. Richard B. Stothers, "The Great Dry Fog of 1783," *Climatic Change* 32 (1996): 80–83; Charles A. Wood, "Climatic Effects of the 1783 Laki Eruption," in C. R. Harrington, *The Year Without a Summer? World Climate in 1816* (Ottawa: Canadian Museum of Nature, 1992), 61; Gilbert White, *The Natural History and Antiquities of Selborne* (London, 1789), 301; G. Manley, "Central England Temperatures: Monthly Means, 1659–1973," *Quarterly Journal of the Royal Meteorological Society* 100 (1974): 389–405; John Grattan and Jon Sadler, "Regional Warming of the Lower Atmosphere in the Wake of Volcanic Eruptions: The Role of the Laki Fissure Eruption in the Hot Summer of 1783," *Geological Society, London, Special Publications* 161 (1999): 164; John Grattan and Mark Brayshay, "An Amazing and Portentous Summer: Environmental and Social Responses in Britain to the 1783 Eruption of an Iceland Volcano," *Geographical Journal* 161, no. 2 (1995): 128–30; J. Grattan, M. Durand, and S. Taylor, "Illness and Elevated Mortality in Europe Coincident with the Laki Fissure Eruption," *Geological Society, London, Special Publications* 213 (2003): 401.
2. Alexander Allardyce, ed., *Scotland and Scotsmen in the Eighteenth Century from the MSS of John Ramsay, Esq. of Ochtertyre*, 2 vols. (Edinburgh, 1888), 2:265; James Fergusson, ed., *Letters of George Dempster to Sir Adam Fergusson, 1756–1813, with Some Account of His Life* (London: Macmillan, 1934), 123–24; *The Correspondence of James Boswell with James Bruce and Andrew Gibb, Overseers of the Auchinleck Estate*, ed. Nellie Pottle Hankins and John Strawhorn (Edinburgh: Edinburgh University Press, 1998), 63.
3. H. H. Lamb, "Volcanic Dust in the Atmosphere: With a Chronology and Assessment of Its Meteorological Significance," *Philosophical Transactions of the Royal Society of London*, A 266 (1970): 442–43; Archibald Geikie, *Text Book of Geology* (London, 1885), 202; Mark Brayshay and John Grattan, "Environmental and Social Responses in Europe to the 1783 Eruption of the Laki Fissure Volcano in Iceland: A Consideration of Contemporary Documentary Evidence," *Geological Society, London, Special Publications* 161 (1999): 180–82; Sigirdur Thorarinsson, "Greetings from Iceland: Ash-Falls and Volcanic Aerosols in Scandinavia," *Geografiska Annaler, Ser. A, Physical Geography*, 63, no. 3/4 (1981): 116; Benjamin Franklin, "Meteorological Imaginations and Conjectures," in *Memoirs of the Literary and Philosophical Society of Newcastle*, vol. 2 (Warrington, 1785), 359–61. At least one periodical reported on Franklin's hypothesis; see Arthur Young, *Annals of Agriculture and Other Useful Arts* (1786): 484.

4. Thorarinsson, "Greetings from Iceland," 116; Franklin, "Meteorological Imaginations and Conjectures," 359–61.
5. James L. Larson, *Interpreting Nature: The Science of Living Form from Linnaeus to Kant* (Baltimore: Johns Hopkins University Press, 1994); John V. Pickstone, *Ways of Knowing: A New History of Science, Technology, and Medicine* (Chicago: University of Chicago Press, 2000), ch. 3 passim; Emma C. Spary, "Political, Natural and Bodily Economies," in *Cultures of Natural History*, ed. Nicholas Jardine, James A. Secord, and E. C. Spary (Cambridge: Cambridge University Press, 1996), 178–96. NLS, MS 23165–66, James Hutton, *Elements of Agriculture*, vol. 1 (MS 1797), 143; Clarence J. Glacken, *Traces on the Rhodian Shore: Nature and Culture in Western Thought from Ancient Times to the End of the Eighteenth Century* (Berkeley: University of California Press, 1967); Vladimir Janković, *Reading the Skies: A Cultural History of the English Weather, 1660–1820* (Chicago: University of Chicago Press, 2000); Jan Golinski, *British Weather and the Climate of Enlightenment* (Chicago: University of Chicago Press, 2007); Janet Browne, "Biogeography and Empire," in Jardine, Secord, and Sperry, *Cultures of Natural History*, 305–21.
6. James Hutton, "Theory of Rain," in *Transactions of the Royal Society of Edinburgh*, vol. 1 (Edinburgh, 1788), 49, 54; NLS, MS 23165–66, Hutton, 1:165; Lisbet Koerner, *Linnaeus: Nature and Nation* (Cambridge, MA: Harvard University Press, 1999), 120; Carl Frängsmyr, *Klimat och karaktär: Naturen och människan i sent svenskt 1700-tal* (Stockholm: Natur och Kultur, 2000).
7. Hutton, "Theory of Rain," 70; Catesby quoted in Joyce E. Chaplin, "Mark Catesby, a Skeptical Newtonian in America," in *Empire's Nature: Mark Catesby's New World Vision*, ed. Amy R. W. Meyers and Margaret Beck Pritchard (Chapel Hill: University of North Carolina Press, 1998), 49; Chaplin, "Knowing the Ocean: Benjamin Franklin and the Circulation of Atlantic Knowledge," in *Science and Empire in the Atlantic World*, ed. James Delbourgo and Nicholas Dew (New York: Routledge, 2008); Benjamin Franklin, *Maritime Observations* . . . (Philadelphia, 1786); Karen Ordahl Kupperman, "The Puzzle of the American Climate in the Early Colonial Period," *American Historical Review* 87, no. 5 (1982): 1262–89; Golinski, *British Weather*, ch. 7 passim.
8. James C. Riley, *The Eighteenth Century Campaign to Avoid Disease* (New York, 1987); G. E. R. Lloyd, ed., *Hippocratic Writings* (New York: Penguin, 1983), 148–69; Lord Kames, *Sketches of the History of Man*, 2 vols. (Edinburgh, 1774), 1:53; Andrea Rusnock, *Vital Accounts: Quantifying Health and Population in Eighteenth-Century England and France* (Cambridge: Cambridge University Press, 2002), ch. 5; Richard Grove, *Green Imperialism: Colonial Expansion, Tropical Island Edens and the Origins of Environmentalism, 1600–1860* (Cambridge: Cambridge University Press, 1995); Simon Schaffer, "Measuring Virtue; Eudiometry, Enlightenment, and Pneumatic Medicine," in *The Medical Enlightenment of the Eighteenth Century*, ed. Andrew Cunningham and Roger French (Cambridge: Cambridge University Press, 1990), 281–318.
9. EUL, La III 352/1a, 8, John Walker to Carl Linnaeus, October 12, 1762; James Headrick, *View of the Mineralogy, Agriculture, Manufactures and Fisheries of the Island of Arran* (Edinburgh: D. Willison, 1807), 351–53.

10. Glacken, *Traces on the Rhodian Shore*, 487–88, 689–90; *Edinburgh Magazine*, January 1787, 6; David Arnold, *The Problem of Nature: Environment and Culture in Historical Perspective* (London: Blackwell, 1996), 152–53; François Jean Chastellux, *Travels in North-America, in the Years 1780, 1781, and 1782*, 2 vols. (London, 1787), 54; Jan Golinski, *British Weather and the Climate of Enlightenment* (Chicago: University of Chicago Press, 2007), 197–99.

11. John Campbell, *A Political Survey of Britain*, 2 vols. (London, 1774), 2:60; James Anderson, *The Bee* 12 (1792): 170–71; Edward Gibbon, *The History of the Decline and Fall of the Roman Empire*, vol. 1 (London, 1776), 218–20; Georges Louis Leclerc Buffon, *Natural History General and Particular*, trans. William Smellie, 9 vols. (Edinburgh, 1780), 9:396–99; NLS, MS 23165–66, 1:645; John Sinclair, *The Code of Agriculture* (London, 1817), 2–3; Sinclair, *Essays on Miscellaneous Subjects* (London, 1802), 174; Glacken, *Traces on the Rhodian Shore*, 669; Theodore S. Feldman, "The Ancient Climate in the Eighteenth and Early Nineteenth Century," in *Science and Nature: Essays in the History of the Environmental Sciences*, ed. Michael Shortland (Stanford in the Vale: British Society for the History of Science, 1993), 23–40; Richard W. Judd, *The Untilled Garden: Natural History and the Spirit of Conservation in America, 1740–1840* (Cambridge: Cambridge University Press, 2009), 232–35.

12. EUL, La III 379, ff. 359–60; John Sinclair, *General View of the Agriculture of the Northern Counties of Cromarty, Ross, Sutherland, and Caithness, and the Islands of Orkney and Shetland; With Observations on the Means of Their Improvement* (London, 1795), 146.

13. James Anderson, *Observations on the Means of Exciting a Spirit of National Industry* (Edinburgh, 1777), 170, 172.

14. John Lightfoot, *Flora Scotica; or, A Systematic Arrangement, in the Linnaean Method, of the Native Plants of Scotland and the Hebrides*, 2 vols. (London, 1777), 1:76, 158–59, 191, 197, 257; D. M. Henderson and J. H. Dickson, eds., *A Naturalist in the Highlands: James Robertson, His Life and Travels in Scotland, 1767–1771* (Edinburgh: Scottish Academic Press, 1994), 34, 118.

15. Margaret M. McKay, ed., *The Rev. Dr. John Walker's Report on the Hebrides of 1764 and 1771* (Edinburgh: John Donald, 1980), 182–83: "A climate more temperate than Gaul"; Benjamin Stillingfleet, *Miscellaneous Tracts Relating to Natural History, Husbandry, and Physick . . .* (London, 1759), 13.

16. Anderson, *Observations on the Means*, 191, 223; for Shetland wool, see chapter 8; on Lightfoot's primitivism, see chapter 3; for Atholl rhubarb, see BM, boxes 49/6/70, 65/1/134, 54/1/25; for Atholl larch, see chapter 6; McKay, *Walker's Report on the Hebrides*, 47–48, 55, 66, 79–80, 100, 103, 118, 133, 161, 173, 188–89, 213. For present views of the climate conditions in Scotland, see David Turnock, *The Making of the Scottish Rural Landscape* (Aldershot, UK: Scolar, 1995), 11–27.

17. Allardyce, *Scotland and Scotsmen*, 2:265; Franklin, "Meteorological Imaginations," 360–61; Wood, "Climatic Effects of the 1783 Laki Eruption," 70–71; R. A. Dodgshon, D. D. Gilbertson, and J. P. Grattan, "Endemic Stress, Farming Communities and the Influence of Icelandic Volcanic Eruptions in the Scottish Highlands," *Geological Society, London, Special Publications* 171 (2000): 267–80; J. A. Kington, "Daily Weather

Mapping from 1781: A Detailed Synoptic Examination of Weather and Climate During the Decade Leading up to the French Revolution," *Climate Change* 3 (1980): 29–32 ; on the pattern of dearth and bad weather in the 1790s, see Roger Wells, Wretched Faces (New York: St. Martin's Press, 1988), 36–38. For the place of Iceland in natural history, see Karen Oslund, "Imagining Iceland: Narratives of Nature and History in the North Atlantic," *BJHS* 35 (2002): 313–34.

18. OSA, 12:473–74, 14:376, 9:487, 489, 17:279.
19. Sinclair, *General View of the Agriculture of the Northern Counties*, 8–9; James Robertson, *A General View of the Agriculture in the County of Perth; With Observations on the Means of Its Improvement* (Perth, 1799), 61, 259; John Smith, *General View of the Agriculture of the County of Argyll* (Edinburgh, 1798), 135–36.
20. For the quantification of the weather in the Enlightenment, see Theodore S. Feldman, "Late Enlightenment Meteorology," in *The Quantifying Spirit in the Eighteenth Century*, ed. Tore Frängsmyr, J. L. Heilbron, and Robin E. Rider (Berkeley: University of California Press, 1990); Marie-Noëlle Bourget, "Measurable Difference: Botany, Climate, and the Gardener's Thermometer in Eighteenth-Century France," in *Colonial Botany: Science, Commerce, and Politics in the Early Modern World*, ed. Londa Schiebinger and Claudia Swann (Philadelphia: University of Pennsylvania Press, 2005); and *KVAH*, 1757–58. Jan Golinski argues for an early start to record keeping but a late emergence of the "scientific credentials to meteorology"; see *British Weather*, 6–7. Jankovic, *Reading the Skies*, 134–35, 156–64. For some scattered series of local Scottish measurements, see NLS, MS 6615, "Notes on Weather, 1719–35"; NLS, Acc 10069, Royal Society of Edinburgh, Robert Mossman, "Meteorological Records, 1735–1808"; and NLS, MS 17254, "Records of Weather at Saltoun, 1772–3, 1777–8, 1818–19," ff. 100–202.
21. John Sinclair, *Queries Drawn Up for the Purpose of Elucidating the Natural History and Political State of Scotland* (Edinburgh, 1790); for an exception to this trend, see Robertson, *General View of the Agriculture in the County of Perth*, 7–10.
22. Jan Golinski, *Science as Public Culture: Chemistry and Enlightenment in Britain, 1760–1820* (Cambridge: Cambridge University Press, 1992), 32.
23. Harriet Ritvo, "Possessing Mother Nature: Genetic Capital in Eighteenth Century Britain," in *Early Modern Conceptions of Property*, ed. John Brewer and Susan Staves (London: Routledge, 1995); Ritvo, "At the Edge of the Garden: Nature and Domestication in 18th- and 19th-Century Britain," *Huntington Library Quarterly* 55 (1992): 363–78; Simon Schaffer, "The Earth's Fertility as a Social Fact in Early Modern England," in *Nature and Society in Historical Context*, ed. Mikulaus Teich, Roy Porter, and Bo Gustafsson (Cambridge: Cambridge University Press, 1997), 124–47.
24. EUL, Dc 2.26, Walker Papers, Lectures, 44:228–29, "Habit in Plants"; Dc 2.17, 71; Dc 2.23, Walker's Natural History, May 3, 1790, 72–73; John Sinclair, *Address to the Society for the Improvement of British Wool; Constituted at Edinburgh, on . . . January 31, 1791*, 2nd ed. (London, 1791), 3; NLS, Liston Papers, MS 5564, 3–69. For a recent history of ecological exchange in Scotland, see Robert A. Lambert, *Species History in Scotland: Introductions and Extinctions Since the Ice Age* (Edinburgh: Scottish Cultural Press, 1998).

25. Robert Maxwell, ed., *Select Transactions of the Honourable the Society of Improvers in the Knowledge of Agriculture in Scotland* (Edinburgh, 1743), xi.
26. Maxwell, *Select Transactions*, xii, 303; cf. *The Bee* 14 (1794): 95–96. For other early modern versions of ecological exchange, see Joan Thirsk, *Alternative Agriculture: A History from the Black Death to the Present Day* (Oxford: Oxford University Press, 1997); and Mauro Ambrosoli, *The Wild and the Sown: Botany and Agriculture in Western Europe, 1350–1850*, trans. Mary McCann Salvatorelli (Cambridge: Cambridge University Press, 1997), 262–336.
27. Henry Home, *The Gentleman Farmer*, 2nd ed. (Edinburgh, 1779), 331–32; Anderson, *Observations on the Means*, 186–87; Campbell, *Political Survey*, 1:60.
28. EUL, Dc 1.57, Walker Papers, "Essays, Transcripts and Other Papers," 3 vols., unpaginated; John Walker, *An Economical History of the Hebrides and Highlands of Scotland*, 2 vols. (Edinburgh, 1808), 1:247.
29. Thomas Pennant, *Arctic Zoology*, 2 vols. (London, 1784–85), 1:iv, xxxi, lxxv, clxvi; Erasmus Darwin, *The Botanic Garden: A Poem, in Two Parts* ... (London, 1791), 33–34; Darwin, *Zoonomia; or, The Laws of Organic Life*, 2nd ed. (London, 1796), 103; Ludmila Jordanova, *Lamarck* (Oxford: Oxford University Press, 1984); Koerner, *Linnaeus*, 44.
30. EUL, Walker, Lectures, Dc 2.20 4:15, 16; Dc 2.26, 166; Dc 2.28, 140–41; EUL, Gen 703D, 9:132–33.
31. Walker, *Economical History*, 1:186–89 (potatoes and wasteland), 217 (bear), 252–71 (potatoes); Walker, "An Essay on Peat, Containing an Account of Its Origin, of Its Chymical Principles, and General Properties; Its Properties as a Manure, and as a Manured Soil; The Different Methods of Its Cultivation; Its Usefulness in Plantation and Gardening, and as a Fuel," *THSS*, vol. 2 (Edinburgh, 1803), 1–137.
32. Richard Drayton, "Knowledge and Empire," in *The Eighteenth Century*, vol. 2 of *The Oxford History of the British Empire*, ed. P. J. Marshall (Oxford: Oxford University Press, 1998), 244.
33. David Mackay, *In the Wake of Cook: Exploration, Science, and Empire, 1780–1801* (New York: St. Martin's, 1985), 14; John Gascoigne, *Science in the Service of Empire: Joseph Banks, the British State and the Uses of Science in the Age of Revolution* (Cambridge: Cambridge University Press, 1998); B. Elliott, "The Promotion of Horticulture," in *Sir Joseph Banks: A Global Perspective*, ed. R. E. R. Banks et al. (Kew: Royal Botanic Gardens, 1994).
34. Mackay, *In the Wake of Cook*, 140.
35. George Métailié, "Sir Joseph Banks—An Asian Policy?" in Banks et al., *Sir Joseph Banks*; Alan Frost, "The Antipodean Exchange: European Horticulture and Imperial Designs," in *Visions of Empire: Voyages, Botany, and Representations of Nature*, ed. David Miller and Peter Hanns Reill (Cambridge: Cambridge University Press, 1996), 64, 75; for the notions of the "portmanteau biota" and "Neo-Europe," see Alfred Crosby, *Ecological Imperialism: The Biological Expansion of Europe, 900–1900* (Cambridge: Cambridge University Press, 1986), 89–90.
36. H. B. Carter, *His Majesty's Spanish Flock: Sir Joseph Banks and the Merinos of George III of England* (London: Angus and Robertson, 1964); John Gascoigne with the

assistance of Patricia Curthoys, *The Enlightenment and the Origins of European Australia* (Cambridge: Cambridge University Press, 2002), 73, 80–85.

37. For some of Banks's Scottish correspondents, see Warren R. Dawson, ed., *The Banks Letters: A Calendar of the Manuscript Correspondence of Sir Joseph Banks . . .* (London: Trustees of the British Museum, 1958), which includes letters to Banks from Matthew Guthrie, John Hope, John Lightfoot, Francis Humberston Mackenzie, Thomas Pennant, and John Sinclair. Note also the dedication to Sir Joseph Banks in Thomas Pennant's *Tour in Scotland and Voyage to the Hebrides, 1772*, ed. Andrew Simmons (Edinburgh: Birlinn, 1998), xxvii–xxviii; and James Headrick's *View of Arran*.

38. Rosalind Mitchison, *Agricultural Sir John: The Life of Sir John Sinclair of Ulbster, 1754–1835* (London: Geoffrey Bles, 1962), 93–94, 112–18; NAS, RH4/49/3, 5:193, 315; RBG, Folder, Letters to Hope 1783, n.f.; D. J. Galloway and E. W. Groves, "Archibald Menzies, MD, FLS (1754–1842): Aspects of His Life, Travels and Collections," *ANH* 14, no. 1 (1987): 3–43; Tim Robinson, *William Roxburgh: The Founding Father of Indian Botany* (Edinburgh: Phillimore, 2008); Harold B. Carter, *The Sheep and Wool Correspondence of Sir Joseph Banks, 1781–1820* (Norwich: Library Council of New South Wales, 1979), 185–88; Carter, *His Majesty's Spanish Flock*, 194–200; Gascoigne, *Science in the Service of Empire*, 174–75, 174.

39. James Anderson, *An Account of the Present State of the Hebrides and Western Coasts of Scotland . . .* (Edinburgh, 1785), v, xii; cf. James Headrick, "On the Practicability, and Advantages, of Opening a Navigation Between the Murray Frith, at Inverness, and Loch Eil, at Fort William," *THSS*, vol. 1 (Edinburgh, 1799), 394.

40. Arthur Young, *Political Essays Concerning the Present State of the British Empire*, (London, 1772), 8, 13–14. The effect of mercantilism on the American colonial economy is treated in John J. McCusker and Russell R. Menard, *The Economy of British America, 1607–1789* (Chapel Hill: University Press of North Carolina, 1985), 35–50. To be fair, Young took an interest in wasteland reclamation in Britain as an alternative to colonial expansion, although his proposals focused on cereal production rather than the acclimatization of cash crops; see *Observations on the Present State of the Wastelands of Great Britain* (London, 1773); and Young, *An Inquiry into the Propriety of Applying Wastes to the Better Maintenance and Support of the Poor* (Bury, 1801).

41. McKay, *Walker's Report on the Hebrides*, 47–48, 55, 66, 79–80, 100, 103, 118, 133, 161, 173, 188–89, 213; James Headrick, "Suggestions Respecting Various Improvements in the Highlands of Scotland," *THSS*, 1:458–62; NAS, GD9/3, ff. 644–46; Pennant, *Tour in Scotland, 1772*, 270; John Spruel, *An Accompt Current Betwixt Scotland and England Ballanced* (Edinburgh, 1705); NLS, MS 11140, 1–2, MS 11198, 86–149; Michael Fry, *The Dundas Despotism* (Edinburgh: Edinburgh University Press, 1992), 63; NAS, RH4.49.2, 323; for the early history of hemp, flax, tobacco, and other forms of diversification in England, see Joan Thirsk, *Alternative Agriculture*; the Atholl larch is discussed in chapter 6; for Highland rhubarb, see BM, boxes 49/6/70, 65/1/134, 54/1/25; on sugar beets, maple, and other substitutes for sugar cane, see *The Bee* 7 (1792): 330; cf. Neil Chambers, ed., *The Scientific Correspondence of Joseph Banks*, vol. 4: *The Middle Period, 1785–1799; Letters, 1790–1799* (London: Pickering and Chatto, 2007), 588–89; for Anderson on Silesian cotton, *The Bee* 13 (1793): 259–63; on cudbear, see Cuthbert

Gordon, *Memorial of Mr. Cuthbert Gordon, Relative to the Discovery and Use of Cudbear, and Other Dying Wares*; NAS, E728/27/1–5, E730/19/1–7, GD113/1/487/3; W. T. Johnston, *Cuthbert Gordon*, rev. ed. (Livingston: Officina, 1995).

Chapter 4. Alternate Highlands

1. Margaret M. McKay, ed., *The Rev. Dr. John Walker's Report on the Hebrides of 1764 and 1771* (Edinburgh: John Donald, 1980), 90, 198. Steven Shapin suggests a Tory connection for Walker but omits to explore the Highland dimension; see Shapin, "Property, Patronage, and the Politics of Science: The Founding of the Royal Society of Edinburgh," *BJHS* 7 (1974): 14–17.
2. Agricola [James Anderson], *Miscellaneous Observations on Planting and Training Timber-Trees; Particularly Calculated for the Climate of Scotland . . .* (Edinburgh, [1777]); Anderson, *Observations on the Means of Exciting a Spirit of National Industry* (Edinburgh, 1777); Anderson, *An Account of the Present State of the Hebrides and Western Coasts of Scotland . . .* (Edinburgh, 1785); *The Bee* 7 (1792): 330; *The Bee* 9 (1792): 160–61.
3. Charles W. J. Withers, "A Neglected Scottish Agriculturalist: The 'Georgical Lectures' and Agricultural Writings of the Rev. Dr. John Walker (1731–1803), *AHR* 33, no. 2 (1985): 132–46; Withers, "Improvement and Enlightenment: Agriculture and Natural History in the Works of the Rev. Dr. John Walker (1731–1803)," in *Philosophy and Science in the Scottish Enlightenment*, ed. Peter Jones (Edinburgh: John Donald, 1988); Withers, "The Rev. Dr. John Walker and the Practice of Natural History," *ANH* 18, no. 2 (1991): 201–20; M. D. Eddy, "Scottish Chemistry, Classification and the Early Mineralogical Career of the 'Ingenious' Rev. Dr. John Walker (1746–1779)," *BJHS* 35, no. 4 (2002): 411–34; Eddy, "Scottish Chemistry, Classification and the Late Mineralogical Career of the 'Ingenious' Professor John Walker (1779–1803)," *BJHS* 37, no. 4 (2004): 373–99.
4. For the Kames-Walker correspondence on natural history, see Alexander Woodhouselee, *Memoirs of the Life and Writings of the Honorable Henry Home of Kames*, 2 vols. (Edinburgh, 1807), 2:23–37, 52–74; EUL, La III 352/4, 1, 35; Dc 1.18, no. 9 (Walker's class lists); *Transactions of the Royal Society of Edinburgh* 1 (1788): 15, 19, 36–37; EUL, DA67, *Proceedings of the Society for the Investigation of Natural History* [Natural History Society of Edinburgh], 15 vols.; EUL, La III 352/3, Agricultural Society of Edinburgh, "Papers, 1790–92"; Charles W. J. Withers, "'Both Useful and Ornamental': John Walker's Keepership of Edinburgh University's Natural History Museum, 1770–1803," *Journal of the History of Collections* 5 (1993): 65–77; D. E. Allen, "James Edward Smith and the Natural History Society of Edinburgh," *Journal of the Society for the Bibliography of Natural History* 8 (1978): 483–93; M. D. Eddy, "The University of Edinburgh Natural History Class Lists, 1782–1800," *ANH* 30 (2003): 97–117; Shapin, "Property, Patronage and the Politics of Science," 24–25; Withers, "Neglected Scottish Agriculturalist," 133–34; Withers, "Walker and the Practice of Natural History," 202, 212–16; Withers, "Geography, Natural History and the

Eighteenth-Century Enlightenment: Putting the World in Place," *History Workshop Journal* 39, no. 1 (1995): 137–67; for Walker and the Highland Society, see NAS, RH4/188/1, "Sederunt Book 1," 240–41, "Sederunt Book 2," 41, 207, 378–79; *THSS*, vol. 1 (Edinburgh, 1799), xxiv, 1–31; *THSS*, vol. 2 (Edinburgh, 1803), 1–137, 164–203, 270–304, 346–76. A list of Walker's correspondents can be found in the University of Edinburgh Special Collections.

5. Allan Macinnes, *Clanship, Commerce and the House of Stuart, 1603–1788* (East Linton, UK: Tuckwell, 1996), 142–51; NAS, GD24/1/564, f. 138, Walker to Kames, August 18, 1764, quoted in Withers, "Geography, Natural History and the Eighteenth-Century Enlightenment," 137.

6. EUL, La III 352/1b, 96; Henry Home, Lord Kames, *The Progress of Flax Husbandry* (Edinburgh, 1766); Walker's observations on raising flax are scattered throughout his report on the voyage of 1764; see McKay, *Walker's Report on the Hebrides*.

7. McKay, *Walker's Report on the Hebrides*, 117; Withers, "Walker and the Practice of Natural History," 206–7; Lisbet Koerner, *Linnaeus: Nature and Nation* (Cambridge, MA: Harvard University Press, 1999), 82–83, 92–93, 97–98, 101, quotation on 93; Staffan Müller-Wille, "Walnuts at Hudson Bay, Coral Reefs in Gotland: The Colonialism of Linnaean Botany," in *Colonial Botany; Science, Commerce, and Politics in the Early Modern World*, ed. Londa Schiebinger and Claudia Swan (Philadelphia: University of Pennsylvania Press, 2005), 34–48.

8. John Lightfoot, *Flora Scotica*, 2nd ed., 2 vols. (London, 1789), 2:692, 767–68.

9. McKay, *Walker's Report on the Hebrides*, 117, 188–89, 212, 217, 218; EUL, Walker Papers, Dc 2.36, John Walker, "Queries Concerning the North of Scotland," 47, 51, 59, 63, 109, 121–23, 136, 165–67, 216. Walker set out his priorities for resource inventory in "A Memorandum Given by Dr. Walker, Professor of Natural History, Edinburgh, to a Young Gentleman Going to India, with Some Additions," *The Bee* 17 (1793): 330–33.

10. McKay, *Walker's Report on the Hebrides*, 35, 195; Walker, *Essays on Natural History and Rural Economy* (Edinburgh, 1812), 94; EUL, La III 352/1a, f. 30, La III 352/5, 2; Paul Baines, "Ossianic Geographies: Fingalian Figures on the Scottish Tour, 1760–1830," *Scotlands* 4, no. 1 (1997): 44–61; Charles D. Waterson, "The Case of Sir George Steuart Mackenzie of Coul, 1780–1848," in *Science and Medicine in the Scottish Enlightenment*, ed. Charles Withers and Paul Wood (East Linton, UK: Tuckwell, 2002), 316; Leah Leneman, "The Effects of Ossian in Lowland Scotland," in *Aberdeen and the Enlightenment*, ed. Jennifer J. Carter and Joan H. Pittock (Aberdeen: Aberdeen University Press, 1987), 358; Thomas Pennant, *A Tour in Scotland and Voyage to the Hebrides, 1772*, ed. Andrew Simmons (Edinburgh: Birlinn, 1998), 255–68, 288; D. M. Henderson and J. H. Dickson, eds., *A Naturalist in the Highlands: James Robertson, His Life and Travels in Scotland, 1767–1771* (Edinburgh: Scottish Academic Press, 1994), 89; John Williams, *An Account of Some Remarkable Ancient Ruins, Lately Discovered in the Highlands, and Northern Parts of Scotland* (Edinburgh, 1777), iii–vii, 7, 18–23; NLS, MS 996, 12–13; NAS, E727/46, 44, 46 (11).

11. Lightfoot, *Flora Scotica*, 2nd ed., 1:96, 159–60, 204, 269, 273, 2:579, 614, 767–68, 830–31; cf. McKay, *Walker's Report on the Hebrides*, 75, 90, 198; Henderson and Dickson, *Naturalist in the Highlands*, 54, 80; Thomas Pennant, *Tour in Scotland and Voyage to*

the *Hebrides*, 1772, ed. Andrew Simmons (Edinburgh: Birlinn, 1998), 273, 312, 412; Sir James Foulis to Thomas Pennant, "Original Letter for the Bee," *The Bee* 13 (1793): 295–98.
12. Charles Withers, "Introduction," in Martin Martin, *A Description of the Western Islands of Scotland Circa 1695 and a Late Voyage to St. Kilda* (Edinburgh: Birlinn, 1999), 4–5; Withers, *Geography, Science and National Identity*, 87–91.
13. Martin, *Description of the Western Islands*, 123, 125–26.
14. EUL, La III 352/1a, f. 3; Lightfoot, *Flora Scotica*, 2nd ed., 1:vii; Harold R. Fletcher and William H. Brown, *The Royal Botanic Garden Edinburgh, 1670–1970* (Edinburgh: HMSO, 1970), 64; Withers, "Geography, Natural History and the Eighteenth-Century Enlightenment," 144, 146–47.
15. Koerner, *Linnaeus*, 57, 60, 71–75, 77, 80–81.
16. Macinnes, *Clanship, Commerce*, 18.
17. Henderson and Dickson, *Naturalist in the Highlands*, 129; Lightfoot, *Flora Scotica*, 2nd ed., 1:viii. For the modern influence of Lightfoot, see D. E. Allen and Gabrielle Hatfield, *Medicinal Plants in Folk Tradition: An Ethnobotany of Britain and Ireland* (Cambridge: Timber Press, 2004).
18. NAS, E721/4, f. 208.
19. John Walker, "An Essay on Peat, Containing an Account of Its Origin, of Its Chymical Principles, and General Properties; Its Properties as a Manure, and as a Manured Soil; The Different Methods of Its Cultivation; Its Usefulness in Plantation and Gardening, and as a Fuel," *THSS*, 2:118–19; cf. Elinor Ostrom, *Governing the Commons: The Evolution of Institutions for Common Action* (Cambridge: Cambridge University Press, 1990).
20. Joseph A. Schumpeter, *History of Economic Analysis* (New York: Oxford University Press, 1994), 263–65, 676n; John Stuart Mill, *Principles of Political Economy*, ed. William Ashley (Fairfield, NJ: Augustus M. Kelley, 1987), 425; René Prendergast, "James Anderson's Political Economy: His Influence on Smith and Malthus," *Scottish Journal of Political Economy* 34, no. 4 (1987): 388–409; Matthew D. Eddy, "The Aberdeen Agricola: Chemical Principles and Practice in James Anderson's Georgics and Geology," in *New Narratives in Eighteenth-Century Chemistry: Contributions from the First Francis Bacon Workshop, 21–23 April 2005*, ed. Lawrence M. Principe, *Archimedes* 18 (2007): 139–56; James Anderson, *Observations on the Means of Exciting a Spirit of National Industry* . . . (Edinburgh, 1777), 376.
21. AUL, James Anderson Papers, typed correspondence, no. 6; Agricola [James Anderson], *Miscellaneous Observations on Planting and Training Timber-Trees; Particularly Calculated for the Climate of Scotland* (Edinburgh, 1777).
22. Gascoigne, *Science in the Service of Empire*, 105–6; Anderson, *Observations on the Means*, 167–68, 403 (critique of Board of Trustees), 100–114 (heat and wool), 185–90 (climate and diversification), 197–207 (Halifax and Highlands), 401–2 (Whiggery).
23. James Anderson, *The Interest of Great-Britain with Regard to Her American Colonies, Considered; To Which Is Added, an Appendix Containing the Outline of a Plan for a General Pacification* (London, 1782), 97; NLS, MS 6602, 9–10.

24. Christopher A. Bayly, *Imperial Meridian: The British Empire and the World, 1780–1830* (New York: Longman, 1989), 11–12, 106–9, 123, 156; John Ehrman, *The Younger Pitt: The Years of Acclaim* (London: Constable, 1969), 351–52; Committee Appointed to Enquire into the State of the British Fisheries, *Third Report from the Committee Appointed to Enquire into the State of the British Fisheries* . . . (n.p., 1785), 48; Peter Jupp, *The Governing of Britain, 1688–1848: The Executive, Parliament and the People* (London: Routledge, 2006), 217–19; Seymour Dreischer, *The Mighty Experiment: Free Labor Versus Slavery in British Emancipation* (Oxford: Oxford University Press, 2002), 5; William Cobbett, *The Parliamentary History of England*, vol. 25 (London, 1815), 920–34.
25. James Anderson, *An Account of the Present State of the Hebrides and Western Coasts of Scotland* . . . (Edinburgh, 1785), iv-v, 121–25; WN, 1: book 3 passim. On the idealization of Dutch society, see Steve Pincus, *1688: The First Modern Revolution* (New Haven: Yale University Press, 2009).
26. Anderson, *Present State of the Hebrides*, 68–69; David R. Raynor, "Adam Smith: Two Letters to Henry Beaufoy, MP," *Scottish Journal of Political Economy* 43, no. 5 (1996): 586–88; WN, 1:405.
27. WN, 1:343–44, 418, 422; Anderson, *Present State of the Hebrides*, 45, 71–74.
28. For Buccleuch's personal copy signed by Anderson, see NLS, Bdg. M 51; *The Bee* 8 (1792): 76; 13 (1793): 205–8. Anderson was introduced to the Prussian minister Herzberg by the Earl of Buchan; see EUL, La II 588, E35. Committee Appointed to Enquire into the State of the British Fisheries, *Third Report*, 53–54 (subsidies), 57 (bounties); cf. Anna Gambles, "Free Trade and State Formation: The Political Economy of Fisheries Policy in Britain and the United Kingdom, circa 1780–1850," *Journal of British Studies* 39, no. 3 (2000): 299.
29. Jean Dunlop, *The British Fisheries Society, 1786–1893* (Edinburgh: John Donald, 1978), 18–22, 115–16; John Ehrman, *The Younger Pitt: The Years of Acclaim* (Stanford, CA: Stanford University Press, 1969), 351–52; Anderson, *Present State of the Hebrides*, lxv, lxix, lxxviii, lxxxvi, xiv, lxxi, lxxiv–lxxv, lxxxvi, 19, 81; John Knox, *View of the British Empire and Scotland*, 3rd enl. ed. (London, 1787); Knox, *Observations on Northern Fisheries* (London, 1786); Knox, *A Discourse on the Expediency of Establishing Fishing Stations* (London, 1786), 33–34, 43.
30. Cobbett, *Parliamentary History*, 925; GUL, Cullen Papers 215.
31. Anderson, *Present State of the Hebrides*, 162; Cobbett, *Parliamentary History*, 923–24; Committee Appointed to Enquire into the State of the British Fisheries, *Third Report*, 48 (open market); for Anderson's disappointment, see Buchan's biographical sketch in NLS, Adv 29.3.17, f. 8; Ehrman, *Younger Pitt*, 351, n. 2.
32. James Anderson, *Observations on Slavery; Particularly with a View to Its Effects on the British Colonies, in the West-Indies* (Manchester, 1789); Anderson, *Observations on the Effects of the Coal Duty on the Remote and Thinly Peopled Coasts of Britain* . . . (Edinburgh, 1792).
33. For Buchan's contributions, see NLS, Adv 29.3.17, 5–7; on Callendar, see Bob Harris, *The Scottish People and the French Revolution* (London: Pickering and Chatto, 2008), 62.

34. AUL, MS 2787/4/1/1/13; cf. *The Bee* 1 (1791): viii.
35. See the following issues of *The Bee*: 14 (1793): 96 (gradual acclimatization); 8 (1792): 304–7 (poppies); 8 (1792): 111–13 (larch); 17 (1793): 88–90 (larch); and 13 (1793): 259–62 (cotton substitute).
36. *The Bee* 7 (1792): 330, 333; AUL, James Anderson Papers, typed correspondence, no. 6.
37. Kames, *Gentleman Farmer*, 391–92, 393–96; Rosalind Mitchison, *Agricultural Sir John: The Life of Sir John Sinclair of Ulbster, 1754–1835* (London: Geoffrey Bles, 1962), 135–36.
38. David Young, *National Improvements upon Agriculture, in Twenty Seven Essays* (Edinburgh, 1785), 207, 247–50, 272–73, 343–47, 405–12 ("List of Subscribers").
39. Dunlop, *British Fisheries Society*, 22–25, 102, 208–9; James R. Coull, "Fishery Development in Scotland in the Eighteenth Century," *Scottish Economic and Social History* 21, pt. 1 (2001): 2.
40. A Member of the Highland Society in London, *The Necessity of Founding Villages Contiguous to Harbors . . . on the West Coast of Scotland* (London, 1786), 6–8. Jan de Vries and Ad van der Woude, *The First Modern Economy: Success, Failure, and Perseverance of the Dutch Economy, 1500–1815* (Cambridge: Cambridge University Press, 1997), 235–36, 243–54; Bob Harris, "Patriotic Commerce and National Revival: The Free British Fishery Society and British Politics, c. 1749–58," *English Historical Review* 114 (1999): 285–313; NAS, GD9/3, ff. 433–35, "List of Subscribers in India to the British Society for Extending the Fisheries." James Fergusson, ed., *Letters of George Dempster to Adam Fergusson, 1756–1813* (London: Macmillan, 1934), 182; T. M. Devine, *Scotland's Empire, 1600–1815* (London: Penguin, 2003) 335; Devine, *The Transformation of Scotland: The Economy Since 1700* (Edinburgh: Edinburgh University Press, 2005), 31–32; Gambles, "Free Trade and State Formation," 294–98.
41. Anderson, *Present State of the Hebrides*, xxxviii–xxxix, xlvi–xlvii, liii, lvi–lviii; AUL, MS 2787/4/2/12a; George Dempster, *A Discourse Containing a Summary of the Proceedings of the Directors of the Society for Extending the Fisheries . . . Together with Some Reflections Intended to Promote the Success of the Said Society, by John Gray* (London, 1789), 49.
42. Dunlop, *British Fisheries Society*, 140–42, 150–51.
43. Knox, *Tour Through the Highlands*, ciii; Knox, *Discourse on the Expediency*, 36–37, 35; Anderson, *Present State of the Hebrides*, 260–61.
44. NAS, GD9/3, "Extracts of Letters Addressed to the Deputy Governor [Breadalbane] of the British Fisheries Society in Answer to the Printed Queries Circulated by the Court of Directors of the Society," 49–143 passim, 50 (Argyll's quota), 69 (Lovat's potherbs), 74, 109 (spade), 113 (Lovat's potato ground)
45. NAS, GD9/3, ff. 69–70.
46. NAS, GD9/3, 74–81, ff. 108–12; Joyce Appleby, *Economic Thought and Ideology in Seventeenth-Century England* (Princeton, NJ: Princeton University Press, 1978), 168–69; David Hume, *Political Essays*, ed. Knud Haakonsen (Cambridge: Cambridge University Press, 1994), 101; John Henderson, *General View of the Agriculture of Sutherland . . .* (London, 1815), 206, 209–11, 213; Eric Richards, *Patrick Sellar and the*

Highland Clearances: Homicide, Eviction and the Price of Progress (Edinburgh: Polygon at Edinburgh, 1999), 39, 389n10.

47. NAS, GD9/3, ff. 89–92, 123–24.
48. NAS, GD9/3, f. 97; on the size of gardens, see also Dunlop, *British Fisheries Society*, 53, 69 70.
49. NAS, GD9/3, f. 40; Knox, *Discourse on the Expediency*, 35; Dunlop, *British Fisheries Society*, 52–53, 69–71, 219, 221; Malcolm Gray, *The Highland Economy, 1750–1850* (Edinburgh: Oliver and Boyd, 1957), 111–12. Gray stresses that not every fishing community in the northwest devolved into crofting, see 214–16.
50. NAS, RH4/188/1, "Sederunt Book 1," 240–41, "Sederunt Book 2," 41, 207, 378–79, "Sederunt Book 3," 107, 152, 339, 436, 441, 670.
51. Alexander Ramsay, *History of the Highland and Agricultural Society of Scotland with Notices of Anterior Societies for the Promotion of Agriculture in Scotland* (Edinburgh, 1879), 45–50, 539–48, 549–51; *DNB*, s.v. "James Grant of Grant," by Andrew Mackillop.
52. *THSS*, 1:ii–iii; "Sederunt Book 1,"206; Adam Smith, *The Theory of Moral Sentiments*, ed. D. D. Raphael and A. L. Macfie (Oxford: Oxford University Press, 1976), 45.
53. J. M. Bumsted, *The People's Clearance: Highland Emigration to British North America, 1770–1815* (Edinburgh: Edinburgh University Press, 1982), 41–43.
54. John Walker, "Essay on Kelp . . . Delivered to the Society in 1788," *THSS*, 1:1–31; "Sederunt Book 1," 174–75, 241, 246; "Sederunt Book 2," 86–89, *THSS*, vol. 4 (Edinburgh, 1820), 1–121 passim. For Black's dismissal of kelp, see EUL, Gen 873/III, ff. 50–51 (draft letter to Alexander Eason, October 1787).
55. "Sederunt Book 2," 3, 9, 24–25, 39, 41, 56, 62, 67–80, 92, 106; AUL, MS 2787/4/2/12c.
56. "Sederunt Book 2," 207, 217, 267, 308, 347, 422, 426–27; "Sederunt Book 3," 45, 149, 151, 176, 246, 251, 258, 276, 278–79, 344–50, 361–63, 429, 441. A list of wasteland premiums offered by the society between 1791 and 1871 can be found in Ramsay, *History of the Highland and Agricultural Society of Scotland*, 115–18, 584–89.
57. "Sederunt Book 2," 207.

Chapter 5. Rival Ecologies of Global Commerce

1. B. Faujas Saint-Fond, *Travels in England, Scotland, and the Hebrides; Undertaken for the Purpose of Examining the State of the Arts, the Sciences, Natural History and Manners, in Great Britain . . .* , 2 vols. (London, 1799), 2:244–46; John Rae, *Life of Adam Smith* (London: Macmillan, 1895), 373; Ian Simpson Ross, *The Life of Adam Smith*, 2nd ed. (Oxford: Oxford University Press, 2010), 424–27; James Buchan, *Crowded with Genius: The Scottish Enlightenment* (New York: HarperCollins, 2003), 294; E. C. Mossner and I. S. Ross, eds., *The Correspondence of Adam Smith* (Oxford: Oxford University Press, 1977), 59.
2. Pehr Kalm, *Travels into North America: Containing Its Natural History and a Circumstantial Account of Its Plantations and Agriculture . . .*, Translated into English by John Reinhold Forster, 3 vols. (Warrington, 1770–71), 1:31; Alfred Crosby, *Ecological Imperialism: The Biological Expansion of Europe, 900–1900* (Cambridge: Cambridge

University Press, 1986), 11. Compare with the confusion of Linnaeus in Lapland 1732; see Linnaeus, *Iter Lapponicum*, in *Skrifter af Carl von Linné: Utgifna af. Kungl. Vetenskapsakademien*, ed. Thomas M. Fries, vol. 5 (Uppsala: Almqvist and Wiksell, 1913), 106–7; Staffan Müller-Wille, *Botanik und weltweiter Handel: Zur Begründung eines Natürlichen Systems der Pflanzen durch Carl von Linné (1707–78)* (Berlin: Verlag für Wissenschaft und Bildung, 1999), 187–88.

3. Sverker Sörlin and Otto Fagerstedt, *Linné och hans apostlar* (Stockholm: Natur och Kultur, 2004), 57–66; Lisbet Koerner, *Linnaeus: Nature and Nation* (Cambridge, MA: Harvard University Press, 1999), 117–23; Staffan Müller-Wille, "Walnuts at Hudson Bay, Coral Reefs in Gotland: The Colonialism in Linnaean Botany," in *Colonial Botany: Science, Commerce, and Politics in the Early Modern World*, ed. Londa Schiebinger and Claudia Swan (Philadelphia: University of Pennsylvania Press, 2004); John Gascoigne, *Joseph Banks and the English Enlightenment: Useful Knowledge and Polite Culture* (Cambridge: Cambridge University Press, 2003), 98–107; Frans A. Stafleu, *Linnaeus and the Linnaeans: The Spreading of Their Ideas in Systematic Botany, 1735–1789* (Utrecht: A. Oosthoek's Uitgeversmaatchappij, 1971), 199–240 passim; Charles Withers, "Improvement and Enlightenment: Agriculture and Natural History in the Works of the Rev. Dr. John Walker (1731–1803)," in *Philosophy and Science in the Scottish Enlightenment*, ed. Peter Jones (Edinburgh: John Donald, 1988); Charles Withers, "Geography, Natural History and the Eighteenth-Century Enlightenment: Putting the World in Place," *History Workshop Journal* 39 (1995): 137–64; H. J. Noltie, *John Hope (1725–1786): Alan G. Morton's Memoir of a Scottish Botanist*, new rev. ed. (Edinburgh: Royal Botanic Garden, 2011); Emma Spary, *Utopia's Garden: French Natural History from the Old Regime to the Revolution* (Chicago: University of Chicago Press, 1999); Richard Grove, *Green Imperialism: Colonial Expansion, Tropical Island Edens and the Origins of Environmentalism, 1600–1860* (Cambridge: Cambridge University Press, 1995).

4. Mark Overton, *Agricultural Revolution in England: The Transformation of the Agrarian Economy, 1500–1850* (Cambridge: Cambridge University Press, 1996), 93, 107–9, 116–21.

5. Koerner, *Linnaeus*, 48–49; Sten Lindroth, *Svenska Vetenskapsakademiens historia, 1739–1818*, vol. 1 (Stockholm: Kungl. Vetenskapakademien, 1967), 258–60; *Pehr Kalms brev till friherre Sten Carl Bielke*, ed. Carl Skottsberg (Åbo: n.p., 1960), 12, 47, 56–57; Martti Kerkkonen, *Peter Kalm's North American Journey: Its Ideological Background and Results* (Helsinki: Finnish Historical Society, 1959), 40; Carolus Linnaeus, *Pan Svecicus* (Uppsala, 1749), partly translated in Benjamin Stillingfleet's *Miscellaneous Tracts Relating to Natural History, Husbandry, and Physic*, 184–201 (a book owned by Adam Smith).

6. Kalm, *Travels into North America*, 1:102–3, 184–86, 343–45; 2: 192–95 and passim, 3:5–7, 241–43; contrast with *William Byrd's Natural History of Virginia; or, The Newly Discovered Eden*, ed. Richmond Croom Beatty and William J. Mulloy (Richmond, VA: Dietz, 1940), 18; Koerner, *Linnaeus*; Lisbet Rausing, "Underwriting the Oeconomy: Linnaeus on Nature and Mind," in *Oeconomies in the Age of Newton: Annual Supplement to Volume 35 History of Political Economy*, ed. Margaret Schabas

and Neil De Marchi (Durham, NC: Duke University Press, 2003); Schabas, *The Natural Origins of Economics* (Chicago: University of Chicago Press, 2005), 30–31; William Beinart, *The Rise of Conservation in South Africa: Settlers, Livestock and the Environment, 1770–1950* (Oxford: Oxford University Press, 2003), 66–68; Virginia DeJohn Anderson, *Creatures of Empire: How Domestic Animals Transformed Early America* (Oxford: Oxford University Press, 2004); Brian Donahue suggests that New England agriculture was careful rather than negligent; *The Great Meadow: Farmers and the Land in Colonial Concord* (New Haven: Yale University Press, 2004), 92, 208.

7. WN, 1:167 (artificial grasses), 240–41, 245 (North America). Smith was not the only reader of Kalm in Scotland; see NAS, GD253/144/11/9, 25 (John Hope); EUL, Dc 1.58, [John Walker], "Professor Peter Kalm's Travels to North America in 1748–49"; and William Robertson, *The History of America*, 2 vols. (Edinburgh 1777), 1:364.

8. Richard Drayton, *Nature's Government: Science, Imperial Britain, and the "Improvement" of the World* (New Haven: Yale University Press, 2000), xv–xvi, xviii, 272; Kenneth Pomeranz, "Introduction," in *The Environment and World History*, ed. Edmund Burke III and Kenneth Pomeranz (Berkeley: University of California Press, 2009), 10–11; James Scott, *Seeing Like a State: How Certain Schemes to Improve the Human Condition Have Failed* (New Haven: Yale University Press, 1998), 2.

9. I use the word *ecology* here as shorthand for such eighteenth-century terms as the *balance* of nature and the *economy* of nature. Compare Donald Worster, *Nature's Economy: A History of Ecological Ideas*, 2nd ed. (Cambridge: Cambridge University Press, 1994); for the wider range of "economy," see Emma Spary, "Political, Natural and Bodily Economies," in *Cultures of Natural History*, ed. Nicholas Jardine, James A. Secord, and E. C. Spary (Cambridge: Cambridge University Press, 1996), 178–96; Frank N. Egerton, "Changing Concepts of the Balance of Nature," *Quarterly Review of Biology* 48, no. 2 (1973): 322–50; Richard W. Judd, *The Untilled Garden: Natural History and the Spirit of Conservation in America, 1740–1840* (Cambridge: Cambridge University Press, 2009), 187–90.

10. Istvan Hont, *The Jealousy of Trade: International Competition and the Nation-State in Historical Perspective* (Cambridge, MA: Harvard University Press, 2005), 154–55; Koerner, *Linnaeus*, 1.

11. Schabas, *Natural Origins of Economics*, 67–68, 70–71, 105–10; Joseph Schumpeter, *History of Economic Analysis* (New York: Oxford University Press, 1994); Koerner, *Linnaeus*, 15, 25–26, 39–40, Richard Grove, *Green Imperialism: Colonial Expansion, Tropical Island Edens and the Origins of Environmentalism, 1600–1860* (Cambridge: Cambridge University Press, 1995), 188, 198, 206, 219–21; David Mackay, "Agents of Empire: Banksian Collectors and the Evaluation of New Lands," in *Visions of Empire: Voyages, Botany and Representations of Nature*, ed. David Philip Miller and Peter Hanns Reill (Cambridge: Cambridge University Press, 1996); Michael Dettelbach, "Humboldtian Science," in Jardine, Secord, and Sperry, *Cultures of Natural History.*

12. Koerner, *Linnaeus*, 4–5; Gascoigne, *Joseph Banks and the English Enlightenment*, 105; Drayton, *Nature's Government*, 108–21; Spary, *Utopia's Garden*; Harold J. Cook, *Matters of Exchange: Commerce, Medicine, and Science in the Dutch Golden Age* (New Haven: Yale University Press, 2007); E. R. Brann, *The Political Ideas of Alexander*

von Humboldt: A Brief Preliminary Study (Madison, WI: Littel, 1954); Aaron Sachs, *The Humboldt Current: Nineteenth-Century Exploration and the Roots of American Environmentalism* (New York: Viking, 2006), 82–85; Keith Thomson, *A Passion for Nature: Thomas Jefferson and Natural History* (Monticello, VA: Thomas Jefferson Foundation, 2008).

13. Crosby, *Ecological Imperialism*; Crosby, *The Columbian Exchange* (Westport, CT: Greenwood, 1972); Antonio Barrera Osorio, *Experiencing Nature: The Spanish American Empire and the Early Scientific Revolution* (Austin: University of Texas Press, 2006).

14. Gascoigne, *Science in the Service of Empire: Joseph Banks, the British State and the Uses of Science in the Age of Revolution* (Cambridge: Cambridge University Press, 1998), 142–44; Alan Frost, "The Antipodean Exchange," in *Visions of Empire*.

15. Koerner, *Linnaeus*, 82–85; Grove, *Green Imperialism*, ch. 5 passim; Gregory Barton, *Empire Forestry and the Origins of Environmentalism* (Cambridge: Cambridge University Press, 2002), 47; Beinart, *Rise of Conservation in South Africa*, 28; T. C. Smout, *Nature Contested: Environmental History in Scotland and Northern England Since 1600* (Edinburgh: Edinburgh University Press, 2000), 37; Richard W. Judd, *Untilled Garden*; Fredrik Albritton Jonsson, "Adam Smith in the Forest," in *The Social Lives of the Forest: The Past, Present and Future of Woodland Resurgence*, ed. Susanna Hecht, Kathleen Morrison, and Christine Padoch (Chicago: University of Chicago Press, 2013).

16. Clarence J. Glacken, *Traces on the Rhodian Shore: Nature and Culture in Western Thought from Ancient Times to the End of the Eighteenth Century* (Berkeley: University of California Press, 1967); Alessa Johns, *Dreadful Visitations: Confronting Natural Catastrophe in the Age of Enlightenment* (London: Routledge, 1999); Matthew Mulcahy, *Hurricanes and Society in the British Greater Caribbean, 1624–1783* (Baltimore: Johns Hopkins University Press, 2005); Charles F. Walker, *Shaky Colonialism: The 1746 Earthquake-Tsunami in Lima, Peru, and Its Long Aftermath* (Durham, NC: Duke University Press, 2008); Lee Alan Dugatkin, *Mr. Jefferson and the Giant Moose: Natural History in Early America* (Chicago: University of Chicago Press, 2009).

17. Glacken, *Traces on the Rhodian Shore*, 658–63; Karen Ordahl Kupperman, "The Puzzle of the American Climate in the Early Colonial Period," *American Historical Review* 87, no. 5 (1982): 1262–89; Müller-Wille, "Walnuts at Hudson Bay," 42–43; Joyce E. Chaplin, "Mark Catesby, a Skeptical Newtonian in America," in *Empire's Nature: Mark Catesby's New World Vision*, ed. Amy R. W. Meyers and Margaret Beck Pritchard (Chapel Hill: University of North Carolina Press, 1998), 47–51; Chaplin, *The First Scientific American: Benjamin Franklin and the Pursuit of Genius* (New York: Basic Books, 2006), 323; Theodore S. Feldman, "Late Enlightenment Meteorology," in *The Quantifying Spirit in the Eighteenth Century*, ed. Tore Frängsmyr, J. L. Heilbron, and Robin E. Rider (Berkeley: University of California Press, 1990); Marie-Noëlle Bourget, "Measurable Difference: Botany, Climate, and the Gardener's Thermometer in Eighteenth-Century France," in Schiebinger and Swann, *Colonial Botany*; Jan Golinski, *British Weather and the Climate of Enlightenment* (Chicago: University of

Chicago Press, 2007), 170–202 passim; Dettelbach, "Humboldtian Science"; Sachs, *Humboldt Current*, 45.

18. WN, 1:259 (Columbian exchange), 174 (tobacco), 259, 177 (potato), 237–40 (cattle), 169 (kitchen gardening), 111–13 (stationary state), 363–64 (soil fertility), 527 (drought), 254 (silver mines), 586 (plow on plantations).

19. WN, 1:258 (land), 380 (capital), 376 (opulence). A count of some frequent keywords in the text offers a rough sense of how closely linked commerce and agriculture were in Smith: trade (312), corn (147), nature (125), merchants (103), agriculture (74), and cattle (72). The word search data is taken from the 1776 London edition of WN in *The Making of the Modern World* database; cf. Edward Puro, "Use of the Term 'Natural' in Adam Smith's Wealth of Nations," *Research in the History of Economic Thought and Methodology* 9 (1992): 73–86.

20. Smith's views on agriculture have been examined by a number of scholars, including Istvan Hont and Michael Ignatieff, "Needs and Justice in the '*Wealth of Nations*,'" in Hont, *Jealousy of Trade*; E. P. Thompson, "The Moral Economy of the English Crowd in the Eighteenth Century" and "The Moral Economy Reviewed," in *Customs in Common: Studies in Traditional Popular Culture* (New York: New Press, 1993); David McNally, *Political Economy and the Rise of Capitalism: A Reinterpretation* (Berkeley: University of California Press, 1988); Donald Winch, *Riches and Poverty: An Intellectual History of Political Economy in Britain, 1750–1834* (Cambridge: Cambridge University Press, 1996), 80–89, 175–85; Keith Tribe, *Land, Labour and Economic Discourse* (London: Routledge and Kegan Paul, 1978); E. A. Wrigley, *Continuity, Chance and Change: The Character of the Industrial Revolution in England* (Cambridge: Cambridge University Press, 1988), 47–50; Wrigley, "The Limits to Growth: Malthus and the Classical Economists," *Population and Development Review* 14 (1985): 30–48; John Robertson, *The Case for the Enlightenment: Scotland and Naples, 1680–1760* (Cambridge: Cambridge University Press, 2005), 390–92; Vernard Foley, *The Social Physics of Adam Smith* (West Lafayette, IN: Purdue University Press, 1976); Stefano Fiori, "Visible and Invisible Order: The Theoretical Duality of Smith's Political Economy," *European Journal of the History of Economic Thought* 8 (2001): 1429–48; Colin A. M. Duncan, "Adam Smith's Green Vision and the Future of Global Socialism," in *New Socialisms: Future Beyond Globalization*, ed. Robert Albritton et al. (New York: Routledge, 2004), 90–104; Schabas, *Natural Origins of Economics*, 88, 92.

21. WN, 1:236 (Pliny), 240 (Kalm), 173 (Poivre), 243, 2:560; James Bonar, *A Catalogue of the Library of Adam Smith* (London, 1894); Hiroshi Mizuta, *Adam Smith's Library: A Supplement to Bonar's Catalogue with a Checklist of the Whole Library* (Cambridge: Cambridge University Press, 1967); Simon Schaffer, "The Earth's Fertility as a Social Fact in Early Modern England," in *Nature and Society in Historical Context*, ed. Mikulaus Teich, Roy Porter, and Bo Gustafsson (Cambridge: Cambridge University Press, 1997), 138–41; *Edinburgh Review for the Year 1755*, 2nd ed. (London, 1818), 128–29; Brian Bonnyman, *The Third Duke of Buccleuch and Adam Smith: Estate Management and Improvement in Enlightenment Scotland* (Edinburgh: Edinburgh University Press, 2013); Ian Simpson Ross, *The Life of Adam Smith*, 2nd ed. (Oxford:

Oxford University Press, 2010). For some contacts between Black, Cullen, and Lord Kames, see EUL, Gen 873/I–IV; Jan Golinski, *Science as Public Culture: Chemistry and Enlightenment in Britain, 1760–1820* (Cambridge: Cambridge University Press, 1992), 11–49; Buchan, *Crowded with Genius*, 272–77; NLS, MS 23165, James Hutton, *The Elements of Agriculture*, vol. 1 (1797), 236/684, 256/704, for the reference to *The Wealth of Nations*; Jean Jones, "James Hutton's Agricultural Research and His Life as a Farmer," *Annals of Science* 42 (1985): 573–601; and Charles Withers, "On Georgics and Geology: James Hutton's 'Elements of Agriculture' and Agricultural Science in Eighteenth-Century Scotland," *AHR* 42, no. 1 (1994): 38–48.

22. Gary M. Anderson, William F. Shughart II, and Robert D. Tollison, "Adam Smith in the Customhouse," *Journal of Political Economy* 93, no. 4 (1985): 740–59. For the letter from Smith to Black, see EUL, Gen 873/III, 7–8. Compare William Ashworth, *Customs and Excise: Trade, Production, and Consumption in England, 1640–1845* (Oxford: Oxford University Press, 2003), 91.

23. WN, 1:332; Wrigley, *Continuity, Change, Chance*, 45–50; Schabas, *Natural Origins of Economics*, 29–31, 91–92, 94–95; Rausing, "Underwriting the Oeconomy," 185–86, 188, 191. For providence, see Ryan Patrick Hanley, *Adam Smith and the Character of Virtue* (Cambridge: Cambridge University Press, 2009), 183–84; and A. M. C. Waterman, "Economics as Theology: Adam Smith's Wealth of Nations," *Southern Economic Journal* 68 (2002): 907–21.

24. Schabas, *Natural Origin of Economics*, 49.

25. Kalm, *Travels into North America*, 1:102–4 (degeneration), 291–93 (shrinking populations). Other notions of imbalance or instability include the idea of American degeneration, worries about dessication on Mauritius, and fears of adverse climate change in the Highlands.

26. Douglas Irwin, *Against the Tide: An Intellectual History of Free Trade* (Princeton, NJ: Princeton University Press, 1996), 11; Jacob Viner, *Essays on the Intellectual History of Economics*, ed. Douglas Irwin (Princeton, NJ: Princeton University Press, 1991), 42.

27. WN, 1:458.

28. WN, 1:458; NAS; on Hope, see chapter 2.

29. WN, 1:174; NLS, MS 11198; Michael Fry, *The Dundas Despotism* (Edinburgh: Edinburgh University Press, 1992), 63; Robert Douglas, *General View of the Agriculture in the Counties of Roxburgh and Selkirk* (Edinburgh, 1798), 105–6.

30. WN, 1:259, 177.

31. Quesnay quoted in Tribe, *Land, Labour and Economic Discourse*, 96.

32. WN, 1:363–64, 427.

33. WN, 1:376–80, 343–44, 2:686–87; Wrigley, *Continuity, Change, Chance*, 46.

34. WN, 1:167, 237–40, 411–27, 2:687.

35. WN, 1:240–41, 245; [Arthur Young?], *American Husbandry*, 2 vols. (London, 1775), 1:144–49, 275–76; Mark Stoll, *Larding the Lean Earth: Soil and Society in Nineteenth-Century America* (New York: Hill and Wang, 2002); in Alfred Crosby's account, European fodder grasses spread without the aid of human agency, see Crosby, *Ecological Imperialism*, 156–63.

36. WN, 1:167 (artificial grasses), 2:556, 593–94 (Greek colonization).

37. David R. Raynor, "Who Invented the Invisible Hand?" *Times Literary Supplement*, Aug. 14, 1998, 22; Hont, *Jealousy of Trade*, 404–5; Emma Rothschild, *Economic Sentiments: Adam Smith, Condorcet, and the Enlightenment* (Cambridge, MA: Harvard University Press, 2001), 72–86.
38. Keith Wrightson, *Earthly Necessities: Economic Lives in Early Modern England* (New Haven: Yale University Press, 2000), 199–200, 263; WN, 1:524–26. Smith owed some of his data on grain markets to David Dalrymple, Lord Hailes; see Mossner and Ross, *Correspondence of Adam Smith*, 139, 145–50.
39. WN, 1:539. Istvan Hont and Michael Ignatieff argue that Smith saw manufacturing and international trade as the best means to move "forever beyond the closed limits of nature"; see "Needs and Justice in the Wealth of Nations," in Hont, *Jealousy of Trade*, 414. Edmund Burke, *Thoughts and Details on Scarcity, Originally Presented to . . . William Pitt, in the Month of November, 1795* (London, 1800), 17–18, 44; [T. R. Malthus], *An Essay on the Principle of Population, as It Affects the Future Improvement of Society . . .* (London, 1798), 139–40; Jeremy Bentham, "Defense of a Maximum," in *Jeremy Bentham's Economic Writings*, ed. Werner Stark, vol. 2 (London, 1954), 255–58; Thompson, "Moral Economy of the English Crowd, and "The Moral Economy Reviewed," 281n1; Karl Gunnar Persson, *Grain Markets in Europe, 1500–1900: Integration and Deregulation* (Cambridge: Cambridge University Press: 2000); Steven Kaplan, *Bread, Politics and Political Economy in the Reign of Louis XV*, 2 vols. (The Hague: Nijhoff, 1976); Nicolas de la Mare, *Traité de la police*, 3rd ed., 4 vols. (Amsterdam, 1729), 2:566.
40. John F. Richards, *Unending Frontier: An Environmental History of the Early Modern World*, 33–34; Christopher Bayly, *Indian Society and the Making of the British Empire* (Cambridge: Cambridge University Press, 1988), 32, 51, 66–67.
41. David Arnold, "Hunger in the Garden of Plenty: The Bengal Famine of 1770," in *Dreadful Visitations: Confronting Natural Catastrophe in the Age of Enlightenment*, ed. Alessa Johns (New York: Routledge, 1999); W. W. Hunter, *Annals of Rural Bengal*, 5th ed. (London, 1872), app. A, "Bengal in 1772, Portrayed by Warren Hastings," 381, quoted in Arnold, "Hunger in the Garden," 107. The account of the Bengal famine in the *Gentleman's Magazine* was reprinted in the *Annual Register . . . for the Year 1771* (London, 1772), 205–8. Smith owned a copy of the *Register*, see Mizuta, *Adam Smith's Library*, 67.
42. *Middlesex Journal or Chronicle of Liberty*, August 10, 1771; WN, 1:91, 527, 223.
43. Ranajit Guha, *A Rule of Property for Bengal: An Essay on the Idea of Permanent Settlement*, 2nd ed. (Durham, NC: Duke University Press, 1996), 7.
44. Alexander Dow, *The History of Hindostan, from the Death of Akbar, to the Complete Settlement of the Empire Under Aurungzebe* (London, 1772), xlvi, 141–42, 168, 341; Henry Pattullo, *An Essay upon the Cultivation of the Lands* (London, 1772), 13–14; Robert Orme, *A History of the Military Transactions of the British Nation in Indostan*, 2 vols. (London, 1763), 1:54. Smith stressed the importance of "inland navigation" but did not go so far as to endorse state management of water; see WN, 1:36–37, 2:838.
45. Arnold, "Hunger in the Garden of Plenty," 82.

46. For Hope's students in India, see H. J. Noltie, *John Hope (1725–1786): Alan G. Morton's Memoir of a Scottish Botanist*, new rev. ed. (Edinburgh: Royal Botanic Garden, 2011), 29–31; Marika Vicziany, "Imperialism, Botany and Statistics in Early Nineteenth-Century India: The Surveys of Francis Buchanan (1762–1829)," *Modern Asian Studies* 20, no. 4 (1986), 649; James Anderson, *The Bee* 8 (1792): 32–36; NLS, MS 9819, 8; Charles Francis Greville, *British India Analyzed*, 3 vols. (London, 1793), 2:498–99; Gascoigne, *Science in the Service of Empire*, 137–38; on the shifting perception of Bengal, cf. Arnold, "Hunger in the Garden of Plenty," 91, 105; Banks quoted in Gascoigne, *Science in the Service of Empire*, 88.
47. Greville, *British India Analyzed*, 2:503–4; Alexander Dalrymple, *Oriental Repertory*, 2 vols. (London: 1793–97?), 1:ii–iii, 2:33–34; James Rennell, "An Account of the Ganges and Burrampooter Rivers," *Philosophical Transactions of the Royal Society of London* 71 (1781): 98, 100; Tim Robinson, *William Roxburgh: The Founding Father of Indian Botany* (Edinburgh: Phillimore, 2008), 187–208 passim.
48. Thomas Forrest, *A Treatise on the Monsoons in East-India* (London, 1783); William Nicholson, *Sundry Remarks and Observations Made in a Voyage to the East-Indies* (London, 1773); William Roxburgh, "A Meteorological Diary, &c. Kept at Fort St. George in the East Indies," *Philosophical Transactions of the Royal Society of London* 68 (1778): 180–93; BL, Eur Mss 95/1, Robert Kyd, "Some Remarks on the Soil and Cultivation of the Eestern Side of the River Hooghly"; BL, IOR Mss Eur D 72, 154, 161; Guha, *Rule of Property for Bengal*, 184; Grove, *Green Imperialism*, 332–35; Grove, "Revolutionary Weather: The Climatic and Economic Crisis of 1788–1795 and the Discovery of El Niño" in *Sustainability or Collapse? An Integrated History and Future of People on Earth*, ed. Robert Costanza, Lisa J. Graumlich, and Will Steffen (Cambridge, MA: MIT Press, 2007), 151–68; Grove, "The East India Company, the Raj and the El Niño: The Critical Role Played by Colonial Scientists in Establishing the Mechanisms of Global Climate Teleconnections, 1770–1930," in *Nature and the Orient: The Environmental History of South and Southeast Asia*, ed. Richard Grove, Vinita Damodaran, and Satpal Sangwan (New York: Oxford University Press, 1998), 301–23; Arnold, "Hunger in the Garden of Plenty," 92; Richard Drayton, *Nature's Government*, 117; Gascoigne, *Science in the Service of Empire*, 137; James Anderson, *The Conclusion of Letters on the Culture of Silk, with Additional Accounts of Both Kinds of Bread Fruit Trees and the Distribution of Nopal . . .* (Madras, 1792), 15. On potatoes, see Ray Desmond, *The European Discovery of the Indian Flora* (Oxford: Oxford University Press, 1992), 215–16.
49. T. R. Malthus, *An Essay on the Principle of Population; or, A View of Its Past and Present Effects on Human Happiness . . .* (London, 1803), 341, 349–50; Malthus, *An Essay on the Principle of Population . . .* , vol. 2 (London, 1817), 485, 507; Winch, *Riches and Poverty*, 332–35; BL, Add 78784 A, Malthus, "Queries Relative to India, 1804," ff. 142.
50. William J. Barber, *British Economic Thought and India, 1600–1858: A Study in the History of Development Economics* (Oxford: Clarendon Press, 1975), 146; Barton, *Empire Forestry*, 46–47; S. Ambirajan, *Classical Political Economy and British Policy in India*, 59–61, 67, 70–72; Martha McLaren, *British India and British Scotland, 1780–1830: Career-Building,*

Empire-Building, and a Scottish School of Thought on Indian Governance (Akron, OH: University of Akron Press, 2001); Grove, *Green Imperialism*, 446–47; Manu Goswami, *Producing India: From Colonial Economy to National Space* (Chicago: University of Chicago Press, 2004), 45–61; Elizabeth Whitcombe, "Irrigation," in *The Cambridge Economic History of India*, vol. 2: 1757–1970, ed. D. Kumar and T. Raychaudhuri (Hyderabad: Cambridge University Press, 1983), 693–95, cited in William Beinart and Lotte Hughes, *Environment and Empire* (Oxford: Oxford University Press, 2007), 136–37; Ian Stone, *Canal Irrigation in British India: Perspectives on Technological Change in a Peasant Economy* (Cambridge: Cambridge University Press, 1984), 239–77; Grove, *Green Imperialism*, 383, 423–24, 446, 449; David Gilmartin, "Scientific Empire and Imperial Science: Colonialism and Irrigation Technology in the Indus Basin," *Journal of Asian Studies* 53, no. 4 (1994): 1127–49; Mike Davis, *Late Victorian Holocausts: El Niño Famines and the Making of the Third World* (London: Verso, 2001), 331–40; Amartya Sen, *Development as Freedom* (New York: Anchor Books, 2000), 168–75, 178–84.

51. T. C. Smout, "Famine and Famine-Relief in Scotland," in *Comparative Aspects of Scottish and Irish Economic and Social History, 1600–1900*, ed. L. M. Cullen and T. C. Smout (Edinburgh: John Donald, 1978), 26–29; John Knox, *A View of the British Empire, More Especially Scotland . . .*, 2 vols. (London, 1784), 2:616, quoted in Smout, "Famine and Famine-Relief in Scotland," 29; Robert Dodgshon, "Coping with Risk: Subsistence Crises in the Scottish Highlands and Islands, 1600–1800," *Rural History* 15, no. 1 (2004): 5; John Sinclair, *Queries Drawn Up for the Purpose of Elucidating the Natural History and Political State of Scotland* (Edinburgh, 1790), 4; Rosalind Mitchison, *Agricultural Sir John: The Life of Sir John Sinclair of Ulbster, 1754–1835* (London: Geoffrey Bles, 1962), 43; NAS, GD248/358/3/80; Henry Mackenzie, *The Anecdotes and Egotisms of Henry Mackenzie, 1745–1831*, ed. Harold William Thompson (London: Humphrey Milford, 1927), 12.

52. Fry, *Dundas Despotism*, 138; NAS, RH4/188/1, "Sederunt Book 1," 1–3.

53. Mossner and Ross, *Correspondence of Adam Smith*, 262, 266; WN, 1:31–32, 94, 96–97, 2:874. Compare A. E. Youngson, *After the Forty-Five: The Economic Impact on the Highlands* (Edinburgh: Edinburgh University Press, 1973), 64; Jacob Viner, *Guide to John Rae's "Life of Adam Smith"* (1895; reprint ed., New York: Augustus M. Kelley, 1965), 101; and David R. Raynor, "Adam Smith: Two Letters to Henry Beaufoy, MP," *Scottish Journal of Political Economy* 43, no. 5 (1996): 587.

54. *Lectures on Jurisprudence*, ed. R. L. Meek, D. D. Raphael, and P. G. Stein (Oxford: Oxford University Press, 1978), 239, 541, 573. Compare WN, 1:26–29; and *The Complete Works and Correspondence of David Hume*, electronic ed., comp. and ed. Mark C. Rooks, vol. 1: *Letters of David Hume* (Charlottesville, VA: InteLex, 1995), 400.

55. Meek, Raphael, and Stein, *Lectures on Jurisprudence*, 541. Compare WN, 2:700–701, 782–87. Any argument for a radical change in attitude must be tempered by the fact that there are no references to Ossian in any of the editions of *The Theory of Moral Sentiments* between 1759 and 1790. Smith's appreciative remarks on the sentimental novel and modern sensibility in the sixth edition do not mention James Macpherson, *The Theory of Moral Sentiments*, ed. D. D. Raphael and A. L. Macfie (Oxford: Oxford University Press, 1976), 143.

56. WN, 1:165, 243, 420; Raynor, "Adam Smith: Two Letters to Henry Beaufoy, MP," 587.
57. René Prendergast, "James Anderson's Political Economy: His Influence on Smith and Malthus," *Scottish Journal of Political Economy* 34, no. 4 (1987): 388–409; James Anderson, *Observations on the Means of Exciting a Spirit of National Industry . . .* (Edinburgh, 1777), 376; WN, 1:515n28, 516–18; Mossner and Ross, *Correspondence of Adam Smith*, 251; Youngson, *After the Forty-Five*, 104–6. On the 1749 act, see Bob Harris, "Patriotic Commerce and National Revival: The Free British Fishery Society and British Politics, c. 1749–58," *English Historical Review* 114 (1999): 285–313.
58. Committee Appointed to Enquire into the State of the British Fisheries, *Third Report from the Committee Appointed to Enquire into the State of the British Fisheries . . .* (n.p., [1785]), 53–54 (optimal policy), 57 (acceptable bounty), 62–67 (premiums), 69 (total costs); cf. Anderson, *Present State of the Hebrides*, 82–83; WN, 1:397–410, 523.
59. Viner, *Guide to John Rae's "Life of Adam Smith"*; WN, 1:161, 2:701; Youngson, *After the Forty-Five*, 98–99; Raynor, "Adam Smith: Two Letters to Henry Beaufoy, MP," 586–88; NLS, MS 6602, 23–24 (Dempster on Smith to Dundas). On projecting, see WN, 1:357.

CHAPTER 6. LARCH AUTARKY

1. Estimates vary between 14 and 27 million larch trees. *THSS*, vol. 9 (Edinburgh, 1832), 177–78, calculates the number of larches planted by the fourth duke between 1774 and 1826 (excluding the last four years of his life) to be 14,083,378. BM H7, "Abstract of the Duke of Atholl's Woods and Forests 1829," includes a tabulation of the acres planted by the fourth duke. A total of 8,604 (Scots) acres of larch plantations were estimated to contain a minimum of 18.9 million seedlings (at 2,200 plants per acre). But thinning would have reduced this number considerably. One contemporary estimate gives 300–400 trees per Scots acre; see *THSS*, 9:166–67, 186 (planting practices), 196. For other estimates, see Syd House and Christopher Dingwall, "'A Nation of Planters': Introducing the New Trees, 1650–1900," in *People and Woods in Scotland: A History*, ed. T. C. Smout (Edinburgh: Edinburgh University Press, 2003), 139 (14 million larch trees); and James Winter, *Secure from Rash Assault: Sustaining the Victorian Environment* (Berkeley: University of California Press, 1999), 95 (14 million).
2. Samuel Johnson and James Boswell, *A Journey to the Western Islands of Scotland and The Journal of a Tour to the Hebrides* (London: Penguin, 1984), 39; T. C. Smout, *Nature Contested: Environmental History in Scotland and Northern England Since 1600* (Edinburgh: Edinburgh University Press, 2000), 46; Smout, Alan R. MacDonald, and Fiona J. Watson, *A History of the Native Woodlands of Scotland, 1500–1920* (Edinburgh: Edinburgh University Press, 2005), 64; William Boutcher, *A Treatise on Forest-Trees* (Edinburgh, 1775), xxvii–xliii; Fredrik Albritton Jonsson, "Adam Smith in the Forest," in *The Social Life of the Forest*, ed. Kathleen Morrison and Susanna Hecht (Chicago: University of Chicago Press, 2013).
3. M. L. Anderson, *A History of Scottish Forestry*, 2 vols. (London: Nelson, 1967); ; Thomas Hamilton, Earl of Haddington, *A Treatise on the Raising of Forest Trees* (Edinburgh, 1761); Agricola [James Anderson], *Miscellaneous Observations on*

Planting and Training Timber-Trees; Particularly Calculated for the Climate of Scotland . . . (Edinburgh, [1777]), 61, 117; Robert Greenhalgh Albion, *Forests and Sea Power: The Timber Problem of the Royal Navy, 1652–1862* (1926; reprint ed., Annapolis, MD: Naval Institute Press, 1999); NAS, E727/46/7 (6) and /22, John Williams, "Memorial, 1770–71," etc., Report, 12.
4. WN, 1:180, 183.
5. Leah Leneman, *Living in Atholl: A Social History of the Estates, 1685–1785* (Edinburgh: Edinburgh University Press, 1986), 9; Christopher Dingwall, *Blair Castle: A History of the Grounds* (Atholl Estates, 1998), 1–2, 4; *Account of the Larch Plantations on the Estates of Atholl and Dunkeld, Executed by the Late John, Duke of Atholl* . . . (Perth, 1832), 9–10; Anderson, *History of Scottish Forestry*, 1:586–87; for more on Atholl's rhubarb plantation, see Fredrik Albritton Jonsson, "The Enlightenment in the Highlands: Natural History and Internal Colonization in the Scottish Highlands, 1760–1830" (Ph.D. diss., University of Chicago, 2005), ch. 5.
6. *Edinburgh Weekly Amusement* (1771), 11:257–61; 12:129–33, 193–97, 259–62 (larch), 321–323, 358–60; 13:1–4, 65–68, 102–4, 129–30, 164–66, 230–32, 263–65; *Scots Magazine* 33 (1771): 349, etc.; reprinted as [Anderson], *Miscellaneous Observations on Planting*, 116 (prodigious growth); Anderson, *Observations on the Means of Exciting a Spirit of National Industry* (Edinburgh, 1777), 187; the major Scottish writings on planting before 1771, including the Earl of Haddington's *Treatise on the Manner of Raising Forest Trees* (Edinburgh, 1761) made no mention of the larch.
7. [Anderson], *Miscellaneous Observations on Planting*, 56, 122, 134–35, 162–70, 176; Anderson, *The Interest of Great-Britain with Regard to Her American Colonies, Considered; To Which Is Added, an Appendix Containing the Outline of a Plan for a General Pacification* (London, 1782), app., 35.
8. [Anderson], *Miscellaneous Observations on Planting*, 116–18; "A Report from the Committee Appointed to Consider How His Majesty's Navy May Be Better Supplied with Timber, May 6, 1771," in R. J. B. Knight, *Shipbuilding Timber for the British Navy: Parliamentary Papers, 1729–1792* (Delmar, NY: John Carter Brown Library, 1993), 15–52; on the committee of 1771, see Albion, *Forests and Sea Power*, 134; Henry Dundas, *A Letter from Lord Viscount Melville to the Right Honorable Spencer Perceval, on the Subject of Naval Timber* (London, 1810), 4. For the growth rate of larch, see David Welch, *An Audit of Alien Species in Scotland, 2001* (Edinburgh: Scottish Natural Heritage, 2001), 166.
9. AUL, MS 2787/4/2/23; James Anderson, "On the Culture of the Larch Tree and Its Uses," 1789; *The Bee* 8 (1792): 111–13; *The Bee* 17 (1793): 6–9, 88–94, 172–76; THSS, vol. 5 (Edinburgh, 1820), 278 (Kames); James Fergusson, ed., *Letters of George Dempster to Adam Fergusson, 1756–1813* (London: Macmillan, 1934), 109, 166; EUL, La III 379, 442–44; Anderson, *History of Scottish Forestry*, 1:594–96; House and Dingwall, "'Nation of Planters,'" 140–41; William Boutcher, *A Treatise on Forest-Trees* (Edinburgh, 1775), 76–88.
10. John Williams, "Suggestions for Promoting and Improving the Fisheries, upon the Coasts of the Highlands and Isles," THSS, vol. 1 (Edinburgh, 1797), 272; John Smith, "On the Advantages of Planting, and Raising Timber, in the Hebrides, and Other Parts of the West and North-West Coasts of the Highlands," THSS, 1:169–70. Compare

EUL, Dc 6.102.3, George Low, *Orkney Manuscripts*, 24–25; Patrick Neill, "Observations on Different Subjects Connected with the Natural History of Orkney and Shetland," read January 29, 1806, in EUL, *Proceedings of the Natural History Society of Edinburgh*, 15:268–69; and James Robertson, "Report, 1769," in *A Naturalist in the Highlands: James Robertson, His Life and Travels in Scotland, 1767–1771*, ed. D. M. Henderson and J. H. Dickson (Edinburgh: Scottish Academic Press, 1994), 119.

11. Smith, "On the Advantages of Planting," 180–83; cf. Anderson, *Miscellaneous Observations on Planting*, 14–21; Anderson, "The Value and Use of the Larch Tree," *The Bee* 17 (1793): 6–9, 88–89, 176; and Arthur Young, *The Farmer's Tour Through the East of England*, 4 vols. (London, 1771), 1:332–36. For a critique of Anderson's figures, see Anderson, *History of Scottish Forestry*, 1:641.

12. *Account of the Larch Plantations*, 10–11, 25, 31–32, 40; cf. Welch, *Audit of Alien Species*, 166; BM, box 70.10, "Trials of Larch, 1780–1810"; Christopher Dingwall, "Coppice Management in Highland Perthshire," in *Scottish Woodland History*, ed. T. C. Smout (Edinburgh: Scottish Cultural Press, 1996), 162–75.

13. *Account of the Larch Plantations*, 41; BM, box 48/10/113–14; ; BM, H1, "Copy of Questions by the Commissioners of Naval Revision Respecting Oak etc and the Duke of Atholl's Answers, June 1807"; NAS, RH4/188/2, "Sederunt Books 4–5"; Albion, *Forests and Sea Power*, 344; James Anderson, *The Bee* 17 (1793): 176, 137 (error in pagination); John Murray, "Observations on Larch; Transmitted to the Commissioners of Naval Revision in May, 1807," in *Communications to the Board of Agriculture; on Subjects Relative to the Husbandry and Internal Improvement of the Country*, vol. 7, pt. 1 (London, 1811), 277. It should be noted that Atholl seems to have been active in at least one of the political campaigns of the Highland Society of Scotland, the lobbying effort to reform the salt laws; see NAS, RH4/188/1, "Sederunt Book 3," 295. Murray also served as president of the Highland Society of London in 1783 and 1795; see John Sinclair, *An Account of the Highland Society of London . . .* (London, 1813), 62.

14. *Account of the Larch Plantations*, 4–5, 31, 38–44, 52–3; BM, boxes 68/4/27, 68/6/126, 68/2/376; Roger Morriss, *Naval Power and British Culture, 1760–1850: Public Trust and Government Ideology* (Aldershot, UK: Ashgate, 2004), 194, 206, 212–13.

15. BM, H3; John [Murray], the Duke of Atholl, *Observations on Larch; Together with Two Experiments of the Strength and Resilience of the Timber* (London, 1819).

16. On HMS *Atholl*, see BM, J series, esp. J1–2, J4, J14, J17–18, J25, J29. Larch timber was even considered for the purpose of polar navigation; BM, box 69/4/480. On the "Snow Larch," see BM, K1–9.

17. BL, Add MS 41079, ff. 46, 59; Commissioners of His Majesty's Woods, Forests, and Land Revenues, *The Eleventh Report of the Commissioners Appointed to Enquire into the State and Condition of the Woods, Forests, and Land Revenues of the Crown, . . .* (London, 1792), 19, 10, 29–30. To be fair, the *Eleventh Report* also cautioned that no larch should be used in warships "while Oak [could] still be had," 30. Compare Albion, *Forests and Sea Power*, 32–34, 135–36. Oliver Rackham has disputed that naval demand caused a crisis in the timber supply. Other scholars argue the case for a general diminution of woodlands in the eighteenth century from a variety of causes, as did the authors of the *Eleventh Report*. For Rackham's thesis, see *Trees and Woodland in*

the British Landscape: The Complete History of Britain's Trees, Woods and Hedgerows, 2nd ed. (New York: Phoenix Press, 1990).

18. BL, Add MS 37275, ff. 260–61, 303–4; *Eleventh Report*, 19.
19. Dundas, *Letter from Lord Viscount Melville*, 33–39, quotation on 35; NLS, MS 1067, 21; Albion, *Forests and Sea Power*, 33–37, 364–68; Gregory Barton, *Empire Forestry and the Origins of Environmentalism* (Cambridge: Cambridge University Press, 2002), 44–46; NAS, GD51/2/797/1 (Atkins); BL, Add MS 37275, ff. 260–61, 276–300, 308, 328, 334–41, 353–74 (quote about "preventive" on 353), 361–62 (inexhaustible woods), 366–67, 371–73; James Belich, *Replenishing the Earth: The Settler Revolution and the Rise of the Anglo-World, 1783–1939* (Oxford: Oxford University Press, 2009), 444.
20. BM, H1, "Copy of Questions by the Commissioners of Naval Revision respecting Oak etc and the Duke of Atholl's answers June 1807." On Atholl's political support for Dundas, see Michael Fry, *The Dundas Despotism* (Edinburgh: Edinburgh University Press, 1992), 149, 201; for Dundas's imperial strategy, see 226–28. J. M. Bumsted, *People's Clearance*, 191–92; NAS, GD51/139/1–31, esp. 5 (Middleton on Russia).
21. NLS, MS 1067, 21; Albion, *Forests and Sea Power*, 35–37, 364–68; Bernard Pool, *Navy Board Contracts, 1660–1832: Contract Administration Under the Navy Board* (Hamden, CT: Archon Books, 1966), 133; Michael T. Bravo, "Precision and Curiosity in Scientific Travel: James Rennell and the Orientalist Geography of the New Imperial Age (1760–1830)," in *Voyages and Visions: Toward a Cultural History of Travel*, ed. Jaë Elsner and Joan-Pau Rubiés (London: Reaktion Books, 1999), 162–83; Matthew H. Edney, *Mapping an Empire: The Geographical Construction of British India, 1765–1843* (Chicago: University of Chicago Press, 1990), 9–15.
22. NAS, GD51/2/797/1.
23. BL, Add MS 37275, ff. 361–78 (Buchanan's report, quotation on 366, trade with Siam on 371); 260–61 (interview with Philip Dundas), 328 (Philip Dundas on Tipu); Buchanan Hamilton had in fact recommended the conquest of the kingdom of Ava in the late 1790s to Wellesley, see BL, Add 13872, ff. 32–33; Bellich, *Replenishing the Earth*, 444; Barton, *Empire Forestry and the Origins of Environmentalism*, 45–48.
24. Dundas, *Letter from Lord Viscount Melville*, 33, 39; NAS, GD51/16/46/3; Albion, *Forests and Sea Power*, 366–69.
25. BM, box 68/9/227, 287. On Brunel's interest in larch (1821), see BM, box 68/11/107; on the *Diana*, BM, J12, J19, note also J29.
26. A. R. M. Lower, *Great Britain's Woodyard: British America and the Timber Trade, 1763–1867* (Montreal: McGill and Queens University Press, 1973); Belich, *Replenishing the Earth*, 109, 444; Ralph Davis, *The Industrial Revolution and British Overseas Trade* (Leicester: Leicester University Press, 1979), 47–48.

Chapter 7. Coal Exhaustion in 1789

1. *DNB*, s.v. "Williams, John," by H. S. Torrens; Hugh Torrens, "The British 'Mineral Engineer' John Williams (1732–1795)," in *The Practice of British Geology, 1750–1850*, vol. 2 (Aldershot, UK: Ashgate, 2002); NAS, E 727/46/10 (2).

2. T. C. Smout, "Lead Mining in Scotland, 1650–1850," in *Studies in Scottish Business History*, ed. Peter L. Payne (London, 1967); NAS, E721/7, 87, 119, 149; E721/8, 15, 37; E721/9, 38, 171–72; E 727/46/1–4, 6; Annette Smith, *The Jacobite Estates of the Forty-Five* (Edinburgh: John Donald, 1982), 32; Eric Richards, *Patrick Sellar and the Highland Clearances: Homicide, Eviction and the Price of Progress* (Edinburgh: Polygon at Edinburgh University Press, 1999), 71, 88, 126. The mine underwent a brief revival under the earl's daughter Elizabeth of Sutherland. A Newcastle chaldron equaled 53 cwt, or 2,692 kg; see John Hatcher, *The History of the British Coal Industry*, vol. 1: *Before 1700: Towards the Age of Coal* (Oxford: Clarendon Press, 1993), 567.

3. NAS, E727/46/8, 25, 28 (1), 37, 38 (long quotation), 40, 47, 49; see also NAS, RHP 3423, William Morison, "Plan of the Farm of Callart, 1773." For newspaper advertisements, see, e.g., *London Chronicle*, July 19–21, 1774; and *St. James's Chronicle; or, The British Evening Post* (London), August 4–6, 1774. On the success of the Laroch quarry, see OSA, 1:499; and *The New Statistical Account of Scotland: Under the Superintendence of a Committee of the Society for the Benefit of the Sons and Daughters of the Clergy*, 15 vols. (Edinburgh: Blackwood, 1845), 7:247.

4. John Knox, *A Tour Through the Highlands of Scotland, and the Hebride Isles, in MDCCLXXXVI* (London, 1787), cli; James Anderson, *Observations on the Effects of the Coal Duty upon the Remote and Thinly Peopled Coasts of Britain . . .* (Edinburgh, 1792), 28.

5. *Third Report from the Committee Appointed to Enquire into the State of the British Fisheries* (n.p., 1785), 53; NAS, GD9/3, 68, 113, 302; THSS, vol. 1 (Edinburgh, 1797), xiv.

6. Torrens, "British 'Mineral Engineer,'" 166–70; John Williams, "An Essay on the Means of Supplying the Want of Coals, and of Providing Fuel on a Highland Estate, with the Smallest Loss of Time and Trouble," THSS, 1:313–23; NAS, RH4/188/1, Highland Society Sederunt Book 1, 152, 201; Williams, *The Natural History of the Mineral Kingdom*, 2 vols. (Edinburgh, 1789). The book was not actually published until 1790; see Torrens, "British 'Mineral Engineer,'" 170.

7. John Williams, *Prospectus and Proposals for Publishing an Essay Towards a Natural History of the Mineral Kingdom; in Two Parts . . .* (Edinburgh, 1787), 4–5; NLS, MS 996, inserts 1–2; Torrens, "British 'Mineral Engineer,'" 170–71.

8. Torrens, "British 'Mineral Engineer,'" 170; Williams, *Natural History of the Mineral Kingdom*, 1:254, 258, 2:366; Williams, *Prospectus and Proposals*, 3, 7–8; cf. Richard Watson, *Chemical Essays*, 3 vols. (London, 1787), 2:357; Williams may also have held out some hope for coal mines in the isle of Mull. At least he encouraged members of the Highland Society to prospect there; see THSS, 1:259.

9. There had been scares regarding coal exhaustion as early as the sixteenth century, but they were shaped by the expectations of the preindustrial organic economy. Williams's vision of social and economic collapse reflected the new centrality of coal in the mineral energy economy. Williams, *Natural History of the Mineral Kingdom*, 1:158–60, 167–68, 171–73, 174–76, 178–79, 2:378. *Scots Magazine* 53 (1791): 544; William Stanley Jevons, *The Coal Question: An Inquiry Concerning the Progress of the Nation, and the Probably Exhaustion of Our Coal-Mines*, 3rd ed. rev., ed. A. W. Flux (1906; reprint ed.,

New York: Augustus M. Kelley, 1965), 15; for preindustrial fears of exhaustion, see Rolf Peter Sieferle, *The Subterranean Forest: Energy Systems and the Industrial Revolution* (Cambridge: White Horse Press, 2001), 186–87; E. A. Wrigley argues for the persistence of preindustrial views of the economy in the late eighteenth century and beyond; see his *Energy and the English Industrial Revolution* (Cambridge: Cambridge University Press, 2010), 3, 11.

10. Williams, *Natural History of the Mineral Kingdom*, 178–79; *Scots Magazine* 53 (1791): 544.

11. Alan H. Fielding and Paul F. Haworth, *Upland Habitats* (London: Routledge, 1999), 30–33; R. S. Clymo, "The Limits to Peat Bog Growth," *Philosophical Transactions of the Royal Society of London*, B 303 (1984): 606–7; I. G. Simmons, *An Environmental History of Great Britain* (Edinburgh: Edinburgh University Press, 2001), 39–40, 114; *Report of the Committee Appointed by the Board of Agriculture to Take into Consideration the State of Waste Lands and Common Fields of This Kingdom* (London, 1795), 15–17; T. C. Smout, *Nature Contested; Environmental History in Scotland and Northern England Since 1600* (Edinburgh: Edinburgh University Press, 2000), 52–53.

12. Wrigley, *Energy and the English Industrial Revolution*, 223; I. G. Simmons, *The Moorlands of England and Wales: An Environmental History, 8000 BC to AD 2000* (Edinburgh: Edinburgh University Press, 2003), 66, 97; J. W. De Zeeuw, "Peat and the Dutch Golden Age: The Historical Meaning of Energy Attainability," *A.A.G. Bijdragen* 12 (1976): 3–31; Richard W. Unger, "Energy Sources for the Dutch Golden Age: Peat, Wind, and Coal," *Research in Economic History* 9 (1984): 221–53; F. Fraser Darling, *Crofting Agriculture: Its Practice in the West Highlands and Islands* (Edinburgh: Oliver and Boyd, 1945), 5; for additional traditional uses of peat in the Scottish economy, see William Milliken and Sam Bridgewater, *Flora Celtica: Plants and People in Scotland* (Edinburgh: Birlinn, 2004), 271–73.

13. Henry Gray Macnab, *Letters Addressed to the Right Honourable William Pitt, Chancellor of the Exchequer of Great Britain; Pointing out the Inequality, Oppression, and Impolicy of the Taxes on Coal: and A Substitute for These Taxes on All Coals Consumed in England and Scotland* (London, 1793), app.: 15–16, 22–23. Macnab's appendix contained a large number of extracts from OSA on these issues from the first nine volumes of the series.

14. Anderson, *Observations on the Effects of the Coal Duty*, 24 (extracts from OSA, 24–27); OSA, 7:475, 242, 447–48; John Sinclair, *Queries Drawn Up for the Purpose of Elucidating the Natural History and Political State of Scotland* (Edinburgh, 1790), question 136. Sinclair also asked whether the parish had a coal mine (question 33).

15. Anderson, *Observations on the Effects of the Coal Duty*, 28; E. A. Wrigley, *Continuity, Chance and Change: The Character of the Industrial Revolution in England* (Cambridge: Cambridge University Press, 1988).

16. Macnab, *Letters to Pitt*, 96, 4, 31.

17. Macnab, *Letters to Pitt*, 104, 124, app.

18. *Reports by John Clerk . . . and by Messrs Grieve and Henderson, in Consequence of Surveys, Made by Them, of Culross and Valleyfield Collieries . . .* (Edinburgh, 1793), 31; Anderson, *Observations on the Effects of the Coal Duty*, 31; Citizen of Edinburgh,

Considerations on the Present Scarcity and Dearness of Coals in Scotland; and on the Means of Procuring Greater Quantities at a Cheaper Rate (Edinburgh, 1793), 12; Macnab, *Letters to Pitt*, 130.
19. *Scots Magazine* 55 (1793): 380–81.
20. OSA, 12:543–49; Robert Bald, *General View of the Scottish Coal Trade* (Edinburgh, 1808), 94; John Smith, "On the Advantages of Planting, and Raising Timber, in the Hebrides, and Other Parts of the West and North-West Coasts of the Highlands," *THSS*, 1:173; John Walker, *Essays on Natural History and Rural Economy* (Edinburgh, 1812), 416; Jevons, *Coal Question*, 16–19.
21. John Ehrman, *The Younger Pitt: The Years of Acclaim* (London: Constable, 1969), 252–53, Pitt quoted on 252; *Morning Chronicle and London Advertiser*, July 2, 1784; Paul Kelly, "British Parliamentary Politics, 1784–1786," *Historical Journal* 17, no. 4 (1974): 741–42; *Cobbett's Parliamentary History of England*, 36 vols. (London, 1806–20), 25:924; Michael Fry, *The Dundas Despotism* (Edinburgh: Edinburgh University Press, 1992), 166; NLS, Melville Papers, MS 640 (on coal and salt duties); House of Commons, *Third Report from the Committee Appointed to Enquire into the State of the British Fisheries* (n.p., 1785), 114; Archibald Cochrane, *Thoughts on the Manufacture and Trade of Salt . . .* (Edinburgh, 1784); John Dalrymple, *Address and Proposals from Sir John Dalrymple, Bart., on the Subject of the Coal, Tar, and Iron, Branches of Trade* (Edinburgh, 1784); James Anderson, *An Account of the Present State of the Hebrides and Western Coasts of Scotland . . .* (Edinburgh, 1785), 149–50.
22. Michael W. Flinn, *The History of the British Coal Industry*, vol. 2: *1700–1830: The Industrial Revolution* (Oxford: Clarendon Press, 1984), 285, 310; for contemporary complaints about prices, see *Report from the Committee Appointed to Consider of the Coal Trade*, 41–43, 106–18, 120, 127; Citizen of Edinburgh. *Considerations on the Present Scarcity and Dearness of Coals in Scotland; and on the Means of Procuring Greater Quantities at a Cheaper Rate . . .* (Edinburgh, 1793), 1; *Cursory Remarks on Bread and Coal* (London, 1800), 14–15; Matthias Dunn, *An Historical, Geological, and Descriptive View of the Coal Trade . . .* (London, 1844), 28; William J. Hausman, "Market Power in the London Coal Trade: The Limitation of the Vend, 1770–1845," *Explorations in Economic History* 21 (1984): 383–405.
23. *Cobbett's Parliamentary History*, 26:900–901; William Hutton, *An History of Birmingham, to the End of the Year 1780* (Birmingham, 1781), 18; Citizen of Edinburgh, *Considerations on the Present Scarcity*, 4; Macnab, *Letters to Pitt*, 130; *Cursory Remarks on Bread and Coal*, 10–12. For more examples, see David Young, *National Improvements upon Agriculture* (Edinburgh, 1785), 34–35; Adam Anderson, *Historical and Chronological Deduction of the Origin of Commerce*, 6 vols. (Dublin, 1790), 3:626 (Newcastle's "almost inexhaustible" coal); Charles Beaumont, *A Treatise on the Coal Trade* (London, 1789), vii, 2 ("inexhaustible" coal mines); and *Bell's Weekly Messenger* (London), January 25, 1801. Earlier mentions of "inexhaustible" coal include Thomas Salmon, *Modern History, or, The Present State of All Nations*, vol. 4 (Dublin, 1739), 201, 215 (thanks to Will Cavert for this reference). The conviction about the central economic and social importance of coal appears to have emerged gradually over the early modern era, see William Cavert's dissertation, "Producing Pollution:

Coal, Smoke, and Society in London, 1550–1750," (Northwestern University, 2011), ch. 5.

24. *OSA*, 12:545–49. The discussion of coal exhaustion was submitted as a lengthy footnote to the account of Markinch parish. When Thomson returned to the topic in 1800, he seems to have taken a more positive view, stressing the "great abundance of coal" in Fife; see *General View of the Agriculture of the County of Fife* (Edinburgh, 1800), 385. For the price spike in Edinburgh, see Citizen of Edinburgh, *Considerations on the Present Scarcity*, 2.

25. Sieferle, *Subterranean Forest*, 184–85; John Baillie, *An Impartial History of the Town and County of Newcastle* (Newcastle upon Tyne, 1801), 444; James Brindley, *The History of Inland Navigations; Particularly Those of the Duke of Bridgewater, in Lancashire and Cheshire . . .* (London, 1766), 8; *Reports by John Clerk*, 26–27; OSA, 2:270; Bald, *General View of the Scottish Coal Trade*, 94; NAS, GD124/17/581 (Robert Bald to J. M. Erskine, 1818); John Wilson, *General View of the Agriculture of Renfrewshire; with Observations on the Means of Its Improvement, and an Account of Its Commerce and Manufactures* (Paisley, 1812), 23; Flinn, *History of the British Coal Industry*, 1, 29. On the geography of exhausted fields, see Roger Burt, "The Extractive Industries," in *The Cambridge Economic History of Modern Britain*, ed. Roderick Floud and Paul Johnson (Cambridge: Cambridge University Press, 2004), 419; and Williams, *Natural History of the Mineral Kingdom*, 1:168.

26. Williams, *Natural History of the Mineral Kingdom*, 1:174; Macnab, *Letters to Pitt*, 126–27; cf. Richard Watson, *Chemical Essays*, 3 vols. (London, 1787), 2:357.

27. Macnab, *Letters to Pitt*, 132–36.

28. John Bailey and George Culley, *General View of the Agriculture of the County of Northumberland, with Observations on the Means of Its Improvement; Drawn Up for the Consideration of the Board of Agriculture and Internal Improvement* (Newcastle, 1797), 11, 18–19; cf. John Bailey, *General View of the Agriculture of the County of Durham: With Observations on the Means of Its Improvement; Drawn Up for the Consideration of the Board of Agriculture and Internal Improvement* (London, 1810), 27–29; Robert Edington, *An Essay on the Coal Trade . . .* (London, 1803), 23, 30; Edington, *A Treatise on the Coal Trade; with Strictures on Its Abuses, and Hints for Amelioration* (London, 1813), 115, 122, 126, 141–43; Thomas Thomson, "A Geognostical Sketch of the Counties of Northumberland, Durham, and Part of Cumberland," *Annals of Philosophy*, vol. 4, ed. Thomas Thomson (July–December 1814): 410–12; Robert Bakewell, *An Introduction to Geology . . .* , 3rd ed. (London, 1829), 132–35; ; *Report of the Select Committee on the State of the Coal Trade* (London, 1830), 231–47; Jevons, *Coal Question*, 16–19.

29. *Hansard's Parliamentary History*, 3rd ser., vol. 25 (London, 1834), 533–34; Jevons, *Coal Question*, 269, 272–74; Roy Church, *History of the British Coal Industry*, vol. 3: *1830–1913: Victorian Pre-Eminence* (Oxford: Oxford University Press, 1986), 86; E. Kula, *History of Environmental Economic Thought* (New York: Routledge, 1998), 44–46; Donald Worster, *A Passion for Nature: The Life of John Muir* (Oxford: Oxford University Press, 2008), 430; "Catastrophist-Cornucopian Debate" in David J. Cuff and Andrew S. Goudie, *The Oxford Companion to Global Change* (Oxford: Oxford University Press, 2009), 103.

30. Jevons, *Coal Question*, 140, 457, 459–60; Macaulay quoted in David Skilton, "Tourists at the Ruins of London: The Metropolis and the Struggle for Empire," *Cercles* 17 (2007): 116.
31. Williams, *Natural History of the Mineral Kingdom*, 1:xv, 125, 144; Bald, *General View of the Scottish Coal Trade*, [vi], ix, 66, 120–22; Archibald Cochrane, *A Treatise, Shewing the Intimate Connection That Subsists Between Agriculture and Chemistry* (London, 1795), 4–5; on Sinclair, see chaps. 2 and 9.
32. Williams, *Natural History of the Mineral Kingdom*, 1:178–79; OSA, 12:547–48; Bald, *General View of the Scottish Coal Trade*, 106–9; Walker, *Essays on Natural History and Rural Economy*, 416, 592; THSS, 1:173.

Chapter 8. Overpopulation and Extirpation

1. Joseph Townsend, *A Dissertation on the Poor Laws* (London, 1786), 37–41, 53.
2. Benjamin Franklin, *Political, Miscellaneous, and Philosophical Pieces . . . Now First Collected, with Explanatory Plates, Notes, and an Index to the Whole* (London, 1779), 9–10; T. R. Malthus, *An Essay on the Principle of Population; or, A View of Its Past and Present Effects on Human Happiness . . .* (London, 1803), 74–75 (hereafter cited as Malthus 1803). For an overview of the tradition, see Joel E. Cohen, *How Many People Can the Earth Support?* (New York: W. W. Norton, 1995).
3. *DNB*, s.v. "Townsend, Joseph." Curiously, there seems to be no mention of Townsend in the *Chronicles of Tullibardine* or the section of family correspondence for 1769–70 in the Blair Muniments. He does not even appear in the third duke's account book as an employee of the family; see BM 5/139.
4. Townsend, *Dissertation on the Poor Laws*, 43–44, 48–50, 52–53; Townsend, *A Journey Through Spain in the Years 1786 and 1787; with Particular Attention to the Agriculture, Manufactures, Commerce, Population, Taxes, and . . .*, 2nd ed., 2 vols. (Dublin, 1792), 2:120, 384; Leah Leneman, *Living in Atholl: A Social History of the Estates, 1685–1785* (Edinburgh: Edinburgh University Press, 1986), 9.
5. Victor de Riquetti, Marquis de Mirabeau, *L'ami des hommes; ou, Traité de la population* (Avignon, 1756), pt. 1, 172; Richard Cantillon, *Essai sur la nature du commerce en général; traduit de l'anglois* (London, 1755), 110; WN, 1:97.
6. Elinor Melville, *A Plague of Sheep: Environmental Consequences of the Conquest of Mexico* (Cambridge: Cambridge University Press, 1994), 6–7; William Robertson, *The History of America*, 2 vols. (Edinburgh, 1777), 2:337, 394; WN, 1:240–41, 247.
7. Alfred Crosby, *Ecological Imperialism: The Biological Expansion of Europe, 900–1900* (Cambridge: Cambridge University Press, 1986), 75, 91; Martin Martin, *A Description of the Western Islands of Scotland Circa 1695 and a Late Voyage to St Kilda* (Edinburgh: Birlinn, 1999), 27. See also the discussion of rabbits in John Walker, *An Economical History of the Hebrides and Highlands of Scotland*, 2 vols. (Edinburgh, 1808), 2:175–79.
8. Karl Polanyi, *The Great Transformation: The Political and Economic Origins of Our Time* (1944; reprint ed., Boston: Beacon, 2001), 117–18; Glyndwr Williams, *The Great South Sea: English Voyages and Encounters, 1570–1750* (New Haven: Yale University

Press, 2007), 176–78; Crosby, *Ecological Imperialism*, 95. It is revealing that Polanyi in the same passage dismissed any positive role for nature in Smith's *Wealth of Nations*: "Nature in the physical sense was consciously excluded in Smith from the problem of wealth" (117). For Townsend's dual interests in natural history and political economy, see, e.g., NLS, MS 5547, f. 93.
9. Townsend, *Dissertation*, 40–41.
10. [T. R. Malthus], *An Essay on the Principle of Population, as It Affects the Future Improvement of Society* . . . (London, 1798), 14–15, 21–23; Malthus 1803, 6–8.
11. Malthus 1803, 13–14, 74–75, 194, 325–27, 332, 334, 349.
12. Malthus 1803, iv, 2, 562, 568.
13. Eric Richards, *The Highland Clearances: People, Landlords and Rural Turmoil* (Edinburgh: Birlinn, 2002), 46–47; Michael Flinn, "Malthus, Emigration and Potatoes in the Scottish North-West, 1770–1870," in *Comparative Aspects of Scottish and Irish Economic and Social History, 1600–1900*, ed. L. M. Cullen and T. C. Smout (Edinburgh: John Donald, 1978), 47, 54. Compare T. C. Smout, "Famine and Famine Relief in Scotland," in the same collection, 27: "landowners and the middle classes did now have a larger surplus to be generous with" in times of dearth. Arguably, such a surplus should not be defined narrowly as a question of "disposable income" and charity but rather as a problem of state policy, taxation, and entitlements.
14. Richards, *Highland Clearances*, 71.
15. *Oxford English Dictionary*, s.v. "extirpate"; BL, Auckland Papers, Add MSS 34412, f. 352.
16. Claude Rawson, *God, Gulliver, and Genocide: Barbarism and the European Imagination, 1492–1945* (Oxford: Oxford University Press, 2001), 302; David Hume, *The History of England from the Invasion of Julius Caesar to the Revolution of 1688*, 6 vols. (Indianapolis, IN: Liberty Fund, 1983), 1:24, 161, 429; Thomas Innes, *A Critical Essay on the Ancient Inhabitants of the Northern Parts of Britain, or Scotland; Containing an Account of the Romans, of the Britains* . . . (London, 1729), 125; John Millar, *An Historical View of the English Government*, ed. Mark Salber Philips and Dale R. Smith (Indianapolis, IN: Liberty Fund, 2006), 383; Robertson, *History of America,,* 2:346–49; Abbé Raynal [Guillaume-Thomas-François], *A Philosophical and Political History of the Settlements and Trade of the Europeans in the East and West Indies*, 8 vols. (London, 1783), 4:310; Lord Kames, *Sketches of the History of Man*, 2 vols. (Edinburgh, 1774), 2:81.
17. Hume, *History of England*, 1:161, 166, 168, 202–3, 226; cf. Eugene Miller, "Hume on Liberty in the Successive English Constitutions," in *Liberty in Hume's History of England*, ed. Nicolas Capaldi (Dordrecht: Kluwer, 1990), 64–65, 79; contrast with Millar, *Historical View*, 42–43, 212–15, 383.
18. Martin Rudwick, *The Meaning of Fossils: Episodes in the History of Paleontology* (Chicago: University of Chicago Press, 1985), 101; Benjamin Stillingfleet, *Miscellaneous Tracts Relating to Natural History, Husbandry, and Physick* . . . (London, 1759), 95, 63; EUL, Dc 2.20, 4:14–15; EUL, Gen 703D, 9:132–33.
19. Pehr Kalm, *Travels into North America: Containing Its Natural History and a Circumstantial Account of Its Plantations and Agriculture* . . ., Translated into English

by John Reinhold Forster, 3 vols. (Warrington, 1770–71), 1:291, 371, 2:129, 177; Philip J. Pauly, "Fighting the Hessian Fly: American and British Responses to Insect Invasion, 1776–1789," *Environmental History* 7, no. 3 (2002): 485–507; *The Scientific Correspondence of Sir Joseph Banks, 1765–1820*, vol. 3: *The Middle Period, 1785–1799: Letters, 1785–1790*, ed. Neil Chambers (London: Pickering and Chatto, 2007), 407.

20. Thomas Pennant, *British Zoology*, 4 vols. (London, 1768–70), 1:18, 61–64, 70, 92, 98; Pennant, *Arctic Zoology*, 2 vols. (London, 1784–85), 1:iv–v, 2; EUL, Gen 703D, 9:132–33; John Sinclair, *General View of the Agriculture of the Northern Counties of Cromarty, Ross, Sutherland, and Caithness, and the Islands of Orkney and Shetland; With Observations on the Means of their Improvement* (London, 1795), 160. On extirpation, see, e.g., also Margaret M. McKay, ed., *The Rev. Dr. John Walker's Report on the Hebrides* (Edinburgh: John Donald, 1980), 158; Walker, *Economical History of the Hebrides and Highlands of Scotland*, 1:327.

21. Pennant, *British Zoology*, 1:100; Georg J. Krinke, *The Laboratory Rat* (London: Academic Press, 2000), 4–5.

22. NLS, MS 23165, James Hutton, *The Elements of Agriculture*, vol. 1 (1797), 639/425–644/430. For the sugar borer, see *The Scientific Correspondence of Joseph Banks*, vol. 4: *The Middle Period, 1785–1799: Letters, 1790–1799*, ed. Neil Chambers (London: Pickering and Chatto, 2007), 141–42. Other contemporary reports of insect invasions include the report on Asiatic grasshoppers, *Scots Magazine* (January 1782): 46.

23. Kalm, *Travels into North America*, 1:175–76; Hutton, *Elements of Agriculture*, 1:639/425; cf. Pehr Kalm, "Beskrifning på et slages maskar, som somliga år göra stor skada både på frukt-träden och skogarna i Norra America," *KVAH* (April–June 1764): 124–39.

24. Richards, *Highland Clearances*, 75–81, quotation on 79; NLS, MS 6602, 21.

25. NAS, GD51/5/52/4, f. 185.

26. NLS, MS 6602, 21–22. Andrew Munro Lang, *A Life of George Dempster, Scottish M.P. of Dunnichen (1732–1818)* (Lewiston: Edwin Mellen, 1998).

27. NLS, MS 640, Henry Beaufoy, "Remarks on the Scheme of Establishing Fishing Stations on the Western Coasts of Scotland—Suggested by a Tour to That Country in the Year 1787," 168; Beaufoy, *The Substance of the Speech of Henry Beaufoy, Esq. to the British Society for Extending the Fisheries. &c. at Their General Court . . .* (London, 1788), 25, 27; James Anderson, *An Account of the Present State of the Hebrides and Western Coasts of Scotland* (Edinburgh, 1785), xvii–xviii, 168–69, 318; *The Bee* 6 (1791): 201–8, 157–61; Eric Richards, *A History of the Highland Clearances: Agrarian Transformation and the Evictions, 1746–1886* (London: Croom Helm, 1982), 194–96.

28. John Knox, *A Tour Through the Highlands of Scotland and the Hebride Isles, in MDCCLXXXVI* (London, 1787), xc–xci.

29. Knox, *Tour Through the Highlands*, xxxii, xxxvi–xxxvii, lxxi–lxxii; note also 118–19 on the agility of the Highlander, a cardinal trait of light infantry. John Smith, *Galic Antiquities: Consisting of a History of the Druids, Particularly Those of Caledonia; A Dissertation on the Authenticity of the Poems of Ossian . . .* (Edinburgh, 1780).

30. Sinclair, *General View of the Agriculture of the Northern Counties*, 163–64; Rose also contributed to the British Fisheries Society survey of 1787, NAS, GD9/3, ff. 74–81; *Letters of George Dempster to Sir Adam Fergusson*, 167; Richards, *Highland Clearances*, 121–30.

31. NLS, MS 6602, ff. 21–22; George Dempster, *A Discourse Containing a Summary of the Proceedings of the Directors of the Society for Extending the Fisheries and Improving the Sea Coasts* . . . (London, 1789), 5–6, 34, 84–86; EUL, La III 379, f. 355; *Letters of George Dempster to Sir Adam Fergusson*, 173, 194; Dempster acknowledged his debt to William Pulteney, *Reflections on the Domestic Policy, Proper to Be Observed on the Conclusion of a Peace* (London, 1761), 2–6.
32. *The Bee* 11 (1792): 69; NLS, MS 5319, 72; NAS, RH4/49/3, vol. 5, ff. 191, 197; for the wool bill, see John Gascoigne, *Science in the Service of Empire: Joseph Banks, the British State and the Uses of Science in the Age of Revolution* (Cambridge: Cambridge University Press, 1998), 86–87, Holroyd quotation on 77.
33. NAS, RH4/188/1, "Sederunt Book 2," 67, 70, 89; *Report of the Committee of the Highland Society of Scotland, on the Subject of Shetland Wool* (Edinburgh, 1790), 16, 21, 45–46; William Marshall, *The Rural Economy of Glocestershire*, 2 vols. (Glocester [sic], 1789), 2:233, 238; M. L. Ryder, *Sheep and Man* (London: Duckworth, 1983), 531–39.
34. *Report of the Committee on Shetland Wool*, 2–3, 7, 17–20, 52–53; NAS, RH4/188/1, "Sederunt Book 2" 78; B. C. Gournay, *Tableau général du commerce . . . années 1789 et 1790* (Paris, [1790]), 437.
35. Andrew Ker, *Report to Sir John Sinclair . . . of the State of Sheep Farming* . . . (Edinburgh, 1791), 36–37.
36. NAS, MS 23166, James Hutton, *Elements of Agriculture*, 2:760, 763; *Scots Magazine* 50 (1790): 565. A flock of sixty sheep from Leuchars in Fife was crossed with Shetland rams and kept on Cramond Island; see George Robertson, *General View of the Agriculture of the County of Mid-Lothian: With Observations on the Means of Its Improvement* (Edinburgh, 1795), app. 3, 26.
37. John Sinclair, *Address to the Society for the Improvement of British Wool; Constituted at Edinburgh, on . . . January 31, 1791*, 2nd ed. (London, 1791), iii–iv, 2, 6–7, 25; *The Bee* (January 19, 1791): 110–11; [Sinclair], *Observations on the Advantages Which the Public May Expect to Derive, by Means of the Proposed Association for the Improvement of British Wool* (N.p., 1790), 2–3; NLS, MS 5564, ff. 3–53; Robertson, *General View of the Agriculture of the County of Mid-Lothian*, app. 3, 17–28, 30, 38; *Report of the Committee on Shetland Wool*, 3n (quotation), 5. Compare John Gascoigne, *Science in the Service of Empire*, 73; Harold B. Carter, *The Sheep and Wool Correspondence of Sir Joseph Banks, 1781–1820* (Norwich: Library Council of New South Wales, 1979), 208–10.
38. Andrew Ker, *Report to Sir John Sinclair*, 27; Arthur Young, *Annals of Agriculture and Other Useful Arts*, vol. 16 (Bury St. Edmond [sic], 1791), 284. Ker's survey was followed by two others, one by William Redhead with companions to England in 1792 and another by John Naismyth in the south of Scotland in 1794; see Robertson, *General View of the Agriculture of the County of Mid-Lothian*, app. 3, 33.
39. NAS, RH4/49/2, 4:ff. 92, 96. Compare Lord Melville's worry in 1809 to Sinclair: "I heard lately, I hope it is not true that the Cheviot sheep stand the winter worse than the old black faced sheep, so that many more of them die under a severe winter such as the [past] for example" (f. 447).
40. William Redhead, *Observations on the Different Breeds of Sheep, and the State of Sheep Farming in Some of the Principal Counties of England* (Edinburgh, 1792), i–ii;

Young, *Annals of Agriculture*, 397, 399–401; John Sinclair, *Essays on Miscellaneous Subjects* (London, 1802), 114 ("at last ascertained"), 126; Carter, *Sheep and Wool Correspondence*, 185–88, 196, 198–200, 202, 205, 213–14, 220, 229–30, 234; Rosalind Mitchison, *Agricultural Sir John: The Life of Sir John Sinclair of Ulbster, 1754–1835* (London: Geoffrey Bles, 1962), 109–11; James Anderson wrote to Sir Joseph Banks in December 1794, "I have seen several Shetland sheep whose fleece was perfectly free from hair"; see NLS, MS 9819, f. 8.

41. NAS, RH4/49/2, 4:f. 43; Richards, *Highland Clearances*, 80–83, 130–33.
42. Sinclair expressed his faith in the compatibility of sheep and men already in the wool report to the Highland Society, but he had yet to work out the precise details of this accommodation; see *Report of the Committee on Shetland Wool*, 78–79.

Chapter 9. Wasteland Island

1. *Reports from Committees of the House of Commons*, 15 vols. (London, 1803–6), 9:202–3; John Sinclair, *Essays on Miscellaneous Subjects* (London, 1802), 178–79.
2. The term *ghost acre* first appeared in the Swedish population theorist Georg Borgström's work *The Hungry Planet: The Modern World at the Edge of Famine* (New York: Macmillan, 1965), but the concept arguably existed long before the current term, just like the concept of the "tragedy of commons" predates Hardin's term. *Ghost acre* has been popularized in environmental history by Kenneth Pomeranz's use of it in *The Great Divergence: China, Europe, and the Making of the Modern World Economy* (Princeton, NJ: Princeton University Press, 2000), 277; quotation in E. A. Wrigley, *Energy and the English Industrial Revolution* (Cambridge: Cambridge University Press, 2010), 39n38; cf. Wrigley, *Continuity, Change and Chance: The Character of the Industrial Revolution in England* (Cambridge: Cambridge University Press, 1990), 55; Joel E. Cohen, *How Many People Can the Earth Support?* (New York: W. W. Norton, 1994); on island economies and environmental thought, see E. Kula, *History of Environmental Economic Thought* (New York: Routledge, 1998), 202–3.
3. NAS, RH4/188/1, "Sederunt Book 2," 244–46, 253–54, 265, "Sederunt Book 3," 18, 123, 137–41, 213; J. E. Cookson, "The Napoleonic Wars, Military Scotland and Tory Highlandism in the Early Nineteenth Century," *Scottish Historical Review* 78, no. 205 (1999): 60–75.
4. Christopher A. Bayly, *Imperial Meridian: The British Empire and the World, 1780–1830* (New York: Longman, 1989), 123; Michael J. Turner, *The Age of Unease; Government and Reform in Britain, 1782–1832* (Stroud: Sutton, 2000), 80–82; Roger Wells, *Wretched Faces: Famine in Wartime England, 1793–1801* (New York: St. Martin's, 1988); A. D. Harvey, *Britain in the Early Nineteenth Century* (London: Palgrave Macmillan, 1978), 316–19; Thomas Beddoes, *A Letter to the Right Hon. William Pitt on the Means of Relieving the Present Scarcity and Preventing the Diseases That Arise from Meager Food* (London, 1796), 26–32; Count Rumford, *The Complete Works*, 4 vols. (Boston, American Academy of Arts and Sciences, 1870–73), 4:411; Eliza Melroe, *An Economical and New Method of Cookery; Describing Upwards of Eighty Cheap, Wholesome, and*

Nourishing Dishes . . . (London, 1798); Jeremy Burchardt, *The Allotment Movement in England, 1793–1873* (Woodbridge: Boydell, 2002), 33–34.

5. Archibald Cochrane, the Earl of Dundonald, *A Treatise, Shewing the Intimate Connection That Subsists Between Agriculture and Chemistry* (London, 1795), 2–6; *DNB*, s.v. "Cochrane, Archibald."

6. Cochrane, *Treatise*, frontispiece, 3; EUL, Gen 874/IV, 55–57; Archibald and Nan Clow, *The Chemical Revolution: A Contribution to Social Technology* (London: Batchworth, 1952), 389–423.

7. Cochrane, *Treatise*, 180–83, 196, 200–203; Wrigley, *Continuity, Chance and Change*, 47–50.

8. Donald J. Withrington, "What Was Distinctive about the Scottish Enlightenment?" in *Aberdeen and the Enlightenment*, ed. Jennifer J. Carter and Joan H. Pittock (Aberdeen: Aberdeen University Press, 1987), 16; Rosalind Mitchison, *Agricultural Sir John: The Life of Sir John Sinclair of Ulbster, 1754–1835* (London: Geoffrey Bles, 1962), 131; James Burnet, *Antient Metaphysics*, 5 vols. (Edinburgh, 1797) 5:302; John Sinclair, *General View of the Agriculture of the Northern Counties and Islands of Scotland* (Edinburgh, 1795), 31n; on cottagers, see T. M. Devine, *The Transformation of Rural Scotland: Social Change and the Agrarian Economy, 1660–1815* (Edinburgh: John Donald, 1994), 140–41; and Sarah Lloyd, *Charity and Poverty in England, c. 1680–1820: Wild and Visionary Schemes* (Manchester: Manchester University Press, 1829), ch. 7 passim.

9. James Robertson, *A General View of the Agriculture in the County of Perth; With Observations on the Means of Its Improvement* (Perth, 1799), xvi, 59, 67–68, quoted in T. C. Smout, "The Landowner and the Planned Village," in *Scotland in the Age of Improvement: Essays in Scottish History in the Eighteenth Century*, ed. N. T. Phillipson and Rosalind Mitchison (Edinburgh: Edinburgh University Press, 1970), 79, 91, 98–99; James Robertson, "The Parish of Callander," in *OSA*, 11:593–94; Withrington, "What Was Distinctive about the Scottish Enlightenment?" 14; Linda Colley, *Britons: Forging the Nation, 1707–1837* (London: Pimlico, 1994), 296.

10. D. G. Lockhart, "Planned Village Development in Scotland and Ireland, 1700–1850," in *Ireland and Scotland, 1600–1850: Parallels and Contrasts in Economic and Social Development*, ed. T. M. Devine and D. Dickson (Edinburgh: John Donald, 1983), 140; John Sinclair, *General View of the Agriculture of the Northern Counties of Cromarty, Ross, Sutherland, and Caithness, and the Islands of Orkney and Shetland; With Observations on the Means of Their Improvement* (London, 1795), 31–32, 71–72, 132–34, 136; EUL, La III 379; Mitchison, *Agricultural Sir John*, 191–92; John Henderson, *General View of the County of Caithness* (London, 1815), app. (by Sinclair), 54; Daniel Samson, "'The Yoke of Improvement': Sinclair, Young, and the Improvement of the Highlands, New and Old," in *Transatlantic Rebels: Agrarian Radicalism in Comparative Context*, ed. James Scott and Thomas Summerhill (East Lansing: Michigan State University Press, 2004), 92; R. J. Adam, ed., *Papers on Sutherland Estate Management, 1802–1816*, 2 vols. (Edinburgh: Constable, 1972), 2:71; Charles D. Waterston, "Late Enlightenment Science and Generalism: The Case of Sir George Steuart Mackenzie of Coul, 1780–1848," in *Science and Medicine in the Scottish Enlightenment*, ed. C. W. J. Withers and P. Wood (Edinburgh: Birlinn, 2002), 307–8.

The factors who managed the Sutherland Clearances were avid readers of the agricultural literature, including the works of John Sinclair; see Eric Richards, *Patrick Sellar and the Highland Clearances: Homicide, Eviction and the Price of Progress* (Edinburgh: Polygon at Edinburgh University Press, 1999), 297.
11. *Letters of George Dempster*, 208, 216, 246, 251; Huntington Library, PU 174; Anthony Cooke, *The Rise and Fall of the Scottish Cotton Industry, 1778–1914* (Manchester: Manchester University Press, 2010), 4, 35; EUL, La II 379, 363–65, 368–69; *The Bee* 4 (August 24, 1791): 255–56; NAS, RH4/49/2 258, 278, 280, 285, 319; Andrew Munro Lang, *A Life of George Dempster, Scottish M.P. of Dunnichen (1732–1818)* (Lewiston: Edwin Mellen, 1998), 262–66; NLS, MS 9370, 115.
12. James Headrick, *Essay on the Various Modes of Bringing Waste Lands into a State Fit for Cultivation, and Improving Their Natural Productions* (Dublin, 1801), 25–26. Notice Headrick's comment that "wild land," when turned up "for the first time," should be dug with a spade.
13. EUL, La III 379, 355–57; EUL, Gen 873/III, 183, 193, 195; NLS, MS 6602, 22–23; NAS, RH4/49/2, 272, 364.
14. Sinclair, *General View of the Agriculture of the Northern Counties*, 132, 151–52, 158–59; Rev. Mr. Alexander Falconer, "Parish of Edderachylis," *OSA*, 6:288–89; on cottages as a social ideal, see Sarah Lloyd, "Cottage Conversations: Poverty and Manly Independence in Eighteenth-Century England," *Past and Present* 104 (August 2004): 69–108; and John Crowley, "From Luxury to Comfort and Back Again: Landscape Architecture and the Cottage in Britain and America," in *Luxury in the Eighteenth Century: Debates, Desires and Delectable Goods*, ed. Maxine Berg and Elizabeth Eger (London: Palgrave Macmillan, 2003), 135–50.
15. Sinclair, *General View of the Agriculture of the Northern Counties*, 31, 57–59, 71–72, 111; Adam, *Papers on Sutherland Estate Management*, 1:30, 64, 151, 166–67, 179–80, 202–4, 222–23, 229, 2:70–71, 78, 144–45; Sinclair, *Hints Submitted to the Consideration of the Select Committee, to Whom the Survey and Report of the Coasts and Central Highlands of Scotland . . . Including Some Observations on the Advantages of Domestic Colonization* (London, 1803); Sinclair, *Observations on the Means of Enabling a Cottager to Keep a Cow by the Produce of a Small Portion of Arable Land* (London, 1801), 12; Sinclair, *Essays on Miscellaneous Subjects*, 214, 226–28 (little farmers).
16. Christopher Tait, *An Account of the Peat Mosses of Kincardine and Flanders in Perthshire: From the Transactions of the Royal Society of Edinburgh* (Edinburgh, 1792); James Anderson, *A Practical Treatise on Peat Moss: Considered as in Its Natural State Fitted for Affording Fuel, or as Susceptible of Being Converted into Mold Capable of Yielding Abundant Crops of Useful Produce: with Full Directions for Converting It from the State of Peat into That of Mold, and Afterwards Cultivating It as a Soil* (Edinburgh, 1794); Archibald Cochrane [Earl of Dundonald], *A Treatise, Shewing the Intimate Connection That Subsists Between Agriculture and Chemistry* (Edinburgh, 1795); *An Account of the Improvement of Moss . . .*, 2nd ed. (Dunse, 1797); *The Anti-Jacobin Review and Magazine; or, Monthly Politique and Literary Censor* (London, 1800), 48–50; Headrick, *Essay on the Various Modes*; Lord Meadowbank [Allan Maconochie], *Directions for Making Compost Dunghills from Peat-Moss* (Edinburgh, 1802); John

Walker, "An Essay on Peat, Containing an Account of Its Origin, of Its Chymical Principles, and General Properties; Its Properties as a Manure, and as a Manured Soil; The Different Methods of Its Cultivation; Its Usefulness in Plantation and Gardening, and as a Fuel," *THSS*, vol. 2 (Edinburgh, 1803), 1–137; William Aiton, *A Treatise on the Origin, Qualities, and Cultivation of Moss-Earth* . . . (Air, 1811); Robert Rennie, *Essays on the Natural History and Origin of Peat Moss* (Edinburgh, 1807); John Naismith, "An Essay on Peat, Its Properties and Uses," *THSS*, vol. 3 (Edinburgh, 1807), 17–85; [Allan Maconochie], *Directions for Preparing Manure from Peat: Instructions for Foresters* (Edinburgh, 1815); Andrew Steele, *The Natural and Agricultural History of Peat-Moss or Turf-Bog* (Edinburgh, 1826); John Sinclair, *On the Means of Improving the Condition of the Industrious Labourers in Husbandry, and Effectually Relieving Their Distresses* (Edinburgh, 1831). See also T. C. Smout, *Nature Contested: Environmental History in Scotland and Northern England Since 1600* (Edinburgh: Edinburgh University Press, 2000), 20. See also Smout, "The Improvers and the Scottish Environment: Soils, Bogs and Woods," in *Eighteenth-Century Scotland: New Perspectives*, ed. T. M. Devine and J. R. Young (East Linton, UK: Tuckwell, 1999), 217–19.

17. John Ehrman, *The Younger Pitt: The Reluctant Transition* (Stanford, CA: Stanford University Press, 1983), 467–69; John Gascoigne, *Science in the Service of Empire: Joseph Banks, the British State and the Uses of Science in the Age of Revolution* (Cambridge: Cambridge University Press, 1998), 128; Michael Duffy, *The Younger Pitt* (London: Longman, 2000), 146–47; Mitchison, *Agricultural Sir John*, 137–58.

18. Sinclair, *Essays on Miscellaneous Subjects*, 3, 18; Sinclair, *Account of the Origin of the Board of Agriculture, and Its Progress for Three Years After Its Establishment; By the President* (London, 1796), 48–49; Sinclair originally wanted John Walker to write a *General View of the Agriculture of the Hebrides*, but the task fell to James Macdonald instead, see 51; Ian Hacking, *The Taming of Chance* (Cambridge: Cambridge University Press, 1990), 26–28.

19. "Report from the Committee on the Cultivation and Improvement of Waste Lands [1797]," *Reports from Committees of the House of Commons*, 9:225; Mitchison, *Agricultural Sir John*, 157.

20. Sinclair's computation of the national acreage used the Scottish measure of an acre, which was 1.3 times larger than the English equivalent. Mitchison, *Agricultural Sir John*, 154–57, 170–72, 179, 181, 205–7; Sinclair, *Account of the Origin of the Board of Agriculture*, 17, 22 (acreage).

21. Sinclair, Account of the Origin of the Board of Agriculture, "Appendix K: Substance of Sir John Sinclair's Address to the Board of Agriculture, on Tuesday the Twenty-ninth of July 1794," 57–58 (on Vancouver's survey); Charles Vancouver, *General View of the Agriculture in the County of Cambridge* (London, 1794), 193.

22. *Report of the Committee Appointed by the Board of Agriculture to Take into Consideration the State of Waste Lands and Common Fields of This Kingdom* (London, 1795), 15–17 (new numbers from General Reports, Scottish acres on 14); Sinclair, *Address to the Members of the Board of Agriculture on the Subject of Waste Lands of This Kingdom* (London, 1795), 7–8 (acreage in 1795).

23. *The First Report from the Select Committee . . . Appointed to Take into Consideration the Means of Promoting the Cultivation and Improvement of the Waste, Unincloused, and Unproductive Lands* (London, 1796), 10–12; *Reports from Committees of the House of Commons*, 9:223–24.
24. *Reports from Committees of the House of Commons*, 9:223.
25. [T. R. Malthus], *An Essay on the Principle of Population, as It Affects the Future Improvement of Society* . . . (London, 1798) (hereafter cited as Malthus 1798); Malthus, *An Essay on the Principle of Population; or, A View of Its Past and Present Effects on Human Happiness* . . . (London, 1803), 465, 481–82.
26. Malthus 1798, 20–22, 315; Malthus 1803, 6; Boyd Hilton, *The Age of Atonement: The Evangelical Influence on Social and Economic Thought, 1785–1865* (Oxford: Oxford University Press, 1992), 376–77.
27. For Middleton and the timber survey, see chapter 6. For Williams and Macnab, see chapter 7. On agricultural surveys, see W. E. Minchinton, "Agricultural Returns and the Government During the Napoleonic Wars," *AHR* 1, no. 1 (1953): 29–43; Frederick Morton Eden, *The State of the Poor; or, An History of the Labouring Classes in England* . . ., 3 vols. (London, 1797), 1:xvii, xx. Another strategic liability was the hemp supply for the navy. Middleton warned William Pitt in 1786 about the danger of depending on foreign or colonial supplies of hemp. Sinclair in turn proposed three years later that the entire import of the naval store, worth £400,000 per annum, could be replaced with plantations in the Hebrides and Highlands: "The whole Hemp consumed by Great Britain might be produced on 50,000 Scotch acres." See John K. Laughton, ed., *Letters and Papers of Charles, Lord Barham, 1758–1813*, vol. 2 (London, 1909), 222–223; NAS, GD9/3, 644–45.
28. Ted McCormick, *William Petty and the Ambitions of Political Arithmetic* (Oxford: Oxford University Press, 2011), 183; Joyce Appleby, *Economic Thought and Ideology in Seventeenth-Century England* (Princeton, NJ: Princeton University Press, 1978), 135; E. A. J. Johnson, *Predecessors of Adam Smith: The Growth of British Economic Thought* (New York: Prentice Hall, 1937), 120–24; Andrea Rusnock, *Vital Accounts: Quantifying Health and Population in Eighteenth-Century England and France* (Cambridge: Cambridge University Press, 2002); Richard Cantillon, *Essai sur la nature du commerce en général* (London, 1755), 49; Cohen, *How Many People Can the Earth Support?* 212, 402–4. One *arpent* amounted to a little less than one English acre.
29. Bayly, *Imperial Meridian*; Colley, *Britons*; Roger Wells, *Wretched Faces*. On hemp imports, see BL, Add MS 41079, f. 44; NLS, Acc. 11612; and Robert Wissett, *A Treatise on Hemp* (London, 1808).
30. Wrigley, *Energy and the English Industrial Revolution*, 99, 208; Joseph Hume quoted in Boyd Hilton, *A Mad, Bad and Dangerous People? England, 1783–1846* (Oxford: Oxford University Press, 2006), 546.
31. Brinley Thomas, *The Industrial Revolution and the Atlantic Economy: Selected Essays* (London: Routledge 1993), 60, 78, 86–87; Kenneth Pomeranz, *The Great Divergence: China, Europe, and the Making of the Modern World Economy* (Princeton, NJ: Princeton University Press, 2000) 26, 216–17, 220–21 (he defines these pressures as "quasi-Malthusian"—that is, a "serious obstacle to large amounts of further growth,"

26); Mauro Ambrosoli, *The Wild and the Sown* (Cambridge: Cambridge University Press, 1997), 392–95, 412; Ralph Davis, *The Industrial Revolution and British Overseas Trade* (Leicester: Leicester University Press, 1979), 111–15, 125; James Belich, *Replenishing the Earth: The Settler Revolution and the Rise of Anglo-World, 1783–1939* (Oxford: Oxford University Press, 2010), 52. See also Wrigley, *Energy and the English Industrial Revolution*, 32, 39, 87.

32. James Headrick, "Suggestions Respecting Various Improvements in the Highlands of Scotland," THSS, 2:469.

Chapter 10. "A Stationary Condition for Ever"

1. J. M. Bumsted, *The People's Clearance: Highland Emigration to British North America, 1770–1815* (Edinburgh: Edinburgh University Press, 1982).
2. Donald Worster, *Nature's Economy: A History of Ecological Ideas*, 2nd ed. (Cambridge: Cambridge University Press, 1994), 2; T. C. Smout, *Nature Contested: Environmental History in Scotland and Northern England Since 1600* (Edinburgh: Edinburgh University Press, 2000), 7–10.
3. See, e.g., John Wesley Powell, *The Arid Lands* [1878](Lincoln, NE: Bison Books, 2005); and Jared Diamond, *Collapse: How Societies Choose to Fail or Succeed* (New York: Penguin, 2005).
4. NAS, RH4/188/1–2, "Sederunt Book 3," 443–44, also 453, 498, 531–35, 555–68, 665; NAS, GD51/5/52; NLS, Adv 35.6.18; Bumsted, *People's Clearance*, 143.
5. NAS, GD51/5/52; NLS, MS 9646, *On Emigration from the Scottish Highlands and Islands*; Rosalind Mitchison, *Agricultural Sir John: The Life of Sir John Sinclair of Ulbster, 1754–1835* (London: Geoffrey Bles, 1962), 182; John Walker, "An Essay on Peat, Containing an Account of Its Origin, of Its Chymical Principles, and General Properties; Its Properties as a Manure, and as a Manured Soil; The Different Methods of Its Cultivation; Its Usefulness in Plantation and Gardening, and as a Fuel," THSS, vol. 2 (Edinburgh, 1803), 1–137; James Anderson, *Two Letters to Sir John Sinclair . . . on the Subject of Draining Wet and Boggy Lands* (Edinburgh, 1796), 8–13, 22–31; Anderson, "Letter from Dr Anderson Respecting the Prevention of Emigration and Improving the Highlands and Western Isles of Scotland," in Robert Fraser, *Letter to the Rt. Hon. Charles Abbot, Speaker of the House of Commons, Containing an Inquiry into the Most Effectual Means of the Improvement* (London, 1803); Anderson, *Recreations in Agriculture . . .* (London, 1799–1802). The death of his Scottish wife may also have contributed to Anderson's decision to leave for England; see *The Papers of George Washington, The Retirement Series, March 1797–December 1799*, ed. Dorothy Twohig, 4 vols. (Charlottesville: University Press of Virginia, 1998–99), 1:198; Dempster's name is mentioned only once in the Highland Society Sederunt Books, 1800–1808.
6. Mackenzie, *The Man of Feeling* (New York: Oxford University Press, 2001), 65–66, 75–76. On the "cottage politics" of Robert Burns, see Nigel Leask, *Robert Burns and Pastoral: Poetry and Improvement in Late Eighteenth-Century Scotland* (Oxford: Oxford University Press, 2010).

7. NAS, GD51/5/52; NLS, Adv 35.6.18, "State of Emigration from the Highlands of Scotland, Its Extent, Causes, and Proposed Remedy, Anonymous," 20; NLS, MS 9646, *On Emigration from the Scottish Highlands and Isles* [attributed to E. S. Fraser], 5; NAS, RH4/188/1, "Sederunt Book 3," 532; Walker, "Essay on Peat"; James Headrick, "Suggestions Respecting Various Improvements in the Highlands of Scotland," *THSS*, 2:433–69. The Walker and Headrick essays were contributions to the same debate but may not have been read by Melville.
8. NAS, GD51/5/52, esp. 185; NLS, MS 9646,, 59, 103, 111, 139, 171.
9. Andrew Mackillop, *"More Fruitful than the Soil": Army, Empire and the Scottish Highlands, 1715–1815* (East Linton, UK: Tuckwell, 2000), 200, 243–44; Heather Streets, "Identity in the Highland Regiments in the Nineteenth Century: Soldier, Region, Nation," in *Fighting for Identity: Scottish Military Experience, c. 1550–1900*, ed. Steve Murdoch and Andrew Mackillop (Leiden: Brill, 2002); NAS, RH4/188/1, "Sederunt Book 3," 139–41.
10. NAS, GD51/5/52/4.
11. NAS, GD51/5/52/4; cf. NLS, MS 9646, 147 (spade husbandry optimal for poor land); Thomas Pennant, *A Tour in Scotland and Voyage to the Hebrides, 1772*, ed. Andrew Simmons (Edinburgh: Birlinn, 1998), 368–69; John Knox, *A View of the British Empire, More Especially Scotland . . .*, 2 vols. (London, 1784), 14.
12. NAS, GD112/47/2/3, GD112/12/1/5, 17–19; Robert Fraser, *A Letter to the Rt. Hon. Charles Abbot, Speaker of the House of Commons, Containing an Inquiry into the Most Effectual Means of the Improvement* (London, 1803), 15, 37, 49, 73–74; for the Queries of 1787, see chapter 4; Mackillop, *"More Fruitful than the Soil,"* 112–23.
13. NAS, RH4/188/1, "Sederunt Book 3," 153; NAS, RH4/188/2, "Sederunt Book 4," 37, 43–48, 50–51, 172; NAS, GD248/703/2/1; Mitchison, *Agricultural Sir John*, 212–15; John Sinclair et al., *The Poems of Ossian . . .*, 3 vols. (London, 1807).
14. James Headrick, *Report on the Island of Lewis . . . Contained in a Letter to the Right Honorable Lord Seaforth, the Proprietor* (Edinburgh, 1800); Headrick, *Essay on the Various Modes of Bringing Waste Lands into a State Fit for Cultivation, and Improving their Natural Productions* (Dublin, 1801); *THSS*, 2:455, 457–58, 461–64, 469; for the date of this piece, see *THSS*, 2:435: "last year, (1800,)"; J. H. Burns, "Twilight of the Enlightenment: James Headrick (1759–1841)," *Scottish Historical Review* 81, no. 212 (2002): 194–96; for Headrick's Foxite Whig sympathies, see NLS, MSS 682, 126.
15. Walker, "Essay on Peat"; "Sederunt Book 3," 276, 412; EUL, Gen 874/IV, 51–52; EUL, La III 352/1b, 181.
16. Walker, "Essay on Peat," 48–55.
17. Walker, "Essay on Peat," 9–14, 62–72, 90–94; *Report on the Hebrides*, 101–2.
18. Walker, "Essay on Peat," 83, 102–3.
19. William Aiton, *A Treatise on the Origin, Qualities, and Cultivation of Moss-Earth* (Glasgow, 1805), 25 (definition of peat moss) (hereafter cited as Aiton 1805); *A Treatise on the Origin, Qualities, and Cultivation of Moss-Earth . . .* (Air, 1811), 304 (Blair Drummond) (hereafter cited as Aiton 1811).
20. Aiton 1805, title page (poem), 2–7 (climate change); Aiton 1811, 187–89 (fir trees in mosses and moss as soil).

21. Aiton 1811, xxi–xiv (wasteland acreage), 344–45 (food imports).
22. Aiton 1811, 342–43.
23. *Edinburgh Review* 4, no. 7 (1804): 63–75, esp. 63, 66, 68, 72; *THSS*, vol. 2; Biancamaria Fontana, *Rethinking the Politics of Commercial Society: The* Edinburgh Review, *1802–1832* (Cambridge: Cambridge University Press, 1985).
24. *Edinburgh Review* 4, no. 7 (1804): 63–65, 75.
25. *Edinburgh Review* 4, no. 7 (1804): 65, 73; James Anderson, *Observations on the Means of Exciting a Spirit of National Industry . . .* (Edinburgh, 1777), 192; *THSS*, 2:364–69.
26. *Edinburgh Review* 7, no. 13 (1805): 185–202, quotations on 190, 192; the Smith quotation also appears in Thomas Douglas, *Observations on the Present State of the Highlands of Scotland* (Edinburgh, 1805), 36; *WN*, 1:243.
27. Douglas, *Observations*, 3, 71–73, 88–89 (right to carry labor freely), 116, 168, 175; Eric Richards, *The Highland Clearances* (Edinburgh: Birlinn, 2002), 5; Richards, *Patrick Sellar and the Highland Clearances: Homicide, Eviction and the Price of Progress* (Edinburgh: Polygon at Edinburgh University Press, 1999), 115, 122, 233–35; Lucille H. Campey, *The Silver Chief: Lord Selkirk and the Scottish Pioneers of Belfast, Baldoon and Red River* (Toronto: Natural Heritage, 2003), 10, 39; Barbara C. Murison, "Poverty, Philanthropy and Emigration to British North America: Changing Attitudes in Scotland in the Early Nineteenth Century," *British Journal of Canadian Studies* 2, no. 2 (1987): 263–88.
28. Douglas, *Observations*, 25–31 (Highlands), 34–35 (superfluous mouths), 45–47, 58, 87 (silent migration); Malthus, *An Essay on the Principle of Population; or, A View of Its Past and Present Effects on Human Happiness . . .* (London, 1803), 74–75, 349 (hereafter cited as Malthus 1803). On the respective energy content of coal and peat, see E. A. Wrigley, *Energy and the English Industrial Revolution* (Cambridge: Cambridge University Press, 2010), 23.
29. Douglas, *Observations*, 87 (drain), 112–14, 117, 125; Malthus 1803, 7, 326. Presumably, the Highland population would fall to a lower maximum limit once sheep farms had been introduced.
30. Douglas, *Observations*, 121–25; Richards, *Highland Clearances*, 86–91.
31. Douglas, *Observations*, 68, 80, 97, 99–100.
32. Douglas, *Observations*, 3, 68, 70, 72, 205, 209–10.
33. Malthus 1803, 394; Malthus, *Reply to the Chief Objections Which Have Been Urged Against the Essay on the Principle of Population; Published in an Appendix to the Third Edition* (London, 1806), 8, 21; Malthus, *Essay on the Principle of Population*, 5th ed. with Important Additions, 3 vols. (London, 1817), 2:305; R. N. Ghosh, "Malthus on Emigration and Colonization: Letters to Wilmot-Horton," *Economica*, n.s., 30, no. 117 (1963): 61.
34. *The Agricultural Magazine, or Farmers' Monthly Journal of Husbandry and Rural Affairs . . . 1808* (London, 1808), 213; Nathaniel Atcheson, *American Encroachments on British rights; or, Observations on the Importance of the British North American Colonies, and on the Late Treaties . . .* (London, 1808), xxxix; J. C. Loudon, *An Immediate, and Effectual Mode, of Raising the Rental of the Landed Property of England; and Rendering Great Britain Independent of Other . . .* (London, 1808), 51;

James Gordon, *Eight Letters on the Subject of the Earl of Selkirk's Pamphlet on Highland Emigration: as They Lately Appeared Under the Signature of Amicus in One of the Edinburgh Newspapers*, 2nd ed., with supplementary remarks (Edinburgh, 1806), 6–7; J. M. Bumsted, "Another Look at the Founder: Lord Selkirk as Political Economist," in *Thomas Scott's Body, and Other Essays in Early Manitoba History* (Winnipeg: University of Manitoba Press, 2000), 48–49; Richards, *Patrick Sellar and the Highland Clearances*, 103–4.

35. Gordon, *Eight Letters*, 17–18, 31–32, 34–35, 37; Robert Brown, *Strictures and Remarks on the Earl of Selkirk's Observations on the Present State of the Highlands of Scotland* (Edinburgh, 1806), 42; Anonymous, *Remarks on the Earl of Selkirk's Observations on the Present State of the Highlands of Scotland, with a View of the Causes and Probable Consequences of Emigration* (Edinburgh, 1806), 61–62.
36. Gordon, *Eight Letters*, 32.
37. Brown, *Strictures and Remarks*, 42–44, 70–71, n.b. "crofting system" on 42.
38. Brown, *Strictures and Remarks*, 94. Contrast with Bumsted, *People's Clearance*, 108.
39. Gordon, *Eight Letters*, 28, 36; Brown, *Strictures and Remarks*, 79–80, 82; *Remarks on the Earl of Selkirk's Observations*, 63, 244, 248; Douglas, *Observations*, 111.
40. Arthur Young, *The Question of Scarcity Plainly Stated, and Remedies Considered* (London 1800), 76–77; John Sinclair, *Observations on the Means of Enabling a Cottager to Keep a Cow by the Produce of a Small Portion of Arable Land* (London, 1801); John Walker, "A Memorial Concerning the Present Scarcity of Grain in Scotland," in *Essays on Natural History and Rural Economy* (Edinburgh, 1812), 620–21; cf. *WN*, 1:133; Jeremy Burchardt, *The Allotment Movement in England, 1793–1873* (Woodbridge: Boydell, 2002), 11–12 (note that Burchardt makes no mention of Scottish crofting as a form of tenure and social experiment closely related to his subject); T. R. Malthus 1803, 570–80; Robert Owen, *Report to the County of Lanark of a Plan for Relieving Public Distress and Removing Discontent . . .* (Glasgow, 1821), 10–11, 19; William Cobbett, *Rural Rides* (London, 1830), 74; C. E. Trevelyan, *The Irish Crisis: Reprinted from the* Edinburgh Review *No CLXXV January 1848* (London, 1848), 4–9.
41. T. M. Devine, *The Great Highland Famine: Hunger, Emigration and the Scottish Highlands in the Nineteenth Century* (Edinburgh: John Donald, 1988), 125, 251; compare with the discussion of Indian famine relief in chapter 5.
42. Annette Smith, *The Jacobite Estates of the Forty-Five* (Edinburgh: John Donald, 1982), 210; John Sinclair, *Hints Submitted to the Consideration of the Select Committee, to Whom the Survey and Report of the Coasts and Central Highlands of Scotland . . . Including Some Observations on the Advantages of Domestic Colonization* (London, 1803), 7; *Select Committee on Survey and Report of Coasts and Central Highlands of Scotland; Third Report* ([London], 1803), 27, 48–49; *Scots Magazine* (December 1805): 889–90; *A Survey and Report of the Coasts and Central Highlands of Scotland; Made by the Command of the Right Honourable the Lords Commissioners of His Majesty's Treasury, in the Autumn of 1802: by Thomas Telford, Civil Engineer, Edin. F.R.S.* (London, 1803), 20.
43. NAS, GD9/3, 466, GD112/47/2/1, 3, GD112/12/1/5, 17–19; *A Survey and Report . . . by Thomas Telford*, 8, 15, 17, 22–27.

44. WN, 1:163, 179, 2:726–30; Douglas, *Observations*, 58.
45. Anthony Burton, *Thomas Telford* (London: Aurum, 2000), 83–100; Richards, *Highland Clearances*, 109; Michael Fry, The *Dundas Despotism* (Edinburgh: Edinburgh University Press, 1992), 246–48; T. M. Devine, *Scotland's Empire, 1600–1815* (London: Penguin, 2003), 340; Bruce Lenman, *An Economic History of Modern Scotland, 1660–1976* (Hamden, CT: Archon Books, 1977), 150.
46. Richards, *Patrick Sellar and the Highland Clearances*, 54, 60–61, 103–4, 115, 122, 179, 233–35, 264; Richards, *Highland Clearances*, 129–30, 153–54, 160; John Kington, "Weather Patterns over Europe in 1816," in *The Year Without a Summer? World Climate in 1816*, ed. C. R. Harrington (Ottawa: Canadian Museum of Nature, 1992), 368–69.
47. Karen O'Brien, "Colonial Emigration, Public Policy and Tory Romanticism, 1783–1830" in *Lineages of Empire: The Historical Roots of British Imperialist Thought*, ed. Duncan Kelly (Oxford: Oxford University Press, 2009), 155, 161–79; Michael E. Vance, "The Politics of Emigration: Scotland and Assisted Emigration to Upper Canada, 1815–26," in *Scottish Emigration and Scottish Society*, ed. T. M. Devine (Edinburgh: John Donald, 1992), 38–45.
48. Hugh Miller, *Sutherland as It Was and Is, or, How a Country May Be Ruined* (Edinburgh, 1843) 14–15; Eric Richards, "Hugh Miller and Resistance to the Highland Clearances," in *Celebrating the Life and Times of Hugh Miller*, ed. Lester Borley (Cromarty: Cromarty Arts Trust, 2003), 59; William Thomas Thornton, *Over-Population and Its Remedies* (London, 1846), 412; Alexander Mackenzie, *The History of the Highland Clearances* (Inverness, 1883), 32–33, 165, 181; Francis Napier, "The Highland Crofters: A Vindication of the Report of the Crofters' Commission," *Nineteenth Century* 17 (1886): 447, 457; Allan W. MacColl, *Land, Faith and the Crofting Community: Christianity and Social Criticism in the Highlands of Scotland, 1843–1893* (Edinburgh: Edinburgh University Press, 2006), 204–5; Ewan Cameron, *Land for the People: The British Government and the Scottish Highlands, 1880–1925* (East Linton, UK: Tuckwell, 1996), 19–21.

Conclusion

1. On the era of sporting estates, see T. C. Smout, *Nature Contested* (Edinburgh: Edinburgh University Press, 2000), 131–38; and Eric Richards, *The Highland Clearances* (Edinburgh: Birlinn, 2003), 288–90.
2. Compare Nicholas Xenos, *Scarcity and Modernity* (London: Routledge, 1989), 35: "Abundance is the conceptual twin of scarcity."
3. John Williams, *The Natural History of the Mineral Kingdom*, 2 vols. (Edinburgh, 1789), 1:173.
4. Donald Winch, *Wealth and Life: Essays on the Intellectual History of Political Economy in Britain, 1848–1914* (Cambridge: Cambridge University Press, 2009), 63–68; William Stanley Jevons, *The Coal Question: An Inquiry Concerning the Progress of the Nation, and the Probably Exhaustion of Our Coal-Mines*, 3rd ed. rev.

(New York: Augustus M. Kelley, 1965), 15–18; John Stuart Mill, *Principles of Political Economy* (Fairfield, NJ: August Kelley, 1987), 264, 338 (the critique of "cottier system" in Ireland and Scotland), 746–51 (the stationary state); Murray Milgate and Shannon C. Stimson, *After Adam Smith: A Century of Transformation in Politics and Political Economy* (Princeton, NJ: Princeton University Press, 2009), 191–210; John Ruskin, *Fors Clavigera*, "Letter 29," in *Works of John Ruskin*, vol. 27, ed. E. T. Cook and Alexander Wedderburn (London: George Allen, 1907), 527; T. R. Malthus, *An Essay on the Principle of Population; or, A View of Its Past and Present Effects on Human Happiness . . .* (London, 1803), 75, 349.

5. E. A. Wrigley, *Energy and the English Industrial Revolution* (Cambridge: Cambridge University Press, 2010), 1–2; Björn-Ola Linnér, *Return of Malthus: Environmentalism and Postwar Population—Resource Crises* (Isle of Harris, UK: White Horse Press, 2004); Timothy Mitchell, Carbon *Democracy: Political Power in the Age of Oil* (New York: Verso, 2011); Donella Meadows, Jorgen Randers, and Dennis Meadows, *Limits to Growth: The 30-Year Update* (White River Junction, VT: Chelsea Green, 2004); Will Steffen, Paul J. Crutzen, and John R. McNeill, "The Anthropocene: Are Humans Now Overwhelming the Great Forces of Nature?" *Ambio* 36, no. 8 (2007): 614–21; Johan Rockström et al., "Planetary Boundaries: Exploring the Safe Operating Space for Humanity," *Ecology and Society* 14, no. 2 (2009): 1–33; David Archer, *The Long Thaw: How Humans are Changing the Next 100,000 Years of Earth's Climate* (Princeton, NJ: Princeton University Press, 2009); Tim Jackson, *Prosperity Without Growth: Economics for a Finite Planet* (New York: Earthscan, 2009); James Gustave Speth, *The Bridge at the Edge of the World: Capitalism, the Environment and Crossing from Crisis to Sustainability* (New Haven: Yale University Press, 2008).

Index

Aberdeen, 102, 110, 210
Aberdeenshire, 70, 93, 207, 223
abolitionism, 94, 107, 109, 122, 151
acclimatization, 48, 55, 59–63, 66–68, 71, 80–83, 86–87, 96, 103, 108, 150, 152, 206, 262
Africa, 58, 81, 156, 209
Agricultural Society of Edinburgh, 95
Aiton, William, 33–34, 222, 233, 243–45, 253
allotments, 215, 256, 327n40
Ambirajan, S., 140
American War of Independence (American Revolutionary War), 94, 107, 109–10, 119, 132, 144, 157, 181, 202, 213, 216, 229
anachronism, 15
Anderson, Alexander, 66
Anderson, James: acclimatization, 77, 83, 87–89, 93–94; biography, 93–94, 102–3, 234; British Fisheries Society, 16, 48, 54, 94, 104–7, 111–12, 145–46; British Wool Society, 87, 120, 205–11; climate, 74–75, 77; coal duties, 171–72, 177–80; critique of empire, 88–89, 103–4; larch, 147–48, 150–51, 153; Linnaeus, 57; sheep farms, 202–3; *The Bee*, 67, 107–9; wool manufactures, 103, 247

Anderson, James (of Madras), 138–39
Anderson, John, 110
Angus, 151, 177, 240
Annals of Agriculture, 211
Argyll, 79, 152, 178, 201, 210, 225, 237
Arnold, David, 138
Arran, 47, 65, 73, 240
asafetida, 66, 89, 108
Ashworth, William, 14
Atholl estate, 2, 66, 77, 89, 150, 153–55, 159, 162, 190, 201
Atkins, John, 160
aurochs (wild cattle), 199
autarky: coal, 187; food production, 55, 222, 230, 244; hemp, 55, 217, 240; imperial, 4, 157–60, 162–63; indigenous, 58–59, 98–100; national, 4, 44, 50, 149, 151, 154–55, 163, 209, 213, 215–17, 223, 226, 231–32, 240, 244; timber supply, 147, 154–55, 163, 217; wool, 209

Bacon, Francis, 223
Bald, Robert, 181, 183–84, 187
Baltic region, 58, 149, 152, 154, 156, 161–63, 229, 240, 258
Banks, Joseph, 51–52, 57, 62, 67, 85–88, 123, 126–27, 138, 159, 198, 206, 209
Barton, Gregory, 7, 140, 161

331

bear (six-rowed barley, *Hordeum vulgare*), 1–2, 37, 76, 84–85, 246
Beaufoy, Henry, 104, 106, 107, 110, 122, 144, 145, 167, 202, 203
Beddoes, Thomas, 215
beetles, 200–201
Belich, James, 230
Bengal, 49, 95, 126, 136–40, 146, 232
Bentham, Jeremy, 102, 107, 136
Berchtold, Leopold, 55
Berg, Maxine, 284–85n28
Bielke, Sten Carl, 123
Black, Joseph, 17, 65, 119, 130, 208, 220–21, 240
blackfaced sheep, 201, 210–11
Blair, Hugh, 16, 17, 30
Blair Atholl, 201
Blair Drummond, 11, 32–34, 120, 217, 242, 244–45
Board for the Annexed Estates: 28–29; accommodation policy, 31–32, 37–38, 40, 42; assimilation policy, 28–29, 39, 278n36; dismantled, 41, 141; expertise, 47–49, 85–86, 93, 95–97, 168–71; military recruitment, 28, 31–32, 39–40
Board of Agriculture, 56, 77, 79, 109, 213–14, 217–19, 223–25
Board of Trustees for the Encouragement of Fisheries, Arts, and Manufactures in Scotland, 31, 33, 103, 109
Borgström, Georg, 264, 319n2
Boswell, James, 51–53, 70, 148
botanic gardens, 57, 61, 86, 123, 134, 138–39. *See also* Kew Gardens; Royal Botanic Garden of Edinburgh
Bottleneck Panic, 228–30
Boyle, Robert, 55
breadfruit, 86–87, 127
breeding, 25, 71, 81, 85, 124, 202; Gaels, 205, 236. *See also* sheep
British Fisheries Society, 2, 29, 46, 52, 122; coal duties, 167, 171–72; failure, 112, 117, 219; liberal critique of, 144–46, 250–51;

origin, 54, 93–94, 104–7, 110–11; queries of 1787, 112–16; remedy for sheep farming, 202–3, 205; spade husbandry, 114–15, 238, 254, 258–59; urban ideal, 111. *See also photo gallery image 6*
British Wool Society: acclimatization, 82, 209; civil cameralism and, 56; Joseph Banks and, 87–88; origin, 56, 93–94, 206; preserving Shetland breed, 205–8; spread of Cheviot breed, 210–12
Brora, 169–70, 172–73
Brown, Robert, 233, 252–55, 258
Buchanan, John Lanne, 54
Buchanan Hamilton, Francis, 54, 67, 95, 138–39, 160–61
Buckland, William, 183, 186
Buffon, Georges-Louis Leclerc de, 55, 72, 74, 127, 128, 130
Burke, Edmund, 50, 136
Burma, 158
Burnett, James (Lord Monboddo), 12, 17, 18, 20–23, 27, 35, 38, 110, 212, 218. *See also photo gallery image 1*

Caithness, 70, 106, 112, 116, 210–11, 219, 221–22, 243
Caledonian Canal, 2, 54, 239, 249, 257–60, 262
Caledonian Forest, 128, 152, 244
Callander, 79, 194, 218
Callendar, James Thomson, 107
cameralism: civil (Scottish), 56, 68, 147, 149, 224; Prussian, 55, 224; Swedish, 58–59, 99, 124
Campbell, Archibald (captain), 53
Campbell, Archibald (Third Duke of Argyll), 16, 28, 121
Campbell, Colin, 113
Campbell, John (Fifth Duke of Argyll), 54, 56, 74, 110, 113, 117, 119, 174, 177, 207–10, 237–38
Campbell, John (Fourth Earl of Breadalbane), 110, 112–13, 117, 207, 238–39, 258–59

Campbell, John (Third Earl of Breadalbane), 33
Campbelltown, 152
Canada, 74, 82, 163
Cape Breton, 175
Cape Colony, 67, 81, 128, 260
Carlyle, Alexander, 18–19
casa de la contratación, 127
caschrom (crooked spade), 35–38. See also *photo gallery image 3*
caterpillars, 198, 200
cattle, 11–12, 27, 31, 51, 62, 65, 77, 85, 93, 96, 113, 115–16, 120, 123–24, 129, 131, 133–34, 143–44, 149, 191–92, 195, 199–200, 202, 217, 220–22, 226, 232, 239, 243, 250, 254, 256, 258–59, 261
cheviot sheep, 68, 195, 201, 210–11, 219, 222, 240, 262
China, 59, 66–67, 72, 86, 89, 127, 190, 255, 259, 263
Church of Scotland (the Kirk), 16–18, 94, 168. *See also* clergy; General Assembly
civil society, 3–4, 14, 41, 44, 56, 94, 99, 109, 118, 122, 131, 239, 257
clanship (clans), 13, 15, 25, 31, 39, 40–41, 51, 98, 100, 246
clearances (dispossession), 2, 11, 15, 23, 25, 189–90, 201, 205, 214, 257, 262. *See also* Sutherland Clearances
clergy, 8, 16–17, 19, 23–24, 34–35, 47–48, 52, 54–58, 78–79, 93–94, 141, 152, 167, 177–78, 182, 186–88, 190, 206, 218, 243, 246
Clerk, John (Lord Eldin), 110, 118, 170–71, 184, 206
Clerk-Maxwell, George, 29, 168, 170
climate: amelioration of, 48, 60, 68, 70, 72–74, 108, 128–29, 244; character and, 18, 36, 41, 53, 63–64, 99; deterioration of, 77–80, 128, 136, 244, 264; Enlightenment theory of, 70–73; local, 72–74, 80, 97, 238, 246; microclimates and, 51, 72–73, 76, 207; northern, 2, 31, 59, 61–64, 66–67, 75–78, 87–88, 93, 103, 152, 168, 175, 200, 221, 246, 253; pasture and, 64, 74, 93, 103, 203, 247–48; popular memory and, 78–79; Providence and, 96; quantified, 70, 73, 78, 80; South Asia, 139–40; temperate, 74, 88, 160; uncertainty and controversy regarding, 2, 49, 70–71, 75–77, 88, 128, 210, 253; tropical, 73, 128–29, 139–40, 151, 159; zones of, 71–72, 88, 131–32
Club of Rome, 264
coal, 6, 57, 227; duties, 106–7, 114, 145, 177–82, 186; exhaustion, 173–74, 181–84, 228–29, 262–63, 311–12n9, 314n25; fisheries, 106, 172–73; ghost acres, 229; Highland, 142, 168–71, 179, 240, 247–49; husbandry, 174, 187; inexhaustible, 173, 181; peak, 167, 173–74, 249, 263; prospecting, 44, 48, 169–71, 173; quantified, 167, 185–86, 262–63; stock, 175, 263; substitute for wood fuel, 149, 174
Cochin-China (Vietnam), 161–62
cochineal, 127
Cochrane, Archibald (Earl of Dundonald), 176, 180, 187, 214–18, 220–22, 241
Coll, 35, 115
Colonsay, 52, 117
Columbian exchange, 127, 132
conservation, 7–8, 123, 125–28, 140, 147, 149, 161, 186–87, 206–8, 233
conservative Enlightenment, 13–14, 24, 33, 41, 93–94, 187, 189, 206. *See also* paternalism; population politics
consumption, 16, 40, 45–46, 59, 77, 135, 161, 167, 174–75, 179, 182, 185–86, 191, 213, 218–19, 226–27, 229, 240, 264
Cook, James, 44, 51, 86, 123, 241
Cooper, Alix, 5
Corn Laws, 144, 227, 240
cornucopianism: economics and, 186, 264; Scotland and, 1, 4, 44, 49, 262; South Asia and, 158, 160

cottars (cottagers), 19, 22–26, 28, 31–32, 38, 101, 143, 149, 203, 218, 221–22, 238, 247, 249, 250, 254, 256
cotton, 89, 108, 127
cotton manufactures, 209, 220, 245
Cowper, William, 69
crofting system, 3, 26, 34, 41, 176, 238, 242–44, 254–55, 258, 270n4, 279n43, 281n60, 298n49, 327n40
Cromarty, 79, 101, 169–70, 219
Cronon, William, 273n18
Cudbear, 89
Cullen, William, 17, 29, 47, 65, 94, 102, 107, 130, 190, 215
Cuvier, Georges, 197

Dale, David, 34, 245
d'Alembert, Jean Le Rond, 130
Dalrymple, Alexander, 138
Dalrymple, David (Lord Hailes), 17, 27–32, 39, 42, 148
Dalrymple, John, 27
Daly, Herman, 270n6
Darling, Frank Fraser, 176
Darwin, Erasmus, 61, 62, 84
Davis, Ralph, 230
degeneration, 82, 85; cattle, 51; division of labor, 38; flax, 64; luxury and, 53, 112, 218; New World, 72, 123–24, 128, 131; Shetland sheep, 207
Dempster, George, 29, 70, 74, 103, 107, 110, 111, 119, 141, 142, 145, 152, 162, 167, 189, 196, 201, 202, 204–6, 210, 218–21, 234, 240, 262
Denmark, 56, 74, 87, 206, 240
Derham, William, 59
Devine, Thomas Martin, 44–45, 111, 260
Diderot, Denis, 173
diet, 21, 63, 74, 86, 93, 100, 115, 129, 132, 256, 261
Dodgshon, Robert, 37
Don, George, 54
Douglas, Thomas (Fifth Earl of Selkirk), 231–32, 248–57, 259–62

drainage, 11, 56, 73–74, 101, 129, 184, 220–21, 234, 242, 244
Drayton, Richard, 125
drought, 136–39
Drummond, George, 33, 120
Dubos, Jean-Baptiste, 78
Dundas, Henry (Lord Melville): British Fisheries Society, 107, 110, 142; coal duties, 179–82; emigration crisis of 1803, 232–37, 239; famine of 1782, 141–42; memorandum on military recruitment, 39–42; repeals the Annexed Estates Act, 41; Scottish planting, 148, 161; sheep farming, 196, 201–3, 209; support for Highland Society of Edinburgh, 117, 119, 142; South Asia, 138, 158–62; timber supply, 147, 157–62
Dundas, Robert (of Arniston), 28
Dundas, Robert (Second Duke of Melville), 154–55, 162
Dunkeld, 153, 155
Dunnichen, 220, 240
Dutch Republic, 56, 69, 105–6, 111, 134, 144–45, 176, 228

eagles, 199, 208
earthquakes, 128, 139, 220
Easter Island, 233
East India Company, 87, 111, 136–38, 140, 160–61
ecological exchange, 38, 65–67, 70, 81–83, 86–87, 89, 94, 108, 123, 125–27, 132, 206, 291n26
ecological strain (resource strain), 4, 8, 101, 131, 158, 168, 190–93, 214, 228, 230, 233
ecology (economy of nature): 300n9; anti-imperial, 89; Arcadian, 8; cameralist, 123–24; conservative, 4, 14, 93–94; imperial, 8; island, 191–92; liberal (Whig), 93–94, 102, 122, 124, 136, 146, 149, 181, 260; local, 49, 97–97, 153; neo-European, 87; rival, 125, 232; sufficient, 261

economic growth, 4, 8, 16, 19, 47, 49, 59, 105, 114, 125, 131, 133–34, 148, 150, 214, 217, 230, 236, 263–64
Eddy, Matthew, 5
Eden, 24, 60
Eden, Sir Frederick Morton, 228
Eden, William (First Baron Auckland), 39
Edinburgh, 16–18, 39, 65, 109–10, 117, 121, 134, 154, 179, 182–83, 220, 237
Edinburgh Review, 130, 231–32, 245–48, 252, 259
Ehrlich, Paul, 264
Eigg, 78
Eisenstadt, Shmuel, 13
Elliot, Gilbert, 26, 28, 29, 32
Elphinstone, Montstuart, 140
Emerson, Roger, 16
emigration, 2, 20, 39–40, 45, 52–53, 55–56, 100, 103, 111–12, 179, 190, 194–96, 201–2, 218, 230–31, 233, 235–37, 241, 243, 253, 255–57, 258, 260; assisted, 189, 260–61; restrictions on, 26, 42, 233; salutary drain, 232, 248–52, 260, 263
empire, 125–26, 248; climate zones and, 88; conservation and, 7, 161; critique of, 2, 29, 59, 88–89, 103–4, 110–11, 230–31; end of, 186, 213; Highland participation in, 13; liberal reform of, 137, 142; natural history of, 49, 67, 86, 88, 125; peripheries of, 3–4, 257
empty world, 4, 270n6
enclosure, 1, 27, 31, 56, 74, 93, 207, 213, 218, 222–24, 227
energy revolution, 131, 168, 229
England, 3, 12, 14–15, 20, 23–24, 48–49, 69, 73–75, 103, 127, 134–35, 140, 151, 160, 171, 180, 182, 187, 196–97, 206–7, 211, 215, 225, 228–29, 238, 254
entail, 15, 26–27
environmental fragility, 3, 8, 68, 125–26, 131, 174, 181, 233, 262–64, 303n25
environmentalism, 4, 7–8, 233, 262–64, 270n7

environmental stability, 49, 59, 128, 131, 136, 140, 149
Erskine, David Steuart (Eleventh Earl of Buchan), 54, 102–3, 107, 173
Erskine, Henry, 214
Erskine, John Francis (Earl of Mar), 187
exhaustion, 4, 228, 262–64; coal, 173–74, 181–84, 228–29, 262, 311–12n9; peat, 101, 176–79; soil, 100, 124, 217; timber, 147, 151, 158, 161, 228–29
extinction: biological, 197–98; Shetland sheep, 205–9; cultural, 30, 202, 204, 235–36, 251
extirpation, 84–85, 196–200, 207, 220, 250

famine (subsistence crisis), 135, 227; Bengal, 136–38; Highland, 80, 141–42, 194, 257
Faujas de Saint-Fond, Barthélemy, 54, 121
Ferguson, Adam, 16, 19–20, 38, 42
Fergusson, Adam (of Kilkerran), 111
feudalism, 15, 25, 40, 52, 105–7, 126. *See also* entail
Finland, 60, 122
flax, 2, 33, 44, 64, 77, 83, 89, 93, 96, 103, 127, 204, 217, 220, 241, 247, 251
Fletcher, Andrew (Lord Milton), 28, 31–33, 42, 110
Fletcher, Andrew (of Saltoun), 13
floods, 78, 138–39
food chain, 6, 43, 123, 128, 188, 191–93, 198
forests: afforestation, 28, 74, 147–49, 151–52, 181, 187, 200, 244; deforestation, 7, 73–74, 128–29, 148–49, 151, 157, 175, 244; larch, 2, 44, 61, 68, 77, 89, 93–94, 108, 150–63; oak, 68, 89, 103, 149, 151–62; pine, 151–53, 158, 200; scientific forestry, 140; teak, 68, 89, 140, 147, 158–62
Forrest, Thomas, 139
Forster, Johann Reinhold, 52
Fort William, 2, 202, 257–58
foxes, 199, 208
France, 13, 68, 72, 74, 112, 123, 154, 157–59, 182, 213, 223, 228–29, 232, 240, 248

Franklin, Benjamin, 70, 72, 77, 106, 189–90, 227
Fraser, Archibald (of Lovat), 113, 172
Fraser, Edward S., 201, 235–36
Fraser, Robert, 172, 238
Frederick the Great, of Prussia, 224
free trade, 3, 102, 125, 131, 134–35, 137, 145, 149, 304n39
French Revolution, 13, 15, 94, 120, 213, 216
French Revolutionary and Napoleonic Wars, 2, 45, 158, 189, 214–15, 217
frontier, 273n18; American, 191–92, 251; Highland (internal, northern), 8, 176, 189, 201, 210–11, 225, 232, 240–44; Roman, 29; Swedish, 58
full world, 4, 270n6
future: demographic forecast, 227; exhaustion of coal, 173–74, 181–84, 228–29, 262–63, 311–12n9, 314n24; extinction of Gaelic culture, 30, 189, 246; postindustrial, 173–74, 186, 263; prospect, 51; resource husbandry of landowners, 147, 152, 155; resource husbandry of state, 157, 186–87; uncertainty, 48; urban Highlands, 112, 240

gardens and gardening: aristocratic status, 61, 150; Britain as garden, 193, 249, 255; skill and acclimatization, 60, 74, 82; spade culture and, 21; whole planet, 24; winter garden, 66
Garnett, Thomas, 54
Gascoigne, John, 86
General Assembly of the Kirk, 16, 94–95
gentry, 15, 18, 39, 46, 48, 95, 109, 117, 148, 197, 218, 250. *See also* landed interest
Germany, 56, 74, 82, 98, 199, 258
ghost acres, 163, 214, 226, 230, 263, 319n2
Gibson, Alexander, 140
Glasgow, 17–18, 36, 132, 134, 110, 170, 179, 220
Glorious Revolution, 14, 80, 104, 181, 197, 215

goats, 82, 115, 188–89, 191–93, 195
Golinski, Jan, 5
Gordon, James, 252–55
Goswami, Manu, 140
Gower, Elizabeth Leveson (Duchess of Sutherland), 29, 114, 117, 199, 205, 211, 219, 260–61
Graeme, Hugh, 1, 2, 31, 33
grain in the Highlands, 1, 6, 37, 76, 78–79, 83–84, 115, 141, 152, 220, 225, 247–48
grain trade, 129, 133–36, 139–40, 149, 157, 198, 213, 215, 223, 226, 228–30
Grant, Archibald, 15, 148
Grant, James (advocate), 115
Grant, James (of Grant), 113, 117, 141–42, 219, 237, 239
Grantown on Spey, 117, 219
Gray, Malcolm, 270n4
Great Glen, 211, 250
Greece, 99, 134, 139
Grove, Richard, 7–8

Hardin, Garrett, 264, 319n2
Harris, 195
Headrick, James, 54, 73, 80, 220, 222, 231, 235, 240, 247
hemp, 48, 55, 64, 66, 77, 83, 89, 97–98, 108, 127, 217, 228–29, 240, 323n27
herring, 43–44, 94, 104–5, 108, 111–12, 115, 122, 144–46, 240–41
herring bounties, 111, 122, 142, 144–45
Hertzberg, Ewald Friedrich von, 55, 224
hessian fly (*Mayetiola destructor*), 198, 200
Highlanders: diet, 93, 98, 115, 261; Gaelic language, 30; martial spirit, 30, 32, 39–40, 143, 204, 235, 239, 251; as a race, 202, 219–20, 235–36; virtues, 34, 36, 53, 98–99, 204, 261, 283n23
Highland society (basic features), 12–16, 41, 44–46, 195
Highland Society of Edinburgh (of Scotland from 1787), 46, 54, 80; autarky, 231; coal, 172; critique of, 245–47, 251;

emigration crisis of 1803, 232–38, 258; forestry, 152–54, 181, 187; infrastructure, 118, 258; kelping, 118–19; loyalism, 214–15; military recruitment, 41, 235–36, 239; origin, 29, 41, 104, 117–19, 219; Ossian, 239; peat, 85, 101, 240; preserving Highland culture, 118, 235; sheep farming, 56, 206–8; wasteland reclamation, 85, 119–20, 240, 242–43

Highland Society of London, 41, 54

Holroyd, John (Earl of Sheffield), 206, 208–9, 223

Home, Francis, 17, 65

Home, Henry (Lord Kames), 11–12, 15–17, 26–36, 38–39, 42, 44, 63–64, 66, 72, 83, 94–96, 109–10, 113, 120, 130, 151, 169, 179, 190, 196–97, 217, 238, 243–45

Hont, Istvan, 125

Hope, Charles, 232

Hope, John, 17, 21, 29, 47, 54, 57, 64–67, 75, 86–87, 89, 95, 100, 108, 123, 132, 138, 160. See also *photo gallery image 4*

Horn, Jeff, 13

Humboldt, Alexander von, 126–27, 129

Hume, David, 3, 13, 16–21, 23, 26, 30, 42, 49, 78, 114, 125, 129, 135, 143, 179, 196–98, 246, 248

Hume, Joseph, 229

hurricanes, 128

Hutton, James, 71, 74, 95, 130, 172, 199–201, 208

Hutton, William, 182

Iceland, 51, 58, 70, 72, 83, 87, 98

import substitution, 44, 55–56, 64–65, 77, 81, 86, 89, 94, 97, 108, 119, 151–53, 157–61, 172, 209, 216, 249, 284–85n28

improvement, 1, 56, 95–96, 118, 132, 144, 221; historiography, 5, 14; risks of, 20, 22, 207

India, 111, 126–28, 136–41, 158–62

indigenous substitutes, 55, 64, 77, 81, 89, 100–101, 108, 119, 172, 175–76, 179, 241, 249

Industrial Revolution, 14, 167

infrastructure (roads, canals, ports, irrigation, granaries), 29, 46, 54, 106, 118, 136, 138, 140–41, 234, 254, 257, 259. See also Caledonian Canal

internal colonization, 2, 5, 29, 33–34, 38, 46, 55–56, 60, 86–87, 110. See also wasteland reclamation

Inveraray, 121, 177

Inverness, 2, 51, 148

Ireland, 14, 132, 215, 217, 230, 242, 244, 250, 256–58, 263

Irish Rebellion of 1798, 250

irrigation, 73, 136, 140–41

island: climate, 51, 72–73, 75–76, 78, 128; consciousness, 8, 214; cornucopia, 44; ecology, 48, 64, 93, 128, 152, 188–89, 191–93, 262; extirpation and conservation, 196, 199, 206–8, 251; limits, 6, 82, 149, 174, 187–89, 191–94, 214, 222–30, 233, 263; population boom, 45, 188–95, 226–28, 243, 249, 263; self-sufficiency, 99, 193, 217, 226. See also Isle de France (Mauritius); Juan Fernandez; Shetland sheep; *and various entries for the* Western Isles

Isle de France (Mauritius), 123, 128

Jackson, Charles, 89, 132

Jacobites, 12, 23, 28, 40, 143

Jameson, Robert, 54, 95

Jameson, Thomas, 119

Jefferson, Thomas, 108, 127–28

Jevons, William Stanley, 167, 181, 186, 263–64

Johnson, Samuel, 35, 50–53, 148

Juan Fernandez, 188–89, 192–93

Jura, 194, 207

Kalm, Pehr, 60–61, 66, 122–25, 130–31, 134, 191–92, 198, 200

kelp and kelping, 45, 51, 93–94, 97, 117–20, 254–55, 260, 262. See also *photo gallery image 2*

Ker, Andrew, 208, 210–11
Kew Gardens, 61–62, 86, 123
kitchen gardens, 31, 33–34, 110, 112–13, 116, 126, 129, 202, 222, 234, 251
Knox, John, 16, 43–44, 54, 104, 106, 112, 114, 116, 141, 171–72, 179, 202–4
Koerner, Lisbet. *See* Rausing, Lisbet
Kratzenstein, Christian Gottlieb, 70
Kyd, Robert, 139

La Galissonnière, Roland-Michel Barrin de, 124
Laki, 70, 77
Lamarck de Monet, Jean-Baptiste-Pierre-Antoine, 84, 95
Lanark, 34, 245, 256
landed interest (landowning elite), 2–3, 12, 14–15, 17, 24–27, 41–42, 44, 46, 54–56, 61, 89, 93, 95, 101, 103, 105, 107, 112–13, 117–18, 141–42, 147–49, 152, 157, 169, 172, 182, 186–87, 196, 199, 206, 209, 215, 217, 219–20, 223–24, 236–37, 242–43, 246, 248, 251, 254, 257. *See also* gentry
Lapland, 44, 58–60, 63–64, 75–76, 81, 99, 197, 273n18
larch, 2, 44, 61, 68, 77, 89, 93–94, 103, 108, 147–48, 150–63
lazy bed cultivation, 37–38, 242–44
lead, 44, 47, 97, 168, 170–71
Lewis, 35, 37, 44, 117, 202, 235, 240, 254
Lightfoot, John, 47–48, 52, 57, 75, 77, 87, 95–101, 242
lime, 48, 52, 57, 120, 153, 169, 177–78, 219–22, 254
limits to economic growth, 8, 24, 131, 264. *See also* stationary state
Lind, James, 51, 73
linen manufactures, 2, 28, 33, 38, 96, 103, 190, 209
Linnaean Society of London, 67, 95
Linnaeus, Carolus (Carl von Linné), 5, 44, 51, 52, 55, 57–67, 71–72, 75–77, 83–84, 87, 93, 95–96, 99, 122–23, 125–28, 130, 197–98
Little Ice Age, 176
Livesey, James, 284–85n18
local economies, 14, 25, 40, 96–98, 101, 106, 113, 127, 141, 152, 176
local knowledge, 44, 48, 54–56, 58, 61, 64, 66, 71, 93–94, 96–98, 123, 125, 134, 139, 146
Lochbay, 106, 112
Loch Broom, 43, 201, 240
Loch Tay, 238, 258–59
London, 21, 95, 109, 136, 138, 154, 178, 182, 186, 213, 215, 220, 226, 234
Lowlands (Scotland), 12–13, 41, 44, 46, 74, 95, 130, 180, 182, 220, 238, 244, 249, 257; Lowland model of improvement, 3, 28, 31, 35–36, 95, 134–35, 171
luxury, 19–26, 39, 42, 66, 94, 99–100, 109, 143, 237, 254, 277n25

Macdonald, Ranald George (Lord Clanranald), 252, 254
Mackay, David, 86
Mackenzie, Alexander, 261
Mackenzie, Francis Humberston (Earl of Seaforth), 56, 113, 117, 235, 254
Mackenzie, Henry, 15, 39, 42, 117, 141, 142, 232–39, 246, 258
Mackenzie, Margaret (of Delvin), 78
Mackillop, Andrew, 32, 270n4, 279n43
Macleod, Donald, 113, 114, 172
Macnab, Henry Gray, 167, 176, 179, 180, 184–86, 228
Macpherson, James, 29, 30, 50, 51, 97, 106, 122, 143, 204, 239
Malthus, T. R., 4, 6, 8, 24, 126, 129, 136, 139, 140, 167, 189, 193–95, 198, 214, 227–28, 232, 248, 249, 251–52, 255–57, 260, 263–64
marble, 44
marl, 48, 56, 120, 220–21
Marshall, William, 207, 223

Martin, Martin, 35, 37, 64, 98–99, 106, 152, 192, 241
Maskelyne, Nevil, 54
Maxwell, Robert, 15, 82–3
Medical School of Edinburgh, 17, 94
Melon, Jean-François, 6
Menzies, Archibald, 54, 87
merino sheep, 77, 82–83, 87, 94, 102–4, 127, 144, 150, 206, 208–11
Middleton, Charles (Lord Barham), 157–59, 228
military recruitment, 2, 12–14, 22, 25, 28, 31–32, 36, 40–41, 53, 68, 111, 146, 203, 236, 239
militia, 5, 13, 16, 19–20, 23–24, 143, 202
Mill, John Stuart, 4, 102, 263
Millar, John, 79–80, 179, 196
Miller, Hugh, 261
Miller, Thomas, 25–26, 28–29, 39
mineral energy economy, 173–74, 178, 181, 186, 214, 229, 263–64
modernity, 275n6; alternative, 13–15, 38, 243; rival global, 125
Monro, Alexander, 17
monsoon, 139–40
Montesquieu, Charles-Louis de Secondat, 16, 36, 83
moral geography, 2, 13, 34, 40–41, 53, 85, 93–94, 100, 143–44, 218, 234–35, 239, 251, 258
Mughal Empire, 136, 140
mull, 53, 98, 106, 113, 201, 254
Munro, Thomas, 140
Murray, Alexander, 168
Murray, James (Second Duke of Atholl), 150
Murray, John (Third Duke of Atholl), 66, 77, 89, 150
Murray, John (Fourth Duke of Atholl), 2, 68, 110, 147, 150, 153–56, 158–59, 161–63
Murray, Patrick, 27
Mysore, 95, 138, 161

natural history: Board for the Annexed Estates and, 47–49, 85–86, 93, 95–97, 168–71; cameralist, 58–59; Enlightenment and, 2–7; as global knowledge, 125–29; imperial science (neo-mercantilist), 5, 86–87, 125–29, 157–60; parliamentary testimony and, 104–5, 145, 171–72, 183, 186; taxonomy, 57–58, 61, 127
Natural History Museum of Edinburgh, 47, 65, 95
Natural History Society of Edinburgh, 54, 95
neo-Europe, 87, 127, 291n35
New Jersey, 49, 122, 146, 200
New South Wales, 86–67, 127, 250, 261
New Town of Edinburgh, 16, 149
North America, 2, 8, 26, 49, 61, 65–66, 69, 71–72, 84–86, 88–89, 104, 110–11, 122–24, 128, 134, 137, 151, 158, 161–62, 170, 190–92, 197–200, 216, 227, 233, 237, 248–52, 255
Northern Isles (Shetland and Orkney Isles), 178, 206, 219. *See also* Orkney; Shetland Isles
North Rona, 192
North Uist, 98, 195, 254
Norway, 84, 149, 152, 199, 246

oak woods, 68, 89, 103, 149, 151–62
oats, 11, 34, 37, 84–85, 226, 242, 246
O'Brien, Karen, 261
O'Brien, Patrick, 14
Organic Energy Economy, 175–76, 178
Orkney, 100, 177
Ormrod, David, 14
Ossian, 30, 37, 51–53, 97, 122, 143, 204, 239, 283n23
Ostrom, Elinor, 295n19

Parthasarathi, Prasannan, 14
Passenger Vessels Act, 233–34
paternalism, 25, 40, 55, 131, 179, 234, 251

Pax Britannica, 163, 213–14
peat: autarky, 217, 244–45; colonies, 11, 33, 217, 242–43; climate change, 244; exhaustion, 176–78, 179, 181, 228; formation, 175–76; fuel, 52, 101–2, 119, 172, 175–79, 220–21, 243, 247, 249, 254; ghost acres, 214; medical effects, 241; moss husbandry, 1, 11, 31, 33–35, 60, 85, 94, 117, 120, 217, 240–45; natural history and chemistry, 96–97, 222, 240–44, 246; resource management, 101–2; soil amendment, 48, 217, 241–43; tree planting, 1, 152, 244; virtue and, 34, 245
Pennant, Thomas, 43, 47, 48, 50–53, 75, 84, 87, 89, 98, 179, 196, 198, 199, 238
Perth, 110, 202
Perthshire, 2, 11, 30, 33, 69, 77–79, 87, 89, 109, 120, 147, 151, 159, 162, 168–71, 178, 194, 201, 223, 225, 238, 245
Petrusewicz, Martha, 14
physiocrats, 123, 127, 129, 131, 135
Pincus, Steven, 14
pine woods, 151–53, 158, 200
Pitt, William (the Younger), 39, 104, 107, 109–10, 127, 158, 179, 181–82, 215, 223, 253
planned villages, 2, 5, 25–26, 28, 31, 33–34, 43, 46, 55, 104–6, 110–11, 114–19, 145–46, 176, 194, 218–19, 237–38, 241, 251, 254, 262
Pliny the Elder, Gaius, 22, 130, 199
Poivre, Pierre, 123, 126, 128, 130, 136
Polanyi, Karl, 192, 315–16n8
political arithmetic, 152, 184, 212–14, 223, 228–29, 262
political economy, 3–6, 8, 12–14, 16, 24, 33, 49, 61, 93, 97, 102, 105, 107, 113, 125–26, 129–30, 140, 149, 157, 167, 179, 186, 188–92, 195, 214, 223, 227, 232–33, 235, 246, 248–49, 253–54, 261, 263, 273n15. *See also* Anderson, James; Douglas, Thomas; *Edinburgh Review*; Hume, David; Malthus, T. R.; Smith, Adam
Pomeranz, Kenneth, 230, 319n2, 323n31

Poor Laws, 168, 188, 190–91, 195, 256
poppies, 108
population: ancient, 23; depopulation, 21, 196–98, 218, 247, 256; Malthusian trap, 24, 190, 195, 204; overpopulation (surplus population), 167–68, 189, 195, 202–3, 214, 228, 231–32, 255–57, 262–64; population pressure, 228, 316n13, 323n31; rate of population growth, 23, 188–90, 193–94, 218, 227
population politics, 2–3, 11, 14, 24, 26, 30–31, 41, 55, 146, 189, 206, 220, 234–35, 269–70n3
porcelain, 97
Porto Santo, 192
potash, 119, 151
potatoes, 1, 12, 34, 37–38, 41, 56, 60, 74, 77, 83, 85, 87, 93, 100–101, 108, 112–13, 115, 120, 129, 132, 202, 216, 223, 242–43, 256–57
Prince Edward Island, 248, 250–51, 253
Prussia, 55, 224, 240
Pulteney, Richard, 62–63, 67
Pulteney, William, 29, 111
purple moor grass (*Aira coerulea*), 64, 93, 242

quantification: climate, 70, 73, 78, 80; coal reserves, 184–86; environment and economy, 8; ghost acres, 226, 229; population density, 228; population growth, 227; subsistence farming, 22–23, 31, 34, 112–13, 116, 221–23, 256; wasteland, 176, 224–26, 245
Quesnay, François, 133, 135

rabbits, 192
Rackham, Oliver, 309–10n17
Ramsay, John (of Ochtertyre), 69–70, 77
Raspe, Rudolph, 54
rats, 191–92, 196, 199
Rausing, Lisbet, 5, 125, 272n13
Ray, John, 59, 64
Réaumur, René-Antoine Ferchault de, 130

Rebellion of 1745–46, 12, 23, 25, 28, 39, 143, 236
Rennell, James, 139, 159–60
Rennie, Robert, 222, 243
rent, 6, 20, 24, 27, 31, 40, 52, 102, 104, 115–16, 143–45, 195, 201, 203–4, 215, 220, 222, 225, 235–38, 246–47, 251–52, 254, 256
resource management, 7, 100–102, 148–49, 233, 261
rhubarb, 44, 61, 66–67, 77, 87, 89, 108, 150
Ricardo, David, 126, 263
rice, 61, 81, 83, 89, 126, 136–37, 139
Richards, Eric, 195, 201, 211
Ritvo, Harriet, 7–8
Robertson, James (John Hope's student), 47–48, 57, 65–66, 75, 95, 99–101, 128
Robertson, Reverend James, 33, 79, 218–19, 223
Robertson, John, 5–6, 16, 18–19, 269n2
Robertson, William, 17, 54, 65, 128, 191, 196–97
Rockström, Johan, 264
Roman Empire and Republic, 22–23, 29, 35, 83, 99, 110, 197, 244
romanticism, 7–8, 257, 261
Rome, 22, 69, 83
Rose, Hugh, 113–15, 189, 196, 199, 202, 204–5, 219, 221
Ross-shire, 113–14, 151, 172, 177, 201–2, 219, 225, 249–50
Rousseau, Jean-Jacques, 21, 24, 58, 130
Roy, William, 148, 168
Royal Botanic Garden of Edinburgh, 17, 47, 64–67, 87, 89, 108, 132
Royal Society of Edinburgh, 71, 95
Roxburgh, William, 67, 87, 138–39
Rum (Rhum), 64, 78, 93
Russia, 66, 69, 123, 154, 157, 159, 246

Saint-Fond, Barthelemy Faujas de, 54, 121
salt duties, 105–7, 114, 145, 234
Sami, 58–59, 63, 77, 99
savant, 274n2

Scandinavia, 48, 162, 216
Schumpeter, Joseph, 102
Scott, Henry (Third Duke of Buccleuch), 105, 130
Scott, James, 125
Scottish Enlightenment: chronology and definition, 5, 269n2; environmentalism and, 8, 167, 189; geography and, 12; natural history and, 2–4, 6–7, 67–68; paternalist improvement, 15, 41
Select Society of Edinburgh: agricultural improvement, 27–28; alternative modernization, 15; Board for the Annexed Estates and, 28–29; entail, 26; luxury debate, 11–12, 18–23, 277n25; membership, 16–18, 25; militia, 19–20
Selkirk, Alexander, 192–93
Sellar, Patrick, 260
sensibility, 36, 58, 117, 121, 306n55
sentimental: environmentalism, 8; literature, 39, 141, 234–35, 306n55; population politics, 2, 11, 14, 24, 30, 41, 234–35; tourism, 7, 52; unsentimental political economy, 143, 149, 203, 246
serfdom, 105
Seven Years' War, 2–3, 12, 15, 19, 24, 26, 31–32, 66, 120
Shetland Isles, 43, 47, 145, 194, 205
Shetland sheep, 77, 87, 120, 205–12
Siam, 161
Sibbald, Robert, 55, 64, 98
Siberia, 75, 98
Silesian milkweed (common milkweed, *Asclepias syriaca*), 89
silk and silkworms, 83, 89, 99
Sinclair, John: Board of Agriculture, 109, 185–86, 223–26; British Fisheries Society, 111; British Wool Society, 56, 77–80, 87, 120, 205–12; civil cameralism, 56–57; climate and acclimatization, 74, 82; coal duties and peat moss, 175–79; emigration crisis of 1803, 233; famine of 1782, 141; *General View of the*

Sinclair, John (continued)
Agriculture of the Northern Counties, 205, 219–22; Highland poetry, 239; kelping, 119; population growth, 194, 249; *The Statistical Account of Scotland*, 33, 54–57; wasteland reclamation, 176, 213–14, 217–18, 223–26, 229, 243, 245, 256–57, 263
Skibo, 74, 219–20
Skye, 35, 51, 93, 97–98, 106, 113, 142, 195, 202, 249, 254
slavery, 20, 86, 94, 105, 107, 109, 221, 245. *See also* abolitionism
Smith, Adam: acclimatization, 132; agriculture, 15, 17, 105, 124, 129, 133–34; canals, 259; critique of feudalism, 15, 27, 40; East India Company, 137; gardening, 61; grain markets, 135–36; Highland improvement, 13, 49, 121–22, 142–46; natural history, 130–32, 191–92; nature and markets, 3, 6, 8, 49–50, 124–26, 129–32; population, 144, 190–91, 247; pre-industrial model, 174; Select Society of Edinburgh, 16–7; timber, 149, 162. See also *photo gallery image 7*
Smith, Charles, 135, 226
Smith, James Edward, 67, 95
Smith, John, 79, 152–53, 181, 187, 204, 223
Smith, William, 190
Smout, T. C., 7, 17–18, 233
Society of Improvers in the Knowledge of Agriculture in Scotland, the Honorable, 82
soil fertility, 24, 45, 123–24, 131, 133–34, 177, 217, 241–42, 263
Solander, Daniel, 51, 57, 61, 123
South America, 84, 127, 197
Southern Uplands (Scotland), 89, 93, 210
South Uist, 195
spade husbandry, 3, 11–12, 21–22, 26–28, 31–38, 41, 83, 85, 110, 112–17, 120, 212, 216–17, 221–22, 234, 238, 241–44, 254–56, 260. *See also* allotments; *caschrom*; kitchen gardens

Spain, 127, 190, 210
Sparrman, Anders, 128
stadial history (four stages), 3, 15, 20, 30, 36, 38, 50, 52, 97, 100, 106, 134, 140, 143, 193, 221, 263
Staffa, 51
Stanhope, William, 181
state building, 14, 45, 125, 224; cameralism and, 55–56, 122, 124; fiscal-military state, 13, 15, 20, 41, 68; infrastructure, 29, 46, 54, 106, 118, 136, 138, 140–41, 234, 254, 257, 259; natural knowledge and, 3, 5, 12, 19, 28, 44, 48, 50, 55, 100, 105, 124–25, 127–28, 130–31, 138–39, 168–71, 198, 201, 228, 230; neo-mercantilism and, 68, 86–87, 157–63; population policy and, 13–14, 20, 25, 28, 31–32, 39–40, 42, 46, 110, 118, 202, 233–34, 237, 250, 252, 261, 263; resource husbandry and, 7, 68, 100, 124, 128, 136, 138–39, 149, 157–58, 168–71, 174, 179, 182, 186–87, 215, 223–24, 228, 244–45; urbanization and, 118, 145, 179
stationary state, 4, 186, 228, 249, 255–56, 262–64
Statistical Account of Scotland (ed. John Sinclair, 1791–99): clearance, 218; climate, 77–80; coal duties and peat moss, 175–79; coal exhaustion, 181–83, 185, 187; famine of 1782, 141; origins, 33, 54–57; population growth, 194, 249
steam engine, 47, 156, 162, 169, 184, 186, 214, 258, 260
Steuart, James, Sir, 6, 15, 33
Stewart, David (of Garth), 261
Stewart, Dugald, 260
Stillingfleet, Benjamin, 61–63, 130, 198
Stirling, 1, 11, 69
Stornoway, 44
Stuart, Charles Edward (Bonnie Prince Charles), 12
Stuart, John, 52, 57
sugar beets, 89, 94, 108–9
sugar cane, 61, 89, 94, 108

surveys, 47, 54, 64–65, 75, 109, 148, 186, 194, 211, 223–24, 238, 243, 247, 262, 282n8
sustainability, 7
Sutherland, 29, 74, 114, 117, 144, 152, 169–70, 196, 199, 204–5, 211, 219, 250, 260–61
Sutherland Clearances, 144, 205, 211–12, 260–61
Sweden, 5, 44, 57–61, 63–65, 67, 75–76, 81, 99, 123, 152, 197, 200, 209, 240, 273n18
Swinton, John, 27–29, 32, 110

tacksman class, 100, 232, 251, 254
Tahiti, 86–87, 127
Tambora, 260
tar, 151, 153
tea, 59, 67, 86, 89, 99, 108, 127
teak, 68, 89, 140, 147, 158–62
Telford, Thomas, 54, 238–39, 257–59
Thomas, Brinley, 230
Thomas, J. F., 140
Thomson, John Deas (Navy Board), 154, 155, 162
Thomson, Reverend John, 182–83, 187
Thorkelin, Grimur Jónsson, 74
Thornton, William Thomas, 261
Thouin, André, 123
Thunberg, Carl Peter, 61
time travel, 50–3
Tiree, 37, 76, 89, 98, 195
tobacco, 56, 89, 99, 132
Tobermory, 106, 112, *photo gallery image 6*
Tory ideology, 24, 179, 186, 232, 256–57, 259, 260–61. *See also* conservative enlightenment; paternalism
Townsend, Joseph, 24, 167–68, 188–93, 195, 198, 201, 248–49, 262–63
Troil, Uno von, 51
Tucker, Josiah, 55

Ullapool, 106, 112, 116–17
uncertainty, 45, 48–49, 70, 77, 97, 128, 147, 159, 210, 214, 221, 226, 230, 242
ungulate irruption, 6–7, 191–93, 249, 262
United States, 7, 158, 213, 248, 250

University of Edinburgh, 35, 54, 64–65, 81, 93, 160, 179, 198, 208, 260
University of Glasgow, 17, 27, 110, 143, 220
Uppsala, 57, 59–61, 65, 67
urbanization, 23, 27, 111, 118, 262; Adam Smith and, 131, 133–34; consumption and, 226, 230; coal and, 171–72, 174, 176, 179; David Hume and, 18–19; James Anderson and, 94, 104–7, 144–45, 178; sheep and, 202–4
urban mortality rates, 14, 21, 110, 216, 218–20, 245

Vancouver, Charles, 224–25
volcanic eruption, 70, 77, 260. *See also* Laki; Tambora

Wales, 54, 168, 225, 229
Walker, John: acclimatization and climate, 73, 76, 80–86, 89, 96; Board for the Annexed Estates, 29, 35–38, 47, 93–96; coal exhaustion, 181, 187; cornucopianism, 44, 262; critique of Adam Smith, 49–50; expert in the Highland Society of Scotland, 95, 101–2, 117, 119–20; extirpation, 198–99; kelping, 119; Linnaeus and, 63–64, 99–100; peat frontier, 33, 35, 120, 232–33, 235, 240–43, 246, 256; providence and natural advantage, 93–94, 96–97; Select Society of Edinburgh, 17, 21, 35. *See also photo gallery image 5*
Wallace, Robert, 12, 15, 17–19, 23–27, 31, 38, 42, 238, 250
Wargentin, Pehr, 60
wasteland reclamation, 3, 33, 103, 153, 190, 212, 221–27, 240–44. *See also* internal colonization
Webster, Charles, 194, 249
Western Isles (Hebrides), 3, 16, 19, 35–38, 42–43, 45, 47, 49–53, 62–64, 73, 76, 83–85, 89, 93–97, 96, 98, 101, 104–7, 110–12, 120, 141, 144–46, 152, 176,

Western Isles (Hebrides) (continued) 179, 182, 192, 194–95, 203, 207, 233, 254–55. See also *entries for individual islands*
West Indies, 65, 67, 72–73, 86, 89, 94, 109, 111, 127, 151, 199, 217, 221
wheat, 1, 83, 127, 132, 135, 157, 198, 226, 230, 260
Whig ideology, 14–15, 23–24, 107, 138, 159, 179, 181–82, 232, 245
Whitcombe, Elizabeth, 140
White, Reverend Gilbert (of Selborne), 8, 52, 62, 69
Wick, 106, 112
Wight, Andrew, 34, 47, 170
Williams, John, 47, 48, 54, 148, 152, 167–75, 178, 179, 181–84, 186, 187, 202, 228, 229, 247, 249, 262–64
willow, 181, 187
Withers, Charles, 5, 50
wolves, 198–99
woolen manufactures, 103, 144, 209
Worster, Donald, 7–8, 233
Wright, William, 67
Wrigley, E. A., 178, 229

Young, Arthur, 88–89, 102–3, 152, 206, 223, 256
Young, David, 109–10
Young, William, 260